GREEK DRAMA V

Also published by Bloomsbury

ARISTOPHANIC HUMOUR: THEORY AND PRACTICE
Edited by Edith Hall and Peter Swallow

'AUTOMATIC' THEATRE IN ANCIENT GREEK DRAMA
by Maria Gerolemou

GUIDE TO GREEK THEATRE AND DRAMA
by Kenneth McLeish, completed by Trevor R. Griffiths

THE LOST PLAYS OF GREEK TRAGEDY (VOLUME 1)
by Matthew Wright

THE LOST PLAYS OF GREEK TRAGEDY (VOLUME 2)
by Matthew Wright

GREEK DRAMA V

STUDIES IN THE THEATRE OF THE FIFTH AND FOURTH CENTURIES BCE

edited by Hallie Marshall and C. W. Marshall

BLOOMSBURY ACADEMIC

LONDON • NEW YORK • OXFORD • NEW DELHI • SYDNEY

BLOOMSBURY ACADEMIC
Bloomsbury Publishing Plc
50 Bedford Square, London, WC1B 3DP, UK
1385 Broadway, New York, NY 10018, USA
29 Earlsfort Terrace, Dublin 2, Ireland

BLOOMSBURY, BLOOMSBURY ACADEMIC and the Diana logo
are trademarks of Bloomsbury Publishing Plc

First published in Great Britain 2020
Paperback edition first published 2021

Cover design: Terry Woodley
Cover image © Tragedy-related scene, Sicilian calyx-krater, ca. 330s, the Capodarso Painter
(Gibil Gabib Group), Caltanissetta, Museo Regionale 1301bis.

A catalogue record for this book is available from the British Library.

A catalog record for this book is available from the Library of Congress.

ISBN: HB: 978-1-3501-4235-0
PB: 978-1-3501-9371-0
ePDF: 978-1-3501-4236-7
eBook: 978-1-3501-4237-4

Typeset by RefineCatch Limited, Bungay, Suffolk

To find out more about our authors and books visit
www.bloomsbury.com and sign up for our newsletters.

for John Davidson

CONTENTS

Contents

ILLUSTRATIONS

Figures

Tables

CONTRIBUTORS

Rosa Andújar is Deputy Director of Liberal Arts and Lecturer in Liberal Arts at King's College London.

Eric Csapo is British Academy Global Professor at the Dept. of Classics and Ancient History at the University of Warwick.

Francis Dunn is Professor of Classics at the University of California, Santa Barbara.

John Gibert is Associate Professor of Classics at the University of Colorado Boulder.

Paul G. Johnston is a PhD student in Classical Philology at Harvard University in Cambridge, Massachusetts.

Ruggiero Lionetti is a PhD candidate at the Scuola Normale Superiore, Pisa.

Wilfred E. Major is Associate Professor of Classics at Louisiana State University.

Kathryn Mattison is Associate Professor of Classics at McMaster University in Hamilton, Canada.

Hallie Marshall teaches in the Department of Theatre and Film at the University of British Columbia in Vancouver, Canada.

C. W. Marshall is Professor of Greek at the University of British Columbia in Vancouver, Canada.

Sheila Murnaghan is the Alfred Reginald Allen Memorial Professor of Greek at the University of Pennsylvania.

Anna A. Novokhatko is Assistant Professor of Greek and Latin at the Albert-Ludwigs-Universität of Freiburg (Germany).

Eleni Papazoglou is Assistant Professor of Ancient Drama at the Faculty of Fine Arts, Aristotle University of Thessaloniki, Greece.

Brett M. Rogers is Associate Professor of Classics at the University of Puget Sound in Tacoma, WA, USA.

Elizabeth Scharffenberger teaches in the Department of Classics at Columbia University in New York City.

Anna E. Simas is a PhD candidate at the University of Washington, Seattle.

Niall W. Slater is the Samuel Candler Dobbs Professor of Latin and Greek at Emory University.

Anastasia-Stavroula Valtadorou is a doctoral researcher at the University of Edinburgh, Scotland.

Peter Wilson is William Ritchie Professor of Classics at the University of Sydney, Australia.

PREFACE

The first Greek Drama conference was held in Sydney in 1982. It inaugurated a periodic conference that has gathered scholars of classical theatre from around the world, always to investigate and explore new approaches to the study of ancient theatre, representing a range of senior and junior scholars. The second conference was held in Christchurch in 1992, and the third in Sydney in 2002. As a decennial opportunity to bring together scholars, the Greek Drama conference had established itself as the largest conference dedicated specifically to the study of ancient theatre. Ten years may have seemed too long to wait, and so the fourth conference was held in Wellington in 2007. This was now a major event, and one eagerly anticipated by many researchers, for whom the opportunity to have one's ideas critically examined by like-minded and supportive colleagues was eagerly anticipated (and was, for some of us, a wonderful opportunity to visit the southern hemisphere).

As another decade was due to pass without another such conference, we confirmed with our Antipodean colleagues that no other Greek Drama conference was in the works and undertook ourselves to hold Greek Drama V in Vancouver, in July 2017. No longer confined to the southern hemisphere, the Greek Drama tradition remained on the Pacific Rim. We eagerly await to discover where the next conference will be held, in 2027.

Proceedings from Greek Drama III were published as *BICS* Supplement 87 (London, 2006) and from Greek Drama IV with Aris & Phillips (Oxford, 2012). We are proud to present in this volume a selection of papers from the 2017 Vancouver conference. The selection represents an emphasis on fragmentary works, as well as on the reception of Athenian drama in antiquity, both in Greece and beyond.

These emphases, which in different ways unite over half of this volume's contents, can perhaps be embodied by the vase image we have selected for our cover. This vase, a Sicilian calyx-crater, perhaps from the 330s (the Capodarso Painter (Gabil Gabib Group), Caltanissetta, Museo Regionale 1301bis), depicts a scene from a lost tragedy that cannot be identified. Was it an Athenian play? Did it have a Sicilian connection? Was it a fourth-century play, or was it a 'classic', a fifth-century play being reperformed? It simply is not possible to say given information available. The vase is nevertheless striking for the number of apparently unique features that it appears to present. It seems the vase juxtaposes two scenes from the same play within the same image: a young man supplicating a woman on the left, and a messenger relating an offstage event to the same woman on the right (see Taplin 2007, no. 105, and Taplin 2017). The fact that this is the same woman at two different points in the play seems certain, but at the same time it demonstrates the incredible freedom the artist possessed to present both scenes – two two-actor exchanges, and not one four-actor one – in the same visual field. Though the supplicant's hand reaches up for the woman stage right, who appears to be turning away (compare Odysseus' response to Polyxena's supplication in Euripides' *Hecuba*), the artist seems almost cheeky in positioning the outstretched left hand on top of the clothing of the second version of the woman. At the same time, the theatrical context is beyond doubt by the clear presence of a raised stage, which is not usually part of the vocabulary of painted scenes of tragedy, and which would seem to insist on a single theatrical moment. Such stages are regularly seen on the South Italian vases depicting comic theatre, and here again this vase proves exceptional. Though the scenes depicted are conventional (supplications and messenger speeches are found in all the extant tragedians), here we see both, represented for a non-theatrical viewership (whoever it was), who wanted to see these choice scenes on this vase. The movement of various genres of performance across the Mediterranean (from Athens to South Italy in this case), and the many insoluble questions that the vase raises, resonate with many themes that have been given increased prominence in the past ten years and are represented in this collection.

Given that, it is appropriate that the first chapter is the keynote academic lecture by Eric Csapo and Peter Wilson, examining the system of government in place when drama was introduced to the city states of the Greek world. It represents an important contribution that takes us beyond an Athenocentric understanding, and draws heavily on their forthcoming social and economic history of Greek theatre. This chapter also establishes the chronological range of this volume, of the fifth and fourth centuries BCE. **Csapo** and **Wilson** (Chapter 1) explore the political climate in poleis at the time when theatre and dramatic competitions were introduced. This challenges the traditional associations of Athenian theatre as a fundamentally democratic institution and offers many new avenues for understanding the dissemination of literature and culture in the classical period. It also raises the challenging question of how theatre was perceived at the time – whether it was seen to be an Athenian creation.

In the first of three chapters on Sophocles, **Murnaghan** (Chapter 2) discusses how Sophocles manages the conflicted literary pedigree of Ajax the son of Telamon, as seen in Homer, subsequent literature, and cult. By focusing on the short phrase 'since when', she demonstrates the importance of starting points in heroic narrative. **Mattison** (Chapter 3) also considers literary influence on tragedy, identifying important resonances between Sophocles and elegy. She sees Philoctetes advocating an Archilochean response to war, which Heracles needs to correct. Odysseus also adopts an elegiac pose, modelled on Tyrtaeus and Solon. **Papazoglou** (Chapter 4) explores the nature of character within tragedy, looking specifically on Deianira in *Women of Trachis*. Reviewing previous approaches to this question, she challenges both a structuralist reading and a psychological one, and offers a way forward for understanding how character is developed on the Sophoclean stage.

The next three chapters each consider a play by Euripides, though the questions raised have implications for the rest of tragedy as well. **Gibert** (Chapter 5) incorporates Emily Wilson's insight concerning 'tragic overliving' with *Hecuba*. Living beyond one's time, seeing one's children killed or losing the status one possessed formerly effectively turns the Herodotean/Sophoclean adage to count no one happy until they are dead (Hdt. 1.32, quoting Solon; *Oed.* 1528–30, *Trach.* 1–3) inside out. **Dunn** (Chapter 6) describes how suspense is generated in *Electra*. By using a tragedy where the narrative contours had been so well established by Aeschylus' *Libation Bearers*, he provides a model for understanding dramatic suspense in literary narratives. With reference to *Trojan Women*, **Lionetti** (Chapter 7) explores how the communal character of the tragic chorus resonates with the play's Athenian spectators. The collective experience maps onto spectator knowledge of Panathenaic celebrations to create what he calls a 'hybrid perspective' that successfully holds both views (character and audience) in tension.

The theme of Euripides' choruses continues into the next set of three chapters, which are concerned with fragmentary works. **Andújar** (Chapter 8) re-examines the question of a secondary chorus in Euripides' *Phaethon*, and presents a close reading of a song celebrating Phaethon's wedding immediately after his corpse has been brought onstage. 'Choral mirroring' again resonates both within the play and with the audience. **Valtadorou** (Chapter 9) develops a deeper understanding of *erōs* in tragedy through a careful examination of two fragmentary works, Euripides' *Antigone* and *Andromeda*. She demonstrates that in both plays Haemon and Perseus fall in love with their future wives, in a sense that is recognizable to modern audiences. **Sharffenberger** (Chapter 10) provides a rich interpretation of an unplaced tragic fragment (fr. 1063) in which the speaker argues against the domestic isolation of women. She argues that this sentiment emerges in response to a passage in *Thesmophoriazusae* (411 BCE), and could have been written by Euripides (possibly even for his *Antigone*) or by another tragic playwright.

The chapters which follow offer three complementary perspectives on the reception of Aeschylus's *Oresteia* following the initial production in 458 BCE. As reception studies develop as a subfield within the discipline of Classics, these authors remind us of the importance of framing reception in antiquity as well as in more recent times. **Simas** (Chapter 11) looks at the representations of the Erinyes (Furies) in the years immediately after the performance in 458, investigating their apparently beautiful presentation in art and the terrifying effect they have on Orestes. **Johnston** (Chapter 12) explores how the messenger speech in Euripides' *Bacchae* evokes the Aeschylean Furies, as it also draws on hunting and animal imagery that are so prominent in the *Oresteia*. The explicitly metatheatrical nature of this intertextuality therefore builds on the literary studies of Murnaghan and Mattison (Chapters 2 and 3), and seems to depend on audience familiarity with the *Oresteia* through performance. The issue of Aeschylean reperformance is addressed directly by **Rogers** (Chapter 13), whose analysis of Aristophanes' comedy *Clouds* demonstrates a detailed and sustained engagement with the *Oresteia*.

The final three chapters continue the study of comedy begun by Rogers (Chapter 13). **Novokhato** (Chapter 14) describes the way that the technical terminology for genre emerges in comedy, suggesting that it is through the critical examination provided by Aristophanes and his fellow comic playwrights, particularly in the 420s BCE, that 'tragedy', 'comedy', and 'drama' become meaningful terms for audiences. Moving ahead to the period of New Comedy, **Slater** (Chapter 15) surveys the richness of Menander's *Sikyonioi*, positioning the lead character Stratophanes as someone searching for himself. Though the play remains fragmentary, the analysis shows the ways in which Menander draws on tragic precedent in order to integrate Stratophanes successfully as an adult in his community. Finally, **Major** (Chapter 16) positions this process of reintegration into the history of the character of the *miles gloriosus*, the braggart soldier. The soldiers of Greek New Comedy typically return from campaign to wives and communities. Soldiers have been depicted on the comic stage since the fifth century, but this analysis suggests that not all of them were self-obsessed braggarts, and that this stereotype only emerges as dominant in the third century BCE.

This volume presents just a fraction of the sixty-four papers presented at Greek Drama V. We have endeavoured to select papers that reflect the scholarship shared at the conference, from the variety of playwrights and methodologies presented to the ranges of geography and career stages represented by our participants. This collection necessarily provides only a partial snapshot of both the conference and the current state of scholarship on ancient Greek drama. Fortunately, many of the papers presented were part of works in progress, and we look forward to seeing these ideas published in other venues in due course.

What is not represented in this volume, however, are the two other keynote events which sought to showcase the importance of performance and performance-rooted knowledge as part of our methodological toolkit for understanding ancient Greek theatre. In collaboration with C. W. Marshall, Brad Powers, a professor of Design and Production at UBC, along with his graduate students, built a working model of an *ekkyklēma*. In addition to taking the audience through the ancient evidence for the device, and factors that needed to be taken into consideration, such as what kind of ground surface the mechanism would move across, and the calculations required to determine size for various load capacities, the audience were treated to a practical demonstration. Using the scenes of Clytemnestra standing over the body of her husband at the end of Aeschylus' *Agamemnon* and the onstage suicide of Ajax in Sophocles' *Ajax*, the team demonstrated how the *ekkyklēma* might have been used for theatrical effect in antiquity. The conference ended with the performance of scenes from Helen Eastman's adaptation of Euripides' *Phoenician Women*, a work in progress. Particularly striking was her use of a chorus drawn from the UBC community, which included women from the ages of 11 to 80, several of whom had never performed onstage before. The production pointed to the theatrical power of a neglected play, but it also provided insight into how the inclusion of members of a community in the performance alongside professional actors impacts the audience's engagement with and emotional response to theatrical events.

As with all the previous Greek Drama conferences, the opportunity to gather together and share our research, in various stages of development, in a collegial and supportive environment fills us with excitement for the immediate and more distant future of this field of study. We are grateful for financial support to the Social Sciences and Humanities Research Council of Canada, the Peter Wall Institute for Advanced Studies at the University of British Columbia, the Faculty of Arts Visiting Speaker Grant program, the Hampton Co-Funding Grant program, the Department of Theatre and Film, and the

Department of Classical, Near Eastern, and Religious Studies at UBC whose contributions made this conference and this publication possible. Helen Eastman somehow managed to stage a fantastic conference performance with two days of rehearsal with a chorus she had not met. For help at the conference itself, we would like to thank Martin Cropp, Melissa Funke, Florence Yoon, Marios Kallos, the many student volunteers who built sets and helped shepherding stray academics, Cam Cronin for dealing with all the financial paperwork, and our team from Westside Midwives and BC Children's Hospital. For this volume, we would like to thank Alice Wright, Lily Mac Mahon and their team at Bloomsbury Academic for all the support and encouragement they have provided, the heroic work of Martina Treu, and Justin Dwyer and Graham Butler for their exceptional editorial assistance.

This volume is dedicated to John Davidson, who had hoped to attend the conference, but was unable. He has been a guiding figure for the Greek Drama conferences, having participated in the first four, and his collegial and convivial spirit was much missed at Greek Drama V.

NOTE ON TRANSLITERATION
AND NAMES

Most of the works discussed in this volume have titles in Greek, Latin and English by which they might be referred. To maximize accessibility, we have asked authors to refer to ancient works by their common titles, rather than aim for strict uniformity across chapters. The transliteration of Greek characters into English should be consistent within each chapter, as we have allowed authors to present a format that they feel best communicates their material. The contributors in the volume represent the study of Classics and the classical tradition in a wide range of countries, and contributions reflect that diversity in a number of ways, including habits of transliteration.

CHAPTER 1
THE POLITICS OF GREECE'S THEATRICAL REVOLUTION, *c.* 500–*c.* 300 BCE
Eric Csapo and Peter Wilson

Was Greek theatre political?[1] For tragedy opinion is divided, even polarized. For Old Comedy the controversy is not about politics, but whether the politics are 'serious'. New Comedy's 'politics', and even satyr play's, are almost as controversial as tragedy's. The lack of consensus in the case of specific genres offers little encouragement for anyone who would ask the same question about drama or ancient theatre culture in general. But we feel it is worth asking and we offer a different approach to evaluating the question.

In this paper we propose to examine the question of theatre and politics from the perspective of ancient reception. Our sources offer very little explicit comment on how they perceived the politics of drama or theatre, but we think some insight can be gained from the choices communities made in the fifth and fourth centuries as the new medium spread throughout the Greek world. Some states eagerly adopted theatre while others avoided it. Communities that did receive theatre similarly chose to accept or avoid specific theatre genres and practices. For the last twelve years we have collected all forms of evidence for theatre outside Athens.[2] As far as possible we tried to determine a date range for the reception of theatre in a given city. Wherever possible we inquired into the likely political orientation of the city at the time of reception. General trends emerged which help explain the processes by which theatre culture spread. But the sorting of theatre reception by political constitution surprised us by revealing striking disparities that we believe are most easily explained by supposing that politics played a significant role in each state's perception of theatre's benefits and risks.

A short history of the background to our question might begin with the volume *Nothing to Do with Dionysos?* In 1990 it was radically new, at least in Anglophone scholarship, in focusing on the question of theatre's politics in the abstract.[3] But it was also the last major contribution to scholarship that assumed with assurance that only Athens mattered (its subtitle provocatively called drama 'Athenian' not 'Greek' and more than one paper insisted that classical dramas were written exclusively for performance in Athens). The book linked the context and content of tragedy and comedy with Athenian democracy's values and aspirations. But this claim provoked challenges: just how exclusively 'Athenian' or 'democratic' were the theatre and its genres?

The challenge to 'Athenian' and the challenge to 'democratic' followed different paths. One began to explore theatre outside Athens, to quote the title of Kate Bosher's book of 2012.[4] The other questioned whether theatre (and especially tragedy) could be said to be democratic or political at all. Some, like Jasper Griffin, emphasized the timeless, universal, aesthetic and philosophical quality of Greek poetry.[5] Others, like Peter Rhodes, without abandoning the historicist agenda, looked for a deep-structuring context, not in any specific city or constitution, but in the historical formation of the Greek polis.[6] The question becomes particularly urgent when one combines these paths. Referring to several contributions to her volume on theatre in the Greek West, Kate Bosher concluded: 'This work shows that the widely accepted connection between Greek drama and democracy, set out in the 1990 volume, *Nothing to Do with Dionysus?*, for example, does not hold in the west.'[7] Why should democracy or Athens figure large in the account of a phenomenon that embraced many cities and many non-democratic cities?

The view that theatre appealed to many states, including many with non-democratic constitutions, is well substantiated by the evidence. But this fact does not require us entirely to abandon the view of theatre as democratic. Greek theatre was Panhellenic from the fifth century, much earlier than generally thought, but it nonetheless generated a culture that was widely perceived as democratic.[8] We will also argue that the view from outside Athens complicates things greatly and brings important qualifications to the debate, but it does not simply negate the applicability or importance of democracy or even Athens as a context for interpreting ancient performance.

It is well known that contemporary authors say little about the politics of theatre. Aristotle is largely silent. There is notoriously 'no polis in Aristotle's *Poetics*'.[9] Athens is mentioned only three times and democracy once – all in relation to the disputed history of comedy. Less attention has been paid to Plato who definitely sees drama as an essential outgrowth of democratic culture. But in the *Republic* (568c) Plato claims that tragedy, at least, belongs more to autocratic culture: tragic poets 'drag civic constitutions into tyranny and democracy'. Here the word order is deliberate: he goes on to say that tragic poets are honoured 'especially by the tyrants, and *secondly* by the democracies'. But Plato is a biased witness and his perceptions do not often reflect general attitudes.

Is Plato right? A close examination of over one hundred sites outside Attica yielded credible evidence of some form of theatre culture before 300 BCE.[10] We looked for evidence of a building that ancients or moderns identify as a theatre, evidence of performances of the theatre genres of drama or circular choruses (also known as men's and boys' choruses and less often as dithyramb), or some other strong index of theatrical culture as, for example, the prolific comic vase production of Taras which, along with statements from Plato, Aristoxenus and others, makes it more than probable that Taras had theatre throughout the fourth century. In many cases the evidence did not lend itself to precise dating for theatres or precise categorization for constitutions. Of the cities we examined, seventy-one also offered evidence of their political configuration at the date of theatre's initial reception (Figure 1.1). We begin therefore with some broad statistics suggesting general trends but move quickly to specific examples. It must be understood that these statistics are drawn from data whose compilation sometimes involved difficult decisions, given the variable but rarely very good quality of the evidence. We had to decide when theatre first appeared in a locality, what its constitutional shape was at that particular moment, and how that particular constitution might be inserted into the broad tripartite classification of democracy, oligarchy and autocracy. We admit that many steps involved speculative reconstruction, even if guided by a reasoned examination

DEMOCRACY	Possibly Democracy	AUTOCRACY	Possible Autocracy	OLIGARCHY	Possibly Oligarchy
1. Agyrion	Abdera	**Aegae**	Catane	Chios	Megara Hyblaea
2. Argos	Acragas	**Cyprus** (aside Paphos)	Caunus	**Corinth**	
3. **Attica**	Andros	**Dion**	Elea	**Megara**	
4. Byzantium	Cos	**Halicarnassus**	Ephesus	Sparta	
5. Chersonesus	Elis	**Heraclea Pontica**			
6. Cyzicus	Eretria	Ilium			
7. Delos	Erythrae	Messana			
8. Epidaurus	Gela	Nymphaeum			
9. Hephaistia	Leontini	Orchomenos in Boeotia			
10. Heraclea Minoa	Leucas	Panticapaeum			
11. Mantineia	Monte dei Cavalli	Paphos			
12. Megalopolis	Naxos	Pella			
13. **Myrina**	Rhegion	Pherae			
14. Mytilene	Stymphalos	Philippi			
15. **Olbia**		Scepsis			
16. Oropos		**Syracuse**			
17. **Priene**					
18. **Rhodes**					
19. **Salamis**					
20. **Samos**					
21. Siphnos					
22. **Taras**					
23. Tegea					
24. Tenos					
25. **Thasos**					
26. Thebes					

EITHER DEMOCRACY OR AUTOCRACY

Cyme

Cyrene

EITHER AUTOCRACY OR OLIGRACHY

Abydos

EITHER DEMOCRACY OR OLIGARCHY

Calydon

Chaeroneia

Thespiae

Cities for which drama is well attested are listed in **bold**.

Figure 1.1 Theatre in the fifth to fourth centuries: cities by constitution.

of all relevant evidence. The results therefore are open to adjustment in many areas, though we doubt that the overall impression created by the proportions will change much even when better evidence corrects the details. And these proportions are interesting.

Plato may have been right in suggesting that autocracies were the most enthusiastic recipients of theatre culture, but he was wrong if he meant to imply a numerical superiority. Our figures show twice as many democracies receiving theatre as autocracies. But Plato is most vindicated in his implication that theatre did not appeal to oligarchs.[11] Only four certain and another five possible oligarchic cities had theatre, compared with twenty-six to forty-five democracies or with sixteen to twenty-three autocratically governed cities.[12] This does not simply reflect the difference in the numerical ratios of different regimes: Hansen and Nielsen's polis inventory calculates that 32.4 per cent of classifiable fourth-century regimes were oligarchic, against 40.7 per cent democratic.[13] Let us assume that this figure might stand for the fifth and fourth as well as just the fourth century (if anything, a much higher figure for democracies is probable in the fifth).[14] A glance at Figure 1.2 clearly shows that democracy is grabbing more of the theatrical pie (Figure 1.2B) than it deserves according to its prevalence (Figure 1.2A), and this is equally true of autocracies. The percentages do not change visibly when we add the more doubtful cases which we list as 'possible' (Figure 1.2C). The glutton's share of the pie still belongs to democracy. Thus only about 8.7–9.9 per cent of the fifth- and fourth-century cities that had some sort of theatre culture were oligarchies at the time it was introduced, whereas the corresponding figure for democracies is close to 56.5–59.9 per cent.[15] We will see, moreover, that oligarchic theatre cultures are not only sparse but

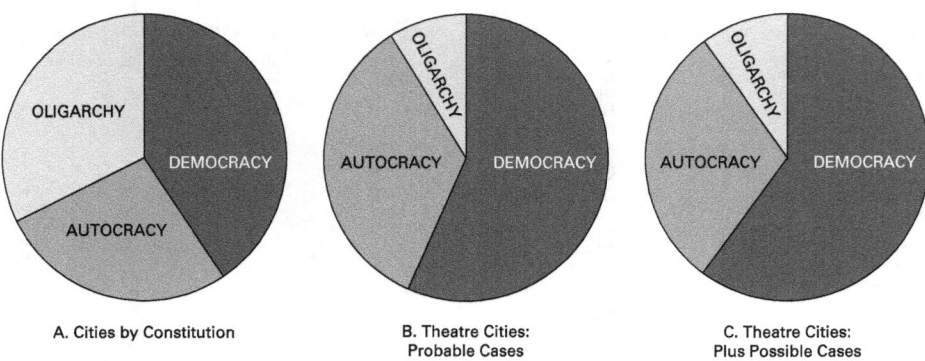

Figure 1.2 Democracies and theatre.

odd and different in other ways. But first let's examine some patterns in the spread of theatre to ancient democracies.

Democracies and Theatre

Athens created one of the primary channels through which theatre spread: in the fifth century, the Athenian Empire and, in the fourth, Athens' Aegean hegemony in the form of the Second Athenian Confederacy. The most direct transfer is through the transplantation of parts of Athens itself. Direct imitation of Athens was normal for Athenian cleruchies and colonies. As Robert Parker points out: 'The cleruchies of the fourth century were little replicas of Athens, with their own councils and assemblies ... and it is scarcely surprising to find such a basic amenity of Attic life as a tragic festival of Dionysos soon attested.'[16] The best examples are Salamis, Lemnos and Samos. Salamis was never incorporated into the Attic deme system. The island was settled by Athenians in the late sixth century and was probably a cleruchy from that time. The Athenians appointed an Archon for Salamis. Aristotle's *Constitution of the Athenians* says that the Archon's single most important duty was to 'run the Dionysia' (54.8). Monuments indicate that Salamis had a choregic system, tragedy and circular choruses by the end of the fifth century.[17]

Lemnos came under Athenian control around 500. The Athenians expelled the non-Greek native population, and planted colonists to make the island entirely theirs. Exploration of the early Hellenistic theatre at Hephaistia has revealed an earlier fifth-century phase.[18] The fifth-century theatre was superimposed upon a native Lemnian sanctuary to a goddess whom the Athenian settlers elsewhere on the island worshiped as a form of Cybele/Demeter and associated with Dionysus, a connection sympathetic to the incorporation of the Lemnian Dionysus within Attic and Eleusinian cult that we find in Euripides' *Hypsipyle*.[19] From 348 inscriptions in Myrina and Hephaistia attest a Dionysia, dramatic competitions, a choregic system and the announcement of public honours in the theatre, but it is likely that these were part of Lemnian life from the fifth century.[20]

Samos spent much of the fifth century as a more or less autonomous ally of Athens and first received an Athenian cleruchy after its revolt in 440, then a second, which involved the expulsion of the local population, around 365 and lasted to 322.[21] The oldest honorific decree from Samos, *IG* XII 6, 253, dated to 350, is by the Athenian cleruchs. It provides for the announcement of honours at the tragic contest of the local Dionysia. Several other states owe their theatre culture to Athenians abroad. Athenian cleruchs probably contributed to the development of theatre in Eretria, Lesbos, Naxos and Andros.[22] This phenomenon may not be limited to the Aegean: Thurii in South Italy is in large part an Athenian foundation in the time of Pericles, and many believe that it was a major transfer point of Athenian culture, including theatre, to the region.[23]

More common in the Aegean is the reception of theatre by democratic states subject to Athens. To reinforce their military and economic interests, Athens attempted to bind her Delian League allies with political and cultural ties. Two policies had important consequences for theatre history. One was Athens' general support for the democratic factions in allied cities.[24] This reinforced Athens' imperial influence not only through the creation of common political values, but also through the subject cities' fear of political instability and oligarchic reprisals that might follow a withdrawal of Athenian support. The other was a more direct involvement of allies within what Peter Rhodes called the 'imperial festival', Athens' own Dionysia.[25] It was to the Dionysia that allied cities brought their tribute, probably beginning immediately after the transference of the treasury from Delos to Athens in 453. Particularly revealing of the care Athens took to involve subjects directly in the festival is an Athenian decree of 372 (*SEG* 31, 67) that required the city of Paros to 'bring a cow and a phallos to the Dionysia *since they are in fact colonists of the people of Athens*'. This requirement for cow and phallos is said to be 'traditional', *kata ta patria*, and we know that colonists were indeed to bring a phallos to the Dionysia from a decree of 445 (*IG* I³ 46) founding the colony of Brea. But the only basis for the assertion that Paros was a colony of Athens was Athens' own mythic claim to be the mother city of all Ionians.[26] The example of Paros strongly suggests that all Ionian cities were subject to the same pressure. The phallos and cow would of course require a chorus or choruses to accompany them in the Dionysian Parade, so the delegations from subject states were reasonably large, adding choreuts to the officials who went to discuss political or military matters with Athens and the other allies.[27] Familiarity with the Athenian Dionysia can be assumed throughout the Empire from the mid fifth century.

It would be a mistake to regard this invitation to the Dionysia as simply a form of Athenian imperial oppression: surely the tribute was, but the Dionysia made that burden sweeter. In fact it seems that the allies embraced the Dionysia as a symbol of the Empire's cultural power. Cities of the Empire are, in any case, the largest and most coherent group in the classical spread of theatre. Some two dozen states are known to have acquired, or can be reasonably suspected of having acquired, some form of theatre culture at the time of the Athenian Empire or under the hegemonic influence of Athens at the time of the fourth-century Athenian Confederacy (see Figure 1.3).[28] In one of our often-cited

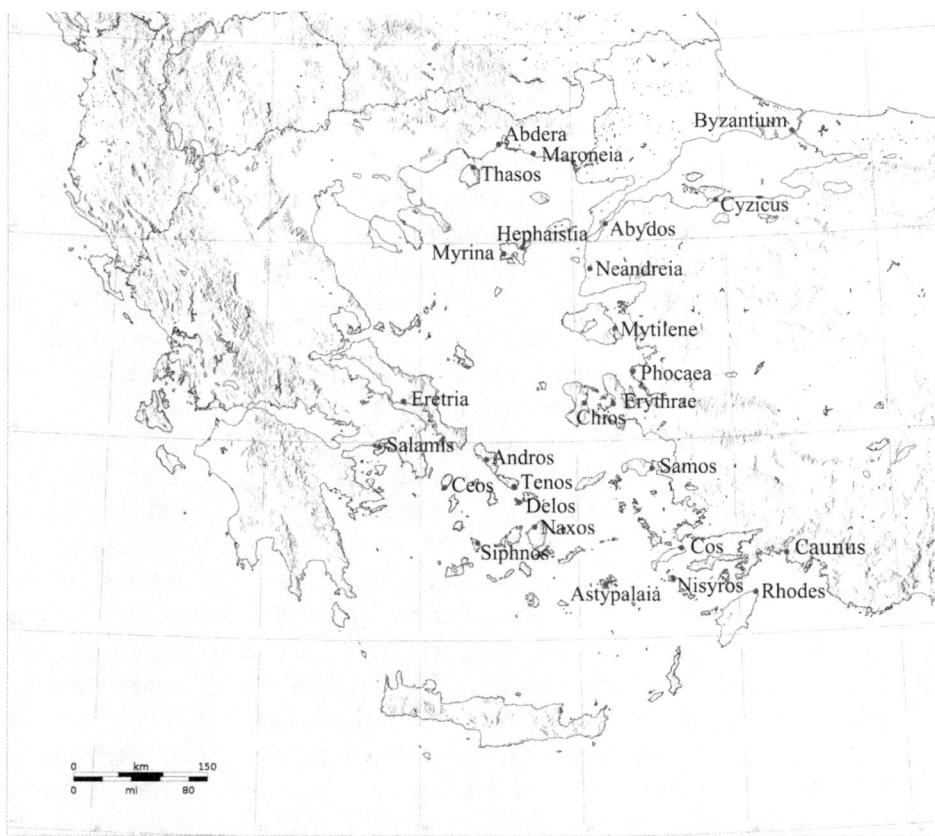

Figure 1.3 Colonies and subject cities that probably acquired theatre culture under Athenian hegemony.

anecdotes about the spread of theatre culture, it is simply assumed that as early as the late fifth century, even a remote and semi-Hellenized city of the Athenian Empire would have better access to Athenian tragedy than a major centre in the Greek West: Plutarch's anecdote in the *Life of Nicias* (29), probably drawn from Philochorus, tells us that even a Caunian ship was only allowed to dock in Syracuse harbour on the promise that the Caunians would teach the Syracusans Euripides' songs.[29] The most recent archaeological evidence from Caunus itself suggests that the Carian city already had a theatre on the north-western slopes of its Great Acropolis at least by the first half of the fourth century.[30]

In general the Aegean region presents several consistent features due to imitation of the Athenian model:

1. All these cities were members of Athens' Aegean empire.

2. All (but Chios) were so far as we can tell certainly or probably democracies at the time theatre is received. Chios is a special case which we will look at later.

3. All the theatrical festivals are initially Dionysia (this is definitely not the case in other regions).[31]

4. Where the evidence exists, the Aegean states resemble the Athenian Dionysia in competitive format, in performance genres (tragedy is almost universally attested but comedy, satyr play and men's and/or boys' lyric choruses appear throughout the region), in their public funding through state-appointed choregoi or in imitation of other Athenian practices.

A striking example comes, not from an Ionian, but from the Dorian city of Rhodes, founded by the synoecism in 408/7 of Ialysos, Kamiros and Lindos. Rhodes may have been a Spartan-dominated oligarchy at its foundation, but before 395 Rhodes revolted against Sparta and became a democracy. Rhodes' founding cities had been members of the Delian League and in 378 Rhodes became a founding member of the Second Athenian Confederacy. Inscriptions show that Rhodes, probably from the beginning of its democracy, but certainly by the 380s, had a Dionysia with a programme comparable to that of Athens. Our information comes unexpectedly from Rome. Twenty fragments of didascalic inscriptions, *IGUR* I 215–234) were mostly recovered from medieval buildings or Renaissance collections but three were excavated in modern times (*IGUR* 215, 220, 221), all from the theatre district of Rome, where the theatres of Pompey, Balbus and Marcellus were located. In the theatre district the temple of Hercules Musarum formed the headquarters of the Roman Artists of Dionysus (or *Artifices Scaenici*). Since other fragments of the same date and style actually mention the Artists, it is believed that this inscription decorated their office.[32] Most fragments of these so-called Roman Fasti deal with the Athenian Dionysia and Lenaea (*IGUR* I 215–222). Less well studied are eight fragments (*IGUR* I 223–230) that include information about the Dionysia at Rhodes: all these were found in the pavement of the church of San Paolo, and seven of them are now lost except for a transcription (Figure 1.4) by Filippo Buonarroti (great grandnephew of Michelangelo) on a page of transcriptions labelled *in pavimento D. Pauli*. The eighth (*IGUR* I 230, or *h* below) was found by Moretti in the same church's collection and its discovery in the pavement was confirmed by local sources.[33] Internal evidence shows that this first-century Roman inscription copies a Hellenistic source.

The inscription proves that by the 380s Rhodes had something resembling the Athenian Dionysia in content and scale.[34] The San Paolo fragments detail the careers of star tragic actors. The actors are listed in the chronological order of their first victory at any of three festivals: the Athenian Dionysia, the Athenian Lenaea and the Dionysia at Rhodes. After each actor's name follow all his first-place finishes in chronological order at any of the three festivals. Next follow second- and third-place finishes, but these may all be Rhodian (see below). In addition to prizes and festivals, the inscription names the plays with which the actor competed and the authors of those plays. Because of uncertainty regarding the length of the lines it is hard to know what parts belong to what competition, but Rhodes is explicitly mentioned in three places (Figure 1.4 *a* line 4 [ἐν] ʽΡόδωι νεμηθείς; *e* line 2 ἐν ʽΡόδ[ωι]; *g* line 5 ἐν ʽΡόδῳ δεύ[τερος]). In two places, the

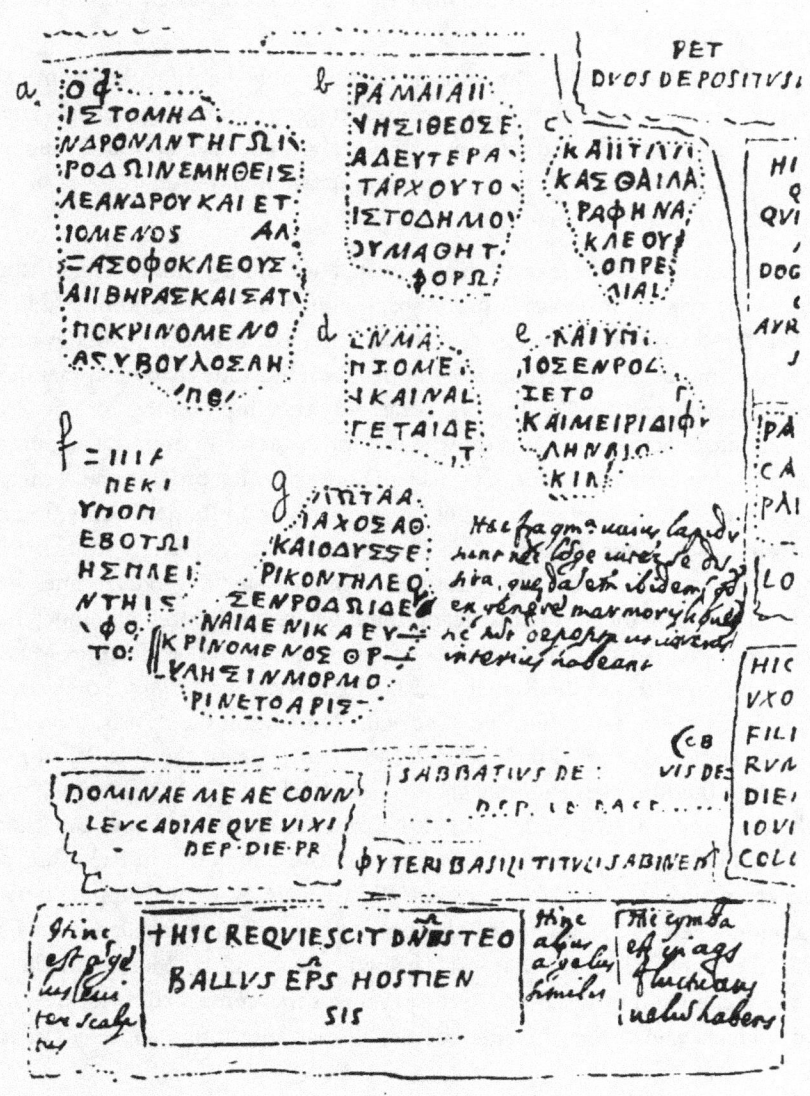

Figure 1.4 Buonarroti's drawing of the fragments from San Paolo (Florence, Biblioteca Marucelliana A 6f. 492). After Moretti 1960: pl. 3. Courtesy of the Ministero per i beni e le attività culturali/Biblioteca Marucelliana di Firenze.

assignment of an actor to a Rhodian tribe is mentioned (Figure 1.4 *a* line 4 [ἐν] ῾Ρόδωι νεμηθείς; *e* line 4 Καμειρίδι φυ[λῆ]), showing that each set of tragedies was publicly funded by the tribes (just as were lyric choruses and later comedy at Athens). Other inscriptions confirm this funding model. There were, therefore, three entries in the tragic competition, each assigned to one of the founding tribes named for the founding cities: Ialysos, Kamiros (cf. *e* line 4) and Lindos. As mentioned, this set of inscriptions also names second and third places as well as rival competitors.[35] But no other source records more than a single prize for actors either in Athens or anywhere else. Therefore, all the information on this list that relates to second and third actors' prizes, or that names competing actors, probably relates to Rhodes. Rhodes had good reason to rank all three competing actors, namely the tribal funding model (in addition to the likelihood that the actors here performed the role of *didaskaloi*).[36] In sum, whereas Athenian records named only the winning actor, Rhodian records appear to have ranked the actors as first, second and third, and thereby gave later antiquity a special window on the careers of the famous classical actors, not only showing who won, but who beat whom. This would explain why the Rhodian list was of particular interest to the Roman actors' guild.

The actors named on the inscription are known from other sources: Mnesitheos, Thrasyboulos, Eupolemos and Kleandros, possibly Aristodemos and Philotades.[37] The poets whose plays they directed are also international stars, but included classics as well as contemporary tragedians. Sophocles is named at least once[38] – judging from the titles, this is the Elder Sophocles[39] – and possibly also Aristarchus. Mentions of Sophocles, if it is the famous Sophocles, must also relate to Rhodes, since at the Athenian festivals revivals fell outside the competition. Note, too, that two satyr plays are named suggesting that at a time when at Athens the genre was obsolescent and only performed in isolation, as a warm-up to and outside the competition, Rhodes was still producing satyr play after a set of tragedies as had once been traditional in Athens.[40]

Other fourth-century Rhodian inscriptions show that the tribes appointed choregoi to sponsor boys' choruses, and later inscriptions show the choregoi supporting men's choruses and comedy.[41] The fragments of the Roman Fasti give no evidence of comedy in early-fourth-century Rhodes, but the fact that Anaxandrides and Antiphanes, two of the most productive comic poets of the first half of the fourth century, are said to be Rhodians suggests that comedy was also a likely feature of the original Rhodian Dionysia. In other words, it looks as if, from the creation of the democracy in 395, or soon after, Rhodes had a full Dionysia with everything and more than contemporary Athens offered, including competitions of men's and boys' lyric choruses, tragic tetralogies with satyr play, comedy, a competition for actors with three prizes, a system of choregic funding, a practice of setting up choregic victory monuments, and accurate public archives recording competitors and winners. In fact, the presence of tetralogies with satyr plays suggests if anything that the Rhodians adopted and preserved a 'classic' fifth-century Athenian format after Athens itself had abandoned it.

This impression is strongly reinforced by information preserved by Diodorus (20.84.3). He tells us that in 305, when under threat from Demetrius the Besieger, the Rhodians passed decrees liberating slaves willing to fight, giving public burial for the war dead and granting a panoply to their sons in the theatre at the Dionysia when they came of age. These provisions are all known from Athens, but the last is of special interest to us because it directly copies a pre-performance ritual of the Athenian theatre from much earlier in the century.[42] Rhodian theatre culture follows the classic Athenian model to the letter and arguably does so, not out of any excess love of Athens, but to adopt Athens' paradigmatically *democratic* theatre culture.

Rhodes demonstrates some characteristics of a third category of theatre reception. There were democracies that appear to have embraced theatre, even though they had no strong connection to Athens, and the circumstances sometimes suggest that they embraced theatre as an expression of democratic culture. The cities of Arcadia, for example, had no part in Athens' Aegean empires. On the contrary, Spartan hegemony sat heavily over Arcadia until the Battle of Leuctra in 371. At that point the Arcadians threw off their Spartan-backed oligarchies and became democracies.[43] In addition, they formed the Arcadian League with a view to resisting a Spartan resurgence and founded Megalopolis to serve as its capital. A monumental theatre stood at the very heart of the new city's design. Even if the precise date of the completion of the stone theatre is disputed, we have compelling evidence for a theatre from the 360s from blocks of the original *skēnē* reused in the later fourth-century *skēnē*. The blocks have cuttings for timbers, indicating a wooden phase.[44] It was the 'largest theatre in Greece', even in Pausanias' day (7.32.1), and a conspicuous emblem of new cultural aspirations. The fifth-century theatre of Mantinea was rebuilt in stone at this time and new theatres were built in Tegea and Orchomenus.[45] It is immediately after the liberation from Spartan hegemony that we first hear of a theatre at Phigaleia where the oligarchic faction, before withdrawing to the safety of Sparta, took bloody revenge on the new democracy by swooping down on their fellow citizens as they sat in the theatre watching a performance.[46] Arcadia, moreover, seems to have adopted a uniform theatre culture: all the Arcadian cities probably had Dionysia and publicly-funded contests, but on a different model from Athens. They were run by agonothetai, and there was a practice of dedicating stone seats in the theatres at the end of their term of office.[47] We do not have evidence of drama, but the Arcadian Polybius (4.20.8–21) attests the popularity in what he considered antiquity of men's and boys' circular choruses, specifically by composers associated with the first great wave of the popular so-called 'theatre music', Philoxenus and the famously Laconophobic Timotheus.

In Boeotia, we find traces of a similar spread of theatrical culture under the impulse of recent democratization and league formation that we saw in Arcadia. Despite its long and rich musical and Dionysian traditions, the earliest evidence for theatre in Thebes comes immediately after the democratic coup in 379 that ousted the Theban oligarchs and the Spartan garrison that secured their position. Right after the coup Epaminondas is reported to have obtained a loan from his fellow conspirators to sponsor a choregia for a men's chorus and then about a decade later found himself in the theatre on trial for exceeding his constitutional powers.[48] It was under the Boeotian League dominated by democratic Thebes that the Panboeotian festival of the Mouseia was developed, if not created, at Thespiae.[49] The theatre and a competition for men's and boys' circular choruses probably date from the period of Theban hegemony. No drama is attested until the end of the third century. The League created another Panboeotian festival, the Basileia, at Lebadeia to commemorate the Boeotian victory over Sparta at the Battle of Leuctra (371). There is (unfortunately undatable) evidence for a theatre and later evidence for musical competitions, though it is likely that both were created at this time.[50]

Oligarchies and Theatre

We noted that oligarchic states with theatre culture were surprisingly few. In fact, Thespiae, as we have just seen, probably acquired its theatre culture in the time of the democratic Second Boeotian League and the same may be true of Calydon and Chaeronea. Abydos was more likely an autocracy.[51] So our focus needs to be on Chios, Corinth, Megara and Sparta. Unlike theatre in democratic states, theatre in oligarchic states is idiosyncratic, though with a few odd characteristics in common:

1. For a small group there are a large number of fifth-century, especially early-fifth-century start dates (Megara, Sparta, maybe Corinth).

2. Most had choral performances in their theatres, but in the fifth and fourth centuries no drama (Sparta, Chios, Thespiae, maybe Corinth).

3. Megara is a major exception as it had comedy, but it was a comedy independent of the Athenian type and probably older. Dick Green posits a regional form of comedy for Corinth as well, based on iconography.[52] Perhaps the one thing oligarchies do have in common is the complete avoidance of tragedy. We have no evidence that any oligarchic state ever initiated a tragic competition. Indeed the only evidence for tragic performance in a fifth- or fourth-century oligarchic state is for Athens in 411, 404–403 and 321–307.[53]

4. Often theatres or theatre festivals were for gods other than Dionysus (Sparta, Corinth, Thespiae, but the theatre festivals were Dionysia in Megara and Chios).

In general, the few oligarchic states that had theatre remained independent of the main trends and independent in their own way. Many possibly developed before one could even properly speak of an Athenian paradigm. Most, if not all (Corinth possibly excepted), seem to have remained aloof from international trends until the Hellenistic period.

By the mid fifth century Megara produced a form of drama that other Greeks identified as *komoidia*, though modern scholarship tends to dismiss it as 'farce', *Possenspiel*, etc. Aristotle notes that both the Megarians of the mainland and those in Sicily claimed the invention of comedy.[54] This probably indicates shared origins in a period of cultural exchange between mother city and colony that necessarily predates the destruction of Sicilian Megara by Gelon in 483. The mainland Megarians of Aristotle's day, though firmly oligarchic, substantiated their claim to the invention of comedy by pointing out that they had a democracy earlier than Athens. By doing so they acceded to a belief that the connection between comedy and democracy was somehow natural or essential (ἀντιποιοῦνται τῆς τε τραγῳδίας καὶ τῆς κωμῳδίας οἱ Δωριεῖς – τῆς μὲν γὰρ κωμῳδίας οἱ Μεγαρεῖς οἵ τε ἐνταῦθα ὡς ἐπὶ τῆς παρ' αὐτοῖς δημοκρατίας γενομένης, 'and for this reason the Dorians are rival claimants both to tragedy and comedy – in the case of comedy the Megarians here, on the grounds that it came into being in the time of their democracy'). There is nonetheless no evidence that the political comedy developed by Cratinus, Aristophanes and Eupolis was ever a feature of Megarian comedy.

Classical Sparta had more than one building that could be called a theatron. One is attested for 486 by Herodotus (6.67) as the place where, during the Gymnopaidia, Demaratus received the public insult that led to his self-exile in Persia. Pausanias (3.11.9) records that the Gymnopaidia took place in a space called the 'Choros' in the Spartan Agora. Kourinou and others have identified the 'Choros' with an archaic construction known as the 'Round Building'.[55] More recently Greco and Voza have argued that the Round Building is the Skias, where Pausanias saw the lyre of Timotheus, with its cut strings, on display, presumably because it was the site of non-choral musical performances. If correct, this is significant as the Skias dates to the mid sixth century. Its position, overlooking the Agora, together with Pausanias' location of the Choros in the Agora, suggests that the Spartan Agora was used for choral performances from at least this time. The theatron was likely temporary wooden seating built around the Agora for choral festivals: such temporary theatra were in fact normal in the fifth century – Athens itself built stands of wooden seats, *ikria,* onto the south slope of the Acropolis until about 340 BCE. In either case Sparta is the site of our earliest 'theatre' construction.[56] Sparta is also the source of the earliest surviving prohedric seat from any theatre, in this case from the sanctuary of Athena Alea.[57]

Sparta's festivals, the Karneia, Gymnopaidia and Hyakinthia, possibly date back to the seventh century. They included local citizen choruses, probably divided by age, tribe and phratry, and supported by a choregic system that Aristotle dates back at least to the post-Persian War period and in which the choregoi served also as the pipers.[58] In addition there were citharodic contests, open to international competitors, at the Karneia, Gymnopaidia and Hyakinthia, dating back possibly to the seventh century. Theatre music in archaic and classical Sparta was connected to Apollo, and possibly also Demeter, Artemis and Athena. Significantly we have no evidence for circular choruses and no evidence for drama until 105 CE.[59]

Chios offers a symmetrical but opposite situation to that of Arcadia and Boeotia. The latter throwing off Spartan hegemony embraced theatre culture when they embraced democracy; Chios endured the yoke of Athenian hegemony but rejected both democracy and theatre. As a non-tributary ally of the Delian League, and then as a member of Athens' fourth-century confederacy, Chios was allowed to retain its oligarchic constitution until about 330 when Alexander imposed democracy. Chios successfully resisted the theatre music that otherwise spread like wildfire across the Aegean. And yet Dionysus was hugely important to this island famous for its wine. Among other things, local legend had it that Dionysus' son Oenopion founded Chios.[60] The magnificence of Chios' Dionysia is attested by the early-fourth-century author Aeneas Tacticus (17.5). The same author, however, singles out a very un-Dionysian feature of its otherwise 'brilliant parades' (πομπὰς λαμπράς). The Chians' anxiety that the licence of the parade might trigger a revolution caused them to regularly 'occupy in advance with guards and copious troops the roads opening onto the marketplace'. Even the icon of Dionysus was kept in chains.[61] After being democratized by Alexander, Chios seems only to have added a competition for boys' choruses to the Dionysia. We have no evidence for drama, nor even men's choruses, at any time in the island's history. The fact that for centuries afterwards public honours were announced at the contest for boys' choruses seems to guarantee the absence of these more prestigious genres.[62] The absence is all the more astonishing given that Ion, one of the most renowned tragedians (and dithyrambists) of the fifth century, was Chian. We can conclude that Ion's tragedies were only viewed by Chians when they visited Athens or other Aegean cities, and it says something of the uneasiness of the relationship between Athens and ally that Ion for political reasons embraced Athenian hegemony to the point of claiming, in his history of the island, that its founder, Oenopion, was a son not of Dionysus but of Theseus.[63] Ion's philathenianism was shared by his son, a leader of the democratic faction, whom the oligarchy put to death in 411 on a charge, Thucydides tells us, 'of being pro-Athenian' (8.38.3). Chian democrats it seems opened their hearts both to Athens and tragedy as readily as the oligarchs closed theirs, and evidently for the same reasons. This conclusion appears true of oligarchies in general.

Autocracies and Theatre

If democrats and oligarchs seem generally to agree that theatre culture and drama in particular are democratic, this view was not shared by autocrats who, as Plato suggested, were even fonder than democracies of tragedy. Drama's success in autocracies certainly proves that there is nothing *essentially* democratic about it, even despite formal links between drama and democratic dialogicity. But, at the same time, we need to judge whether autocratic theatre is quite the same as democratic theatre. Is there some sense in which autocracy converts a dialogic into a monologic form? This is a bigger question than we can properly answer here, but we are able to outline briefly some major differences in the theatre cultures of late archaic and classical autocracies.

The autocracies that received Greek theatre are located on what we might call the barbarian fringe: Sicily, North Africa, Thessaly, Macedon, Caria, the Black Sea and Cyprus. From 485 in Syracuse the tyrants Gelon and Hieron took a keen interest in theatre as later did Dionysius I.[64] Two fifth-century theatres are found in Cyrene, and the excavators now date the earliest *skēnē* to the first half of the fifth century in the time of the Battiad monarchy.[65] Macedon's engagement with theatre begins with the tyranny of Archelaus around 410.[66] There is some evidence for a decree in Magnesia that gave honours to Euripides during his lifetime, so it may be that Thessaly also received theatre about this time, though we only hear of it at Pherae and at Skotoussa in or shortly after 370 in relation to the tyrant Alexander.[67] Theatre and drama first appear in the Pontic region in Heraclea in the time of the Clearchid tyranny as early as the 360s and by 353 in the Cimmerian Bosporus ruled by the Spartocids.[68]

There is a point to be made about this fringe pattern. It is perhaps easiest to make for Macedon, which for Greeks was actually beyond the 'barbarian' fringe. Theatre in Macedon is a remarkable instance of the adoption of a Greek cultural form by non-Greeks, but Greekness was precisely one of theatre's great attractions for the Macedonian rulers. Theatre culture made Archelaus and his successors appear Greek to Greek eyes, and this was no small asset in both the economic and the military sphere. A major component of this Greekness, especially in the early period, was Athenianness, given the income and good will Archelaus was able to generate by providing the raw materials to rebuild the Athenian fleet after its defeat in Sicily.[69] The Black Sea made similar use of theatre. The Spartocids of the half-Scythian Cimmerian Bosporus literally traded upon their Athenianness. They personally controlled the very lucrative export in grain and raw material to Athens to the point that on one occasion Athens directly intervened to save them from a coup and on another turned a blind eye to their occupation of an Athenian outpost, while granting the Spartocids Athenian citizenship and heaping them with other honours.[70]

As with oligarchies, theatre festivals in autocratic realms are normally not Dionysia. In Syracuse the theatres were associated with sanctuaries of Apollo or Demeter and Kore. This in fact appears to be true of all theatres in Sicily, and it is also true of the theatres in Cyrene. In Macedon the first theatre festivals were for Olympian Zeus and for Zeus and the Muses. Only in the Black Sea region are the theatre festivals Dionysia and thus in conformity with the Athenian–Aegean koine.[71]

Unlike oligarchs, autocrats happily received all major genres: tragedy, comedy, circular chorus, even satyr play. The evidence confirms Plato's claim that tragedy had a special appeal for autocrats. We do, however, also find comedy (notably represented by Epicharmus) flourishing under the Syracusan tyrants, though it may be of a less political and more philosophical kind than its Attic counterpart. Comedy is also attested at the Macedonian court, possibly from the time of Archelaus, but certainly under Philip.[72] The life histories of the most famous poets of circular choruses are bound tight with the tyrants of Macedon and Syracuse: Archelaus kept Melanippides and Timotheus; Philip sponsored circular choruses; Dionysius I kept Philoxenus, and it is notably Kinesias who proposes an honorary decree at Athens for the tyrant—that Kinesias acts as much as a poet of circular choruses as an Athenian is suggested by the fact that this is the first decree we know of to have been set up in the Theatre of Dionysus.[73] Alexander sponsored the whole gamut including satyr play.[74] Though the Black Sea autocracies give direct attestation only of unspecified 'drama' and citharodic performances, the presence of Xenotimus, son of Carcinus, in the Bosporan kingdom suggests tragic performance in the early fourth century and a choregic relief indicates comic performance a few decades later.[75] Cyrene, at least in the fourth century, had tragedy, dithyramb and probably also comedy.[76]

Fifth- and fourth-century autocrats began the process of personalizing theatre that characterizes Hellenistic practice. This personalization affects every aspect of performance: the occasion, the performers, the theatrical space and the performance. This is an important contrast to the public nature of democratic theatre.

Occasion: Our sources for Syracusan and Macedonian theatre often imply that festivals were arranged at the whim of the autocrat. For Philip and Alexander literary evidence for theatre performance often takes the form we find in Arrian (*An.* 1.11.1–2): 'having transacted this business, he returned to Macedonia. He conducted the sacrifice to Zeus Olympios which had already been established by Archelaus, and he arranged the games, the Olympics, in Aegae. Some say that he also did a contest for the Muses.' Notices of this kind appear even in the accounts of campaigns in barbarian lands, so there is no question of simply booking in a regular festival.[77] From the very beginning autocrats made theatre occasional and the occasions marked milestones in the autocrats' CVs: the founding of cities, royal weddings, military victories, royal funerals.[78] Even when the festivals are named for gods they seem to be timed to fit the autocrat's, not the god's, busy schedule.

Performers: Syracusan and Macedonian autocrats bound poets and actors to themselves with gifts and favours. Many famous poets like Aeschylus, Euripides and Agathon became their poets in residence. Isocrates' evidence (17.15) of a close connection between Carcinus' theatrical family and Satyrus I, founder of the Bosporan dynasty, seems to tell the same story. Even Pixodaros the Hecatomnid tyrant and satrap of Caria relied on actors as confidants in secret negotiations with Philip.[79] This kind of intimacy was useful if you wanted to conjure up a theatre festival quickly. Consider Plutarch's phrase: 'Alexander dealt with urgent business and once more turned his attention to theatres and festivals, when three thousand scenic artists arrived from Greece' (*Alex.* 72). The scene is distant Ecbatana, 1,500 kilometres from the eastern limit of the Mediterranean. Actors really did drop everything and run, as did Athenodoros, who stood up the Athenian Dionysia in 331, knowing that Alexander would pay his fine for non-appearance and offer other rewards besides.[80] It is no coincidence that at precisely this time Athens starts decreeing civic honours to theatrical performers, prominently citing their fidelity to the Athenian people.[81]

Theatre space: Bosher and Moretti in particular have drawn attention to the monumentality and innovation that marks Sicilian and Macedonian theatre architecture.[82] Gelon may have constructed a monumental theatre that was not only grander than its Athenian counterpart but possibly served as his tomb (the archaeological evidence is hotly debated and only partially published by Giuseppe Voza).[83] Autocrats vied with one another and with non-tyrannical states (especially Athens) to assert geopolitical primacy in what looks like a race to build the largest or most magnificent stone theatre. Moretti, in fact, finds it 'not without some plausibility' that Macedon succeeded in producing a horseshoe-shaped stone theatre before the Lycurgan theatre in Athens and may also have created the first-ever proskenion theatre.[84]

Performance: Autocratic use of theatre for propaganda is notorious: Aeschylus' command reperformance of *Persians* in Syracuse placed Hieron's military achievements in the West on an equal footing with those of the Greeks in repelling Persia in the East; Aeschylus' *Women of Aetna* validated his foundation of the city of Aetna in 476; in the *Archelaus* Euripides spliced the tyrant into the royal lineage of Argos, made him a direct descendent of Heracles and turned Archelaus from tyrant to hereditary king with a firm endorsement by Zeus.

But autocrats insinuated themselves into theatrical performances in more subtle ways: into the processions and ceremonials that precede the competitions, for example, imprinting themselves as head of state and chief transactor of sacrifice to the gods. The unfortunate downside was that the propaganda worked best when the tyrant's dragoons were least visible and so such occasions offered excellent opportunity for assassination as they did in the case of Philip of Macedon and Clearchus of Heraclea.[85] Tyrants could also insinuate themselves into the theatre performances: notoriously Dionysius I of Syracuse and Mamercus of Catane both wrote tragedies.[86] Le Guen speculates that Alexander himself may have commissioned or even written the satyr play *Agen*.[87] Anne Duncan shows that Dionysius' tragedies included openly autobiographical content through which Dionysius depicted himself as a good tragic king.[88] And as the theatre was the main forum in which the autocrat met his subjects face-to-face, image-making and careful orchestration of the tyrant's appearance in the theatre led to a theatricalization of the tyrant: Dionysius I and Demetrius the Besieger are said to have dressed like tragic kings.[89] Dionysius even tried to confuse himself with Euripides. He is said to have acquired the instruments with which Euripides composed his tragedies and, in Hermippus' words, 'dedicated them in the sanctuary of the Muses after inscribing them with his own name and Euripides' (*FGrH* 1026 F84). Dionysius' kinsman and spin doctor Philistus is probably responsible for the false synchronization of Euripides' death with Dionysius' accession to power that appears in Timaeus *FGrH* 566 F 105, a suggestion, if not an actual assertion, of the reincarnation of the poet in the tyrant. Dionysius is probably also the first tyrant to fashion himself as an incarnation of Dionysus, a trick that Alexander, Demetrius, the Ptolemies and the Seleucids picked up to perfect the personalization of theatre.[90]

Before concluding, let us ask if autocratic states had a significant role in the spread of theatre that might rival Athens' role in disseminating theatre to her colonies and imperial subjects. This is obviously true in central and eastern Greece where Philip, Alexander and his successors founded and rebuilt many cities with theatres. The evidence in West Greece is much more mixed. Aetna probably had a theatre from its foundation by Hieron in 476.[91] Dionysius I founded Tyndaris in 396 which may have included a theatre in its original design and also probably Issa in the Adriatic whose Roman theatre is thought to overlie a Greek predecessor and from which a fourth-century comic scene, possibly of local manufacture, was recently published.[92] Despite local promotion by tyrants, classical theatre in West Greece seems just as often to be a phenomenon of democratization. Several cities adopted drama under the democratic regimes that sprang up after the ousting of tyrants or oligarchs: Gela, for example, seems to have created a dramatic festival at the tomb of Aeschylus in a context of what Robinson calls 'vigorous democratization' following the expulsion of the tyrant.[93] Acragas probably adopted theatre after liberation from the tyrant Thrasydaeus in 472.[94] Agyrion, Locri and Rhegion, cities founded or dominated by Dionysius, built theatres only after his death, when their constitutions changed from oligarchic to democratic.[95]

Conclusion

Did fifth- and fourth-century Greece view theatre as democratic? In many, perhaps most, cases yes. Democracy was a major factor driving Greece's theatrical revolution in the late archaic and classical epochs. Athenian colonies embraced theatre as part of their democratic heritage. The democratic cities of Athens' Aegean empire and hegemony also seem generally to have adopted theatre practices as close to the Athenian model as they could afford. Most tellingly, oligarchies either avoided theatre altogether or, if they had theatre, avoided drama, and none, so far as we know, ever received tragedy. There are striking examples of states like Rhodes, Thebes and the cities of Arcadia that embraced theatre as soon as they threw off the oligarchic yoke and became democracies, and examples of oligarchic cities like Chios that remained doggedly theatreless, despite their close integration into Athens' Aegean empires. Oligarchic Megara and Sparta that already had theatre traditions remained idiosyncratic and failed to conform to the common theatre culture that developed about them. All this shows that the spread of theatre (or its failure to spread in some areas) was due to a perception that theatre was linked in some way with democratic culture. Or, at least, this is true in the Greek heartland, the Peloponnese, Attica, the Aegean, and even parts of the Greek West. The autocratic regimes on the fringe of the Greek world, however, clearly saw nothing irremediably democratic in theatre culture, but, on the contrary, embraced it in full as an ideal instrument for maintaining and developing their power and prestige. So, in answer to the question, 'Was Greek theatre culture perceived as democratic in the fifth and fourth century?', one has to say generally 'yes and no' or address the specifics of time, place and purpose.

The question of how broadly and how long theatre culture was perceived as 'Athenian' is more difficult to answer. But certainly this perception is at the heart of the spread through Athenian colonies and cleruchies. Aegean cities might have been tempted, when convenient, to regard theatre as rather more a part of a common heritage than something strictly 'Athenian'. But the reluctance of places like Sparta, Thebes or Megara, traditional enemies of Athens (and its empire), to adopt or adapt their theatre culture may owe something to a perception that Athens was implicated no less than democracy. In the case of the Macedonian and Black Sea autocracies, theatre's Athenianness may in fact have proved part of the initial attraction, not least because they shared strong economic interests with Athens and its empires, particularly through the trade in raw materials. Athens, in turn, can frequently be seen shoring up the autocrats' political and social authority, quite independently of the cultural power it exerted through theatre.

Paradoxically then, the reception of theatre and particularly drama in the rest of Greece, even by autocracies, in many ways affirms rather than undermines the importance of both democracy and Athens in the first two centuries of theatre's history. But, at the same time, it would be a serious mistake to fall back upon the traditional assumption that therefore the only contexts that really matter for interpreting drama or any other form of theatre culture in this period are democracy and Athens. Even if the democratic and Athenian glamour of theatre seems to stick long and hard, each time, place and purpose might allow for a strong or a weak perception of these associations. Indeed Athenian primacy in theatre was frequently and increasingly contested, even in the fifth century, but increasingly in the fourth. Autocrats, especially in Macedon and Sicily, increasingly challenged Athens' economic primacy and moral authority in the theatre industry. Other Greek cities, including oligarchic and autocratic regimes, laid claim to the invention of tragedy, comedy, satyr play and even mime. These challenges, particularly in the case of Syracuse and Megara, were not without some foundation, though, of course, the real issue was never just setting the historical record straight. But the very existence of these challenges to the dominant Athenian narrative of theatre's history also shows just how much, despite its wide distribution and diversity, Greek theatre retained powerful associations with democracy and with Athens in the eyes of all Greece until late in the fourth century.

Notes

1. Our warm gratitude to Toph and Hallie Marshall for their invitation to present our work at Greek Drama V and for their generous hospitality. Numerous scholars and friends have given invaluable assistance to the research behind this chapter: an extensive list can be found in Csapo and Wilson 2019. We renew our thanks to them here, and also acknowledge the support of the following organizations: the University of Sydney, the Australian Research Council, the British Academy, and the Institute for Classical Studies in London.

2. The present context allows room only for a highly selective treatment and we refer the reader for detailed presentation and discussion of the evidence to Csapo and Wilson 2019. A brief survey of the spread of drama throughout Greece and beyond can also be found in Csapo and Wilson 2015. The politics of theatre's reception are frequently addressed in both these works, but only here brought together as the central focus of discussion.

3. Winkler and Zeitlin 1990, especially for tragedy the chapter by Goldhill (anticipated in Goldhill 1987), for comedy the chapter by Henderson, and for drama generally the chapter by Ober and Strauss. Vernant, especially in Vernant and Vidal-Naquet 1972, was seminal for the direction of anglophone studies in the politics of tragedy. Close in time to Winkler and Zeitlin are the important studies by Meier 1988 and Connor 1989.

4. Important studies in this direction are: Easterling 1994; Taplin 1993; Taplin 1999; Allan 2001; Csapo 2004; Bosher 2012; Csapo, Goette, Green and Wilson 2014; Vahtikari 2014; Csapo and Wilson 2015; Stewart 2017; Lamari 2017; Braund, Hall and Wyles 2020.

5. Griffin 1998. Griffin is answered by Goldhill 2000; Seaford 2000.

6. Rhodes 2003.

7. Bosher 2012: 8.

8. E.g. Wilson 2009. Rosenbloom 2011, 2012, 2014 regards tragedy and comedy as both Panhellenic and democratic. Wohl 2015 is an important study of the political (democratic) content of tragic form. Both Rosenbloom and Wohl regard theatre as still essentially Athenian in the fifth century.

9. Hall 1996, answered by Heath 2009.

10. Henceforth all ancient dates will be BCE unless marked otherwise.

11. Frederiksen 2002: 91–2 may give the impression that oligarchies were fonder of theatre than autocrats. But Frederiksen is considering the numerical distribution of theatre buildings in different regions and his point is that in monarchic territories (like Macedon) theatres are confined to the larger centres. He nonetheless seems to suppose a larger distribution of theatres in oligarchic states than we have found, partly perhaps because his survey has a much larger chronological framework.

12. Our count is based on distinct cities and towns with evidence of theatre(s) or theatre culture. It is therefore somewhat inconsistent on our part that we enter Attica as a single entity. In this case we declined to enter Athens plus twenty-one to twenty-four demes as separate entities, though nearly all these theatres and festivals were run independently of Athens.

13. Hansen and Nielsen 2004: 84.

14. See, for example, Robinson 2011: 184–93 figs 4.1–4.4.

15. These figures are arrived at by dividing by two the either/or states in the lower part of Table 1. The overall statistics to a single decimal point are calculated as follows. Of the forty-six reasonably clear cases 56.5 per cent (26) are democracies, 34.8 per cent (16) are autocracies, and 8.7 per cent (4) are oligarchies. Of the seventy-one cases for which we have useful, if not always 'probable', evidence, 59.9 per cent (42.5) are democracies, 30.3 per cent (21.5) are autocracies, and 9.9 per cent (7) are oligarchies.

16. Parker 1994: 343.

17. Piraeus Museum 4229 (ex Salamis Museum 74); *IG* II³ 4, 499.

18. Archontidou and Kokkinoporous 2004.

19. Burkert 1994; Collard, Cropp and Gibert 2004: 178, 249–52 on fr. 758; Csapo 2017.

20. *IG* XII 8, 4 and Cargill 1995: 233–4; *IG* XII 8, 15.

21. Cargill 1995: 17–21.

22. Csapo and Wilson 2019: IV Di, Dvii, Dix, Dx.

23. Csapo and Wilson 2019: IV A Introduction.

24. Robinson 2011: 137–40, 188–200.

25. Rhodes 2010: 94.

26. Cf. Hdt. 8.46–8; Th. 7.57.4; Sch. Dionys. Per. 525.

27. Compare *IG* I³ 71 a decree of 425/4 in which all tributary cities are to contribute a cow and panoply for the Great Panathenaea 'and they are to process them in the procession like colonists', lines 57–8 βō[ν καὶ πανhοπ]λ[ίαν ἀπάγεν ἐς Παναθ]ένια τὰ με[γάλα] hαπάσας· πεμπόντον δ[ὲ ἐν] τ͂ει πομπ͂ει [καθάπερ ἄποι]κ[οι].

28. Delos is included on the map as an exceptional case of a city whose theatrical culture clearly imitated Athens, but seems actually to have been repressed under Athenian domination, possibly out of fear of creating a historically significant and more centrally located rival to Athens' own Dionysia (Csapo and Wilson 2019: IV Dvi).

29. Csapo and Wilson 2019: IV Axi 4–5 and commentary.

30. Csapo and Wilson 2019: IV E Introduction.

31. This is probably also the case on Tenos before drama became part of the Posideia; see Csapo and Wilson 2019: IV Dxv.

32. Coarelli 1997: 452–84; Nocita 2013: 604–5.

33. Moretti 1960: 270.

34. Important studies by: Kaibel 1888; Wilhelm 1906; Moretti 1960; Snell 1966; Nocita 2013. The date range of the victories reported by the inscription is established by the prosopography. Figure 1.4 *a*, to use Kaibel's ordination, as written beside the texts on Figure 3, includes mention of Rhodes within the list belonging to Kleandros, probably in relation to Kleandros' performance at the Rhodian festival. Other recognizable names in these fragments all belong to tragic actors, save only that of Sophocles and the possible Archon Aristodemos (352/1, but there is also an actor Aristodemos). [K]leandros, [M]nesitheos and [Thr]asyboulos are

virtually certain supplements (Figure 1.4 *a* line 5, *b* line 2, *a* line 10). All can be dated to the first half of the fourth century, with Kleandros and Thrasyboulos very early in the century. We can therefore infer that Rhodes was part of a regular festival circuit for top-ranking tragic performers from the 380s if not earlier.

35. Figure 1.4 *b* line 3 [τ]ὰ δεύτερα; *g* line 5 ἐν Ῥόδῳ δεύ[τερος]; *h* line 4 has [— —]όλεμον· τρ[ίτος ἐγένετο? — —] (*h* is not on Figure 1.4). Rival competitors are named but not placed in *a* line 3 [πρὸς Κλέα]νδρον ἀντηγων[ίζετο] and possibly *e* line 3 [ἀντηγωνί]ζετο.

36. Athens offers a close analogy for the interest of tribes in preserving records of the precise order of victory; see Wilson 2000: 278.

37. Kleandros probably appears in Figure 1.4 *a* lines 3, 5; Thrasyboulos in *a* line 10 and possibly *g* 7; Mnesitheos in *b* line 2; Philotades may lie behind *g* line 1; Kaibel suspects Alkimachos is to be restored in *g* line 2 and Moretti would restore Eupolemos to *g* line 6 and *h* line 4 (*h* is not on Figure 1.4). Aristodemos should perhaps be restored to *g* line 9 and conceivably *b* line 5.

38. Figure 1.4 *a* line 7 definitely names Sophocles and line 1 may do so, as may *c* line 4.

39. Sophoclean titles are suspected in Figure 1.4 *g* lines 1, 3 and 4. The Sophoclean title *Captive Women* (*Aichmalotides*) is only evinced by a very invasive emendation by Snell, but two Sophoclean titles name 'Odysseus': *Mad Odysseus* (*Odysseus Mainomenos*) and *Odysseus Struck by a Sting* (*Odysseus Akanthoplex*); and a Sophoclean Telephos trilogy or tetralogy is elsewhere attested. For Figure 1.4 *c* line 5 Snell suggests the restoration '[Sophokles] the El[der]', [Σοφοκλῆς] ὁ πρε[σβύτερος]. But Sophocles the Younger may be meant. Aristarchus seems to be named on *h* (*IGUR* I 230) line 2.

40. Figure 1.4 *a* line 8 καὶ σατυ[ρικόν] seems unavoidable and *g* line 4 [σατυ]ρικὸν Τήλεφ[ον] highly likely.

41. Wilson 2000: 290–1.

42. Aeschin. *In Ctes.* 153–4; Th. 2.46.1; Lys. fr. 129.

43. Robinson 2011: 34–44.

44. Goette 1995: 34–5; Csapo and Wilson 2019: IV Bxii.

45. Csapo and Wilson 2019: IV Bxi–xv.

46. D.S. 15.40.1–2; Csapo and Wilson 2019: IV Bxv.

47. *IG* V 2, 450; *SEG* 11, 1070; *SEG* 11, 1104. For the dating of the inscriptions and the theatres, see Csapo and Wilson 2019: IV Bxii–xiv.

48. Plu. *Arist.* 1.4, *Mor.* 799e–f; Csapo and Wilson 2019: IV Cii, Civ

49. Plu. *Mor.* 578e–9a may imply a start for the Mouseia under Spartan occupation, but this is not a necessary nor even the most common reading. The evidence is detailed in Csapo and Wilson 2019: IV Cv.

50. Schachter 1994: 111–12; Csapo and Wilson 2019: IV C Introduction.

51. Calydon's theatre belongs to the early fourth century (Vikatou, Frederiksen and Handberg 2014: 225, 230) and the city is thought to have become democratic after 366 when Epaminondas conquered the cities of the Achaean Federation. For Thespiae and Chaeronea, see above. On Abydos, see Csapo and Wilson 2019: IV E Introduction, IV Ei.

52. Green 2014: 344–62.

53. We have little evidence for the degree to which a sudden change of constitution can affect theatre already established. In Athens, the brief fifth-century oligarchies seem to have had at most a passing effect on comedy: e.g. the sharp decline in *komoidoumenoi* between 414 and

411 BCE (Ar. *Birds* has sixty-one, but the two plays of 411, *Lysistrata* and *Thesmophoriazusae*, have fourteen and seventeen respectively). But the fourth-century oligarchy transformed the dominant form of comedy altogether (Nervegna 2013: 25–45). One influential institutional change to the Athenian Great Dionysia made after and probably as a result of the oligarchic coup of 411 was the introduction of the award of honorific crowns prior to the contests, with the first being awarded to the assassin of the oligarchic extremist Phrynichos: Wilson 2009.

54. Arist. *Poetics* 1448a30–4; Csapo and Wilson 2019: IV Bi–iii.

55. Martin 1951: 234–5; Kourinou 2000: 114–27; Csapo and Wilson 2019: IV Bix.

56. Greco 2011: 60; Greco and Voza 2016.

57. *SEG* 46, 400; Kourinou-Pikoula 1992–8.

58. Csapo and Wilson 2019: IV Bix.

59. *IG* V 1, 662.

60. Graf 1985: 74–97, 125–6.

61. Polemon *FHG* fr. 90.

62. Ceccarelli 2010: 122 n. 72, 124 n. 79.

63. Ion *FGrH* 392 F 1 (fr. 1 Leurini; fr. 29 W).

64. Wilson 2017; Csapo and Wilson 2019: IV Ai.

65. Ensoli 2012b: 111; Csapo and Wilson 2019: IV Gi.

66. Moloney 2014; Csapo and Wilson 2019: IV Cxii.

67. D.S. 15.75.1; Plu. *Pelop.* 29.7, 9–11, *Mor.* 334a–b; Ael. *VH* 14.40; Paus. 6.5.2–3; *Vita Eur.* 6; Csapo and Wilson 2019: IV Cix–xi.

68. Braund and Hall 2014; Csapo and Wilson 2019: IV Fiii–iv.

69. Moloney 2014: 235–6.

70. Csapo and Wilson 2015: 373–7.

71. Csapo and Wilson 2015: esp. 383.

72. Praxiphanes, *On History* fr. 21 Matelli (18 Wehrli; Marcellinus *Life of Thucydides* 29–30); Dem. 19.192–5.

73. Archelaus: Plu. *Mor.* 334b, 1095c–d; St. Byz. *Ethnika* 452–3; Suda s.v. Μελανιππίδης (μ 454), s.v. Τιμόθεος (τ 620 Adler). Philip: Marsyas *FGrH* 135–6 F 17 (= *PMG* adesp. 840); Dionysius: Luc. *Ind.* 15; *IG* II² 18; LeVen 2014: 127–32, 144–8.

74. Le Guen 2014.

75. Heraclea: Memnon *FGrH* 343 F1.3.2–3; Cimmerian Bosporos: Isoc. 17.15; Polyaen. 5.44.1–10; Macho fr. 11.141–7 Gow; Csapo forthcoming.

76. Csapo and Wilson 2019: IV Gi.

77. For Alexander's campaigns, see Table 1 in Le Guen 2014: 251–5.

78. Csapo 2010a: 172–4.

79. Plu. *Alex.* 10.

80. Plu. *Alex.* 29.

81. Csapo and Wilson 2014: 414–18.

82. Kate Bosher's manuscript on Sicilian theatre will soon be published posthumously by Cambridge University Press; Moretti 2014: 135–7.

83. Voza 2001, Voza 2007, Voza 2008. Voza 2014; Csapo and Wilson 2019: IV Ai.

84. Moretti 2014: 136.

85. Philip: D.S. 16.92–3 is explicit that his bodyguards were ordered to keep their distance as he processed into the theatre. Clearchus: [Chion] *Ep.* 17.1: 'I intend to attack the tyrant at the Dionysia . . . on that day there is a parade for Dionysus and his bodyguard will be less vigilant because of it.' [Chion] is most specific about the Dionysian parade as the venue for Clearchus' assassination; D.S. 16.32.3 simply says 'during the Dionysia while walking to a spectacle', and Memnon *FGrH* 434 F 1.1.3 says when about to perform public sacrifice, which is consistent with his leading the parade.

86. See Mamercus *TrGF* 87.

87. Le Guen 2014: 268.

88. Duncan 2012.

89. On Dionysius' dress: Duncan 2012: 151–3. On Demetrius and others: Chaniotis 1997: 232–4. Cf. the theatricality of Clearchus' use of make-up and dress: Memnon *FGrH* 434 F1 with Braund and Hall 2014: 371.

90. Sanders 1991; cf. Ceccarelli 2004.

91. Csapo and Wilson 2015: 332.

92. Csapo and Wilson 2019: IV A Introduction.

93. Robinson 2011: 100; Csapo and Wilson 2019: IV Aix.

94. Robinson 2011: 92–6; Csapo and Wilson 2019: IV A Introduction.

95. Csapo and Wilson 2019: IV Axv, IV A Introduction.

CHAPTER 2
SELECTIVE MEMORY AND EPIC REMINISCENCE IN SOPHOCLES' *AJAX*
Sheila Murnaghan

Towards the end of the prologue of Sophocles' *Ajax*, Athena issues a triumphant boast.[1] She has just staged a brief pageant for Odysseus, in which Ajax is put on display as a deranged and cruelly vengeful killer.[2] First confirming the report that it was Ajax who had mounted a murderous night-time assault on the Achaeans' common livestock and explaining that he had been trying to kill the Achaean leaders, she has then called Ajax out of the hut and encouraged him to perform his rage and folly in front of Odysseus: at her prompting, Ajax details his punitive plans for a ram that he believes is Odysseus, then airily dismisses her suggestion that he should not be so cruel to poor Odysseus and instructs her always to be his ally – at which point she gloats about what she has accomplished:

ὁρᾷς, Ὀδυσσεῦ, τὴν θεῶν ἰσχὺν ὅση;
τούτου τίς ἄν σοι τἀνδρὸς ἢ προνούστερος
ἢ δρᾶν ἀμείνων ηὑρέθη τὰ καίρια;

Odysseus, do you see how great the gods' power is?
Who, I ask you, could have been found who was more foresightful
than this man, or better at doing the right thing at the right time?

118–20

Athena's first concern here is to stress the magnitude of her own accomplishment as measured by the distance that Ajax has fallen. She formulates her boast in a way that also acknowledges what a narrowly selective portrait of Ajax she has produced, how Ajax has in effect been framed in this opening episode, being captured and put on display at a particular moment that is not necessarily typical. Her past counterfactual construction, 'who would have been found to be *pronousteros*?', with its implicit protasis, 'if he had been judged relative to other people at an earlier point', highlights the way that Ajax appears very differently depending on which part of his story someone tells.

Athena's identification of the mini drama she has staged as a selective snapshot bears in several ways on Sophocles' own project of portraying heroic individuals in brief dramatic works. It relates to his pervasive interest in the question of time, in the relationship between the limitless continuum of time – that is, to evoke the opening word of the play, ἀεί, 'always' – and discrete, marked-off units of time, within the span of history or within the individual lifespan, those consequential moments of crisis around which his plays are built, sometimes encapsulated, as in *Ajax*, in the single day on which something momentous is destined to happen.[3] Sophocles is attentive to the way that people and events look different when seen at different times, something that comes out especially in *Oedipus at Colonus* where we witness Oedipus looking back at his past and observing that on the particular day when he discovered his true identity he judged himself too harshly and punished himself too violently (433–44). Athena's selectivity also bears on two distinctive features of *Ajax* in particular: the play's relationship to Homer and its relationship to ritual.

In terms of literary history, selectivity is a definitive feature of tragedy, which makes brief plays out of a larger mythological tradition that has been previously represented in much longer poems. Here one might invoke the claim attributed by Athenaeus (8.347e) to Aeschylus that his plays were 'slices from the great banquet of Homer' or Aristotle's observation in the *Poetics* (1459b2–7) that many individual tragedies could be made out of the cyclic epics, where he mentions especially the *Cypria* and the *Little Iliad*; the *Little Iliad*, of course, covered the period in the Troy legend following the death of Achilles from which Sophocles drew the plots of both *Ajax* and *Philoctetes*. In terms of ritual, selective framing that allows someone to be defined as unacceptably transgressive, that is to say, scapegoating, is an essential step in the trajectory by which an exceptional individual becomes a cult hero, as is destined to happen with Ajax. While it may be obliquely expressed, Ajax' future heroization is a significant factor in the play: the unfolding of the plot is connected to his destiny as a figure of cult particularly in Athens, where he was worshipped as a hero from the sixth century on and was also the eponymous hero of one of the ten Cleisthenic tribes.[4]

Athena's evocation of Ajax as he would have appeared to someone considering him before this moment under different conditions invites comparison with his treatment in the earlier poetic tradition, beginning with epic. The account of Ajax that we find in epic is marked by sharp discontinuity. In the portion of the Troy legend that leads up to the death of Achilles, which we know from the *Iliad*, Ajax plays a relatively unheralded but extensive role as the community-minded defender of the Achaean army: he is the ἕρκος Ἀχαιῶν, the 'bulwark of the Achaeans' and the next-best fighter after Achilles. Ajax' status as next best after Achilles was a definitive feature of his identity, repeatedly invoked throughout the tradition, as is both illustrated and explicitly noted in a famous Attic skolion:

παῖ Τελαμῶνος Αἶαν αἰχμητά, λέγουσί σε
ἐς Τροίαν ἄριστον ἐλθεῖν Δαναῶν μετ' Ἀχιλλέα.

Son of Telamon, warrior Ajax, they say that you
were the best of the Danaans who came to Troy after Achilles.

PMG 898

Ajax' next best status already shapes his role in the *Iliad,* where he steps in to serve as Achilles' surrogate as the saviour of his fellow Achaeans when Achilles is too angry to do so, playing an especially prominent role in the defence of the ships against Hector's attack and in the fight around Patroclus' body. Ajax, we are told, was ἀνδρῶν … μέγ' ἄριστος … ὄφρ' Ἀχιλεὺς μήνιεν, ('by far the best of men as long as Achilles raged') (2.768–9), and his presence in the narrative is in fact coordinated with Achilles' absence. Ajax appears together with Achilles during the embassy in Book 9, where he speaks eloquently of the importance of giving up even the best-founded grudges, and during the funeral games of Patroclus in Book 23. Otherwise he appears in every book of the *Iliad* except Books 1, 19–22 and 24, the books in which Achilles himself is active.

In *Iliad* 23, Ajax participates in several events at the funeral games for Patroclus, including a wrestling match with Odysseus that Achilles declares to be a draw, although Odysseus is, ominously, doing somewhat better than Ajax. After that, Ajax' next and final appearance in Homer is in Book 11 of the *Odyssey*: there he meets Odysseus with silent resentment, converted into a brooding figure of unremitting anger by the award of Achilles' armour to Odysseus rather than to himself in the competition that followed Achilles' death. The pivotal event of the Judgment of the Arms was included in several of the works that came to form the epic cycle; we know that it figured in both the *Aithiopis* and the *Little Iliad*. We do not have many details, and these will have varied from version to version, but it is clear that the episode (which was generally a favourite moment in the Troy legend for Greek poets and also for vase painters) involved affronted honour (with the award of the arms to Odysseus), consuming rage, destruction (with the attack on the army's livestock), and self-destruction (with Ajax' suicide).[5] These are the events that Sophocles reworked into the plot of *Ajax*, situating his play (as he also did with *Philoctetes*) in the span of time between the events of the *Iliad* and the *Odyssey*.

Fifth-century authors thus looked back to a contradictory poetic legacy that painted a radically different picture of Ajax depending on which point on the trajectory of his epic career one chose to focus on. This is evident in Pindar's divergent accounts of Homer in relation to Ajax, which occur in two separate allusions to the Judgment of the Arms, a decision that Pindar views as a clear miscarriage of justice. In *Isthmian* 4, Pindar stresses the courage of Ajax' suicide, which 'brought him blame among the Achaeans' (or possibly 'brought blame to the Achaeans'), and goes on to add that Homer, however, assured that Ajax would be lastingly honoured:

ἀλλ' Ὅμηρός τοι τετίμα-
    κεν δι' ἀνθρώπων, ὅς αὐτοῦ
πᾶσαν ὀρθώσαις ἀρετὰν κατὰ ῥάβδον ἔφρασεν
θεσπεσίων ἐπέων λοιποῖς ἀθύρειν.

But Homer, to be sure, has made him honoured
    among mankind, who set straight
his entire achievement and declared it with his staff
of divine verse for future men to enjoy.

37–9[6]

Here Pindar looks back in time from the Judgment and identifies Homer with the *Iliad*, where Ajax performs as an exemplary member of the army, in contrast to the cyclic epics where he is dishonoured and compelled to kill himself.

In *Nemean* 7, however, Pindar complains that Homer has overpraised Odysseus, and assured him an inflated reputation among later audiences, and he identifies that later fame with the inflated reputation that gave Odysseus an unfair advantage in the contest for Achilles' armour:

> ἐπεὶ ψεύδεσί οἱ ποτανᾷ τε μαχανᾷ
> σεμνὸν ἔπεστί τι· σοφία
>   δὲ κλέπτει παράγοισα μύθοις· τυφλὸν δ᾽ ἔχει
> ἦτορ ὅμιλος ἀνδρῶν ὁ πλεῖστος. εἰ γὰρ ἦν
> ἓ τὰν ἀλάθειαν ἰδέμεν, οὔ κεν ὅπλων χολωθεὶς
> ὁ καρτερὸς Αἴας ἔπαξε διὰ φρενῶν
> λευρὸν ξίφος· ὃν κράτιστον Ἀχιλέος ἄτερ μάχᾳ ...

[F]or upon his fictions and soaring craft
rests great majesty, and his skill
   deceives with misleading tales. The great majority
of men have a blind heart, for if they could have seen
the truth, mighty Aias, in anger over the arms,
would not have planted in his chest
the smooth sword. Except for Achilles, in battle he was the best ...

22–7

Here, then, Pindar looks forward in time from the Judgment to the *Odyssey*, where Odysseus emerges as the canny survivor who ultimately eclipses his fellow Achaean heroes while Ajax appears as the angry suicide. Pindar shows what is at stake in looking back to Homeric epics with their stress on the competitive ranking of individual heroes and their capacity to confer lasting fame. And he also shows that, in the case of Ajax, the hero's reputation is bound up with selectivity: it depends on where in the Homeric corpus you look.[7]

Athena's reference to the past as the time when a hypothetical investigation would find no one to be *pronousteros* ('more foresightful') than Ajax locates the action of the play that is now beginning in literary historical as well as legendary time, as happening after the events of the *Iliad* are over. In a play which is conspicuously in dialogue with Homer,[8] however, the audience is nonetheless repeatedly reminded of the *Iliad* in a variety of ways. Several characters themselves recall one particular episode from the *Iliad*, the dual between Ajax and Hector narrated in Book 7. In a more subtle and implicit allusion, the encounter between Hector and Andromache in *Iliad* 6 is reworked in the *agōn* between Ajax and Tecmessa.[9] The opening episode of the play, in which the thoughtful, restrained Ajax of the *Iliad* is relegated to the past, is also a replay of the *Iliad*'s own opening, a cruel variation on the episode in *Iliad* 1 in which Athena intervenes to prevent Ajax' counterpart Achilles from attacking one of the Achaean leaders; far from encouraging Achilles to revel in his violent vengeance, she talks him out of killing Agamemnon, getting him to put away his half-drawn sword and use words instead.[10] *Ajax* ends with a reference to *Odyssey* 11, the Homeric end point for several distinguished warriors' careers, so that the play can be said to span, via a sequence of allusions, the entire Homeric corpus and Ajax' entire epic career within it.

Rather than examining these reworked Homeric episodes, this paper considers how the characters in *Ajax* deploy what are in effect allusions to the epic tradition in their own efforts at framing, self-definition and self-positioning. The particular focus of the discussion is the various starting points in earlier time (the time before the action of the play) that they identify for the story that they are all currently participating in, that they are collectively enacting. In *Ajax*, Sophocles confronts us with a figure who is difficult to classify or evaluate: he shows us Ajax in many states of mind, from the delusional arrogance of the prologue to the calm deliberateness of his eventual suicide, and presents him through the eyes of multiple diverse, and sometimes overtly competing, observers. Accordingly he also shows us how different the last act of Ajax' life, the self-chosen death dramatized at the centre of the play, can look depending on how one defines the larger story of which it is the final episode.

Over the course of the play, Odysseus and Ajax reveal an unstated difference of opinion over where the story in which they are both key participants has its starting point. In the concluding episode, when Odysseus shows up to resolve the crisis over whether Ajax should be buried or not, he describes a stretch of time, or a narrative arc, that corresponds to a period of enmity between himself and Ajax. This began with the Judgment of the Arms and is now, as the play reaches its conclusion, coming to an end:

κἀμοὶ γὰρ ἦν ποθ᾽ οὗτος ἔχθιστος στρατοῦ,
<u>ἐξ οὗ</u> ᾽κράτησα τῶν Ἀχιλλείων ὅπλων·
ἀλλ᾽ ...

For this man was once for me, too, the most hateful in the army,
<u>from the point at which</u> I gained control of the arms of Achilles,
but ...

1336–8

Odysseus' conception of the events dramatized in *Ajax* as the final phases of a story that begins with the Judgment of the Arms is also voiced by other characters. As the play opens, Athena explains to Odysseus that Ajax' mad assault on the livestock that he believes to be the Achaean leaders has its origins in his anger over the judgment (41). Later the chorus responds to the discovery of Ajax' corpse with the recognition that Ajax has fulfilled a longstanding destiny, then locates the consequential point of origin, the μέγας ... χρόνος, 'momentous ... time', at which that process of fulfilment began in the *agōn* concerning the arms (934–6).

At the beginning of *Antigone*, Sophocles uses a similar phrase – not ἐξ οὗ, but ἐξ ὅτου – to mark out the stretch of time with which that play's action will be concerned. When Antigone asks Ismene if she has heard about Creon's proclamation, Ismene unwittingly defines the starting point of a plot in which she is about to be unwillingly caught up. She answers that, as far as she knows, nothing has happened – there has been no μῦθος, no 'word', ἐξ ὅτου | δυοῖν ἀδελφοῖν ἐστερήθημεν δύο, | μιᾷ θανόντοιν ἡμέρᾳ διπλῇ χερί· ('since the point | at which the two of us were deprived of two brothers, | killed on a single day by a double blow') (12–14). Ismene does not realize that the death of her brothers is not just the end of one story but also the beginning of another, Creon's prohibition of the burial of Polynices, which will then form the action of *Antigone*.

That this wording can delineate the shapes of poems as well as the experiences of characters is already evident at the very beginning of the Greek poetic tradition, in the opening lines of the *Iliad*, the poem with which *Ajax* has an unmistakable intertextual relationship. Having called on the Muse to sing the wrath of Achilles and having indicated that this story corresponds to the fulfilment of Zeus' will, the poet specifies a starting point: ἐξ οὗ δὴ τὰ πρῶτα διαστήτην ἐρίσαντε | Ἀτρεΐδης τε ἄναξ ἀνδρῶν καὶ δῖος Ἀχιλλεύς, ('from the point at which the two squared off quarrelling: | the son of Atreus, ruler of men, and godlike Achilles') (6–7). The poet uses the phrase ἐξ οὗ, 'from the point at which', as he asks the Muse to separate out and make known to him a particular segment of time out of the limitless continuum over which she has an undivided, synoptic command. Scholars disagree over whether ἐξ οὗ in line 6 should be taken with ἄειδε, 'sing', in the first line of the poem, as indicating at what point the Muse should start her song, or with ἐτελείετο in the fifth line, as indicating when the will of Zeus started being fulfilled; in either case, however, the poet uses the phrase to mark out the starting point of the story he plans to tell with the Muse's help.[11]

All three of these points 'since when' align with a particular form of human crisis: the resolution of a longstanding rivalry, whether between Achilles and Agamemnon in the *Iliad*, Eteocles and Polyneices in *Antigone*, or between Ajax and Odysseus, that rivalry that ends in a draw in Book 23 of the *Iliad*, but is resolved in the Judgment of the Arms. Unresolved rivalry allows for a kind of stasis or status quo, however uneasy, but once there is point of decision – once Achilles seizes the upper hand over Agamemnon, or the sons of Oedipus die with one of them as the invader and the other the defender of Thebes, or Odysseus beats Ajax for the arms of Achilles – a new sequence of events is launched. Similarly, in Sophocles' *Trachiniae*, Deianeira is living out a story that began when the contest between her two suitors, Heracles and Achelous, was decided and to which she herself gives a new impetus after a period of inactivity when she is faced with Iole as a rival and acts to resolve their competition.

The idea that *eris* or rivalry forms the starting point of narrative is deeply embedded in the Greek tradition: the gods repeatedly impose *eris* on human beings and spark the particular episodes of conflict and destruction that make up human history and provide the subjects of poems.[12] One reflection of this can be seen in the participle ἐρίσαντε, 'quarrelling', that also appears in the sixth line of the *Iliad*. The idea that realignments imposed by episodes of *eris* should determine the shapes of stories seems particularly germane to Sophocles, who several times invokes the transformation of friendship into enmity, or its reverse, as an inescapable event that punctuates the continuous flow of human history (*Ajax* 678–82, *OC* 607–20).

Returning to Odysseus at the end of *Ajax*, we see him using the phrase ἐξ οὗ, 'since when', to indicate a story that begins with a quarrel, from which he himself emerged victorious and which he is now bringing to an end with his efforts to assure Ajax' burial. He follows that with an allusion that evokes a longer narrative trajectory with the same starting point: the whole story of the Trojan War after the death of Achilles up to and including the *nostos* of the last hero to return from Troy:

ἀλλ᾽ αὐτὸν ἔμπας ὄντ᾽ ἐγὼ τοιόνδ᾽ ἐμοὶ
οὐκ ἀντατιμάσαιμ᾽ ἄν, ὥστε μὴ λέγειν
ἕν᾽ ἄνδρ᾽ ἰδεῖν ἄριστον Ἀργείων, ὅσοι
Τροίαν ἀφικόμεσθα, πλὴν Ἀχιλλέως.
ὥστ᾽ οὐκ ἂν ἐνδίκως γ᾽ ἀτιμάζοιτό σοι·

But even though that's how he stood towards me,
I would not do him the dishonour of denying
that I saw him as the single best man of the Argives,
of all of us who came to Troy, except Achilles.
So it would not be right for him to be dishonoured by you.

1338–42

This speech recalls – or, looked at another way, anticipates – Odysseus' generous assessment of Ajax as he tells of their meeting in the underworld in *Odyssey* 11. There, too, he honours his angry dead rival by acknowledging his traditional status as the next best warrior after Achilles:

ὡς δὴ μὴ ὄφελον νικᾶν τοιῷδ᾽ ἐπ᾽ ἀέθλῳ·
τοίην γὰρ κεφαλὴν ἕνεκ᾽ αὐτῶν γαῖα κατέσχεν,
Αἴανθ᾽, ὃς πέρι μὲν εἶδος, πέρι δ᾽ ἔργα τέτυκτο
τῶν ἄλλων Δαναῶν μετ᾽ ἀμύμονα Πηλεΐωνα.
τὸν μὲν ἐγὼν ἐπέεσσι προσηύδων μειλιχίοισιν·

I wish I had never won that contest,
so great was the man who lies underground because of that armour:
Ajax, who stood out for his powers and his actions
above all the other Danaans, next after the peerless son of Peleus.
I approached him with conciliatory words.

548–52

In the *Ajax* passage, Odysseus does not express outright regret about the contest, as he does in the *Odyssey*, but he does acknowledge the basis of Ajax' claim by praising him as next best after Achilles, and he is announcing the end of their rivalry. Sophocles here looks back to the underworld scene in the *Odyssey* as a telling moment in the later phase of the Troy legend, in which Odysseus emerges as the dominant figure, the ultimate taker of Troy and the hero who stands apart from the others for his survival skills and strategic self-effacement – and so a prime instance of what Pindar saw as the *Odyssey*'s overrating of Odysseus.[13] In *Ajax*, as the ending of the play is identified with that moment, there, too, Odysseus speaks as an accomplished survivor, alive and forgiving, while Ajax is dead and still resentful, as we are reminded when Teucer declines Odysseus' request to participate in the burial.

Ajax himself, however, asserts a different starting point for the story in which he is the central character in his so-called 'deception speech', using the same phrase, ἐξ οὗ, 'since when'. Announcing that he is going to the shore to bury his sword (the same sword that he used to slaughter the livestock), he explains that ever since – ἐξ οὗ – he received that sword from Hector, his relations with his fellow Argives have been compromised or, as he puts it, he has received nothing good from them:

ἐγὼ γὰρ ἐξ οὗ χειρὶ τοῦτ' ἐδεξάμην
παρ' Ἕκτορος δώρημα δυσμενεστάτου,
οὔπω τι κεδνὸν ἔσχον Ἀργείων πάρα.

For ever since the point at which
I took in my hand this gift from my worst enemy, Hector,
I have never received anything good from the Argives.

661–3

In contrast to Athena, Odysseus and the chorus, Ajax sees his story as beginning, not with the Judgment of the Arms, but with a different competition, his duel against Hector – not in the volatile post-Iliadic stretch of time between the death of Achilles and the taking of Troy, but in an earlier moment that is firmly located in a particular, memorable episode in Book 7 (7.37–312) of the *Iliad*, when Achilles is out of the action and Ajax is shining in his place, fulfilling his role as next best. In the *Iliad* that duel ends without a decision. There is a series of exchanges in which Ajax clearly outperforms Hector (and which lead him to consider himself the victor (312)): he manages to graze Hector's neck with his spear and draw blood and he knocks him down with a stone. Apollo raises Hector up again, and as they are closing in on each other with swords, the heralds on both sides separate them, pointing out that night is falling and that Zeus evidently loves them both. They stop fighting on the understanding that one day they will meet again and fight to a conclusion. For now they part in friendship and exchange gifts: Ajax gives Hector his belt and Hector gives Ajax that fateful sword. Homer raises and then forecloses the possibility that Ajax could transcend his status as next best and usurp Achilles' destined role as Hector's destroyer.

In the 'deception speech', Ajax here turns an inconclusive moment in the *Iliad*'s first long day of fighting, a section of the narrative which generally shows how difficult it is to bring the war to an end, into a decisive turning point in his own life. As one critic puts it, the receipt of Hector's sword 'has split Ajax' life down the middle into the time before he owned it and the time "ever since"'.[14] Ajax' reformulation of his life story into these sharply distinct units is an act of self-assertion at a point in the play in which he is displaying increased agency as he accepts the divinely imposed scenario into which he has been forced. One of the most remarkable features of his anomalous onstage suicide is how deliberate it is, in contrast to the violent, despairing offstage suicide of Deianeira in *Trachiniae* or the suicide we would have heard about if Ajax had killed himself at once offstage, as we are led to expect he will after his contentious encounter with Tecmessa. When he does come to kill himself in a different spirit and on different terms, he is very much in control – and one sign of this is his careful placement of the sword where it will serve him best, or as he puts it, where it will be εὐνούστατον, 'most well disposed' (822).

By dating his troubles to his duel with Hector, Ajax asserts control over his own story at a time when he is also beginning to assert control over the manner and significance of his death. He redefines the narrative that culminates in his suicide as having begun not at a moment of disgrace, his loss of the arms to Odysseus, but at a moment of honour, his equal contest with Hector. In this way he redescribes his death as the resolution of an honourable rivalry with an external enemy rather than as the necessary sequel to his dishonourable hostility towards those who were supposed to be his friends. This may explain something that has puzzled commentators, which is why he stresses, as he positions the sword, that it is δῶρον μὲν ἀνδρὸς Ἕκτορος ξένων ἐμοὶ | μάλιστα μισηθέντος ('the gift of Hector, who was of foreigners the man | most hated by me') (817–18).[15] By linking his death to his duel with Hector, Ajax re-establishes the connection, which has been severed by his attack on the Atridae, to his highly respected, highly valued Iliadic self, the reliable mainstay of the army. In order to do this, he has to rewrite literary history: he turns the aborted victory that he savours in the *Iliad* into a defeat, and he projects onto the past – or onto earlier tradition – a state of estrangement from the other Achaeans immediately following the duel, long before the death of Achilles destabilized relations within the Achaean camp. At the same time, however, he reclaims his traditional status as not quite Achilles' equal and he gives the death that Athena has forced on him a more honourable position within the body of historical narratives through which heroes like himself are characterized and remembered.

Ajax' project of re-establishing a connection to his Iliadic self is picked up and continued by his champion Teucer in the later sequences of the play. When he comes upon Ajax' body, Teucer immediately identifies Hector as the killer (1026–7), and when he stands up to Agamemnon and speaks in defence of Ajax' right to a proper burial, he again looks back to the Ajax of the *Iliad*. He reminds Agamemnon of Ajax' exemplary service with a condensed and somewhat enhanced epitome of Ajax' behaviour at the Achaeans' most precarious moment, defending the cornered Achaeans as the Trojans, led by Hector, broke through their wall and threatened their ships with fire; a few lines later, he brings up Ajax' courageous willingness to face Hector in single combat. This set of poetic reminiscences serves to correct a fictional failure of memory. Teucer begins his speech by lamenting the ingratitude that leads Agamemnon no longer to remember Ajax and he introduces his first examples by asking οὐ μνημονεύεις ('do you not remember when . . .') (1273). Directing Agamemnon's attention back in time, Teucer tries to counter Agamemnon's own wilfully selective vision, his determination to see only that version of Ajax that Athena has shown to Odysseus. References to the *Iliad* become a touchstone for a fuller appraisal of Ajax that incorporates the earlier identity that more recent events have seemingly obliterated.

If Agamemnon never achieves that broader view, Odysseus does: he allies himself with Teucer to promote Ajax' burial, looking back to confirm Ajax' Iliadic identity as the next best after Achilles and choosing to overlook the more recent past. At the same time, Odysseus also reasserts the alternative starting point of the Judgment of the Arms and so makes the action of *Ajax* correspond with the period of his own triumph. This is in keeping with Odysseus' traditional identity as the favourite of Athena, a status which is strongly emphasized as the action of the play gets underway.

When she appears at the beginning of *Ajax*, Athena is not only the traditional divine partisan of the Homeric Odysseus. She is also the divine patron of Athens orchestrating the future role of Ajax in Athenian cult. Divine hostility at the point of the hero's death is an important element in the process of heroization; accordingly, Athena's traditional favouritism towards Odysseus is here overlaid with an intensely vicious but also short-lived antagonism towards Ajax. Odysseus, as he responds with horror and humane sympathy, is being primed to participate in Ajax' heroization by assuring the burial that has to follow Ajax' revelation as transgressive and his self-punishment by suicide. As the plot of *Ajax* reaches its *telos*, Odysseus unwittingly plays a role that was not envisioned for him in Homer. Athena herself hints at her plans for Ajax when she points out how selectively Ajax is being portrayed at this particular moment: as she revels in the disjunction she has brought about between the Ajax of the *Iliad* and the Ajax of this play, she in effect acknowledges that he is being subjected to the undeserved dishonour that anticipates the status of cult hero.

Not only does Athena eclipse the *Iliad* with her play within a play, putting a new and different Ajax on display, but she also implicates him in a new and different storyline. Alongside its clear allusions to the two actual Homeric epics, *Ajax* sketches the contours of an alternative Trojan War narrative focused on Ajax that is more closely tied to Salamis, and therefore to Athens, in which he plays a much less appealing role than in the actual *Iliad*. We are introduced to this narrative and learn of Athena's close interest in it indirectly, through the report of the messenger who brings the news that Athena's intense anger at Ajax will last only for the rest of that one day. According to this messenger, Calchas has explained Athena's anger through an account of Ajax' past behaviour that takes the form of a few select and damning episodes of inappropriately boastful and intemperate speech. This begins on Salamis, at a classic narrative starting point, the warrior's departure from home, recalling the episode in *Iliad* 9 in which Phoenix reminds Achilles of his own departure for Troy and his father Peleus' advice at that time (438–43): κεῖνος δ᾽ ἀπ᾽ οἴκων εὐθὺς ἐξορμώμενος | ἄνους καλῶς λέγοντος ηὑρέθη πατρός ('just as he was setting out from home, | he was found to be heedless (*anous*), when his father gave him good advice') (762–3).

The connection between this moment and Athena's cruel treatment of Ajax as enacted at the beginning of the play is reinforced through a verbal echo. In her boast, Athena stresses the point that Ajax is acting rashly through the counterfactual suggestion that, if someone had looked earlier, Ajax would have been found – ηὑρέθη – to be the most *pronous* member of the army (or, as she puts it, no one would have been found to be *pronousteros*). In the messenger's speech, this apparent reference to Ajax's behaviour at Troy as known from the *Iliad* is superseded by an account of how someone actually did look at the even earlier and definitive moment of his departure from home and he was found on that occasion – ηὑρέθη – to be *anous*, the opposite of the way he is portrayed in the *Iliad* and similar to the way he is made to appear by Athena. Calchas does not specify who did this looking and arrived at this judgment, but certainly Athena is the one whose reception of this episode matters most. This earlier episode underlies and justifies the later moment when, as she proudly boasts, she intervenes to make him behave in a way that is uncharacteristic but damning. The story that Calchas tells can also be understood in the context of framing or scapegoating. Ajax does speak foolishly and arrogantly when he rejects his father's advice, and on another isolated occasion that Calchas also brings up, when in the middle of a battle he tells Athena to help someone else who needs her more (770–5). Two rash speeches are hardly adequate to explain Athena's exceedingly cruel response, unless they are understood as part of the dynamic of extraordinary divine anger followed by extraordinary divine favour that underwrites cult heroism.[16]

The two forms of εὑρίσκω in the passive that bracket Athena's damning portrayal reveal the connection between Sophocles' treatment of Ajax and the accounts he gives in other plays, some more explicit than others, of an exceptional human being drawn into a divine plan that he does not necessarily will or control. One especially telling parallel for this idea of being found out, of someone being revealed to be different from the way he was, or he appeared to be, at all other times can be found in *Oedipus Tyrannus*.[17] There the chorus tells Oedipus that ἐφηῦρέ σ᾽ ἄκονθ᾽ ὁ πάνθ᾽ ὁρῶν χρόνος ('all-seeing time found you out, without you willing it') (1214). Here time itself is figured as doing the looking, or as Jebb puts it in his note on this line: 'Time is here invested with the attributes of the divine omniscience and justice.' This suggestion of a divine perspective resonates with *Ajax*, where Athena is the one who sees and judges.

Athena's view of Ajax is shaped by two episodes of transgressive behaviour that are designated as revelatory or definitive and are linked causally as the source and the fulfilment of Athena's anger: his arrogant speech when he left for Troy, when he was found to be *anous*, and his attack on the livestock, when he was not found – or rather could not have been found – to be *pronous*. The idea that on those occasions he was not just acting but was also being found out by an unseen judging presence indicates his passivity, his lack of control, and it also points to the idea that behaviour on his part that seems aberrant or uncharacteristic really is not: it reflects a latent aspect of his nature that has been present all along but has only, at these select points in time, become visible. Here the parallel case of Oedipus being found out by time is especially instructive because Oedipus has for a long stretch of time preceding the action of the play really been a guilty criminal who appeared to be a benign ruler, someone who had a guilty secret even though he did not know it, a figure who embodies paradox and ambiguity. Oedipus can be both a polluted sinner and a saviour as Ajax can be both *pronous* and *anous*.

The second, battlefield episode of Athena's alternative Salaminian epic, in which Ajax dismisses Athena with heedless overconfidence, also effaces the *Iliad*'s account of Ajax, inserting an episode into the fighting around Troy that is incompatible with Homer's portrayal. This past episode links up with the drama that Athena stages at the beginning of *Ajax*, in which Ajax speaks similarly to her, an episode that is, as we have seen, presented as countering and eclipsing the *Iliad*'s version of Ajax. Ajax himself, in the subsequent early episodes of the play, when he is just emerging from the madness imposed on him by Athena and still overwhelmed by the consequences of what she has done to him, seems almost self-consciously to place himself in that unflattering narrative as well. In his initial lament, he produces again the same kind of boastful speech for which Calchas condemns him:

ὦ Σκαμάνδριοι
γείτονες ῥοαί,
εὔφρονες Ἀργείοις,
οὐκέτ' ἄνδρα μὴ
τόνδ' ἴδητ', ἔπος
ἐξερῶ μέγ', οἷον οὔτινα
Τροία στρατοῦ δέρχθη χθονὸς μολόντ' ἀπὸ
Ἑλλανίδος·

O neighbouring
streams of the Scamander,
friendly to the Argives,
you will never see
this man again – I will pronounce
a great boast – a man whose equal
Troy did not see in the army that came
from Greece.

419–26

In this case, his boast takes the form of denying his signature identity in the *Iliad* and throughout the tradition as the second-best member of the army after Achilles. A few lines later, as he assesses his options in iambics, Ajax himself summons up a Salamis-oriented version of the Troy legend, involving traditions about Telamon and his stellar role in the first Trojan War, the war led by Heracles against Laodemon, who had refused to give him the horses promised for the rescue of Hesione.[18] In some versions of this story, Telamon was the first to breach the walls of Troy and in fact received Hesione (who became the mother of Teucer) as a reward for that. This story stretches back to the epic cycle – we know that it figured in a work by the seventh-century poet Pisander – and was especially prized at Salamis and at Aigina, Telamon's birthplace, from which he migrated to Salamis. Both Trojan Wars were depicted on the pediments of the temple to Aphaea on Aegina, when it was rebuilt sometime around 500: the first on the east pediment, prominently featuring Telamon, the second on the west pediment, prominently featuring Ajax, with Athena playing a central role in both.[19]

When Ajax looks back to the first Trojan War in *Ajax*, there is none of the implied equivalence between father and son found on the Aphaea temple; rather, the comparison is very much to his detriment:

καὶ ποῖον ὄμμα πατρὶ δηλώσω φανεὶς
Τελαμῶνι; πῶς με τλήσεταί ποτ᾽ εἰσιδεῖν
γυμνὸν φανέντα τῶν ἀριστείων ἄτερ,
ὧν αὐτὸς ἔσχε στέφανον εὐκλείας μέγαν;

How can I show my face to my father
Telamon? How will he be able to look at me
Appearing naked, without the prize of valour,
For which he gained the great garland of victory?

462–5

In this non-Iliadic account of the war at Troy, the hero faces a shameful *nostos* that matches his shameful departure from home. He is unable to match the achievement of his father, as a successful aristocratic warrior must. It is only later, beginning in the deception speech, as he begins to glimpse, however imperfectly, a more positive future for himself involving reconciliation with Athena, that Ajax can reassert his Iliadic self.

Unlike the highly selective snapshot produced by Athena, Sophocles' own play offers, within the brief compass of a tragedy, a portrait of Ajax that is not one-sided. This multifaceted portrait does justice to the ups and downs of his changing fortunes and to the intrinsic doubleness of heroic figures, whether in epic or in cult, as both protectors of their community and as embodiments of single-minded, destructive anger. Sophocles achieves this in part by projecting and subsuming into his play multiple epic narratives, each with its own particular slant and selective vision, defined in each case by the particular earlier moment that is presented as the starting point of a trajectory that has the events of *Ajax* – disgrace, suicide and imminent burial – as its conclusion: in one case, a familiar moment from the *Iliad*, Ajax' duel with Hector, that epitomizes Ajax' identity as the reliable second-best warrior in the army; in another, the Judgment of the Arms, which initiates the period of Odysseus' ascendency in the wake of Achilles' death and leads both to Ajax' humiliation and his achievement of burial through Odysseus' humane intervention; and in yet another, Ajax' departure from Salamis, a moment of rashness and overreaching that marks him as inescapably offensive to Athena and so sets him on the course to his remarkable death and its exceptional aftermath.

Notes

1. Versions of this paper were delivered at the Columbia University Seminar in Classical Civilization and the Penn Classical Studies Colloquium during the autumn of 2017, as well as at

the Greek Drama V conference. I am indebted to many audience members on those occasions for their responses, to Seth L. Schein for helpful comments on a written version, and to the editors of this volume for their patience and astute guidance during the process of revision.

2. The metatheatrical character of this scene has often been noted. See, for example, Easterling 1993: 82; Falkner 1993; Ringer 1998: 31–7.

3. On the dramatic significance of the single day in *Ajax*, see van Erp Talmaan Kip 2007.

4. The play's muted but telling intimations of Ajax' future as a cult hero are discussed by Burian 1972; Henrichs 1993; Seaford 1994: 129–30; Krummen 1998; and, more cautiously, Currie 2012: 333–6. For Ajax' role in Athenian religion and civic organization, see Shapiro 1989: 154–7; Kearns 1989: 46, 80–91, 140–1; Kowalzig 2006: 85–9; Kron 1976: 171–6; Parker 1996: 118–19.

5. For a survey of versions of Ajax' fate following the death of Achilles from the archaic and classical periods, see Gantz 1993: 629–35.

6. Quotations and translations of Pindar are taken from Race 1997 with slight adaptation.

7. On the complexity and contingency of Pindar's presentation of Homer, see Nisetich 1989, especially p. 22 for the conclusion that in *Isthmian* 4 'Homer' means the poet of the *Iliad*, in *Nemean* 7 the poet of the *Odyssey*. On Sophocles as evoking Pindar's treatment of Ajax, see Cairns 2006: 108.

8. Hesk 2003: 24–34.

9. Easterling 1984.

10. Barker 2009: 284–90.

11. For the debate, see Pagliaro 1963 and Redfield 1979, both of whom favour ἐτελείετο in line 5 as the point of reference.

12. On *eris* as a theme that pervades early Greek epic, see Thalmann 2004: 362–82; Christensen 2018: 11–13.

13. On Odysseus' dominance in the later phases of the Trojan War legend, see Holt 1992: 327.

14. Mueller 2016: 25. In keeping with her focus on significant objects, Mueller argues that what has happened 'ever since' is that Ajax has become subject to the hostility of Hector, which is embodied in the sword: even though he has changed his mind about the suicide when he delivers the 'deception speech', Ajax is finally compelled by the sword to kill himself after all. In my view, this interpretation gives too little weight to Ajax' agency in shaping his own story.

15. For various attempts to explain ξένων, 'foreigners' at 817, see Finglass 2011: 378. On Ajax' 'recharacterization' of the sword, see Cohen 1978: 31–4; on the developing representation of Ajax' suicide as the completion of his duel with Hector, see Hesk 2003: 80.

16. For other assessments of the gravity of Calchas' reports, see Winnington-Ingram 1980: 12–13; Cairns 108–10. On the dynamic of divine anger giving way to favour, see Seaford 1994: 130 n. 121.

17. Cf. also Heracles' lament at *Trachiniae* 1075 that νῦν δ᾽ ἐκ τοιούτου θῆλυς ηὕρημαι τάλας ('now after being like that [i.e. after a long career of heroic self-restraint] in my misery I have been found to be a woman').

18. On Telamon in early Greek myth, see Gantz 1993: 221–5.

19. On the pediments in relation to poetic traditions about the Aeacids, see Burnett 2005: 29–44. For an account of the first Trojan War that foregrounds Telamon's role over that of Heracles and stresses his connection to Salamis and Athens, see Eur. *Tro.* 799–819.

CHAPTER 3
ELEGY AND SOPHOCLES' *PHILOCTETES*: A REFLECTION ON GENERIC RESONANCE
Kathryn Mattison

Tragedy is the quintessential Athenian genre, the origins of which are notoriously difficult to pin down with any certainty.[1] In this chapter, I propose that archaic elegy was one of the influences on fifth-century tragedy in that elegy provided tragedians with a model of engaging with Homeric themes in a contemporary setting. This study is the beginning of the vast undertaking of a detailed analysis of extant tragedy alongside archaic elegy in an attempt to more fully understand the relationship between the two genres. For now, I offer this case study of Sophocles' *Philoctetes* and its possible relationship to the themes expressed in three different elegies: the 'New Archilochus' fragment (*P.Oxy* LXIX 4708), Tyrtaeus 9, and Solon 3. With Archilochus, I focus particularly on how he and Sophocles present the individual dealing with a moment of crisis. With Tyrtaeus and Solon, I explore how Sophocles is engaging with their presentation of group cohesion. This is not to say that Sophocles was thinking specifically of any of these poems while composing *Philoctetes*; rather, that these kinds of elegies form Sophocles' poetic foundation. While this is a focused discussion of one tragedy, it suggests that tragedians were engaging with a poetic tradition that included elegy, and that tragedy could engage with elegy and the elegiac presentation of the individual in the same way that it could with Homeric epic. The engagement may not be identifiable in every tragedy; my aim is to suggest the possibility of a connection and to encourage the consideration of tragedy developing as part of a poetic tradition that includes elegy.[2]

I have selected Sophocles' *Philoctetes* as the tragedy through which to examine these generic connections for two reasons: it is very Homeric,[3] and it engages with themes that are present in elegy. In particular, it has echoes of exhortation, such as we find in Tyrtaeus and Solon, and of flight or desertion, such as we find in the New Archilochus. Selecting a particularly Homeric tragedy may seem counter-intuitive, but it is important to show how elements of the Homeric tradition can combine with the thematic interests of the elegiac tradition. These two traditions are not at odds with one another, but are instead part of a continuing and evolving poetic voice, of which tragedy is yet another evolution. That *Philoctetes* is such a late play (with a secure date of 409)[4] and still grapples with the questions that the elegiac poets were concerned with demonstrates the lasting impact of the elegiac voice. While my focus below is on the fragmentary New Archilochus, I cannot say with any certainty that Sophocles or his audience knew that precise poem.[5] The Archilochus fragment provides us with evidence, however, of a mythological paradigm in elegy, by an elegist who was not previously known to use them. This, in turn, suggests the possibility of the widespread use of myth by elegists, creating a link in the chain of poetic use of mythology between the Homeric epics and tragedy.

The New Archilochus presents a mythological paradigm in defence of military flight.[6] It tells of the Achaeans' first attempt at finding Troy and landing at Mysia instead, and their subsequent defeat by Telephus. The paradigm is offered after Archilochus reassures the reader in line 4 of the fragment that there is such a thing as the right time to flee (φεύγ[ειν δέ τις ὤρη·). The line is context of an unnamed collective flight, which Archilochus describes in the first-person plural.[7] He then goes directly into the mythological paradigm, highlighting Telephus' strong solo effort in routing the Achaean forces. Because of its fragmentary nature, certain conclusions about its content are impossible,[8] and the extent of the mythological content in particular is difficult to ascertain. Laura Lulli argues that the mythological reference does not exceed the extant fragment, since any such content in elegy is typically concise and complementary to the other elements of the poem (such as historical content, as appears to be the case in this fragment).[9] Along with the mythological paradigm, Archilochus is clearly addressing a contemporary audience, and he is including himself: at line 4 there is a first-person plural, [εἴμ]εθα.[10] And so he straddles the line between myth and his contemporary time. The poem as a whole reads, very simply, as a defence of flight: even the Achaean army was put to flight by Telephus, so it is reasonable for Archilochus and his men to run away, too.

Almost as soon as the fragment was published, it was understood to be a part of a conversation with Homeric heroism. One of the earliest instances of this approach to the new fragment was Barker and Christensen in 2006,[11] who argue that the fragment is evidence in support of the tradition of poetic rivalry with Archilochus explicitly taking on Homeric epic.[12] They argue that this poem presents Archilochus' personal voice, which is in competition with the narrative voice in Homer, resulting in an anti-Iliadic approach to flight, a theme that Archilochus appropriates from the epic tradition.[13]

Laura Swift has issued a rebuttal of this reading, arguing instead for a reading of the poem in which we are meant to focus more on Telephus' solo heroism in fending off the Achaeans than on the Achaean flight.[14] Swift identifies the narrator's 'anxiety about flight' and emphasizes the 'extreme' circumstances that lead to flight.[15] According to this reading, the poem is entirely serious. While Swift's argument is compelling, given the fragmentary nature of the poem, it is difficult to judge its tone, particularly when the ending, where we might expect a twist to undermine any perceived seriousness, is missing entirely. There are other fragments from Archilochus' corpus that have a serious tone (and, in the case of the Lycambes poems, a truly sinister tone even): many of his military-themed fragments are remarkable for their light-heartedness as they play with an audience's expectations of military conduct. It seems possible, therefore, that this poem, too, ultimately played with the audience's expectations of military discussion through mythological paradigm. This is significant because it marks a true departure from the Homeric model and suggests an interest in engaging with both mythology and epic themes in a new way. This, then, establishes a precedent for tragedians, by showing a distinct poetic voice operating within a long-standing tradition. Tragedy's typical method of reworking characters and situations familiar from epic poetry in a way that is unique and deliberately situated in the contemporary world is, I suggest, following in the tradition of elegiac poetry.

While the nature of Archilochus' engagement with the Homeric epics is a valuable point of discussion, of greater interest for my discussion of *Philoctetes* is that Archilochus does not appear to be interested in the fallout of his contemporary flight. The mythological paradigm he presents is not the best example of flight because the Achaeans were wrong to be there in the first place; Mysia was not the battle they were supposed to be fighting, and so their flight is little more than an embarrassing redirection. The selection of this particular paradigm suggests that Archilochus is diverting his audience's attention from the consequences of flight and is focusing instead on the ease of flight with a connection to the mythological world. Sophocles, on the other hand, presents a myth that demonstrates an agonizing portrait of a young man trying to decide whether or not he should abandon his position in the army, with the full knowledge of the consequences of his actions. Sophocles' focus on consequences in this military context highlights the shift we see in tragedy away from the Archilochean encouragement to focus on the present and suggests that tragedy more broadly rejects elegy's simple solutions that elide the examination of the effect of the present action.

Far from suggesting that flight is easy, *Philoctetes* demonstrates both how agonizing the decision to take flight is and how wrong it is. In Sophocles' mythological paradigm of choice in this play, flight is far more consequential than it was in the New Archilochus fragment. Here, if Neoptolemus leaves with Philoctetes, the entire Achaean effort at Troy could be undermined, and so Sophocles takes his audience through Neoptolemus' decision-making only to have Heracles arrive at the end to deliver the final command to return with Philcotetes to Troy. In the tragic version of army desertion, there is no easy way out; instead there is a rather cold proclamation that confirms the primacy of the military mission over the desires of the individual. To fully demonstrate this, Sophocles creates a complicated character in Neoptolemus and shows the audience his wavering allegiance, as he goes from pretending to have deserted the army at Troy at the beginning of the play to actually being about to desert it by taking Philoctetes home at the end. Neoptolemus is coached in the pretend desertion by Odysseus in the prologue:

τὴν Φιλοκτήτου σε δεῖ
ψυχὴν ὅπως δόλοισιν ἐκκλέψεις λέγων.
ὅταν σ᾽ ἐρωτᾷ τίς τε καὶ πόθεν πάρει,
λέγειν, Ἀχιλλέως παῖς· τόδ᾽ οὐχὶ κλεπτέον·
πλεῖς δ᾽ ὡς πρὸς οἶκον, ἐκλιπὼν τὸ ναυτικὸν
στράτευμ᾽ Ἀχαιῶν, ἔχθος ἐχθήρας μέγα

You must manoeuvre the mind of Philoctetes and deceive him with beguiling words. When he asks who you are and where you come from, tell him you're the son of Achilles – that should never be hidden – but say you are heading home and you have abandoned the Greek war fleet, bearing a great grudge.

54–9

Neoptolemus' initial story to Philoctetes shows that he has been a good student:

τοιαῦτ᾽ ἀκούσας κἀξονειδισθεὶς κακὰ
πλέω πρὸς οἴκους, τῶν ἐμῶν τητώμενος
πρὸς τοῦ κακίστου κἀκ κακῶν Ὀδυσσέως.

Abused and insulted, I am sailing for home, deprived of what is rightfully mine by that bastard son of bastards, Odysseus.

382–4

He appears to be going along with Odysseus' plan and at this stage he demonstrates no hesitation with the deception. It is difficult not to hear an echo of Achilles from *Iliad* 9 in these lines, as the son who has never known his father gives a plausible imitation of his father's stubborn temper.[16] But Neoptolemus does not share his father's temper in this play. Once he has spent time with Philoctetes away from Odysseus' influence, we begin to see how malleable he is, in stark contrast with the Iliadic Achilles. He is, rather, quick to change his mind in the face of Philoctetes' perspective and wishes to return to Greece rather than to rejoin the army. It is easy to see him as a young, easily influenced man who changes allegiance depending on who he is with, but I posit that Sophocles uses Philoctetes as a kind of elegiac poet: he is speaking directly to an individual about a particular situation, and he asks him to focus on the present rather than considering the longer-term consequences to the army.

In the same way that Archilochus assures his audience that flight is acceptable, Philoctetes persuades Neoptolemus to take him home by not mentioning the army and emphasizing only the good deed Neoptolemus would be doing for him personally: νῦν δ᾽, εἰς σὲ γὰρ πομπόν τε καὐτὸν ἄγγελον | ἥκω, σὺ σῶσον, σύ μ᾽ ἐλέησον ... ('But now in you I have an escort and a messenger, save me, take pity on me ...') (500–1). Neoptolemus appears to agree to go along with this (524–99), though this initial agreement is part of the deception plot, as Neoptolemus confirms when he confesses the plan to return Philoctetes to Troy at 915–16.[17] When Philoctetes learns the truth he is furious (his lengthy excoriation is 927–62), but continues to try to keep Neoptolemus focused on the immediate situation: οὐκ εἶ κακὸς σύ, πρὸς κακῶν δ᾽ ἀνδρῶν μαθὼν | ἔοικας ἥκειν αἰσχρά· ('You're not bad, but I think you've learned from wicked men and come here for shameful actions;') (970). By focusing on Neoptolemus and trying to reach him on a personal level, Philoctetes again maintains his emphasis on the present in an attempt to keep Neoptolemus from thinking of the larger-scale issue of the army at Troy. In the end, after a lengthy attempt to persuade Philoctetes to sail to Troy willingly, Neoptolemus agrees to take him home (1402). It is unclear precisely why he agrees to do this, except that Philoctetes has successfully appealed to his sense of personal honour and created enough cognitive distance between the present circumstances and the consequences that will occur as a result of their present action. Neoptolemus may have his doubts about the correctness of this course of action, but he has ultimately been assuaged by the elegiac techniques that Philoctetes has used. It takes Heracles *ex machina* to remind us that Philoctetes' personal wish to return home cannot supersede the army's need of Philoctetes, Neoptolemus and the bow. Just like Archilochus presented an inappropriate paradigm for fully evaluating the propriety of flight, Philoctetes presented an inappropriate reason for Neoptolemus to abandon the army.

To summarize up to this point: Sophocles is presenting a version of the New Archilochus fragment with Philoctetes as the elegist, urging the propriety of flight based on the wrong reasons, which Heracles is required to correct in the end. This shows that tragedy could engage with elegy by suggesting that the focus on the present without a consideration of future consequences was misplaced. But it also shows how effective that focus could be in manipulating people. In spite of his reservations, Neoptolemus decides to help Philoctetes in a course of action that would have been disastrous for his army if followed through. Sophocles is correcting that elegiac perspective by emphasizing the importance of following through with difficult actions for the benefit of the group, but also suggests the importance of being able to tell when such manipulative words are used.

It may seem at this point that, while tragedy may be rejecting an Archilochean style of elegy, it adheres more to exhortation-style elegy that is closely linked to building or strengthening bonds within a community. And yet, I suggest here that Sophocles positions Odysseus as an advocate for elite group membership that is based on exclusion, rather than inclusion, and that is, in the end, no better than the narrow perspective offered by Philoctetes. Scholars identify two basic kinds of exhortation in elegy: military and civic. In both cases, a poet calls upon men in a particular group to keep up morale or to improve their behaviour. The question of whom, in particular, the poets are addressing has been a matter of debate for some time. Ewen Bowie, followed by Elizabeth Irwin, has argued persuasively for a private performance context for both military and civic exhortation elegies.[18] This proposition suggests that West's more complex explanation of the different possible performance contexts is overly complicated and requires too literal a reading of the poems.[19] Bowie argues that there were elegies performed in public that spoke to the shared ancestry of the audience or the achievements of the city, elegies performed in a private, sympotic context that spoke to the lifestyle of the aristocracy.[20]

Irwin goes even further to delineate the way that symposia, and the elegies performed at them, were venues for creating social cohesion, but only within the group of participants.[21] That is, the elegies performed in symposia were used to affirm the elite status of the participants. The military exhortation poems, therefore, have little to do with any immediate military threat, but instead speak to the shared experience of the attendees. By drawing on that shared experience, the poems help to create a sense of social cohesion that unites the men. Irwin offers a similar explanation with respect to civic exhortation, suggesting that it engages with the tradition of military exhortation and draws attention to the dangers that can come from within the polis as opposed to the dangers that come from outside of the polis.[22] In both cases, there is an aspect of heroic role playing to the poetry that suggests a self-conscious poetic voice that highlights the nearly dramatic nature of the poems.[23]

Irwin argues that Tyrtaeus 9, and other poems like it, were for a private audience, and the poet was not interested in fostering a sense of community spirit or suggesting any obligations the audience might have towards the polis. Rather, as a sympotic poem, it flatters its audience, which is comprised not of the entire population of citizens but of a select elite. This kind of elegy, Irwin argues, gives its audience the means to represent themselves as the heroic elite.[24] Accordingly, therefore, elegy creates unity among group members, but division and stratification within the broader community. Consider, in this context, *Philoctetes'* Odysseus, who goes about creating unity in a particular group of men with whom he is like-minded, but also creating division and stratification within the community as he relies on epic ideals of heroism to try to recruit and retain Neoptolemus for his purposes.

Like Philoctetes, Odysseus can be read as an elegiac poet, exhorting Neoptolemus to do the deed and earn membership in an elite group. From the prologue, and in every other appearance he makes in the play, he repeats one message: Philoctetes has to come back to Troy, deception is the best way to achieve that and Neoptolemus will be honoured if he succeeds. For example, at 83–5, Odysseus says:

νῦν δ᾽ εἰς ἀναιδὲς ἡμέρας μέρος βραχὺ
δός μοι σεαυτόν, κᾆτα τὸν λοιπὸν χρόνον
κέκλησο πάντων εὐσεβέστατος βροτῶν.

Now give me just one little day of shamelessness, and for the rest of time you will be known as the most virtuous of all living men.

In these lines he is attempting to create a certain intimacy and connection with Neoptolemus, suggesting that through this shared secret (the deception), Neoptolemus can gain fame. He recruits Neoptolemus into his inner circle while keeping Philoctetes outside the group. We can compare Tyrtaeus 9:

οὐδέ ποτε κλέος ἐσθλὸν ἀπόλλυται οὐδ᾽ ὄνομ᾽ αὐτοῦ,
ἀλλ᾽ ὑπὸ γῆς περ ἐὼν γίγνεται ἀθάνατος,
ὅντιν᾽ ἀριστεύοντα μένοντά τε μαρνάμενόν τε
γῆς πέρι καὶ παίδων θοῦρος Ἄρης ὀλέσῃ.

His name and good fame never die, but even though he's under the earth he becomes immortal, whomever furious Ares kills while he behaves nobly and fights for the sake of his country and children.

31–4

Just as Neoptolemus is promised the reward of honour in exchange for a deed that will benefit the army, so these soldiers are promised a life and death of honour in exchange for their military duty. Odysseus, like Tyrtaeus, is feeding Neoptolemus the ideal of heroism, suggesting that the young man will be welcomed into a group of heroes if he does as Odysseus says. Odysseus' purpose may overall be one of unity, as he is working towards Greek success at Troy, but his means of achieving it involves creating division by trying to ensure that Neoptolemus is on his side and not Philoctetes'.

But Odysseus' posturing does not work in this play. His exhortations inspire Neoptolemus at first, but the influence is not sustained. Neoptolemus' sympathy for Philoctetes and Neoptolemus' instinct to follow his own *phusis* rather than Odysseus' counsel suggests that he has not been entirely won over by the appeal to membership in an elite social group. Read against the background of elegy, Sophocles is highlighting the division that such elite groups create: there can be no unity when membership in the group means creating uncomfortable exclusions. It is significant that Neoptolemus, the young man from a new generation, is the one to reject the divisions that Odysseus is trying to create since it allows Sophocles to demonstrate how a new generation might resist the norms of social division in the past. Neoptolemus appears to be trying to find a way to remove himself from such things and to be demonstrating that divisions are not always helpful, but can lead to conflict. It is also significant that tragedy, the younger poetic genre, is rejecting the divisions that elegy created. *Philoctetes* suggests that one man's song directed at a predefined group is not an effective way of creating social unity since it encourages a lack of dialogue with others who may not share one's social group. Multivocal tragedy, on the other hand, is more suited to encouraging dialogue, and showing different perspectives.

The new conflict that Neoptolemus creates when he turns away from Odysseus' influence is most evident in Odysseus' angry reaction to Neoptolemus at the end of the play. Because he has not understood the situation leading to Odysseus' actions, Neoptolemus now risks alienating himself from Odysseus and, by extension, the Greek army at Troy. At first, Odysseus simply expresses anger: ὦ κάκιστ᾽ ἀνδρῶν, τί δρᾷς; ('You traitor, what are you doing?')[25] (974). But later, when Neoptolemus has returned to give Philoctetes back the bow, Odysseus positions himself as the representative of the Greek army, which he says is now against Neoptolemus: ξύμπας Ἀχαιῶν λαός, ἐν δὲ τοῖς ἐγώ ('the entire Achaean host, and myself among them') (1243). He then backs out of making any decisions, saying just that the Greek army will deal with Neoptolemus: καίτοι σ᾽ ἐάσω· τῷ δὲ σύμπαντι στρατῷ λέξω τάδ᾽ ἐλθών, ὅς σε τιμωρήσεται ('I want no more of this. I will inform the army of this, and they will deal with you') (1258–9). With this kind of language, Odysseus creates a strongly divided community, and places Neoptolemus on the outside of the inner circle. The result of Neoptolemus' attempt to circumvent the group that Odysseus was advocating is simply that he has been excluded. He has not successfully united anyone, nor has he opened any dialogue on the issue; he has instead revealed the deep complexities involved in social divisions.

When Odysseus makes his final exit, he is walking away from what he has told Neoptolemus is the only way to ensure the Greeks take Troy: that is, with Philoctetes and his bow. He is also cutting Neoptolemus out of his social circle, which creates tension with the heroic role playing that Irwin argues is present in military exhortation elegies: one can play the hero only by staying within very particular boundaries. This Odysseus presents a very firm set of rules for what heroism is, and for him Neoptolemus' betrayal of the group is cause to remove him from the group entirely. This suggests how deceptive the simple message of group cohesion is in elegy: when faced with a difficult decision to make outside of Odysseus' protective supervision, Neoptolemus is easily swayed by another. Neither elegiac strategy, both of which advocate operating in a kind of isolation that ignores what anyone who does not agree might think, achieves its goal.

Solon's civic exhortation seems to speak in favour of the exact opposite of stratification as he bemoans the problems that arise within the city when the people are not unified, voicing his contemporary political concerns. Solon's 'Eunomia' poem (Campbell 3) says:

τοῦτ᾽ ἤδη πάσῃ πόλει ἔρχεται ἕλκος ἄφυκτον,
ἐς δὲ κακὴν ταχέως ἤλυθε δουλοσύνη,
ἥ στάσιν ἔμφυλον πόλεμόν θ᾽ εὕδοντ᾽ ἐπεγείρει,
ὅς πολλῶν ἐρατὴν ὤλεσεν ἡλικίην·
ἐκ γὰρ δυσμενέων ταχέως πολυήρατον ἄστυ
τρύχεται ἐν συνόδοις τοῖς ἀδικοῦσι φίλαις.

This wound is now coming to the whole city, it's inescapable, and she's falling quickly into evil slavery, which causes strife and awakens slumbering war, destroying so many men in the prime of their life. In the hands of its enemies, the beloved city is quickly being brought down amid conspiracies that are dear to the unjust.

17–22

And yet, of course, these are highly divisive words: we have the enemies of the city and its protectors. Solon's poem urges unity, but reveals deep divisions and suggests that unity can only be achieved if the enemies come around to a more sensible point of view.[26] The wound in the lines above is a perfect metaphor for Sophocles' *Philoctetes*. The wound, the pestilence, of one man cannot be avoided by the community as a whole even, as in *Philoctetes*, when that man is physically removed from the community. Indeed, we learn through Heracles that Philoctetes can be healed when he rejoins the army in Troy (1425), and so wound becomes the physical manifestation of the division within the army. The decision to abandon Philoctetes has grown into an inescapable problem for the Greeks, and Odysseus' plan to use Neoptolemus and the promise of elite group membership against Philoctetes does not solve the problem. In order to solve it, the disparate groups must come together instead of continuing their rejection of one another.

I have tried to argue for a connection between *Philoctetes* and the elegies of Archilochus, Tytaeus and Solon in order to establish elegy as one of tragedy's influences. This is a specific study, and yet the basic premise can be applied to other tragedies. I suggest that the elegiac voice is present and being confronted by tragedians when one or more character is forced to face the consequences of their actions, rather than to act in a way that ignores consequences, and when elite and exclusive social groups are questioned. This helps to place tragedy in a dialogue with another genre, in addition to the Homeric epics and choral poetry, to show how tragedy continued to position itself at the pinnacle of poetic expression. I argue that Sophocles presents Odysseus and Philoctetes as different types of elegiac poets, who both act inappropriately and in a way that makes the situation more complicated for Neoptolemus. Tragedy's multivocal nature can show the messiness of the conflict created by these two characters, and in so doing it can show the deep struggles involved in making the right decision. On stage, characters have the benefit of the gods to steer them, and they often act as tragedy's final corrective stance against the divisive nature of elegy.

Notes

1. An informative place to start with a variety of approaches is Csapo and Miller 2007.

2. Herington 1985: 39 notes that there is no 'unbridgeable gap' between early Greek poetry and fifth-century drama. Where Herington is primarily interested in the connection between elegy and other forms of early Greek poetry and tragedy through poetry's performance context and the level of 'impersonation' involved in poetic performance from the time of the Homeric epics onwards (51), I am drawing the connection of thematic development.

3. It takes place during the Trojan War, but has strong connections to the *Odyssey*. See Davidson 1995; Schein 2013: 15–18.

4. Schein 2013: 10–12 has a good, concise discussion of *Philoctetes'* original performance context at the first Dionysia after the restoration of the democracy.

5. Though other sources from the fifth century and beyond have a clear knowledge of Archilochus' poetry. See, for example, Herodotus 1.12; Pindar *Pythians* 2.52–6; Dio Chrysostom 33.11–12.

6. The performance context of this poem is still uncertain. For the most recent discussion and bibliography, see Bowie 2016. He suggests that it was meant for public, possibly cultic, performance, and that it is too long for a sympotic context. Nobili 2016: 55, however, reminds us that even public elegies could be reperformed in private sympotic settings. See also Swift 2014 for the possibility of a performance on Thasos or Paros.

7. Swift 2014: 433 suggests that Archilochus is connecting with 'implicit mockery' the battle that the Achaeans fight on Mysia with the contemporary military operations on Paros.

8. See Obbink 2006. I follow this edition here.

9. Lulli 2016: 197–8.

10. Bowie 1986: 16 notes that Archilochus evokes situations that his audience would have been familiar with. This is not in reference to the new fragment, but there is no reason to doubt the observation's continued significance.

11. The question of Archilochus' connection to Homer has extensive roots, with scholars arguing both that his work is anti-heroic (for example, Dover 1964; Burnett 1983) and not (for example, Fowler 1987; Toohey 1988).

12. It is impossible to know with certainty whether Archilochus would have known the *Iliad* specifically. Garner 2005 provides a good overview of what Archilochus may have been familiar with (see 389–92 in particular). See also West 2006.

13. While not directly addressing this fragment, it is useful to note that Garner 2011: 81 suggests the possibility of elegy complementing the epic tradition rather than being derived from it. He is talking about the technical compositional elements of the poetry, though, rather than the thematic content.

14. Swift 2012.

15. Swift 2012: 145.

16. Hamilton 1975; Roisman 1997; Belfiore 2000; and Allan 2011 have noted the connections between Neoptolemus and Achilles.

17. Easterling 1983 discusses Neoptolemus' dishonesty and how the constant interplay of honesty and dishonesty creates depth to his character (see 1983: 143 especially).

18. Bowie 1986 and 1990; Irwin 2005.

19. This is in response to West 1974 in particular.

20. Bowie 1986: 33.

21. Irwin 2005: 32–5.

22. Irwin 2005: 111.

23. Irwin 2005: 49.

24. Irwin 2005: 28.

25. 'Traitor' is Peter Meineck's 2014 translation of κάκιστ᾽ ἀνδρῶν. It captures the tone of Odysseus' outrage nicely.

26. Bowie 1986: 34 argues that the symposium was a place where group bonds were strengthened.

CHAPTER 4
A DRAMATURGY OF THE SELF: DEIANIRA BETWEEN THE GRID AND THE COUCH
Eleni Papazoglou

To Pat Easterling

The nature of the tragic character has been intensely debated within classical studies,[1] generating a polarity which can be distinguished broadly as one between a non- or anti-psychological (non-realistic, 'dehumanized') dramatic subject and a psychological (realistic, 'humanized') one.[2] According to anti-psychologists, the conventions of the tragic genre, from the use of masks and space to the form of speech and dialogue, preclude realistic, individualistic and introvert modern perspectives in favour of a more formalistic, impersonal and abstract extroversion,[3] which results in a 'meagreness'[4] in characterization that applies to tragedy as a genre. This concept is seen to conform to Aristotle's idea of *muthos* over *ēthos* (*Poet.* 1450a 16–39) or the structuralist prioritization of action over psychology.[5] Two further distinctions have also been employed: that between ancient (and more 'objectivist/participant') and modern (and more 'subjectivist/individualist') concepts of selfhood;[6] and that between real and fictional personalities.[7] Still, some of the anti-psychologists concede to a developmental process from Aeschylus to Euripides, which leads to psychologically deeper characters in the work of the younger playwright.[8] However, it has also been argued that Sophoclean characters have an intricate selfhood which is much more psychologically economical than that of their Euripidean counterparts.[9] For more determined psychologists, tragic heroes, despite the genre's formalism, can be seen to enjoy an idiosyncratic psychological depth not entirely dissimilar to that of characters in modern drama or, indeed, real life.[10] Furthermore, it has been argued that tragic personae (or, at least, some of them) display their idiosyncrasy through grammar and intonation,[11] and such individuality has been explored through the application of linguistic theory to reveal the characterizing potential of tragic diction.[12]

In what follows, I shall attempt to revisit the psychologists' camp in order to approach Sophocles' Deianira in *Women of Trachis*, taking my lead from Charles Segal's 'Pentheus and Hippolytos on the Couch and on the Grid' (1978). Segal argued that structuralism and psychoanalysis are parallel, analogous and complementary systems of thought: employing an opposition between culture and nature, structuralism aims at revealing the underlying and rational syntax of myth, focusing on the relation between myth and society. Focusing on the hidden and irrational fractures of the unconscious, on the other hand, psychoanalysis aims at exploring an inner syntax, as it were, of the individual's soul. Both approaches, as Segal puts it, 'deal primarily with the mechanisms of thought and feeling through which ambiguous and contradictory aspects of reality are forced into bearable, coherent forms for the inner life of man. [...] Freud reads souls as Levi-Strauss reads myths and societies.'[13] Building on Segal's parallelism between structuralism and psychoanalysis, I shall explore how anthropological crisis opens the space to the emergence of the psychological subject, with a focus on Deianira.

In the following discussion, two words shall function as key terms: *prosōpon* and 'self'. *Prosōpon* is etymologically connected to the idea of the other's gaze ('that with which I am seen by others'), and requires it to signify human subjectivity as a social role: human personality defined relationally, always *pros heteron*, and based on its dependence on shared and social values, principles and stereotypes.[14] In contrast, 'self' shall signpost here a more introverted, individualized subjectivity, which sets one person apart from another and may enjoy self-consciousness, yet does not have full awareness of its 'self': i.e. what we commonly understand with the word 'character'. Western thought has oscillated (and continues to do so) between defending the Self and proclaiming its 'death', but the present day, more than ever before, is ready to accept that social role(s) overdetermine individual subjectivity and compromise any sort of unitary and stable selfhood which enjoys self-sufficiency. In my terms, 'self' and *prosōpon*, personal idiosyncrasy and social identity, are inextricably linked. This subjectivity can be seen to emerge on the tragic stage, too.

Endorsing the idea that not all tragic personages are the same,[15] I would suggest that tragic heroes who display a psychological depth often appear to negotiate their subjectivity through experiences that problematize ritual processes, specifically funeral rites and rites of passage from puberty to adulthood. In ancient life, the main function of such rites was to produce subjects who would conform to identities that were considered appropriate and instrumental in the social and cultural context: funeral rites aimed at the separation between the living and the dead; the rites of male *ephēbeia* at the formation of the adult citizen/soldier; the wedding rituals at the formation of the virgin girl into a woman. Such rites ensured the configuration of human subjects: they provided social roles and shared values, through which they could recognize and communicate their subjectivity. Rituals, in other words, produced *prosōpa*: they precluded individuality, ignored idiosyncrasy and bypassed personal memories, experiences and psychic complexes.

However, as many have argued, rituals on the tragic stage appear systematically perverted, producing a ritual crisis.[16] If the (ab)use of ritual language and action in tragedy indicates a moral and social disorder,[17] then the perversion of initiation rites produces the deconstruction of the tragic *prosōpon*. In my view, ritual perversion forces (and, at the same time, allows) the tragic subject to seek and shape his/her subjectivity away from collective and social values, identities and roles, and to display the psychological profile of an idiosyncratic 'I': this is the 'dramaturgy of the self'.[18]

Deianira's individuality is signposted already in the prologue:

It was long ago that someone first said:
You cannot know a man's life before the man
has died, then only can you call it good or bad.

But I know mine before I've come to death's house
and I can tell that mine is heavy and sorrowful.

1–5[19]

Deianira distances herself from timeless and universal human experience,[20] as she also does a few lines later, when she emphasizes that she feared of marriage 'as no other Aetolian woman' (7–8): here is a person with emphatic consciousness of her unique position.[21]

On the Grid

Trachis is a space which, as telegraphed by its name, is a 'rough' (τραχύ), wild space,[22] even bereft of a polis: its agora seems to be located in pastures (*Trach*. 188),[23] and no king or dynastic *oikos* appears to organize it as a political institution. It is this anthropological frame that allows monsters to be so dangerously close to the humans: the savage figures of Acheloos and Nessos can be part of Deianira's world, entering into the innermost recesses of her house, her soul, her memory and her body,[24] precisely because the world of the play has not safeguarded the barrier between civilization's *nomos* and wilderness's *phusis*, as a key thematic of the plot is 'the repeated interaction between the protected, domestic sphere and the mysterious, natural (and sometimes magical) world, which threatens its existence'.[25]

Furthermore, Deianira is bereft of a safe and stable *prosōpon*: the *prosōpon* that the social role of a woman and wife could give her in the context of a normal *oikos*. On the one hand, her marriage to Heracles does not provide her with such an integration: abandoned to solitude and continuous anxiety, Deianira feels like an 'outlying field' (*Trach*. 32–3), closer to wild nature than to civilization.[26] Deianira is essentially homeless: she is exiled (39) in Trachis, outside a polis and an *oikos*, without her own *oikos*.[27] Deianira 'never achieves the *eudaimonia* of incorporation':[28] she feels as if she does not have a roof above her head. This is why, at the crucial moment, she will ask for the *stegē* ('roof', and so shelter) that the chorus' silence will give her (μόνον παρ' ὑμῶν εὖ στεγοίμεθ', 596). Without a polis and an *oikos* there can be no gaze, and so Deianira never achieves the security of a proper *prosōpon*, the construction of identity that comes from the other's gaze. This lack necessitates, and in turn allows, the formation of a 'self' within her – the emergence of an idiosyncratic 'I' – which, prey to turbulent emotions, decides to conquer Heracles by sending him the fatal gift.

The absence of a stable *oikos* problematizes the genders of both spouses.[29] Deianira's erotic boldness invests her with a sort of 'manliness',[30] and equally masculine is her decision to use erotic magic: in antiquity, it was men who sought to 'bind' their erotic partners with magic and less often the opposite.[31] The reality of Trachis disturbs the very constitution of the human subject: marriage failed to control Deianira's fear and sexuality, and it didn't give her the security and the integration of an *oikos*. Iole's appropriation of her space completes her exposure: marriage will not prove capable of putting Deianira's desire under control; everything is placed at the centre of the stage, exposed, fluid, continuously shifting.

Deianira's anthropological idiosyncrasy is also linked to the perversion of her wedding rite: the procedure through which she should have made the transition from puberty to adulthood and, thus, assume a safe female *prosōpon*. The wedding rite carried the bride from the status of virgin to the status of wife, and was articulated according to Van Gennep's pattern of Separation (from the paternal *oikos*) to Transition to Reintegration (into the conjugal *oikos*). First came the prenuptial bath (or the sprinkling) of the bride with river water. Given that rivers connoted male sexuality and fertility, this water 'cleansed' the bride of her maidenhood,[32] preparing her symbolically for the sexual act. The rite sought to ease the fear of the girl and initiated her into a sexual identity, which she would assume as a wife. The transition was represented by the procession from one *oikos* to the other, during which the bride was considered to be suspended between life and death: she 'died' as a maiden to be 'reborn' as a wife.[33] In my terms, the bride is here between two *prosōpa*: having abandoned the protection of the paternal *oikos* but not yet enjoying the integration into that of the husband, at an institutional *limen* (threshold) where divine protection was temporarily suspended, the bride was extremely vulnerable to the profane and the anomic. The procession through the streets of the city was crucial to the successful performance of the ritual: a *numphagōgos* ('bride-carrier', i.e. the groom or an escort of his) took the bride from her house, grabbing her by her wrist, and lifted her in the air in order to place her in the wedding chariot (the 'bride-lifting rite').[34] This symbolic abduction connoted the girl's unwillingness to abandon the security of the paternal *oikos*, and alludes to the abduction of that paradigmatic bride, Persephone. At the same time, the bride-lifting rite denoted the suspension of the souls of the dead, and the figurative and literal 'manipulation' of the bride aimed at securing her safety. The *numphostoloi*, the group of relatives and friends who escorted the wedding chariot with apotropaic dances and songs, ensured that the bride was sufficiently protected during this period in which she remained liminal, while also easing her transition. Songs during the procession had sexual references, aimed at familiarizing the bride with sexuality. Third and finally, the *anakaluptēria*, which signifies both the gifts which the groom offered to his future wife (the wedding cloak being the most important of them) and the rite of his literally 'dis-covering' her: lifting her veil to look her in the face.[35] Through the gaze of the various participants in the wedding rite, the bride now had a *prosōpon*: that of a wife.[36]

For Deianira, however, all these ritual aspects which were normally symbolic, controlled and appeasing, have been made real, uncontrolled and traumatic. When the shape-changing river Acheloos sought to marry her, she had 'an agonizing fear of marriage':[37] 'in my unhappiness I constantly prayed for death | before I should ever come to *his* marriage bed [πρὶν τῆσδε κοίτης ἐμπελασθῆναί ποτε]' (16–17).[38] Acheloos' different forms reveal the sexual connotations of the river: the phallic 'twisting' snake (ἑλικτός, 12), the bull (symbol par excellence of male sexuality), and the liquids that overflow from his thick-shaded beard.[39] If the ritual bath aims at the bride's familiarization with male sexuality and appeases her fear, its perverted version in Deianira's case has the opposite result.

Heracles, of course, intervenes and defeats Acheloos. But the spectacle of their duel terrifies Deianira so much that she cannot watch it (22–4). In the chorus' fantasy, this is an eroticized duel (514–23): the opponents look alike, they lose their individuality and merge in one and the same body, the same legs, the same cries, in a hold which refers to wrestling but also to the sexual act.[40] What drives them to fight is their lust ('desiring/striving for beds': ἱέμενοι λεχέων, 514),[41] and precisely this monstrous sexuality terrifies Deianira. The choral narrative ends before the conclusion of the duel, fixed on the desolate bride: 'And then she was gone from her mother, like a calf that is lost [ἐρήμα]' (529–30), with *erēma* denoting 'the state of the bride abandoned by her kin and not yet incorporated into a new relationship'.[42] The image of the bride as a calf constituted a basic topos in wedding imagery. Here, the topos appears perverted: it is no longer a metaphor, but real trauma. A canonical wedding ritual would allow the bride to overcome the fear of *erēmia*, offering her new integration. However, the suspension of the choral narrative, with its 'close-up' on Deianira waiting at the shore, and her desperate gaze extending to infinity, indicates that 'the anxiety of the bride at her *erēmia* has spilled out over the limits that should have been set to it by the ritual and has engulfed her whole life'.[43]

Ritual perversion emerges also in the procession, which carried Deianira from Pleuron to her new home. Deianira's procession never took place:[44] 'my father sent me away from home, alone [εὖνις], to follow Heracles' (562).[45] Without the support and participation of community, and in the wild landscape beyond the polis, she experiences an anomic *numphagōgos*: it is Nessos, a 'dark-chested' centaur (δασυστέρνου, 558),[46] who lifts Deianira on his shoulders and attempts to rape her, in a perverted version of the 'bride-lifting rite': Deianira's *numphagōgos* is a wild animal (θήρ, 568), who, far from protecting her from evil, incarnates it.[47] In this anomalous procession, Deianira is exposed to the profane, invested with the violence of male sexuality.

Deianira exists in a world in which metaphors become literal – a paranoid world. And this collapse between literal and metaphorical lies at the core of Deianira's fatal gift. Erotic magic, as attested in the ancient *katadesmoi*, would 'bind' the erotic object, through a process which, at first, brought the erotic object pain and anguish.[48] This pain is spectacularly similar to the effect that Nessos' philtre has on Heracles' body: as attested in a magical papyros, a man, burning myrrh, aspires to 'sear [the] innards [of the woman he desires], her breast, her liver, her breath, her bones, her marrow, till she comes to [him] longing to please [him]' (*PGM* 4.1496–1595).[49] But, if, in the ritual context, the burning is metaphorical, in Sophocles' Trachis it proves fatally literal. This collapse of the symbolic and the real lies at the centre of a reality in which 'the monstrous figures of the remote mythical past return as the inward monstrousness of present lust',[50] overwhelming a subject bereft of a *prosōpon*.

This is why Deianira remains liminal throughout the play, and this liminality lies at the heart of her two crucial acts: her gift to Heracles and her suicide. Given that gift-giving in the wedding context belonged to the responsibilities of the groom, Deianira 'takes over the male role in the marriage ceremony'.[51] Heracles' throwing off of his garments and 'uncovering' his tortured and 'feminized' body in the exodos (1075;

1078–80) can be seen to be a perverted form of *anakaluptēria*.[52] This ritual inversion underscores Deianira's gender ambiguity (which, as we saw, is also manifested in her desire), as does the manner of her suicide: choosing to kill herself on the marital bed, undressing her body as she always did when Heracles visited her, Deianira chooses to kill herself as a female sexual partner (εὐνάτριαν, 922). At the same time, she does it in a way that befits better the *prosōpon* of a man: piercing her side with a sword.[53] This is the suicide of an 'I' which has never known the security of a safe and stable identity. Let us, therefore, examine more thoroughly how an individualized and complex self can be seen to emerge from within this anthropological liminality, from the fractures of the *prosōpon*.

On the Couch

Acheloos can be seen to symbolize a virgin girl's terrified fantasies about the sexual act.[54] Deianira seems fixated on this fear – and this fixation is underlined by her idealization of girlhood (144–50).[55] Deianira's exposure to the hyper-masculine Nessos and Heracles (all figures of monstrous sexuality) deepens her terror, and intertwines it with her own disturbed/traumatized sexuality. 'I kept them', she says of the Centaur's directions, 'like an inscription on bronze that cannot be washed away' (ἀλλ' ἐσῳζόμην χαλκῆς ὅπως δύσνιπτον ἐκ δέλτου γραφήν, 683); if *deltos* connotes the vulva and the act of writing has sexual connotations,[56] then Nessos seems to seal not only Deianira's memory, but her very body – an inscription/experience which, thus, eludes conscious awareness. It is in this complex interior that the depth of Deianira's character is rooted. There are things in herself that Deianira knows and speaks about; there are others that she knows but does not reveal, not even to herself; and, finally, there is a space inside her, which is totally unseen and unseeable, unsaid and unsayable. From this *muchos* emerges both her paralysis and her hastiness, her terror and her naiveté, the impulse of her despair and the coolness of her deceit, her obsession with grief.[57]

One moment accentuates this darkness to the spectator: when, at the end of the first episode, Deianira deceivingly asserts that she is reconciled with Heracles' erotic passion for Iole, and invites Lichas into the house in order to give him 'gifts worthy of his gifts' (ἀντὶ δώρων δῶρα χρὴ προσαρμόσαι, 494). What does she mean? What could be a gift worthy 'of such an escort' (496)? Has she already conceived the plan with Nessos' philtre or not? And, if so, does she know that the philtre must burn Heracles painfully (and drive him to experience a sort of a perverted sexual union) before delivering him full of desire to her?[58] Or, perhaps, her motives and decisions are as yet not clearly formed in her consciousness. This suspension between clarity and vagueness, this uncertainty that the reader and the spectator feel towards a person who suddenly loses her transparency, serves as a vehicle through which we are drawn to speculate on and, thus, explore Deianira's inner or hidden 'self'.[59]

The complex psychological depth of Deianira is traced in the impressive variety of tones, moods and styles with which Sophocles enriches her speech and the finesse with which he draws her character. There are moments when she becomes poignantly ekphrastic, as in her dialogues with the chorus: her speech becomes lyrical, with poetic overtones, at times spasmodic, as emotion breaks out and seems to corrode the grammatical normality of her phrasing. But there are times, also, where she adopts a controlled rhetoric, and this happens when she confronts the men around her, most notably Lichas. This alternation between different tones emerges within a single speech, at the beginning of the second episode, a speech which illustrates spectacularly this delicate layering in both soul and syntax:

> Dear friends, while our visitor is in the house
> talking to the captured girls before he leaves,
> I have come out to you, unobserved. I want
> to tell you the work my hands have done, but also to have
> your sympathy as I cry out for all I suffer.   535
> For here I have taken on a girl – no,
> I can think that no longer – a married woman, as
> a ship's master takes on cargo, goods that outrage my heart.
> So now the two of us lie under the one sheet [χλαίνης[60]]
> waiting for his embrace. This is the gift my brave   540
> and faithful Heracles sends home to his dear wife
> to compensate for his long absence!
> And yet, when he is sick as he so often is with this same sickness,
> I am incapable of anger. But to live
> in the same house [τὸ δ' αὖ ξυνοικεῖν[61]] with her, to share the same marriage
> that is something else. What woman could stand that?   546
> For I see her youth is coming to full bloom
> while mine is fading. The eyes of men love to pluck
> the blossoms; from the faded flowers they turn away.[62]
> And this is why I am afraid that he may   550
> be called my husband but be the younger woman's man.
> But no sensible woman, as I've said before,
> should let herself give way to rage. I shall tell you,
> dear friends, the solution I have to bring myself relief.   555
> [...]
> I am not a woman who tries to be – and may
> I never learn to be – bad and bold. I hate
> women who are. But if somehow by these charms,
> these spells I lay on Heracles, I can defeat   585
> the girl – well, the move is made, unless you think
> I am acting rashly [*lit.* 'unless I seem to you acting rashly']. If so, I shall stop.

> *531–87*

A variety of styles is here combined with an impressive alternation of mood and tone: '[h]er language, superficially resigned, reveals beneath the surface undercurrents of conflict which grow in intensity as her speech proceeds.'[63] There aren't many other speeches in ancient drama which orchestrate with such economy and density so many diverse and finely layered emotions. Lyricism and prosaic cynicism are here combined in order to produce a very complex 'I', torn between desire and anger. Deianira despairs and envies, and her pain acquires suddenly aggressive – and, I add, grammatically spasmodic – tones of cynicism (536–8), while at the same time drives her to insanity (538, λωβητὸν ἐμπόλημα ἐμῆς φρενός: lit. 'merchandise that destroys my mind').[64] She longs to embrace a man who, however, infuriates her to the point of sarcasm ('my "brave" | and "faithful" Heracles', 540–2, a variation on the aristocratic formula καλὸς κἀγαθός). The next moment she tries to control this anger (543), only to give in once again to cynical bitterness (543–4) before arriving immediately at despair (545), and then on to the deceit. Her speech concludes impressively: careful to safeguard her female *prosōpon* (582–4), she gives in immediately afterwards to an antagonistic aggression ('But if [. . .] I can defeat [ὑπερβαλώμεθα] that girl [παῖδα]', 584–6),[65] before arriving finally at a carefully formulated restraint, where the gaze of the other is dominant ('unless I seem [εἰ μὴ δοκῶ] to you acting rashly. If so, I shall stop', 586–7). The tone, the mood, the style change almost at every line, creating an extremely eloquent relief of a self who strives in vain to secure her social role (*prosōpon*) but also her self-consciousness: Deianira is prey to her psychic complexes.[66] Suspended between conflicting feelings, between paranoia and deceit, she loses entirely her control over her actions and decisions. Her speech, her mood, her 'self' modulate between anger and despair, claim and resignation, embroiled in the violence of erotic frustration and the violence of erotic antagonism.

Not Giving an Account of One's Self: Deianira's Silence

> When the 'I' seeks to give an account of itself, it can start with itself, but it will find that this self is already implicated in a social temporality that exceeds its own capacities for narration; indeed, when the 'I' seeks to give an account of itself, an account that must include the conditions of its own emergence, it must, as a matter of necessity, become a social theorist.
>
> The reason for this is that the 'I' has no story of its own that is not also the story of a relation – or set of relations – to a set of norms.[67]

One of the trademarks of tragic characters – especially those of Euripides – is their gnomic rhetoric: careful to articulate their experience, their point of view and their choice of action alongside gender, social and cultural principles, such characters become, indeed, 'social theorists'. In my terms, they meticulously appear as *prosōpa*. They are 'I's with a story' – *hypokritai* rather than *prattontes*. This remains true until they enter the stage building in order to act, becoming invisible and silent to the audience.[68] Sophoclean heroes are more economical in their use of *gnōmai* – Deianira being markedly laconic, and most spectacularly so in her final scene: having realized that she 'alone' is killing Heracles (μόνη γὰρ αὐτόν [. . .] ἐγὼ δύστηνος ἐξαποφθερῶ, 712–3), it takes a couple of two-line *gnōmai* (on female reputation: 721–2; on the futility of hope for the guilty: 725–6) and no less than eighty-one lines of silence for her to display onstage her decision to kill herself.

The moment that Deianira recognizes herself as the crucial 'I' behind the events, she also recognizes that she has been a mere instrument of Nessos. She embodies her name (*dēi* from *dēioō* or *dēoō* [= kill] and *aneira* from *anēr* [= man]) and becomes a 'manslayer'. This is a very thin 'I': against Hyllos, who confirms her loss of the *prosōpon* of a wife and, furthermore, deprives her of that of a mother,[69] Deianira does not defend her 'self', because she cannot define her 'self'. Deianira therefore becomes the mirror image of the 'silent' (ἄναυδος, 860) Kypris: part of a world which has an undecipherable interior. A blind world, which forbids vision, and forbids *prosōpa*.[70]

It is precisely this loss that her final gestures, as narrated by the Nurse, reveal: when Deianira enters the house to kill herself, she is bereft of all identities that her family, her household, her gods could allow her to assume and sustain: she hides to avoid other people's eyes (903). She is no longer a mother: denied by Hyllos, she now sees him preparing his father's stretcher, cut off from her, negligent of her (903), and she laments her 'childlessness' (911).[71] She is no longer a *despoina* (mistress) in her household: seeing her servants she breaks into tears (908–9). She kneels at the altars not as a supplicant but in order to lament their becoming deserted (905):[72] this is the gesture of someone who has lost all contact with the gods.

Deianira has lost all *prosōpa* with which to see and to be seen, all identities that could allow her to relate to others. The only thing that she is left with is her body: the body that at the beginning of the play 'nurtured fear' (28) and, subsequently, erotic desire; the body that was inscribed by Nessos. This is why, in her final moment, she focuses on her identity as a sexual partner: 'O my bed, O my bridal chamber farewell | now forever, for never again will you take me | to lie as a wife [or better: 'as a lover', εὐνάτριαν]' (919–22). In her final words, Deianira is reduced to the identity that her body gives her. She can only kill herself.

Against Conclusion(s): Between Text and Performance

The principles and methodologies of anthropology and psychology need not be mutually exclusive when examining the tragic subject. The two intersect, as crisis in the former leads to fruition in the latter, shaping what I suggested as a 'dramaturgy of the self'. In Deianira's case, ritual perversion leads to a world in which the distinction between the symbolic and the real (the distinction upon which ritual relies) collapses, producing a world and a subject which remain vulnerable to destructive forces from without as well as from within. Unable to adopt a safe and stable *prosōpon*, bereft of the safety net that this could provide to her motives and actions, trapped in a reality where beasts and humans, male and female, are confused, Deianira reveals a striking psychological complexity: traumatized, impulsive, ambivalent until she becomes an 'I' bereft of a story.

A storytelling puzzle of sorts seems to mark the experience of Deianira's readers, too, while, possibly, not the experience of her spectactors. The psychological appraisal of

Deianira's character is not unanimous in contemporary scholarship: despite the fact that no one now endorses Errandonea's famous conviction about her Klytaemnestrian *ēthos*,[73] the exact proportions of her despair and anger are debated.[74] Some see a gentle heart-broken (and somewhat naive) woman in despair, while others (including myself) argue for a more complicated psychological profile, torn between opposing and frustrating sentiments and deliberations.

For example, at lines 539–40, Deianira imagines her position with and alongside Iole: 'So now the two of us lie under the one sheet waiting for his embrace.' According to Fraenkel, the line recalls the indignant words of Klytaemnestra in *Agamemnon* 1446–7 ('to me he has given | a delicate excitement to my bed's delight', trans. R. Lattimore); according to Easterling, it reveals 'pathos'; according to Kamerbeek, 'a graphic and rather cynical bitterness'.[75] These are significantly different readings, which lead to crucially different assessments of Deianira's character and her subsequent action: is she aggressive, incensed and cynical, or resigned and pathetic? Is her mood melancholic or erotic? Or, perhaps, is she incapable of controlling herself and her feelings, being beyond herself? The answer is not obvious, and it is not so because the text could support diverse performances.

Bernd Seidensticker has argued that tragic characters often display their individuality through grammar and intonation.[76] Tragic language can have a psychological perspective, revealing often personal idiosyncrasies, with regard to both text and performance. Deianira's language can be seen to support Seidensticker's view. The diversity of tone and emotion that different scholars read in her lines shows that the determining factor behind meaning is *performative*: it relies on the particular quality of the actor's voice, allowing it to be extremely crucial to character portrayal. Yet, no matter how revealing of intention the words can be, their exact delivery is totally lost to us, forbidding watertight assessments of 'character'.

Despite the fact that the objections to the psychological nature of the dramatic personage are based on refined arguments, it is equally important to keep in our minds something simple, yet fundamental: that theatre is not text, it is above all performance, and this is a parameter that language-centred and text-centred approaches struggle to take into account.[77] And the performance, as Easterling once suggested with an argument which failed to get the attention it deserved, always comes to enrich the two-dimensional subject of the text with the real body of the actor.[78] The process 'from page to stage', leading to the 'embodiment' of the role, displays an 'intelligible' human being:[79] a 'self' which may be illusory, but which, like the self of real life, is rooted on 'the existential ground' of a body.[80] This is a being which is not and cannot be registered in the script alone. And this is an idea that scholars must always bear in mind, despite the hermeneutic frustration it might entail.

Notes

1. I am deeply grateful to Pat Easterling, Bernd Seidensticker and Kostas Valakas for giving me the opportunity to discuss earlier drafts of this paper and avoid various misjudgements. I also

thank Hallie and Toph Marshall for their editing, which improved considerably my arguments' phrasings and flow. Responsibility for any erroneous claims remains obviously my own.

2. The polarity 'humanized'/'dehumanized' is in Culpeper 2014 [2001], who, combining linguistics with cognitive psychology, social psychology and stylistics, argues for the humanizing potential of literary and dramatic language (see also Culpeper 2002 and Culpeper and McIntyre 2010). For a more detailed overview of the character debate within classical studies, see Thumiger 2007, who discusses the portrayal of the self not only in tragedy, but also in epic and lyric poetry.

3. Jones 1980; Gould 1978; Wiles 2000.

4. Thumiger 2007: 6.

5. Chatman 2009.

6. Gill 1996: 11–12.

7. Gould 1978; Goldhill 1990.

8. See Jones 1980 and Thumiger 2007.

9. Even John Gould, an emblematic anti-psychologist, admits that the language of Sophocles' heroes, relieved from the gnomic (hence impersonal) rhetoric and the formal rigidity of Euripides' heroes, allows for the development of some sort of character continuity and coherence (Gould 1978: 51–4).

10. Easterling 1977, 1978, 1990; Seidensticker 2008.

11. Seidensticker 2008: 341.

12. van Emde Boas, 2017; De Temmerman and van Emde Boas 2017.

13. Segal 1978: 129–30.

14. My use of the word *prosōpon* avoids its technical meaning (mask) and is, to an extent, more akin to Goffman's concept of 'face' as 'an image of self, delineated in terms of approved social attributes' (Goffman 1959: 213). This is not so far from Thumiger 2007, who defines the subjectivity of the tragic personages in terms of 'a continuum of man and world' (Thumiger 2007: 10) shaped by the characters' response to divine power and their integration into the community and its values (Thumiger 2007: 10). 'Self', on the other hand, is a term loaded with many and diverse definitions and it often stands for 'I'/'Ego'/'Person'/'Personality' (cf. Carrithers, Collins and Lukes (eds) 1985; Arweiler and Möller (eds) 2008; Gallagher 2011; Mansfield 2000; Seigel 2005). Here, I employ the word 'self' in order to juxtapose to *prosōpon* an interiority (a psychological 'depth') which corresponds to '[t]he ensemble of psychological practices and attitudes that give an interior dimension and a sense of wholeness to the subject' (Vernant 1991: 321 on the meaning of *Moi*). Seigel's definition of Self emphasizes individuality and coherence: 'the particular being any person is, whatever it is about each of us that distinguishes you and me from others, draws the parts of our existence together, persists through changes, or opens the way to becoming who we might or should be' (Seigel 2005: 3).

15. Seidensticker 2008.

16. See, for example, Seaford 1995 and Henrichs 2004.

17. Easterling 1988: 101.

18. I have explored elsewhere this perspective with regard to Sophocles' Neoptolemos and Electra (Papazoglou 2014: 378–90 and 391–9 respectively) and Aeschylus' Danaids (Papazoglou 2019). But it is in Deianira's case that the 'dramaturgy of the self' proposed here achieves its most comprehensive application.

19. Passages from the play are taken from M. Jameson's translation, in Grene and Lattimore 1957: 63–120.

20. Gnomic wisdom is usually employed by tragic characters in order to depersonalize their point of view and choice of action, and avoid personal commitment (van Emde Boas 2017: 44). Deianira's rejection of the Solonian *gnōmē* appears strikingly personalized.

21. According to Wohl 1998: 50, Deianira, here, 'declares her subjectivity: she knows herself'. Wohl argues that Deianira, finding herself in a 'homosocial' world dominated by males, where she is merely a (passive) 'object' of 'exchange', will claim for herself the role of the (active) 'subject'. Wohl also finds psychoanalytical perspectives in Deianira's subjectivity, yet in totally different terms than mine.

22. Segal 1999: 62.

23. See Knox 1983: 7.

24. Cf. 'to keep (σῴζειν) this drug [. . .] always deep in the house (ἐν μυχοῖς)' (685–6): *muchos* 'suggests the dark and destructive power of female sexuality' (Easterling 1987: 19); *sōzein* (cf. *esōzomēn*, 682) means 'keep/safeguard' but also 'save/keep alive'.

25. Conacher 1997: 22.

26. Segal 1999: 75.

27. See Beer 2004: 83.

28. Seaford 1987: 119.

29. Beer 2004: 85.

30. According to Segal 1998: 83, Deianira 'veers towards the negative model of female sexuality in marriage, the Aeschylean Clytaemnestra'. Cf. Foley 2001: 95: 'The self-control of the proper Greek wife depends on the moderation of erotic feeling for her spouse.' Valtadorou, in this volume, argues that amorous reciprocity appears in tragic weddings; however, her examples focus on the feelings of men, not those of women or virgins (the latter, as she admits, not being clearly detected in our texts). Yossi 1996: 116 attributes Deianira's erotic boldness to the Amazonian nature of her mythical identity.

31. Winkler 1991: 227–8; Dickie 2000.

32. Oakley and Sinos 2002: 15; Currie 2002.

33. Van Gennep 2004 [1906]: 186; Foley 1982a with ref. to Rose 1927; Rehm 1994.

34. Sourvinou-Inwood 1973, Jenkins 1983.

35. Toutain 1940.

36. See Oakley and Sinos 2002: 30.

37. νυμφείων ὄκνον | ἄλγιστον ἔσχον (7–8): *oknos*, combined with *algistos*, signifies a fear which is so strong as to resemble a physical pain; *numpheia* signifies wedding rituals, but also the bridal chamber, i.e. the sexual aspect of marriage as such. According to Yossi 1996: 92–3, 'fear for wedding [refers to] the Amazonian nature of the mythical Deianira.'

38. *Koitē* refers simultaneously to bed and river bed; *empelasthēnai*, here, has sexual connotations (Easterling 1982 on 15–17).

39. Wender 1974: 4–5.

40. Cf. Hamstead 2012: 208–9, Easterling 1982 on 517–22, Wohl 1998: 18–20.

41. An erotic variation on the epic expression ἱέμενοι νίκης ('desiring/striving for victory'). Cf. Wohl 1998: 20.

42. Seaford 1986: 58.

43. Seaford 1986: 58. Cf. also Ormand 1999: 42: 'For Deianira to be a bride is to experience separation and to resent it.'

44. Armstrong 1986.

45. *Eunis* signifies the wife, but also the orphan, the deserted, one who is bereft of relatives (cf. the scholiast on 562). The first time that the word acquires also the meaning of the 'bride' is here: this means that the ambiguity was active to the spectators of the play (Armstrong 1986: 101).

46. This adjective connects Nessos to darkness, but also to male sexuality (cf. also Acheloos' 'thick-shaded beard', 13).

47. Without acknowledging the motifs of ritual distortion, Armstrong 1986 sees Nessos as a *nymphostolos*.

48. Faraone 1994.

49. See Carawan 2000: 207–8.

50. Segal 1999: 63.

51. Segal 1995: 83.

52. See Loraux 1995: 39–40; Seaford 1986: 57.

53. Cf. Loraux 1995: 41: 'Deianira dies like an hoplite.' Wohl 1998: 49 sees Deianira's manly death 'as an example of the impossibility of an uncompromised female subject'.

54. Wender 1974: 5.

55. According to Wohl 1998: 51, Deianira's Sapphic description of girlhood 'seems to offer [her] a female community and a potential locus for a female subjectivity' (in my terms: it offers her a *prosōpon*). For a Freudian – yet, perhaps, rather crude – psychoanalytic reading of Deianira's cathexis, see Scott 1995: 20.

56. Dubois 1988: 151–6.

57. Choosing to discuss traits and scenes different from mine (and especially the Deianira–Iole scene), Wohl 1998 psychoanalyzes Deianira's search for a subjectivity, focusing on the fragile alterity of the female and her effort (and failure) to establish a secure relation between 'self' and 'other'.

58. Carawan 2000.

59. On the idea that ambiguity based on *aposiōpēsis* becomes a dramaturgical tool for the construction of a psychologically deep and interesting interiority, see Easterling 1977.

60. *Chlaina* denotes a piece of cloth which covers two lovers (Scheid and Svenbro 1996: 53–82).

61. The use of a substantiated infinitive carries 'a note of indignation' (Easterling 1982 on 545–6).

62. Both foot and eye have phallic connotations (Henderson 1991: 129–30).

63. Long 1968: 118.

64. '[A] metaphor which is passionate and derogatory, as well as highly coloured' (Long 1968: 120). The idea of madness has already been introduced with οὐ καλῶς φρονεῖ (442) and μαίνομαι (446); cf. Easterling 1982 on 536–8.

65. *huperbalōmetha* belongs to the male vocabulary of the battle (note also the somewhat self-aggrandizing use of the plural). This makes Deianira's reference to Iole as *paida* (while, a moment earlier, she was referred to as 'married' and not 'virgin') sound insulting and antagonistic.

66. Scott 1995 and 1997 picks up the dynamic between sorrow and anger in this passage, but does not discuss the other emotional layers of the text, claiming that Deianira 'unconsciously' intends indeed Heracles' destruction but 'turns a blind eye' to her real desire. Dubois 1991: 100

argues that Deianira's sexual ambivalence reflects the ambivalence of Greek women towards their husbands, and that '[l]ike Clytemnestra and Medea, she is a murderess, albeit against her conscious desires'. In my opinion, such narratives throw light where Sophocles opts for silence and darkness – not because he avoids psychic 'depth', but precisely because he wants it to be abysmal.

67. Butler 2005: 7–8.

68. On the idea that the (undecipherable) spatial interior of the stage building corresponds to the (undecipherable) psychic interior of the tragic character, see Segal 1984 and Padel 1990.

69. 'Mother! I wish I could have found you not as you are | but no longer alive, or safe but someone else's | mother, or somehow changed and with a better heart than now' (734–6); 'For why should she | maintain the pointless dignity of the name | of mother when she acts in no way like a mother?' (817–8).

70. It is possible (although, of course, impossible to prove) that, during Hyllos' rhesis, Deianira is covering her face/mask with her veil (compare the woman in the Sicilian calyx krater by the Capordaso Painter, Museo Archeologico Regionale 'P. Orsi', Syracuse, 66557; for which, see also Taplin 2017). If this were the case in the play's performance, then the loss discussed here would have been embodied in a most theatrical language. My analysis here is exactly the opposite to Wohl 1998: 55, who argues that Deianira's refusal to speak in front of Hyllos is her 'futile attempt to preserve any space for her subjectivity'.

71. The text is disputed here (see Easterling 1984 on 910–11), but it appears to refer to Deianira lamenting some sort of *apaidia*.

72. The manuscripts read (quite plausibly in my view) γένητ' ἐρήμη (cf. ἐρήμα, 530).

73. Errandonea 1927.

74. Bibliography and discussion in Carawan 2000.

75. Fraenkel 1962 on 1446f.; Easterling 1968: 63; Kamerbeek 1959 on 539–40.

76. Seidensticker 2008: 341.

77. Cf. Gould (1978: 44): 'For dramatic persons, to be is to "say a few words"' (citing Austin 1975: 7).

78. Easterling 1973: 6–7.

79. Cf. Easterling's idea of 'human intelligibility' (Easterling 1973).

80. The idea belongs to Csordas 1994 ('the body is the existential ground of the self') and is employed by Fischer-Lichte 2005 in her analysis of the 'Page to Stage' process.

CHAPTER 5
TRAGIC OVERLIVING AND DEFERRED FUNERARY RITUAL IN EURIPIDES' *HECUBA*
John Gibert

In tragedy, characters often live through experiences worse than death, things that happen after they 'should' have died. Emily Wilson calls this 'overliving', a word she borrows from Milton's *Paradise Lost*.[1] The term is etymologically equivalent to 'survival', but it usefully captures a set of themes and plot motifs different from what we normally mean by survival. Wilson writes:

> Survival paints the concept of continued existence with positive connotations, 'overliving' with tragic ones. The object of the verb 'to survive' is usually some event that might have been expected to destroy the survivor. One survives earthquakes and shootings; one overlives oneself. 'Survival' implies that continued existence is an unexpected triumph; 'overliving' implies that it is a paradox.[2]

Tragedies that foreground overliving vary in countless ways, but they regularly feature paradoxes such as confusion of the boundary between life and death, a mixed-up sense of time, and unexpected inversion of the values and outcomes normally associated with dying and living, respectively. In her book, Wilson offers subtle and insightful readings of the paradoxes of overliving in Sophocles' two *Oedipus* plays, Euripides' *Heracles* and Seneca's *Moral Epistles* and *Hercules*, Shakespeare's *King Lear* and *Macbeth*, and Milton's *Samson Agonistes* and *Paradise Lost*. Euripides' *Hecuba* is not one of her case studies, but, as I will show, it could well have been. Moreover, tragic overliving in *Hecuba* goes hand in hand with an aspect of theatrical production not high on Wilson's agenda, but very much at the heart of *Greek Drama V*: staging. Specifically, the treatment of dead bodies – or rather, neglect of them, especially through deferral of funerary ritual until after the end of the play – reinforces the sense that Hecuba not only lives to experience horrors she would have been better off never experiencing, but also attains an end state that is neither (ordinary) death nor life. The (mis)treatment of bodies visually reinforces the tragedy's manipulation of the tropes of revenge, including its many denials of a sense of closure.

I begin by illustrating Wilson's notion of overliving further with the example of Euripides' *Heracles*.[3] The title figure of this play returns from the underworld, kills his wife and children in a fit of madness, and faces the choice whether to live on or commit suicide. The words in which he chooses life over suicide are transmitted as ἐγκαρτερήσω θάνατον (1351), often translated 'I will endure death.' This does not sound like a good way to say, 'I choose life,' and almost all recent editors adopt a simple solution: they change 'death' to 'life'.[4] But the Greek verb does not mean 'I will endure,' but something like 'I will brave,' 'I will stand up to,' or 'I will defy.' As an exquisite paradox entirely characteristic of tragic overliving, it should be left in the text.[5] Paradox and other symptoms of overliving show up elsewhere in the play as well. For example, Euripides makes Heracles' twelve labours precede the killing of his family. This is a departure from the most familiar (later) versions of the myth; its effect is that killing his loved ones and refusing suicide become Heracles' thirteenth labour, and a new kind of labour. At the same time, these actions double the twelfth labour, retrieving Cerberus, which is pointedly only half finished when the events of the play occur (Eur. *Her.* 614–17, 1386–8). On first waking up, Heracles thinks he may be in the underworld again (1101–4). Just as fetching Cerberus is an unfinished encounter with death, Heracles' madness, murder of his family and overliving are another. He accepts a new home in Athens, where he will eventually be worshipped as a god or hero (1324–33). This can be seen as the second youth the chorus earlier wished were attainable for men like Heracles (655–72), and it fits his mythical marriage to Hebe, Youth. But, in another paradox, Heracles leaves the stage looking like one of the broken old men of the chorus (1394–1404). All this and more is tragic overliving.

It is easy to show that Hecuba, too, overlives. Early in the play, she says she ought to have died (Eur. *Hec.* 231–3):

κἄγωγ' ἄρ' οὐκ ἔθνηισκον οὗ μ' ἐχρῆν θανεῖν,
οὐδ' ὤλεσέν με Ζεύς, τρέφει δ' ὅπως ὁρῶ
κακῶν κάκ' ἄλλα μείζον' ἡ τάλαιν' ἐγώ.

I did not die, it now appears, when I ought to have died, and Zeus did not kill me but keeps me alive, poor wretch, only to see new misfortunes still greater than the old![6]

Then, in a series of passages, she expresses the wish to die instead of or along with Polyxena (383–8, 391, 396, 505–6). Such a wish is a common response to a situation like hers; likewise, there is nothing unusual in some of her formulations of the idea that she is already dead (e.g. 683 ἀπωλόμην δύστηνος, οὐκέτ' εἰμὶ δή 'I am utterly destroyed, my life is gone!'). Other passages, however, insist on the paradox of being 'dead' while still alive. Thus Hecuba says to Polyxena (431), τέθνηκ' ἔγωγε πρὶν θανεῖν κακῶν ὕπο ('I am already dead before my death, killed by my misfortunes'). Similarly, Hecuba's Slave says to her (668–9),

δέσποιν', ὄλωλας κοὐκέτ' εἶ, βλέπουσα φῶς,
ἄπαις ἄνανδρος ἄπολις ἐξεφθαρμένη.

You are lost, mistress; though you see the light of day you are dead, without child, without husband, without city, utterly destroyed!

At 882, Hecuba tells Agamemnon that she will avenge herself on Polymestor with the help of fellow captive Trojan women. But, instead of naming Polymestor, she calls him, according to the unanimous manuscript reading, τὸν ἐμὸν φονέα 'my murderer'. If kept in the text, this is the most vivid of all the expressions that rank Hecuba among the 'living dead'.[7]

Foils for Hecuba highlight the theme. Thus at 357–8, Polyxena says that she would rather die than live as a slave and, at 375–8, that the once-fortunate man who has become a slave θανὼν δ' ἂν εἴη μᾶλλον εὐτυχέστερος | ἢ ζῶν 'would be luckier dead than alive'. In the same speech, Polyxena pleads with Hecuba (372–4),

μῆτερ, σὺ δ' ἡμῖν μηδὲν ἐμποδὼν γένηι
λέγουσα μηδὲ δρῶσα, συμβούλου δέ μοι
θανεῖν πρὶν αἰσχρῶν μὴ κατ' ἀξίαν τυχεῖν.

Mother, do not oppose me by word or deed, but rather share my wish that I should die before I meet with a disgrace my rank does not deserve.

The words συμβούλου δέ μοι | θανεῖν πρὶν ... τυχεῖν are correctly translated 'share my wish that I should die before I meet with . . .', but an equally valid translation, anticipating Hecuba's explicit wish to die, is 'share my wish to die before meeting with . . .'.[8] Later, the Greek herald Talthybius, another foil, likewise wishes to die before disgrace (497–8). Polyxena, of course, does have to die – or rather, does get to die. In a series of passages, she imagines herself in Hades (418, 422, cf. 551–2). This afterlife, however, is neither overliving nor survival but (ordinary) death.[9]

We can also see Polyxena as a foil for Hecuba in another way. At 550–2, Talthybius reports that Polyxena demanded to be set free before she was killed. She thus achieved qualified freedom in a death she chose over life as a slave. The recollection of this exchange is fresh when Agamemnon asks Hecuba what she wants and says he can easily set her free (754–5).[10] In reply, Hecuba says that she would rather live as a slave, as long as she gets revenge on Polymestor, who killed her son Polydorus and threw his dead body into the sea.[11] Revenge plots and tragic overliving are often connected. As Wilson puts it, 'Revenge is often presented as a possible solution to overliving. One tragic subgenre can begin to mutate into another.'[12] But she adds that revenge rarely is the solution it appears to be; instead, it can 'increase the feeling that all action is only repetition',[13] a feeling typical of tragedies of overliving. Several controversies swirl around Hecuba's revenge, but I do not intend to reopen the questions of whether revenge degrades and dehumanizes her, whether her predicted transformation into a dog is an emblem of degradation, or whether it is degrading for her to use the fact that Agamemnon has sex with Cassandra to persuade him that he owes her a favour.[14] Instead, I turn now to dead bodies to show that their treatment, both as themes and as stage properties, adds an important dimension to Hecuba's overliving.[15]

In the Prologue, the ghost of Polydorus says that Hecuba will look upon 'two corpses of two children' (45), a prediction not fulfilled within the play.[16] Hecuba only hears Talthybius' account of Polyxena's death, and her daughter's body is never brought onstage. She does look upon the corpse of Polydorus, however, when her Slave discovers it and brings it onstage. Hecuba seeks, and Agamemnon grants, permission to bury it. One might expect, then, that at some point the body will be carried off in a stage version of a funeral procession.

Greek tragedy offers many variations on death ritual performed, denied, curtailed, compromised, perverted or displaced. These often occur at the ends of plays, where they can gesture strongly towards closure. At the same time, the variations can undermine the sense of closure by suggesting that something is amiss. For example, at the end of Aeschylus' *Agamemnon*, Clytemnestra says that she and Aegisthus will bury Agamemnon and exclude other family members from the rites; the exclusion becomes a recurrent theme in *Libation Bearers* (*Agam.* 1551–9; *Cho.* 8–9, 429–33). At the end of Euripides' *Medea*, Medea takes charge of her children's bodies and refuses to let Jason touch, mourn or bury them (*Med.* 1377–81, 1399–404, 1410–12). At the end of Sophocles' *Ajax*, the hero's body is carried offstage ceremoniously, but the exclusion of Odysseus works against closure by perpetuating the theme of Ajax' undying enmity (*Aj.* 1394–401). At the end of Euripides' *Heracles*, Heracles excludes himself from participating in the burial of his family (*Her.* 1361–5, 1389–93). After studying these and other examples, Deborah Roberts concludes that in all of them 'exclusion from burial thwarts or complicates the closural effect of burial and lamentation – but in different ways'.[17]

In *Heracles*, as Francis Dunn has shown, a further complication is that Theseus promises Heracles sacrifices and monuments, but fulfilment of this promise is deferred until after the hero's death, that is, 'as an audience raised on stories of Heracles' apotheosis will realize, [until] a time that does not really exist' (*Her.* 1326–33).[18] Helene Foley, in an influential article on Euripides' *Suppliant Women*, in which there is a great deal of more or less proper death ritual, argues that exclusion of the Argive mothers from a part of it in which Athenian women would have expected to participate carries great political significance.[19] Euripides' *Trojan Women*, a play largely built around ritual lamentation, ends in a stage-proper and only somewhat reduced lament for Astyanax, followed by a fuller lament not for a corpse but for the city of Troy itself (*Tro.* 1216–37, 1287–352). Here a twist on ritual lamentation partly makes up for the absence of other typical gestures of closure.[20]

It would be easy to add to these examples. But here it must be acknowledged that at the ends of several plays the text gives no indication whether dead bodies visible to the spectators are left onstage or removed as surviving characters make their final exits. In some cases, the difference for modern spectators, used to a final curtain or blackout, is far from trivial. Until near the end of Sophocles' *Antigone*, for example, Creon holds and laments the bodies of Haemon and Eurydice. It is possible that he makes his final exit down an *eisodos*, and that attendants remove the bodies along with him. This would approximate a funeral procession and be unmistakably closural.[21] Most scholars, however, prefer to have Creon exit into the palace. In this case, the closing of the stage building's doors behind him makes a satisfying ending, as his self-imposed confinement to a domestic interior mirrors the condition he would have imposed on Antigone and the play's other female characters.[22] If the bodies of Creon's dead son and wife are brought inside with him, we see an apt summation of his tragedy as the family closes in on itself.

Could the bodies instead be left onstage? We do not know for certain what Athenian spectators took as definitively signalling 'The End'. In a modern context, a stage on which the last thing seen is two corpses and a stage left empty by closing doors create quite different effects, and a director must choose. In a play like *Antigone*, where the treatment of dead bodies is an inescapable theme, the difference matters, and that was probably true in the ancient context as well, even if it is hard for us to say exactly how.

Similarly, the text of Sophocles' *Electra* does not indicate what becomes of the body of Clytemnestra, visible to spectators near the end of the play in the highly theatrical moment when Aegisthus, believing it to be the body of Orestes, unveils it and realizes that he is face to face with his wife's – and his own – killers (1474–5). The abrupt exit of the principals into the palace soon afterwards raises issues of interpretation that have been much discussed.[23] It is possible to use the *ekkyklēma* to wheel Clytemnestra's body into the palace behind the departing actors, but, if it was possible instead for the play to end with the body on view and neglected by avengers still busy with the murder of Aegisthus about to take place offstage, this would be a powerful (visual) statement in a play that notoriously has so little to say (verbally) about matricide. In this respect, Euripides' *Electra* ends rather differently, although here, too, it is possible either to leave the dead, in this case both Clytemnestra and Aegisthus, on view or to wheel them inside on the *ekkyklēma*.[24] The text seems to indicate that Electra and Pylades exit by one of the *eisodoi*, enacting Castor's instructions to go to Pylades' home in Achaea and be married there (1284–7), while Orestes exits by the other, to go first to Athens, where he will be tried and acquitted, and then as an exile to Arcadia, where a city will eventually be named after him (1250–75). The killers, then, will not tend to the bodies of their victims, but Castor gestures adequately towards closure by announcing that the Argives will bury Aegisthus, and Menelaus and Helen will bury Clytemnestra (1276–80). None of these characters are present, but, in the face of such dispensations, it may matter less whether the bodies remain visible or are removed.[25]

With all this in mind, I now ask: where are the bodies in *Hecuba*? So far I have only mentioned the bodies of Polyxena and Polydorus, but Hecuba's revenge takes the lives of Polymestor's two young sons, who are briefly seen onstage alive, before they enter the fatal tent with their father, and then again later as corpses.[26] Here are the facts and problems concerning these bodies. First, Polyxena. Talthybius winds up playing the role of messenger in *Hecuba* because the Greeks send him to Hecuba to tell her to bury her daughter (503–10). After he describes Polyxena's death, Hecuba tells him to tell the Greeks not to touch the body, and she tells her Slave to fetch seawater so she can wash the body and lay it out for burial (604–13), adding that she will collect jewellery from her fellow captives to adorn it (614–18). But the body of Polyxena never comes onstage.

Next, Polydorus. The Slave discovers the body at the shore. She brings a veiled dummy onstage, and Hecuba initially mistakes it for Polyxena (658–75). Like the unveiling of Clytemnestra's body near the end of Sophocles' *Electra*, the unveiling of this corpse is a big theatrical moment, played for maximum shock. Hecuba's reaction, to which I return below, lasts until Agamemnon arrives at 726. The body is covered again and remains onstage at least until Agamemnon leaves, as deictic pronouns and rhetorical gestures show.[27] But scholars are divided as to whether it is removed by the king's attendants when he exits. If it is removed, this will seem to fulfil Hecuba's request that Agamemnon put off the burial of Polyxena so that she can bury both children together (894–7). If the body is not removed, it must remain onstage until the end of the play, and only one passage gives a clue as to what happens to it. At 1287–8, Agamemnon tells Hecuba to 'go and bury' the corpses of her two children (στείχουσα θάπτε). She cannot leave behind a body she has just been told to 'go and bury', so those who keep the corpse onstage until this point have the chorus or extras carry it off with her, a proper stage version of a funeral procession and a strong gesture towards closure.[28] But the other possibility, that the body of Polydorus was carried off by Agamemnon's men after line 904, is preferable. The arguments in favour of this choice are all essentially from silence, and there are three of them. First, Polymestor's opening words as he arrives onstage are (953–5)

ὦ φίλτατ' ἀνδρῶν Πρίαμε, φιλτάτη δὲ σύ,[29]
Ἑκάβη, δακρύω σ' εἰσορῶν πόλιν τε σὴν
τήν τ' ἀρτίως θανοῦσαν ἔκγονον σέθεν.

Priam, dearest of men, and you, dearest of women, Hecuba, I weep as I see you and your city and also your daughter lately slain.

Again we have two valid translations. 'I see ... your daughter lately slain' could mean that Polymestor misidentifies the veiled body of Polydorus as Polyxena, but 'I see ... that your daughter has been slain' (indirect discourse) is a mental insight and does not require a body onstage. The latter is preferable because there is no deictic pronoun and, for good theatrical reasons, no example in Greek tragedy of a wrongly identified stage body that is not correctly identified later.[30] Second, Hecuba never refers to the body of Polydorus in the trial scene. If it is there, it silently undermines Polymestor's credibility, but it seems more likely that Hecuba would point to it and rhetorically rub Polymestor's nose in it if it were present.[31] The third argument again concerns lines 1287–8. 'Go and bury the two corpses' is a less than obvious way to say 'Take this child to where your other child is and bury them both.' If that is what Euripides meant, he could easily have been clearer. It is probably better, then, not to have the body of Polydorus still onstage to be removed in a funeral procession at the end of the play. In this case, the visual closure provided by a stage version of a funeral procession is withheld. In any case, both burials are undeniably deferred until after the end of the play, and Agamemnon earlier drew a great deal of attention to Hecuba's delay in burying Polyxena (726–32).

That leaves the bodies of Polymestor's murdered children. It would be possible never to bring them onstage, but there is not much in favour of this option. Hecuba says we will see them (1051), they are referred to twice by deictics (1118, 1255) and they give a visual focus to the horror stirred by Hecuba's revenge. Battezzato argues that they are only visible through the *skēnē* doors when the blinded Polymestor comes out on all fours for his frenzied solo (1056–1106), but the arguments against requiring spectators to see anything important, or really anything at all, through the central doors are well known.[32] There is a good parallel in Euripides' *Electra* for characters who enter on foot, with dead bodies rolled out behind them on the *ekkyklēma*, and that is the best choice here, too.[33] Near the end, then, we have corpses onstage, and they must be either wheeled silently back into the *skēnē* or left on view. I suggest that the latter is preferable, as a bleak testament to Hecuba's revenge and another example of death ritual deferred.[34] The two bodies onstage balance the two offstage, which Hecuba neglects while pursuing the revenge that gives her so much new life and energy.[35]

Observation of a few further denials of closure will bring my two themes together and lead to a conclusion. I maintain that all the instances of closure denied, including the neglect of dead bodies, can be taken as symptoms of Hecuba's overliving. First, the way in which Polymestor lives on is not mere survival but overliving. As a somewhat two-dimensional foreign villain, he is not, like Hecuba, a focus of tragic sympathy, but neither is he a mere foil. After all, he sings (1056–106), delivers a lengthy *rhēsis* (1132–82) and reveals unpleasant prophetic truths (1259–84). We might think of him as a 'foil plus', used to suggest the unsettling resemblance between victim and perpetrator (a regular trope in revenge tragedy). In support of the suggestion that he overlives, note that at the end of his song, he wishes he were dead (1105–6), and the chorus leader responds that, when someone suffers calamity too great to bear, suicide is pardonable (1107–8) – a thought they could just as well have expressed to Hecuba. At 1120–1, Polymestor says Ἑκάβη με ... | ἀπώλεσ' – οὐκ ἀπώλεσ' ἀλλὰ μειζόνως ('Hecuba ... destroyed me – not destroyed me but more than that'). Here we recognize the familiar struggle to find language adequate to tragic overliving. The jewellery Hecuba said she would gather for Polyxena's funeral has been used to blind Polymestor instead (614–18 ~ 1169–71), as revenge has caused mourning to be deferred and one tragic subgenre has replaced another. Through his predictions, Polymestor approximates a *deus ex machina*, something this play lacks. The events he prophesies, Clytemnestra's revenge murder of Agamemnon (1279–81) and Hecuba's future transformations (1259–65, 1270–3), are all anti-closural. Finally, Polymestor is not killed but relegated to an island, a living death and a perfect figure for overliving (1284–6).[36]

The point that Hecuba's revenge displaces expected mourning merits brief elaboration. Hecuba's initial reaction to the unveiling of her son's body (684–720) bears the formal markers of lament. She sings dochmiacs while the Slave and chorus leader speak, and she uses poetic resources like anadiplosis, polyptoton, rhetorical question and references to her own singing. It is possible, as Mossman and Gregory suggest, to have her bend over the body and embrace it, although the text does not insist.[37] One might instead choose to keep her physically distant, to suggest that her lament is slightly off-key, or at any rate curtailed. At under forty lines, it is short for a formal lament, and it belongs to a category Elinor Wright calls 'included'.[38] What Wright means is that it is incorporated in a different Euripidean type-scene, the 'reaction to bad news', which has its own conventions. The first words Hecuba sings ('Alas, my child, my child: the melody of frenzy (νόμον βακχεῖον), now I begin it', 684–7) signal that she is singing a new, Dionysiac tune, which marks the start of her transformation into a revenge heroine. After the short lament, she ignores the body of Polydorus except when using it to score rhetorical points with Agamemnon.

Some scholars interpret Hecuba's single-minded pursuit of fierce revenge as evidence of moral degradation, while others see this is a misunderstanding of ancient Greek moral attitudes towards revenge, a misguided or oversimplified response to the revenge tragedy subgenre, or both.[39] While continuing to avoid taking a stand on this issue, I would like to make one last point, motivated by Wilson's demonstration that tragedies of overliving tend to express themselves in paradox. At 1270, Hecuba asks whether she will be alive or dead when her canine self, after falling from the mast of Agamemnon's ship, is swallowed by the sea. Polymestor replies that she will be dead, and her tomb will become known as 'Hound's Grave, a mark for sailors to steer by' (κυνὸς ταλαίνης σῆμα, ναυτίλοις τέκμαρ, 1273). There is textual trouble with line 1270, and again it is a matter of life and death. The manuscripts have Hecuba ask, 'Shall I complete my life (ἐκπλήσω βίον) by dying or living here?' Kovacs, Matthiessen and Battezzato adopt Weil's φάτιν for βίον, so that 'complete my life' becomes 'fulfil the prophecy'. Others conjecture words meaning 'fate', πότμον or μόρον.[40] In this case, we may be able to take the point that Hecuba 'fills out' a fate that lasts beyond the point when she should have died, that is, that she overlives. But if we translate transmitted ἐκπλήσω βίον as 'fill out my life', it is not so obvious that the text ('Shall I fill out my life alive or dead?') is flawed. It is just possible that Euripides is once again straining language to the breaking point to give paradoxical expression to the tragedy of overliving.

Notes

1. Wilson 2004. For helpful comments and suggestions, I would like to thank Lauri Reitzammer, the students in my Spring 2016 class on Euripides at the University of Colorado Boulder (especially Joseph Frankl), the organizers of the Vancouver conference, and the anonymous reader for the press. Before the conference, Luigi Battezzato kindly allowed me to see and cite his since-published commentary on *Hecuba*.

2. Wilson 2004: 2.

3. Some of the observations in this paragraph are found in Wilson 2004: 66–87; others were made independently by others, including me (Gibert 1995 and 1997).

4. βίοτον, conjectured by Wecklein. Heimsoeth conjectures πότμον, which Musgrave conjectures at Eur. *Hec.* 1270, discussed at the end of this paper.

5. Gibert 1997 studies the semantics of ἐγκαρτερεῖν and offers a full defence of the manuscript reading. The only other classical occurrence of the verb followed by accusative is at Eur. *Andr.* 262, where the translation 'defy' is appropriate.

6. Here and throughout, the Greek text is Diggle's; translations are from Kovacs 1995, occasionally modified.

7. Most editors, however, accept Scaliger's conjecture ἐμῶν and understand Hecuba to be calling Polymestor 'the murderer of my [family members]'. In support of this change, Diggle, Gregory and Battezzato all cite 750, where Gregory and Battezzato interpret τέκνοισι τοῖς ἐμοῖσι as a genuine plural in Hecuba's remark that she cannot accomplish her revenge for her 'children' without Agamemnon's help. Euripides may indeed want to make revenge on Polymestor, who killed only one of Hecuba's children, appear (to Hecuba, spectators or both) to compensate Hecuba for the loss of *both* Polydorus and Polyxena, but should we follow Scaliger in

introducing this conceit by conjecture, especially when τέκνοισι can be explained differently, as 'allusive' plural (that is, a plural form alluding to just one person, cf. Smyth §1007)? Of course, ἐμῶν at 882 can also be taken as 'allusive', as it is by Collard. Matthiessen, who ultimately prefers Scaliger's conjecture, seems right to concede at least the possibility of understanding τὸν ἐμὸν φονέα metaphorically (for which he compares Soph. *OT* 534).

8. Hecuba's wish comes just after this, at 383–8. Τὸ πρὶν αἰσχρῶν μὴ κατ' ἀξίαν τυχεῖν ('before meeting with a disgrace my rank does not deserve') compare Hecuba's claim at 231–3 that she ought to have died already (quoted above).

9. In her long speech explaining her wish to die, Polyxena contrasts her present misery with her former happiness, when Trojan women and girls looked on her with admiration, and she was ἴση θεοῖσιν πλὴν τὸ κατθανεῖν μόνον ('like the gods in all but my mortality') (356). Insofar as her mortality is itself a foil for Hecuba's overliving, the implication that she is even now 'like the gods' (that is, unusually fortunate) is another paradox. Battezzato compares Hecuba's lament for Hector at Hom. *Il.* 22.434–6. For more on Polyxena's death as a variation on the epic καλὸς θάνατος ('fine/noble/beautiful death'), see Papastamati 2017.

10. Actually, what Agamemnon says he can set free is Hecuba's αἰών, her lifetime (but the word can refer to any long period of time). The periphrasis is typically tragic, but here resonates with two of the tragic overliving theme's typical tendencies: to confuse the boundary between life and death and to mix up the sense of time.

11. Lines 756–7 are missing from some mss. and deleted by Diggle, who then transposes 758 and 759; Gregory, Kovacs and Matthiessen retain the lines, while Battezzato deletes all of 756–9.

12. Wilson 2004: 15.

13. Wilson 2004: 15.

14. In connection with another much-discussed topic not directly related to my argument, the play's uses and abuses of rhetoric, note that Odysseus serves as yet another kind of foil for Hecuba. Hecuba reminds him that she could have killed him when she caught him spying in Troy and, at 245–50, we learn that he supplicated her with such tenacity that his hand 'went numb' in the folds of her robe (250 ἐνθανεῖν, lit. 'died on'). Odysseus was willing to say and do anything to stay alive. The difference between him and Hecuba is that while he survives she overlives.

15. *Hecuba*'s 'somatics', that is, its discourse of living bodies, has been well studied by Segal 1990 (= 1993: 157–69), Zeitlin 1991 (= 1996: 172–216), and Rehm 2002: 175–87, among others. There are suggestive connections between this work and the play's discourse of dead bodies.

16. In addition to the ghost of Polydorus, who appears onstage, *Hecuba* features the ghost of Achilles, who does not. Ghosts are obviously well suited to complement the theme of overliving.

17. Roberts 1993: 585.

18. Dunn 1996: 118.

19. Foley 1993. For further reflections on this aspect of *Suppliant Women*, see Loraux 1986: 47–50 (cf. 107–9), Pelling 1997: 230–5, and Sourvinou-Inwood 2004: 184–6.

20. Wright 1986: 115–17, Suter 2003, Dunn 1996: 101–14.

21. Two other Sophoclean plays, *Ajax* and *Trachinian Women*, end with stage actions that approximate funeral processions. The same is probably true of Euripides' *Hippolytus*, *Andromache*, *Trojan Women*, and [*Rhesus*], as well as *Suppliant Women* and *Heracles* (with the complicating exclusion of the Argive mothers and Heracles, respectively, as noted above). The end of *Bacchae* is too mutilated for certainty regarding the reassembled corpse of Pentheus,

but the body may remain on view as Cadmus and Agave exit down the *eisodoi* to exile. On Aeschylus' *Oresteia* and Sophocles' and Euripides' *Electra* plays, see further below.

22. So Blundell 1998: 75 n. 2 (= Blondell 2002: 88 n. 216), 103; cf. Tyrrell and Bennett 1998: 152. Several commentators (e.g. Jebb, Kamerbeek, Brown) adopt this staging without argument.

23. References in Finglass 2007 on [1510].

24. For use of the *ekkyklēma* in this scene, see Hourmouziades 1965: 107, Cropp on 1172–232.

25. The case of Aeschylus' *Oresteia* seems even easier. Near the ends of both *Agamemnon* and *Choephori*, dead bodies are on view, probably on the *ekkyklēma*. If there was a means of indicating to spectators that they are 'still there' when the plays end, we will have no trouble interpreting this as an anti-closural gesture appropriate to the first two plays of a thematically connected trilogy – and then taking the processional ending of *Eumenides* as confirming our sense of how a cycle of dramatic events definitively ends.

26. Eur. *Hec.* 998–1007. The boys come onstage at 953 and exit into the tent at 1022, as 998–1007 demonstrate; cf. 891–4.

27. From its clothing/covering, Agamemnon judges that the veiled body is that of a Trojan man (733–5). The body is referred to at 760–3, 833–5, 871.

28. Those who keep Polydorus' body onstage until the end include Mossman 1995: 60, 64; Gregory 1999, on 903–4, 955; Synodinou 2005, on 953–5; Matthiessen 2010, on 904, 955, 993. Those who have it removed by Agamemnon's men after line 904 include Collard 1991: 105 and on 902–4; Kovacs 1995: 481; Battezzato 2018, on 904, 954–5.

29. Some follow Nauck in deleting 953. The case against imagining that the body of Polydorus is present (*ex hypothesi* misrecognized as that of Polyxena) may receive a slight boost if Polymestor's opening address is to the certainly absent Priam, but it does not depend on this support.

30. The only comparable case is in fact the unveiling of Clytemnestra's body already discussed (Soph. *El.* 1474–5). Battezzato 2018, on 954–5, documents the use of εἰσορᾶν (+ accusative + participle) for 'realizing' rather than literally 'seeing'. It may be relevant that Agamemnon correctly identified the veiled body as that of a man at 733–5 (above, n. 27).

31. So Battezzato 2018, on line 904.

32. Battezzato (2018, on 1051–3); see Garvie 1986: lii–liii, with references.

33. Above, n. 24.

34. As one of his reasons for not bringing the corpses of Polymestor's children onstage in the first place, Battezzato maintains that 'Forgetting the dead children in plain view at the end of the play ... would be very awkward' (2018, on 1051–3). It is exactly this awkwardness that the present interpretation seeks to exploit. Of course, Polymestor denied burial to Polydorus, and it fits his crime that nobody tends to the bodies of his sons. My contention is that we can take this point and at the same time see in the neglected bodies a more general denial of closure, applicable to Hecuba as well.

35. Scholars generally assume that when Hecuba makes her final exit, she is accompanied by the chorus, whether or not the body of Polydorus is present to be carried in procession; by use of a different *eisodos*, her exit can be made to contrast with Polymestor's forcible removal after Agamemnon's orders at 1284–6. Another staging is possible, however. Immediately after Polymestor's removal, Agamemnon instructs Hecuba to 'go and bury' her children; σὺ δ᾽ 'and you' (1287) contrasts with αὐτόν 'him' (1285). Agamemnon next instructs the women of the chorus to go to the tents of their masters; here δεσποτῶν δ᾽ ὑμᾶς χρεὼν | σκηναῖς πελάζειν (1288–9) indicates a destination that is not the same as the place where Hecuba will 'go and bury'. Hecuba, then, could leave the stage alone, by the *eisodos* not taken by the chorus, and, in this case, having

her use the same *eisodos* as Polymestor will express visually the resemblance of perpetrator and victim in the revenge plot, as well as Hecuba's tragic isolation as future dog and nautical landmark.

36. Wohl 2015 also emphasizes the play's denial of closure, which she sees as a refusal to end with justice and ethical balance. She writes, 'Our pleasure in the play's beautiful suffering becomes a sadistic investment in injustice; our pity for Polyxena's beautiful death makes us take satisfaction in the punishment of a man who bears no responsibility for it, even as our desire for the beautiful symmetry of *dikē* helps us to accept the corrupt verdict that judges this brutal vengeance just. . . . Beauty, then – the beauty of tragic suffering or of legal recompense – may make us long for justice, but it does not in itself make us just; and it is Euripides' pointed refusal of the particular beauty of formal unity that reminds us of the crucial difference between the two' (Wohl 2015: 61–2). Wohl's argument about beauty and justice is compatible with mine about overliving and deferred ritual.

37. Mossman 1995: 61 and Gregory 1999, on 716–20.

38. Wright 1986: 154–5.

39. Proponents of the first view include Reckford 1985, Nussbaum 2001: 397–421, Michelini 1989: 131–80, Segal 1993: 157–69. For the second view, see e.g. Kovacs 1987: 108–12, Burnett 1994 and 1998: 157–76, Gregory: xxxiii–xxxv, Matthiessen 2010: 27–34. The judicious discussions of Mossman 1995: 164–203 and Battezzato 2018: 14–18 aim to strike a balance.

40. Conjectured by Musgrave and Brunck, respectively. Gregory adopts μόρον and suggests that it is used here in its root sense, 'fate, destiny', as a variation of μοῖρα, rather than in its usual tragic sense, 'death'. Diggle and Collard obelize.

CHAPTER 6
AFFECTIVE SUSPENSE IN EURIPIDES' *ELECTRA*
Francis Dunn

This essay is part of an attempt to rethink the role of suspense in Euripides. The playwright has long been recognized for his skill in creating and heightening suspense,[1] especially in so-called 'intrigue plays' such as *Ion, Electra, Iphigenia among the Taurians* and *Helen*. These plays centre upon the recognition and reunion of two characters, which may be an end in itself, as when Ion and Creusa are belatedly discovered to be mother and child, but more often is the means to an end, as when the reunited couples conspire to escape in *Iphigenia* and *Helen*, or when the siblings in *Electra* plot their revenge. Scholarly interest in these plays has focused primarily on complications in the plot, with spectators held in suspense until the protagonists are first reunited, and then able to carry out their schemes. On this view, suspense is a plot device generating uncertainty about events; yet equally important – it seems to me – is suspense about the characters involved, and uncertainty concerning their affective bond. From this perspective, what I call 'affective suspense' causes us to ask how a bond can be established between two individuals who are related but do not know one another, and how the relation can then enable a murder or an escape.

My interest is thus in certain dramatic examples of suspense, and my argument is that they can better be understood by attending to their emotional and psychological dimensions. I am not advancing an argument about suspense in general, although it may help to frame my argument by distinguishing the internal psychology of suspense in plays such as *Electra* from the external psychology of suspense emphasized by some recent scholars. Whereas theorists of suspense have tended to focus on the reader's or viewers' uncertainty about how events will unfold, thus regarding suspense as a narrative tension that is largely epistemological, Aaron Smuts argues that the tension is largely affective, and consists in a frustration of readers' and viewers' desire for a particular outcome. He cites many examples, especially from Hitchcock films, where 'we often feel suspense in response to narratives [even] when we know their outcomes ("the paradox of suspense")'.[2] In such cases, he argues, suspense cannot arise from uncertainty as to how events will unfold. I find Smuts' essay persuasive, yet my interest here is not in explaining how suspense generally affects readers and viewers, but in showing how emotional dynamics *within* a particular drama contribute in important ways to that external tension or apprehensiveness.

Euripides' intrigue plays build suspense or narrative tension concerning two characters' recognition and reunion. In *Ion, Electra* and *Iphigenia among the Taurians*, there is a nominal relation between sister and brother or mother and child, yet because they were separated in infancy or childhood no effective bond had a chance to develop, and each play asks if, and how, it can do so now. In *Helen*, Menelaus arrives in Egypt to find a Helen with whom he has no significant bond because she is the new, chaste Helen created by the poet, whereas he is the husband of the traditional and unfaithful Helen who sailed off with Paris for Troy. In various ways, affective suspense invites us to consider how a relation may be established that will sustain the protagonists in the challenges they face.

In this essay I focus in particular on Euripides' *Electra*, attending to the potential development of an emotional bond between Electra and Orestes and the role of affective suspense in motivating the action. Yet, of the four intrigue plays, only *Electra* is a drama of revenge, and I therefore complement my discussion of the bond between siblings with that of a different kind of affect, namely the anger and hostility that motivate revenge. Indeed, matricide is an especially problematic undertaking which entails its own form of suspense, as we wonder how and when the protagonists can bring themselves to kill their own mother. As we shall see, affective suspense concerning these hostile emotions accompanies that concerning the siblings' reunion, and plays out in a similar manner in the final stages of the drama.

To see fully and clearly how affect motivates the drama, I thus separate, for the sake of discussion, two interrelated aspects of the plot. Electra and Orestes want to be reunited with one another in large measure so they can be avenged on Aegisthus and Clytemnestra. Yet I shall trace, first, uncertainties about creating a positive bond between the siblings, showing how these carry on past the recognition to the final episode of the play. I shall turn, second, to complications in the more negative or hostile impetus for revenge, showing that these arise even before the reunion and continue in the scenes that follow. These very different emotions, and the suspense that accompanies them, nevertheless follow similar arcs that converge in a powerful closing scene.

In *Electra*, suspense concerning the bond between Electra and her brother has two stages: first, we wait to see whether brother and sister, who parted so young they cannot recognize one another (283–4), can at this late stage form an emotional bond. And, then, we wonder if their relationship can enable their revenge. The potentially crucial nature of the bond between them can be illustrated, by contrast, at the moment of recognition in *Libation Bearers*, when Electra says to Orestes:[3]

ὦ τερπνὸν ὄμμα, τέσσαρας μοίρας ἔχον
ἐμοί· προσαυδᾶν σ᾽ ἐστ᾽ ἀναγκαίως ἔχον
πατέρα τε, καὶ τὸ μητρὸς εἰς σέ μοι ῥέπει
στέργηθρον – ἣ δὲ πανδίκως ἐχθαίρεται –
καὶ τῆς τυθείσης νηλεῶς ὁμοσπόρου·
πιστὸς τ᾽ ἀδελφὸς ἦσθ᾽, ἐμοὶ σέβας φέρων·

Oh joyful vision, with four parts
for me; for I must address you
as my father, and to you falls the love

due my mother – whom I justly hate –
and that for my sister, cruelly sacrificed;
and you were a faithful brother, bringing me respect.

Aeschylus, Libation Bearers *238–43*

Orestes embodies for Electra all natural affective bonds rolled up into one, and on this basis she can immediately embrace him and immediately join in his preparations for revenge. In Euripides, by contrast, the recognition and subsequent scheme are both problematic, and both issues are tied up with the problem of establishing reliable affective bonds.

The long-delayed reunion between Orestes and Electra builds suspense and irony as Orestes withholds from his sister knowledge shared with the audience from the start. In doing so, it foregrounds the problem of establishing a bond between them. Towards the end of their long stichomythia, after Electra expresses her resolve to help murder Clytemnestra (279–81), Orestes exclaims: 'Ah! If only Orestes were here to hear that!' (φεῦ· εἴθ' ἦν Ὀρέστης πλησίον κλύων τάδε, 282[4]). Electra then interjects, 'But stranger, I wouldn't know him if I saw him' (ἀλλ', ὦ ξέν', οὐ γνοίην ἂν εἰσιδοῦσά νιν, 283), and her brother answers, 'Nothing unusual – you were separated from him when you and he were young' (νέα γάρ, οὐδὲν θαῦμ', ἀπεζεύχθης νέου, 284). The exchange draws attention to the fact that what is at stake is not the re-establishment of a previous emotional bond between the siblings, but the formation of a bond between people who are essentially strangers. When Electra continues by adding that only the old tutor would now recognize Orestes (285, 287), she not only paves the way for the ensuing recognition, but also anticipates the fact that it will depend more on the Old Man than on a bond between brother and sister.

The distance to be overcome in establishing a bond is underscored in what follows.[5] When Orestes asks what news he should bring back to Electra's brother, she delivers a short speech detailing her own woes and the abuses of her mother and Aegisthus, and frames her remarks by addressing him as 'stranger' and adopting the pose of a suppliant. 'Since you prompt my story,' she begins, 'I supplicate you, stranger, announce to Orestes my evils and his' (ἐπεὶ δὲ κινεῖς μῦθον, ἱκετεύω, ξένε, | ἄγγελλ' Ὀρέστῃ τἀμὰ κἀκείνου κακά, 302–3). She concludes with almost identical words and pose, 'But stranger, I supplicate you, announce these things' (ἀλλ', ὦ ξέν', ἱκετεύω σ', ἀπάγγειλον τάδε, 332). In resorting to the formal and unequal bond of supplication, she underscores the absence of an equal and affective bond between siblings.

As the play proceeds, the viability of an affective bond between brother and sister is put in doubt by Orestes' continuing reluctance to reveal anything about himself, by Electra's abrupt dismissal of the reported tokens at their father's tomb, and by the Old Man who steps in to play the active role in their reunion that properly belongs to one or both of the siblings. After patiently coaxing Electra over some thirteen lines (563–75) to recognize Orestes by his scar, the Old Man adds, 'and you still hesitate to embrace one so close?' (ἔπειτα μέλλεις προσπίτνειν τοῖς φιλτάτοις; 576). His question finally provokes a recognition scene that is exceedingly short (577–81), unusually prosaic (all in trimeters) and entirely lacking in expressions of feeling.[6] Instead, both siblings remark on the unexpected nature of their reunion (El. 'I never expected,' οὐδέποτε δόξασ', Or. 'I never hoped,' οὐδ' ἐγὼ γὰρ ἤλπισα, 580), and in the climactic half-lines that follow, to Electra's question, 'Are you really he?' (ἐκεῖνος εἶ σύ;), her brother replies – not with any expression of affection, nor even with any reference to their family relation – by saying, 'Your only ally' (σύμμαχός γέ σοι μόνος, 581). Indeed, the word σύμμαχος stands where we might have expected to hear σύγγονος, 'close relative', and the aural substitution underscores the absence of an emotional bond between them. The military term σύμμαχος then leads to a brief comment on the task ahead (582–4), followed by the briefest of lyrics (585–95). Yet in place of a recognition duet expressing the feelings of Orestes and Electra for one another,[7] these lyrics are a song by the chorus – a song, furthermore, that does not comment on their reunion but celebrates Orestes' return (585–9) and looks forward to his revenge (590–5).

The ensuing plan for revenge does not rely on an affective bond between the siblings, since the Old Man devises the murder of Aegisthus, just as he engineered the recognition, while Electra plans the murder of Clytemnestra. And although three characters take part in the scene, it is divided into two sections of stichomythia, one in which the Old Man advises Orestes concerning Aegisthus (612–40) and one in which Electra instructs the Old Man about her mother (649–67), so that brother and sister do not even speak to one another.

Even at a moment of shared emotional excitement, it is not the bond of siblings that unites Orestes and Electra. After a messenger reports the murder of Aegisthus and announces that Orestes is about the appear with the corpse, Electra cries out with joy, then goes into the house to fetch garlands, 'since I shall crown the head of my victorious brother' (στέψω τ' ἀδελφοῦ κρᾶτα τοῦ νικηφόρου, 872), using the term proper to a victorious athlete. On returning she exclaims, 'O glorious in victory, Orestes, born from a victorious father' (ὦ καλλίνικε, πατρὸς ἐκ νικηφόρου | γεγώς, Ὀρέστα, 880–1), applying the term νικήφορος this time to Agamemnon and addressing her brother with the athlete's epithet καλλίνικε. As she crowns him, she adds, 'You have come after running no idle lap in your competition' (ἥκεις γὰρ οὐκ ἀχρεῖον ἔκπλεθρον δραμὼν | ἀγῶν', 883–4), and then offers a crown to Pylades as well, since he shared in the contest (887–9). Athletic metaphors are commonly used in describing success of all kinds, but here Electra takes them literally, holding actual crowns and placing one ceremoniously on Orestes' head: 'Receive this wreath for the locks of your hair' (δέξαι κόμης σῆς βοστρύχων ἀνδήματα, 882).[8] The formal and unequal relation of celebrant and athlete is thus made concrete and explicit, upstaging any more affective relation even at this moment of heightened feeling.

The pattern of affective failure is further underscored when Orestes balks at killing his mother. When he realizes that Clytemnestra is approaching the cottage and the trap they have laid for her, Orestes doubts his ability to kill the mother who bore him (969), questions the rightness of Apollo's oracle (971, 973, 981) and fears the pollution and exile he will incur as a matricide (975, 977):

Ορ.	φεῦ·	
	πῶς γὰρ κτάνω νιν, ἥ μ' ἔθρεψε κἄτεκεν;	
Ηλ.	ὥσπερ πατέρα σὸν ἥδε κἀμὸν ὤλεσεν.	970
Ορ.	ὦ Φοῖβε, πολλήν γ' ἀμαθίαν ἐθέσπισας.	
Ηλ.	ὅπου δ' Ἀπόλλων σκαιὸς ᾖ, τίνες σοφοί;	
Ορ.	ὅστις μ' ἔχρησας μητέρ', ἣν οὐ χρῆν, κτανεῖν.	
Ηλ.	βλάπτῃ δὲ δὴ τί πατρὶ τιμωρῶν σέθεν;	
Ορ.	μητροκτόνος νῦν φεύξομαι, τόθ' ἁγνὸς ὤν.	975
Ηλ.	καὶ μή γ' ἀμύνων πατρὶ δυσσεβὴς ἔσῃ.	
Ορ.	ἐγὼ δὲ μητρὶ γ' οὐ φόνου δώσω δίκας;	
Ηλ.	τί δ' ἢν πατρῴαν διαμεθῇς τιμωρίαν;	
Ορ.	ἆρ' αὖτ' ἀλάστωρ εἶπ' ἀπεικασθεὶς θεῷ;	
Ηλ.	ἱερὸν καθίζων τρίποδ'; ἐγὼ μὲν οὐ δοκῶ.	980
Ορ.	οὐ τἂν πιθοίμην εὖ μεμαντεῦσθαι τάδε.	
Ηλ.	οὐ μὴ κακισθεὶς εἰς ἀνανδρίαν πεσῇ.	

Or.	Ah!
	How can I kill her who bore and raised me?
El.	Just as she killed your father and mine.
Or.	O Phoebus, your oracle was so ignorant!
El.	Where Apollo is foolish, who is wise?
Or.	But he decreed I kill my mother, which is wrong.
El.	How are you harmed by avenging your father?
Or.	I shall be exiled as matricide, though clean before.[9]
El.	And you won't escape if you dishonour your father.
Or.	But won't I be punished for a mother's murder?
El.	How can you avoid avenging your father?
Or.	So a demon said to do it, one resembling a god.
El.	Sitting on the holy tripod? I don't think so!
Or.	I cannot believe those oracles were good.
El.	Do not play the wicked coward!

969–82

The emotional distance between them is reinforced, as Evert van Emde Boas points out, by rhetorical and logical disjunctions.[10] Yet Electra has no sympathy: he should kill his mother as she killed their father (970); if Apollo is foolish, who is wise? (972); and she concludes by warning him not to be a coward (982).

All this changes in the epilogue. Emerging from the house with the bodies of their victims, Orestes and Electra sing together for the first time.[11] But the emotional bond conveyed by the lyrics is one of grief, not happiness. Together they bewail the deed of murder (1177–89), together they bewail the consequences (1190–205), together they recall the act itself:[12]

Ορ.   ἐγὼ μὲν ἐπιβαλὼν φάρη κόραις ἐμαῖς
       φασγάνῳ κατηρξάμαν
       ματέρος ἔσω δέρας μεθείς.
Ηλ.   ἐγὼ δέ <γ'> ἐπεκέλευσά σοι
       ξίφους τ' ἐφηψάμαν ἅμα.   1225
Χο.   δεινότατον παθέων ἔρεξας.
<Ορ.> λαβοῦ, κάλυπτε μέλεα ματέρος πέπλοις
       <καὶ> καθάρμοσον σφαγάς.
       φονέας ἔτικτες ἄρά σοι.
Ηλ.   ἰδού, φίλα τε κοὐ φίλα   1230
       φάρεα τάδ' ἀμφιβάλλομεν.
<Χο.> τέρμα κακῶν μεγάλων δόμοισιν.

Or.   I placed my cloak before my eyes
      and with a sword performed the sacrifice,
      thrusting into my mother's throat.
El.   I urged you on
      and grasped the sword with you.
Cho. You did the most terrible of deeds.
<Or.> Take and cover mother's body with robes
      and close up the slaughter.
      So, you gave birth to your murderers!
El.   Look, I wrap the cloak around
      one both dear and not dear.
<Cho.> The end of your family's great evils.

1221–32

In killing their mother, brother (1222) and sister (1225) both held the murder weapon, and together Orestes (1227) and Electra (1231) now cover their mother's body in a caring gesture acknowledging their bond with one 'both dear and not dear' (1230).[13] Aegisthus' body is presumably onstage together with Clytemnestra's but is never mentioned, while Clytemnestra's body now paradoxically enables a belated bond between brother and sister.[14]

No sooner are these emotions expressed than a god interrupts them; no sooner do the siblings form a belated bond than Castor sends them in opposite directions – Orestes is instructed to go to Athens where he will eventually be acquitted of murder, Electra is told to go to Arcadia and marry Pylades. Supervising this denouement are the Dioscuri, whose ambivalent status as divine authorities and family members, and ambivalent comments concerning the matricide, result 'not in clarification or illumination, but rather in confusion and lack of knowledge'.[15] We might add that they arrive, neither as uncles to Orestes and Electra, nor in Castor's case as Electra's former betrothed (cf. 312–13), but as Clytemnestra's brothers (1239–40). As such, they are briefly drawn into the situation, but show no interest in any potential bond with Electra or Orestes, and Castor addresses only the latter.

As for the siblings, after Castor's lengthy speech they briefly question the god above, and receive 'tired clichés' in response.[16] So they turn to one another and Orestes exclaims:

ὦ σύγγονέ μοι, χρονίαν σ' ἐσιδὼν
τῶν σῶν εὐθὺς φίλτρων στέρομαι
καὶ σ' ἀπολείψω σοῦ λειπόμενος.

Oh my sister, I have seen you at last
and at once am robbed of your affections.
I shall leave you and be left by you.

1308–10

Although Castor delivers a few more lines (1311–13, 1319–20), Orestes and Electra speak only to one another. First, each asks the other to embrace for a precious moment:

Ηλ. περί μοι στέρνοις στέρνα πρόσαψον,
     σύγγονε φίλτατε;
     διὰ γὰρ ζευγνῦσ' ἡμᾶς πατρίων
     μελάθρων μητρὸς φόνιοι κατάραι.
Ορ. βάλε, πρόσπτυξον σῶμα· θανόντος δ'
     ὡς ἐπὶ τύμβῳ καταθρήνησον.

El. Join your breast to my breast,
     dearest brother,
     since our mother's murderous curses
     divide us from our ancestral home.
Or. Hold, clasp my body, and lament
     as if at a dead man's tomb.

1321–6

Then after Castor expresses divine pity (1327–30), each says they will never see the other again:

<Ορ.> οὐκέτι σ' ὄψομαι.
Ηλ.   οὐδ' ἐγὼ ἐς σὸν βλέφαρον πελάσω.
Ορ.   τάδε λοίσθιά μοι προσφθέγματά σου.

<Or.> I shall see you no more.
El.   I shall not come before your eye.
Or.   These are your last words to me.

1331–3

So they say goodbye to one another and to Pylades and the chorus (1334–41), and thus – save for parting lines by Castor and the chorus – the play is over.

The play reaches its emotional climax in this closing scene, as Whitehorne argued many years ago. Yet its power derives not, as he concluded, from the contrast between mortals and gods, between human suffering and divine indifference,[17] but from the heart-rending end to which affective suspense finally leads. The bond that, we feel, can and should arise between Electra and Orestes, even though they are essentially strangers, and that, over and over again, fails to develop, finally emerges at the very moment when they realize they will never have a chance to enjoy or make use of that relationship.

The bond between Electra and Orestes is not the only component of the drama's suspense. It deserves special attention because we expect the relationship to develop and strengthen, and in this way contribute progressively to the plot of revenge. Other emotive factors contribute to the plot in a more static fashion. In a drama of revenge, hatred and anger are central motivating forces, and suspense will consist, in part, of uncertainty concerning how and when these emotions will translate into violent action. It might be possible in some contexts for the hatred directed against a foe to develop progressively, but in Euripides' *Electra*, as in other versions of the story, years have passed since the murder of Agamemnon and the grounds for revenge have not changed. The emotive force urging revenge may be revived by recalling his past murder, or reinforced by describing the present conduct of his killers, yet suspense consists not in waiting for hostility to arise but for an occasion where hostile parties may strike. Despite these differences, however, the suspense associated with hatred in *Electra* complements in some important ways that involved in the siblings' reunion.

In the opening scenes, the Farmer, Electra and Orestes establish the burden of the plot by alluding to the murder of Agamemnon, the threat of revenge, and abuses by Aegisthus and Clytemnestra. Yet the affect each reports or expresses is different. The Farmer speaks of the murderers' fears – fear that Orestes may return to avenge his father's murder, and fear that Electra might bear a son to do the same (22–42). Electra expresses her own resentment at Aegisthus and Clytemnestra for mistreating her and banishing her to the countryside (54–63). Orestes speaks of Agamemnon's murder and his own goal of revenge (82–101) – and does so in relatively neutral language: 'returning murder to my father's murderers' (φόνον φονεῦσι πατρὸς ἀλλάξων ἐμοῦ, 89). The difference between Electra and Orestes reflects their own experiences, the former living not far from the usurpers and daily feeling humiliated by them, the latter wandering far from the scene of the old crime he has come to avenge. This difference plays out in subsequent episodes. Orestes is cautious in scouting the area, while she insists that now is the time to act (275); he takes the Old Man's lead in planning revenge, she interrupts to instruct the Old Man. Most telling is the contrast between Orestes' dispassionate murder of Aegisthus and reluctance to kill Clytemnestra, and his sister's angry tirades over the body of Aegisthus and in front of her mother.

All this is familiar, of course, as reflecting Euripides' distinctive characterization of the two protagonists.[18] What I would like to parse is their role in terms of affective suspense. To do so, let us return briefly to the model of Aeschylus' *Libation Bearers*. In that play, the place of emotion in the scheme of revenge is powerfully registered in the *kommos*, where

Orestes, Electra and the chorus attempt to summon the dead Agamemnon by recalling the horror of his death and demanding bloody retribution. All involved, even the absent dead, share the same strong feelings about what has happened and what now must be done, and the action that follows fairly straightforwardly realizes those desires. In Euripides, by contrast, there is no such emotional consensus. There is a logical consensus that Agamemnon's murder must be avenged, but the difference between Electra's vehemence and her brother's reluctance precludes an emotional basis for revenge.

Electra's attitude in the opening scenes, for example – acting out her misery while refusing the support of those around her – squanders or misdirects feelings that might be put to better use. She enters carrying a water jug, and immediately proclaims that she does so, 'not that I have come to this degree of want, but to show the gods Aegisthus' abuse' (οὐ δή τι χρείας ἐς τοσόνδ' ἀφιγμένη | ἀλλ' ὡς ὕβριν δείξωμενΑἰγίσθου θεοῖς, 57–8). In her righteous anger at Aegisthus she takes on burdens that are, as the Farmer reminds her (64–6), self-imposed. Likewise she claims that her squalid condition prevents her from attending the festival of Hera, even though the chorus women offer her suitable clothing (190–2) and suggest that honouring the gods might help her gain revenge (193–7). Whereas Electra indulges her hostile feelings, Orestes cuts his short. He describes his task of revenge as returning murder (89, above), then backtracks and says his plan is two-fold: to secure escape (96–7) and find his sister (98–101) so with her as murder accomplice he can learn of affairs in the city (καὶ φόνου συνεργάτιν | λαβὼν τά γ' εἴσω τειχέων σαφῶς μάθω, 100–1). Thus gaining knowledge takes the place, for now, of seeking to act on hostile intentions.

In her exchange with the disguised Orestes, Electra provides information – and misinformation – calculated to arouse in her absent brother a passion for revenge, yet he fails to take the bait. When Orestes asks if Agamemnon found a tomb (288), Electra implies he was left unburied ('he found what he found, cast out from the house', ἔκυρσεν ὡς ἔκυρσεν, ἐκβληθεὶς δόμων, 289), presumably trusting that such horrific treatment would rouse his son to action. Yet her brother reacts to the false news not by saying how angry Orestes will be, but how sad – or, rather, impersonally, that news can be sad:

οἴμοι, τόδ' οἷον εἶπας· αἴσθησις γὰρ οὖν
καὶ τῶν θυραίων πημάτων δάκνει βροτούς.

Oh what a thing you said! For awareness
even of others' grief can pain a person.

290–1

Thus after his initial outburst, οἴμοι, τόδ' οἷον εἶπας, Orestes deflects any emotional response with a gnomic platitude. The generalizing language helps to protect Orestes' disguise, as van Emde Boas observes,[19] and at the same time indicates an emotional register quite different from his sister's. He nevertheless invites Electra to speak out so he can bring news to her brother (292–3), and she obliges with a catalogue of woes. She describes her own squalor and hard labour, her mother's luxury and her father's maltreatment, claiming that his blood remains in the house and his tomb has never received an offering or libation (304–25). In case this is not enough to stir the anger of her brother, she caps it with an outrageous scenario:

> μέθῃ δὲ βρεχθεὶς τῆς ἐμῆς μητρὸς πόσις
> ὁ κλεινός, ὡς λέγουσιν, ἐνθρῴσκει τάφῳ
> πέτροις τε λεύει μνῆμα λάινον πατρός,
> καὶ τοῦτο τολμᾷ τοὔπος εἰς ἡμᾶς λέγειν·
> Ποῦ παῖς Ὀρέστης; ἆρά σοι τύμβῳ καλῶς
> παρὼν ἀμύνει; ταῦτ' ἀπὼν ὑβρίζεται.

> Soaked in booze, my mother's husband,
> the famous one, they call him, jumps on the tomb
> and pelts with stones our father's stone memorial,
> and dares to speak these words against us:
> 'Where is your son Orestes? Doing a good job being here
> to protect your tomb?' And he, being absent, is abused like this.

> *326–31*

The vivid and overblown account[20] – especially in taunting Agamemnon over the absence of his son – is cleverly calculated to rouse Orestes to fury and revenge, however distant he may be.[21] But Orestes is actually right here, and he says and does nothing. Instead, the chorus notice the Farmer returning home, he notices the strangers near his house, and the moment is lost as conversation now turns to the question of entertaining guests.

The emotional disparity between Electra and Orestes carries over into the execution of revenge. In the messenger's report of Aegisthus' murder, Orestes is all business, displaying fine technical skill in slaughtering the sacrificial victim and repeating the performance over the equally helpless man.[22] When the king's servants rush to attack the assassin, he says:

> Οὐχὶ δυσμενὴς
> ἥκω πόλει τῇδ' οὐδ' ἐμοῖς ὀπάοσιν
> φονέα δὲ πατρὸς ἀντετιμωρησάμην
> τλήμων Ὀρέστης· ἀλλὰ μή με καίνετε,
> πατρὸς παλαιοὶ δμῶες.

> I have come
> not as enemy to this city nor to my attendants
> but I, suffering Orestes, took revenge against
> my father's murderer. So do not kill me,
> old servants of my father.

> *847–51*

Orestes does not bolster his appeal by invoking grief for Agamemnon or hatred for Aegisthus, but simply identifies himself to the slaves and points out the chain of command: those who were once Agamemnon's servants are now Orestes'.

When Orestes returns in person with the body of Aegisthus, he announces rather flatly to his sister, 'I have come, after killing Aegisthus not in word but in deed' (ἥκω γὰρ οὐ λόγοισιν ἀλλ᾽ ἔργοις κτανὼν | Αἴγισθον, 893–4), then invites Electra to mutilate the corpse with no suggestion that he harbours corresponding hostile emotions towards the man he has just killed:

> αὐτὸν τὸν θανόντα σοι φέρω,
> ὃν εἴτε χρῄζεις θηρσὶν ἁρπαγὴν πρόθες,
> ἢ σκῦλον οἰωνοῖσιν, αἰθέρος τέκνοις,
> πήξασ᾽ ἔρεισον σκόλοπι· σὸς γάρ ἐστι νῦν
> δοῦλος, πάροιθε δεσπότης κεκλημένος.

> I bring you the dead man himself
> whom, if you wish, set out as prey for wild animals
> or post him as spoil for the birds, children
> of the sky, fixed to a stake; for he is now your
> slave, who before was called your master.

895–9

When she hesitantly proposes verbal rather than physical abuse of the dead, Orestes actively encourages her with no evident inclination to do the same (900–6). The speech that Electra then delivers, insulting and mocking Aegisthus, sneering at his pretty looks and impugning his masculinity, is bursting with hostile emotions that nevertheless seem misplaced. The murder of Agamemnon and the subsequent mistreatment of his children – the actions which above all others justify the emotions and actions of revenge – are tossed aside in Electra's opening lines, 'You ruined me, and left me and my brother bereft of our dear father' (ἀπώλεσάς με κὠρφανὴν φίλου πατρὸς | καὶ τόνδ᾽ ἔθηκας, 914–15), as she turns instead to petty and personal slurs.[23]

As Clytemnestra approaches, Orestes complains that it is both difficult and wrong to kill his mother but, browbeaten by his sister, reluctantly goes inside to do the deed. The lack of strong emotional impetus in this exchange with Electra is striking, especially by contrast with the corresponding scene in Aeschylus. In *Libation Bearers*, Orestes confronts his mother immediately after killing Aegisthus and announces he will kill her (892, 894–5), but is abruptly stopped short by Clytemnestra's emotional appeal to the bond between them and the breast which embodies it. When Pylades ventriloquizes the commands of Apollo and says he should 'consider all people hateful/enemies rather than the gods' (ἅπαντας ἐχθροὺς τῶν θεῶν ἡγοῦ πλέον, 902), he recovers his resolve and tells his mother that she will die and rest with Aegisthus, 'since you love this man, and the one you ought to love you hate' (ἐπεὶ φιλεῖς | τὸν ἄνδρα τοῦτον, ὃν δὲ χρῆν φιλεῖν στυγεῖς, 906–7; cf. 894–5, φιλεῖς τὸν ἄνδρα; τοιγὰρ ἐν ταὐτῷ τάφῳ | κείσῃ). In the exchange that follows, he responds to her pleas by insisting that her treatment of her husband and of Orestes requires revenge. In Euripides, however, Orestes debates with his sister rather than his mother, and does so with the language of law rather than of love and hate: what the oracle instructed was not right (973), and Orestes will be banished (φεύξομαι, 975) and will pay the penalty (δώσω δίκας, 977, above).

Orestes' apparent lack of emotional investment is accompanied by an excess on Electra's part. After Orestes goes indoors, Electra welcomes Clytemnestra by proclaiming her status as slave and outcast (1004–5), then responds to her mother's speech justifying her actions with a heated speech of her own. She begins with guilt by association, claiming that Clytemnestra has the same good looks as her sister Helen – and the same vanity, and the same lack of virtue (1062–4). Invoking the sacrifice of Iphigenia was an empty pretext, she continues, since even before then Clytemnestra was tending to her looks, an obvious sign of loose morals (1070–5). In fact, her mother was guilty of treachery, rooting for the enemy, since she did not want Agamemnon to return from Troy (1076–9). She concludes by threatening murder, since if it was right to avenge Iphigenia by killing Agamemnon, Electra and Orestes will be right to kill their mother (1093–6). Electra's tirade is fully motivated by hostile feelings which seem lacking in her brother, yet these feelings are also misplaced – less a burning anger at the death of Agamemnon than a snide, perhaps even jealous, resentment of her mother's station and outward trappings.[24]

Electra ushers her mother inside the cottage and, after a brief choral ode, she and Orestes emerge with the bodies of Aegisthus and Clytemnestra. Orestes sings of his 'bloody and loathesome deeds' (ἴδετε τάδ' ἔργα φόνιμα μυσαρά, 1178–9) and Electra agrees, singing, 'very lamentable … wretchedly I burned against my mother' (δακρύτ' ἄγαν … διὰ πυρὸς ἔμολον ἁ τάλαινα ματρὶ τᾷδ', 1182–3). Orestes laments the exile he will suffer (1194–7), Electra her social exclusion (1198–200). Together they recall the murder itself (1214–26, above), and together they cover the body of their enemy and mother, one both dear and not dear (φίλᾳ τε κοὐ φίλᾳ, 1230). The trajectory of negative affect (hatred for enemies) thus ends up converging with that of positive (love for kin). Suspense regarding realization of the negative emotions was not so much deferred or interrupted as torn between two equally unsatisfactory drives towards their goal: Orestes' emotional detachment and Electra's misplaced vehemence. Yet in the wake of the second murder, just as brother and sister belatedly form an emotional bond with one another, they also share, for the first time, the same feelings about their enemies – namely horror and regret at what they have done (1177–232, cf. above). Thus, for the first time, the plot, with all its complications, reaches a point that seems emotionally appropriate.

Electra is a suspenseful and powerful play, and its power derives in part from complications in the plot that require us to wait and see how and when the siblings will be reunited, then how and when they will undertake the task of revenge. Yet the power of the play as a whole, and above all the emotional power of its ending, derives from affective suspense by which we must wait to see, on the one hand, how and when Electra will form an emotional bond with the brother she was separated from as an infant and, on the other hand, how and when the hostile feelings impelling revenge will reach an emotionally suitable outcome. Delays in the progressive movement towards the bonding of Electra and Orestes, and inconsistencies between their more static hostile stances, are only resolved at the very end of the play in a wrenching aftermath played out over the body of Clytemnestra and under the eyes of Castor.

Notes

1. See, for example, Diller 1962, Arnott 1973, Goward 1999: 141–7 and Wright 2005: 56–157.

2. Smuts 2008: 281. A variation of his argument is offered by Uidhir 2011.

3. The Greek text follows that of West 1990a. Translations here and elsewhere are my own, with some debts to that of Cropp 2013.

4. The Greek text follows that of Cropp 2013.

5. Compare Halporn 1983 on the physical separation of Electra and Orestes, and Cropp 2013: 13 on their relatively limited interaction.

6. The siblings' rejoicing is 'brief and almost perfunctory', in the words of Solmsen 1967: 45, who attributes this to Electra's self-centred character.

7. Contrast the lengthy recognition duets in *IT* 827–99, *Ion* 1439–509, *Helen* 625–97, *Hypsipyle* fr. 759a. 1579–632 *TrGF* and Sophocles, *Electra* 1232–87.

8. On athletic imagery more broadly in the play, see Arnott 1981: 187–9, Swift 2010: 156–72. Thury 1985: 9 connects Electra's desire to crown Orestes with her materialism more generally. Marshall 1999/2000: 333 notes metatheatrical aspects of the gesture.

9. Denniston on 975 takes φεύξομαι in the legal sense, 'I shall stand my trial.'

10. van Emde Boas 2017: 215–17.

11. As Mossman 2001: 382–3 observes, it is striking that in a lament the male, Orestes, has a much larger part.

12. Their belated bond is reinforced by 'some striking symmetries of content and phrasing in each strophic pair', Cropp 2013: 227.

13. Of the oxymoron, Denniston *ad loc.* observes, 'This type of expression ... is rather a mannerism of Euripides; but here its pathos is most moving.'

14. Allen-Hornblower 2014 points out further paradoxes in the *kommos*: that it has the function of a messenger speech while acting out the reported deed, and that a lament for the dead is sung by the victim's killers.

15. Andújar 2016: 185. Thury 1985, by contrast, sees the Dioscuri as bringing appropriate rewards and punishments, and a soothing understanding.

16. Andújar 2016: 185.

17. Whitehorne 1978, esp. 10–14.

18. Much debated is how we should respond to this characterization of Electra and Orestes. Some argue that character traits are designed to portray them in a negative light, as for example Kitto 1961: 333–41, or as a means to criticize traditional values, as Arnott 1981. Lloyd 1986, by contrast, argues that these traits are normal by literary and cultural standards, and in this is followed by Papadimitropoulos 2008. The view presented here is that Electra and Orestes do indeed speak and act in unsettling ways, not in order to elicit our condemnation but to

complicate our response to them and their actions. Compare van Emde Boas 2017 who is concerned, however, with 'patterns of miscommunication' and their contribution to narrative suspense.

19. van Emde Boas 2017: 171–4.

20. Arnott 1981: 183–4 goes so far as to call Electra a liar.

21. Compare van Emde Boas 2017: 121: 'These violent face assaults are superficially directed at Agamemnon; but . . . the offence is to be felt by Orestes just as strongly.'

22. Porter 1990 suggests that Euripides' account alludes to sacrifice at the Bouphonia, and is thus marked as perverse and disturbing.

23. Cropp 2013: 206 aptly calls the speech a 'kakology' in which Electra indulges her spite.

24. On the language and rhetoric of her speech, see Mossman 2001 and van Emde Boas 2017: 248–68.

CHAPTER 7
THE FALL OF TROY, THE GLORY OF ATHENS: CHORUS AND COMMUNITY IN EURIPIDES' *TROJAN WOMEN*
Ruggiero Lionetti

Euripides' *Trojan Women* has been intensively investigated in the light of the events or, more generally, of the political climate of the central years of the Peloponnesian War.[1] On the whole, these interpretations of the play presuppose a kind of identification, on the one hand, between the Greeks of the myth and fifth-century Athenians, and, on the other, between the Trojans and the communities annihilated, oppressed or threatened by Athenian imperialism.[2] I will proceed in a different direction. What I aim to do is shed light on the interaction between the two communities involved in the first production of *Trojan Women* at the City Dionysia of 415 BCE: the fictitious community of Troy, *praesens in absentia* throughout the whole tragedy, and the Athenian civic body, as symbolically embodied by the heterogeneous public who witnessed dramatic competitions.[3] Naturally, critics have not failed to observe that in this tragedy the Trojan characters are the object of a 'sympathetic' representation, which transcends ethnic boundaries.[4] My thesis, however, is a slightly more radical one: within the choral interventions of *Trojan Women*, Euripides projects Athens onto Troy, blurring the borders between their civic identities. This is consistent with other classical art and literature,[5] and is made possible by the dramatic chorus' ability to act as a bridge between the audience and the world of the play[6] and – as this paper argues – was designed to ensure a more intense and involving theatrical experience for the prevalently Attic audience members.

On the basis of both empirical and experimental evidence, we know that a certain degree of proximity (i.e. similarity) between two subjects acquires a catalysing function within the dynamics of emotional engagement.[7] In Aristotle's *Rhetoric* (2.1386a25–7) similar reasoning is applied to the feeling of pity (ἔλεος): τοὺς ὁμοίους ἐλεοῦσιν κατὰ ἡλικίαν, κατὰ ἤθη, κατὰ ἕξεις, κατὰ ἀξιώματα, κατὰ γένη· ἐν πᾶσι γὰρ τούτοις μᾶλλον φαίνεται καὶ αὐτῷ ἂν ὑπάρξαι ('men [. . .] pity those who resemble them in age, character, habits, position or family; for all such relations make a man more likely to think that their misfortune may befall him as well').[8] Aristotle here does not posit any mechanism of emotional sharing between the pitier and the pitied, but – as Konstan points out – 'simply requires that we believe that we may suffer a misfortune like that now being experienced by the pitied'.[9] As regards ancient theatre, in particular, it is worth bearing in mind that one crucial precondition for the correct enjoyment of the performance was precisely a certain 'safe distance' between the audience and the dramatic action.[10] For this reason, the present discussion will not assume any mechanism of 'identification' with or 'projection' onto the *dramatis personae* on the part of the audience. Rather, what is being referred to by 'emotional engagement' is that paradoxical situation which Gorgias so effectively describes in *Encomium of Helen* (B11.9 D-K [= D24.3 L-M]), whereby the person who enjoys a work of poetry (or, to be more precise, the person's ψυχή) experiences a direct involvement in the vicissitudes of its fictional characters. Stigmatizing this tendency in his *Republic* (10.605c9–d5), Plato explicitly associates it with lamentation scenes in tragedy (both sung and spoken), in addition to epic.[11]

In the light of these considerations, it is possible to gain a fuller understanding of the peculiar choral technique that Euripides uses in *Trojan Women*. The otherness of the barbarian chorus in this tragedy is constantly brought back within the framework of the perspective and experiences of the fifth-century Athenian audience. By adopting an Athenian point of view, the chorus can become integrated within the Athenian civic body, with a different effect in the parodos and in the second stasimon. Even more striking, albeit less explicit, is the strategy that Euripides adopts in the first stasimon, where the chorus evokes the episodes of the capture of Troy: as I will endeavour to show, the images and situations recurring in this stasimon appear to be modelled after the rituals of the Panathenaia.

1. The chorus as a collective experience: Trojan and Athenian perspectives

The chorus of *Trojan Women* is made up of figures relegated to the margins of the dramatic action:[12] barbarian women who have been brought into slavery and are about to be transported to the victors' homelands. Despite this – and despite the violent end met by Troy – the chorus preserves its traditional role as an authoritative mouthpiece of the community.[13] The event of the women's recent enslavement enables the chorus to preserve a strong link with the city:[14] on the one hand, the Trojan prisoners can already regard themselves as slaves of the Greeks (e.g. 158–9) and raise a 'dirge' for Troy (ᾠδὰν ἐπικήδειον, 514); on the other hand, they fear the moment in which they will be separated from the city (or what remains of it) for good (e.g. 156–89, 233–4).

The first stasimon uses 'choral projection'[15] to evoke Troy concretely in the *hic et nunc* of the dramatic representation. Leaving aside this aspect, to which I will return later, I note here how, at lines 522–6, the chorus proves capable of (literally) lending voice to its community. This occurs at the moment of the discovery of the horse:

> ἀνὰ δ' ἐβόασεν λεὼς
> Τρῳάδος ἀπὸ πέτρας σταθείς·
> Ἴτ', ὦ πεπαυμένοι πόνων,
> τόδ' ἱερὸν ἀνάγετε ξόανον
> Ἰλιάδι Διογενεῖ κόραι.

> The people shouted aloud
> from where they stood on Troy's citadel,

'Come, you whose labours are over,
bring this holy statue
to Troy's Zeus-begotten daughter!'[16]

895–9

The peculiarity of this passage lies not in the use of the *oratio recta* – a common feature of Euripides' late lyrics[17] – but rather in the fact that it is a whole community (λεώς)[18] that is speaking here.[19] By vocalizing the point of view of the Trojan people as a whole,[20] the chorus women confer ominous ambiguity to the Trojans' last words: the expression, 'you whose labours are over' (ὦ πεπαυμένοι πόνων, 524), seems to trigger the same mechanism of tragic irony already exploited in the first episode, where Polyxena's death was described in terms of 'relief' from pains (ἀπηλλάχθαι πόνων, 271). In this passage, the chorus of *Trojan Women* is not only abstractly representative of Troy but is able to embody and give voice to the people of Troy as a corporate whole despite the destruction of the city.

We thus reach the second level of our analysis: how does the chorus of *Trojan Women* – and hence the fictitious community it embodies onstage – stand vis-à-vis the civic community of Athens? The first element that ought to be taken into account is the remarkable place of Athens in the choral sections of the tragedy. Athens receives encomiastic mentions both in the parodos (207–9, 218–9) and in the second stasimon (799–803), which is to say at the beginning of the play and roughly halfway through. A similar situation, however, is to be observed even in the third and last stasimon, where we find a lamentation on Troy that offers fewer possibilities of deviating from the dramatic context. In this case, what lends the ode an Attic flavour is the mention of Salamis, the control of which was one of the cornerstones of Athenian political discourse:[21] in the second strophe the island is referred to as 'holy' (ἱεράν, 1096)[22] and set in contrast to Doric Corinth, which is defined only in geographical terms (ἢ δίπορον κορυφὰν | Ἴσθμιον, 'the peak of the Isthmus with two paths,' 1097–8) and in relation to myth (ἔνθα πύλας | Πέλοπος ἔχουσιν ἕδραι, 'where stand the gates to Pelops' home,' 1098–9).[23] Overall, the picture that emerges seems quite extraordinary, even considering the Attic chauvinism of Greek tragedy.[24] Putting aside *Hecuba*, which I will discuss later, a distant parallel is only to be found in tragedies set in Attica or somehow connected to Athens.[25]

The exceptional nature of the situation becomes clearer in the light of the specific position of Athens in this tragedy. In *Trojan Women* the Athenians are not just to be found in the ranks of the destroyers of Troy but, as Poseidon emphasizes in the prologue, the Theseids, the 'leaders of the Athenians' (Ἀθηναίων ... πρόμοι), have taken part in the allotment of the Trojan captives (28–31). Dué argues that this first mention of Athens, which struck more than one ancient commentator as eulogistic,[26] had the effect of problematizing the reception of the play by involving the Athenian audience in the crimes of the Greek army.[27] However, if we consider the passage in question in the context of the tragedy as a whole – in which there is no criticism of Athens to be found, but rather extensive praise[28] – another interpretation becomes possible, for the ancient spectator as much as for the modern interpreter. The inclusion of the Theseids among the recipients of the war prisoners could be intended as a way to introduce – and somehow confer plausibility to[29] – the statements that shortly the chorus will express in its first lyrical intervention.

In the second strophic pair of the parodos, the chorus women express – twice and very emphatically – their desire to be sent in their enslavement to Athens, which is called 'famous' (κλεινάν, 208), 'blessed' (εὐδαίμονα, 209), 'holy' (ἱεράν, 218) and 'sacred' (ζαθέαν, 219); Thessaly, too, is good destination, yet only second best (τὰ δὲ δεύτερα, 218).[30] There is no doubt that the discourse of the chorus in this passage reflects the political situation in 415 from a patently Athenian perspective, drawing a sharp contrast between Dorian and non-Dorian Greece (juxtaposed in strophe and antistrophe), and displaying a disparaging attitude towards Sparta, which is 'most hateful' (ἐχθίσταν, 211), and Corinth, which plays hardly any role in the Trojan saga.[31] Be that as it may, the eulogistic and anachronistic mention of southern Italy, represented by Syracuse and Thurii, can hardly be regarded as a mere *captatio beneuolentiae*.[32] Rather, it reflects the Athenian interest in these western localities on the eve of the expedition against Syracuse.[33] Gibert points out that this passage is perfectly in line with the prevalently cultural (or 'analogic') mode of Greek self-definition employed in *Trojan Women*: in other words, Greek identity, which in this passage corresponds to Attic identity, is a matter of values and customs, rather than of ethnicity. The effect of this tour through the Greek world was to shorten the distance between chorus and audience, superimposing the perspective of the latter onto the former.

This technique of eliding choral viewpoint with an Attic viewpoint had already been adopted by Euripides about a decade earlier in *Hecuba*, another tragedy dealing with the aftermath of the Trojan War. Battezzato has examined the shifts in the chorus' perspective across the three stasima of the tragedy. In the first stasimon, the women of the chorus picture themselves working on the Panathenaic peplos in Athens (466–74), here referred to as 'Pallas' city' (Παλλάδος ... πόλει, 466).[34] As Battezzato observes, the adoption of an Athenian perspective here constitutes a 'risky move',[35] which indirectly implies the possibility that Athens might be conquered like Troy. But shifting the focus, in the second stasimon, the chorus juxtaposes the cities of Troy and Sparta, which are mentioned along with their rivers Simoeis (641) and Eurotas (650), and then focuses on the Spartan women's mourning (649–56). Finally, in the third stasimon, the chorus includes Troy among the 'unsacked' cities (ἀπορθήτων, 905), thereby usurping the historical record conventionally assigned to Sparta.[36] Recalling their brusque awakening on the night of the capture of Troy, the chorus described themselves as 'wearing only a peplos like a Dorian girl' (μονόπεπλος ... Δωρὶς ὡς κόρα, 933-4).[37] The overall result of this juxtaposition between Troy and Sparta is to suggest that Sparta 'one day, might be destroyed just like Troy'.[38] In *Trojan Women*, Euripides undertakes a much bolder operation, which challenges the expectations of his audience.

2. The first stasimon: a Panathenaic reading

This leads us to the first stasimon, which consists of a vivid narrative of the last hours of Troy. Unlike the parodos, the chorus' perspective is now completely Trojan. I will argue, however, that this time it is the (prevalently Attic) audience that is called, in a sense, to assume a Trojan point of view through the catalyst provided by images pertaining to Athenian cultic praxis – i.e. ones that have become entrenched through their iteration in the spectators' ritual memory.[39]

2.1. General factors (choral projection and Athena)

There are at least two general strategies that could facilitate an assimilation between Athens and Troy in this ode. The first is the use of choral projection. The chorus describe the fall of Troy as taking place amid musical and choral performances: joyful songs (529), the sound of the 'Libyan pipe' (544), 'Phrygian tunes' (545), a chorus of virgins singing a joyful song (545–7) and, above all, a choral performance executed in honour of Artemis (551–5) by the same dramatic chorus (ἐγὼ ... | ... ἐμελπόμαν | χοροῖσι). The fall of Troy, as related by the chorus, ends up overlapping with the performative context of the play in a festival whose primary elements were choruses and songs.

The second strategy is tied to the role played by Athena. In the poetic tradition, the goddess has an ambivalent attitude towards Troy. Notoriously, she played a crucial role in the capture of the city:[40] this aspect is especially stressed in the whole first part of *Trojan Women*, where Athena is presented almost as the only one responsible for the capture of Troy.[41] On the other hand, the relationship between Athena and Troy, as described in *Iliad* 6, could not but resemble – and obviously so in the perspective of a fifth-century Athenian – the patterns of Attic civic cult: we hear of a temple on the Acropolis (6.90–2, 288–95), a cult statue (92), a priestess put in charge by the civic community (300), and, above all, (the promise of) sacrifices (93–4, 308–9) and the offering of a peplos (90).[42] In the first stasimon, the memory of this traditional link between Athena and Troy is conveyed by the epithet 'Iliadic' (Ἰλιάδι, 526).[43] The explicit association of Athens with Troy was not necessary and could have been easily avoided: in the *Odyssey*'s version of the fall of Troy, for instance, the horse is said to be an offering to the gods in general (*Od.* 8.509). Euripides instead chose to follow a version of the myth[44] which, by juxtaposing the figure of Athena and the 'the slaughters about the altars' (562), would have made the reception of the episode more problematic for Athenians living in the city of Pallas Athena.

2.2. The procession

Euripides not only insists on the presence of Athena – a deity shared by Athens and Troy – but he also deploys Panathenaic imagery in this choral song.

In narrating the conveyance of the horse to the rock of Troy, the chorus emphasize the spatial dimension of the events: the Trojans stand up and raise their shouts 'from the rock of Troy' (Τρωϊάδος ἀπὸ πέτρας, 523); from the exhortation at lines 524–6 it can be inferred that they move to the gates of the city, where the Greeks have placed the horse (ἔλιπον ἵππον ... ἐν πύλαις, 'they left the horse at the gates', 519–21). The conveyance of the horse is described in terms of an ascent towards Athena's temple: the Trojans are urged to 'carry it up' (ἀνάγετε, 525).[45] Generally speaking, the episode had already taken a fixed form in the poetic tradition, as represented by the *Odyssey* (8.504) and by Stesichorus' *Sack of Troy* (fr. 103.33 Finglass).[46] Compared to these two antecedents, the Euripidean version stands out not just for its wealth of details, but because it describes the movement of the horse through the city in terms of a procession with joyful songs (κεχαρμένοι δ' ἀοιδαῖς, 'rejoicing in songs', 529) and the general mobilization of the Trojan community. The latter is represented by two extreme categories, young girls and elders: 'which of the girls did not go, | which of the old men, out of his house?' (τίς οὐκ ἔβα νεανίδων, | τίς οὐ γεραιὸς ἐκ δόμων; 527–8).[47]

It is known, on the basis of both literary and archaeological evidence, that the Panathenaic procession followed a route comparable to that described by Euripides, proceeding from outside the Dipylon Gate to the Acropolis, where solemn sacrifices took place and, at least at the Great Panathenaia,[48] a new peplos was offered to the statue of Athena Polias.[49] The procession was perceived of and described as an ascent as indicated by the use of the verb ἀνάγειν also in Plato's *Euthyphro* (6c): τοῖς μεγάλοις Παναθηναίοις ὁ πέπλος ... ἀνάγεται εἰς τὴν ἀκρόπολιν ('at the Great Panathenaia the peplos is carried up to the Acropolis').[50] Furthermore, the Panathenaic procession was characterized by the involvement of all sectors of the population, from young girls (e.g. as 'basket bearers', κανηφόροι) to elders (as 'olive branch bearers', θαλλοφόροι). All this is vividly portrayed on the Ionic frieze of the Parthenon, which is almost universally regarded as a representation of the Panathenaic procession.[51] The central role played by music is highlighted by the presence, in the northern frieze, of a group of musicians with auloi and kitharai.[52]

2.3. The Panathenaic 'ship'

The second Pananthenaic detail is the use of nautical imagery in the description of the horse: the horse, previously presented as a 'holy statue' for Athena (ἱερὸν ... ξόανον, 525) and compared to a 'four-footed vehicle' (τετραβάμονος ὡς ἀπήνας, 516),[53] is carried to the temple of Athena 'with nooses of spun flax like the dark hull of a ship' (κλωστοῦ δ' ἀμφιβόλοις λίνοιο ναὸς ὡσεὶ | σκάφος κελαινὸν, 538–9). To date, scholars have explained the use of nautical terms and the simile of the chariot in terms of the adoption and redevelopment of the Iliadic model.[54] I would argue, however, that the imagery is most influenced by the rituals of the Panathenia, though that is not to deny the presence of epic colouring.

The most symbolic moment of the Panathenaia was surely the above-mentioned offering of the peplos to the statue of Athena Polias.[55] In the Hellenistic period, the Panathenaic peplos was carried up to the Acropolis by a real ship on wheels, but, probably, this was a late innovation.[56] What about the classical period? Here the Parthenon frieze is of no help: not only is the peplos scene (slab 5 of the east frieze) highly idealized, but in all likelihood it represents only the last moment of the ceremony, when the peplos was received on the Acropolis.[57] The earliest literary source concerning the conveyance of the Panathenaic peplos is a fragment from Strattis' comedy *Macedonians* or *Pausanias*:

τὸν πέπλον δὲ τοῦτον
ἕλκουσ᾽ ὀνεύοντες τοπείοις ἄνδρες ἀναρίθμητοι
εἰς ἄκρον ὥσπερ ἱστίον τὸν ἱστόν.

And innumerable men hoist this peplos by hauling it up with ropes like a sail to the top of a mast.

Strattis fr. 31 K–A

Strattis was active roughly from the late fifth century to the first decades of the fourth.[58] The alternative title *Pausanias* refers, in all likelihood, to the lover of the tragedian Agathon, whose death is dated to between 405 and 399.[59] If this reasonable identification is correct, the comedy was staged in the last few years of the fifth century, only a decade or so after the staging of *Trojan Women*. One could argue that the simile was chosen precisely because a real vessel was not used. However, the nautical imagery and lexicon (e.g. τοπείοις, 'ropes')[60] clearly implies the use of some kind of vehicle that could at least be assimilated to a ship – precisely like the Trojan Horse of this first stasimon.[61]

2.4. The nocturnal revel (παννυχίς)

According to the chorus of *Trojan Women*, the offering of the horse was followed by a nocturnal ceremony: a dance and the joyful song performed by a group of virgins when it was 'the dark of night' (νύχιον . . . κνέφας, 544):

. . .   παρθένοι δ᾽
ἄειρον ἅμα κρότον ποδῶν
βοάν τ᾽ ἔμελπον εὔφρον᾽ . . .

and maidens as they lifted their feet in dancing
sang a song of joy . . .

545–7

A similar description can be found in the third stasimon of *Children of Heracles*, where the chorus describes a nocturnal revel (παννυχίς) celebrated on the Acropolis as the last elements of the Panathenaia:[62]

ἀνεμόεντι δ᾽ ἐπ᾽ ὄχθωι
ὀλολύγματα παννυχίοις ὑπὸ παρ-
    θένων ἰαχεῖ ποδῶν κρότοισιν.

On the wind-swept hill loud shouts of gladness resound to the beat of maiden dance steps the whole night long.

Here, too, the παννυχίς consists of dance performances and vocal expressions of joy by maidens (βοάν, 'song of joy' ~ ὀλολύγματα, 'loud cry, mostly of joy' [LSJ *s.vv.*]).

781–3

The actual position of the παννυχίς within the Panathenaic calendar is controversial. Scholars mostly assume that it preceded the procession of the 28th of Hekatombaion; yet this assumption is entirely based on one passage from a fourth-century sacred law concerning the Smaller Panathenaia (*IG* II^3 447 lines 59–60 [cf. II^2 334]) where the procession seems to start in the wake of the παννυχίς: τοὺς δὲ ἱεροποιοὺς ... | ... ποεῖν τὴν πα[ννυχίδα] ὡς καλλίστην τῆι θεῶι καὶ τὴν πομπὴν πέμπε[ιν ἅμα ἡ]λίωι ἀνιόντι ('the religious officials ... are to make the all-night revel as fine as possible for the goddess and to conduct the procession at the rising of the sun').[63] Pritchett, however, argues that the παννυχίς took place the night following procession and sacrifices: at line 56 of the same inscription – he observes – the παννυχίς is mentioned not before but after the festival as such (περὶ τὴν ἑορτὴν καὶ εἰς παννυχίδα, 'for the festival and an all-night revel'); in analogous rites, furthermore, the nocturnal revel was a climactic ceremony that followed the sacrifice.[64] If Pritchett's suggestion is correct, this would mean there is a perfect correspondence between the sequence of the Panathenaic rituals and that of the events described in the stasimon. However, this is not strictly necessary: the above-mentioned passage of *Children of Heracles*, where the παννυχίς is mentioned after the sacrifices to Athena, either also reflects the precise order of events or proves that the precise position of this rite was not relevant to its recognition.[65] Furthermore, in the context of the narrative, the sequence 'παννυχίς – procession' would have made no sense, since the discovery of the horse is a completely unexpected event.

3. A hybrid perspective: Final remarks

As we have seen, in the first stasimon of *Trojan Women* various concomitant factors (the poetic tradition, choral projection and memories of the Panathenaia) were intended to encourage the assimilation of Trojan women's perspective on the part of the Athenian audience – with additional support for this assimilation provided in the parodos: the events of the capture of Troy, as transmitted by the epic tradition, could thus be perceived more vividly by the spectators, having been brought closer to their own experiences. It may be assumed, moreover, that other, extra-scenic factors heightened the impact of the dramatic performance. It is plausible, for example, that at the time of the staging of *Trojan Women* a bronze statue of the Trojan Horse, the Δούριος Ἵππος of Strongylion, already stood on the Acropolis, opposite the sanctuary of Artemis Brauronia.[66] A reference to extra-dramatic reality is certainly found in the third stasimon when the chorus mentions the Athenian Acropolis (ὄχθοις ἱεροῖς, 801), at the foot of which the play was staged.[67] Though, as pointed out at the outset of the paper, in conventional theatre such as that of Attica, the stage and real life remained clearly distinct.

In the third stasimon (799–859), we reach a sort of 'hybrid perspective',[68] which is to say a balanced blending of the perspectives of both the chorus and the audience. The first strophic pair of this complex ode focuses on the episode of the expedition against Troy led by Heracles and Telamon. The latter is solemnly addressed at the beginning of the stasimon:

μελισσοτρόφου Σαλαμῖνος ὦ βασιλεῦ Τελαμών,
νάσου περικύμονος οἰκήσας ἕδραν
τᾶς ἐπικεκλιμένας ὄχθοις ἱεροῖς, ἵν' ἐλαίας
πρῶτον ἔδειξε κλάδον γλαυκᾶς Ἀθάνα,
οὐράνιον στέφανον λιπαραῖσί <τε> κόσμον Ἀθάναις

O Telamon, king of bee-nurturing Salamis,
who dwelt in a wave-washed isle
that lies opposite the holy hill where the shoot
of the grey-green olive was first revealed by Athena,
a heavenly garland and a glory for gleaming Athens.

799–804

The chorus' focus immediately shifts from Salamis to Athens, which is praised with epinician terms and images (στέφανον, κόσμον).[69] Judging from its occurrences in Pindar and, especially, Aristophanes, the adjective 'gleaming' (λιπαραῖσι), applied to Athens, must have been a key term in Athenian civic imaginary.[70] Nevertheless, the chorus maintains a coherent Trojan identity despite this evocation of Athenian imagery. The ode creates a juxtaposition between Athens and Troy, which almost symmetrically share the first strophe and antistrophe. In the second strophic pair, the chorus exploits the exempla of Ganymede and Tithonus to emphasize the contrast between the destinies of Athens and Troy: Athens is blessed by the gift of the olive (801–2), whereas Troy was deserted by the gods.[71] The balance achieved in this stasimon, however, is a precarious one. Indeed, the figure of Athena provides here some sort of common ground between the two cities, and a possible assimilation of the two communities: although the goddess is mentioned here as a benevolent patroness who has adorned Athens through the gift of the olive tree, at this point of the play no one can ignore what she is capable of.

This is only a partial reading of *Trojan Women* through the choral songs punctuating the tragedy. Spectators and readers continued to sympathize with the Trojan women of this play beyond the fifth century, outside Athens, and independently of the chorus' performance: in a famous anecdote reported by Plutarch, for instance, the cruel tyrant of Pherae, Alexander, abruptly leaves a theatre where an actor was performing *Trojan Women* for fear of being seen by his fellow citizens 'weeping for the sufferings of Hecuba and Andromache'.[72] Further, an increasing number of studies offer an evaluation of Attic tragedy – and, specifically, of this play – as a Panhellenic rather than local phenomenon.[73] Throughout this chapter, I have tried to stress how the members of Euripides' first audience were expected to elaborate the meaning of the play actively with the choral songs serving a central role in that process.

Notes

1. I am especially grateful to Luigi Battezzato and Donald Mastronarde for reading and commenting on various versions of this paper. I also wish to thank Patrick Finglass, Anna

Magnetto, Glenn Most and Sheila Murnaghan for valuable criticism and suggestions, and the volume editors, C. W. Marshall and Hallie Marshall, for their insightful comments and several formal improvements; and Sergio Knipe for his careful proofreading of the English.

2. See especially Delebecque 1951: 255–62, Croally 1994: 232–4, Dué 2006: 108, 148, Rosenbloom 2006, Athanassaki 2018. Most scholars today accept the 'Melos interpretation' of the tragedy (e.g. Goff 2009: 33), even though it poses certain chronological difficulties (van Erp Taalman Kip 1987: cf. Mastronarde 2010: 77 n. 27) and challenges the inner coherence of the drama (Rabinowitz 2017: especially 209–10). For a rejection of the traditional historicist readings, see Kovacs 1997 and 2018: 2–16; J. Roisman 1997.

3. The symbolically representative character of the public was not invalidated by the presence of non-Attic spectators: e.g. Rosenbloom 2011: 359 ('The rhetoric of performance at the City Dionsysia addressed audiences as Athenians, identifying their interests with those of Athens and vice versa'). Cf. Taplin 1999: 48.

4. E.g. Hall 1989: 217–23, Croally 1994: 103–15, Gibert 2011: 387–8. Dué 2006: 116 acutely notes that, with *Trojan Women*, 'the Athenians can explore their own sorrows by witnessing the suffering of others'. The possibility that the Athenians were identified with the Trojans, however, is ruled out: 'Whereas [. . .] shortly after the Persian Wars Athens could identify with Troy as the city wrongfully sacked, the Athenians can now, after more than fifty years of empire, be equated with the Achaeans who did the sacking' (149).

5. See Ferrari 2000 and Dué 2006: ch. 3. On the episode of the sack of Athens at the hands of the Dioskouroi, who had come to Helen's rescue, see Anderson 1997: 97–101.

6. See, at least, Mastronarde 2010: 93–8 (on the dramatic and extra-dramatic factors that might have favoured the identification between audience and chorus), Bierl 2009: 47 (on choral self-referentiality), Nagy 2013 (on choral mimesis).

7. See e.g. Preston and de Waal 2002: 16 (with literature). On the peculiarity of ἔλεος compared to the modern notions of 'compassion' and 'sympathy'/'empathy', see, at least, Konstan 2001: ch. 2 ('the audience feels *for* the characters, not *with* them', cit. 72) and 2006: 213. Cf. LaCourse Munteanu 2011: 152 (pity is enacted 'through a mental process of inference rather than of projection').

8. Translation by Freese. For examples of the use of this concept in Greek poetry, see LaCourse Munteanu 2011: 122–5.

9. Konstan 2001: 128–36 (cit. 131). An explanation can thus be offered for why the similarity argument is only applied to fear in *Poetics* (1453a5–6): see Konstan 1999 (with further discussion and literature).

10. E.g. Finkelberg 2006: 21–3, discussing the case of Phrynichus, who was sanctioned for having brought the public face to face with 'its own ills' (οἰκήια κακά, Hdt. 6.21).

11. These and other considerations are advanced in Finkelberg 2006: 21–2.

12. On Euripides' marginalization of the choral voice, see Mastronarde 2010: 98–152.

13. E.g. Neitzel 1967: 64, Sienkiewicz 1978: 85, Murnaghan 2017: 415.

14. Mastronarde 2010: 124–5.

15. On choral projection in *Trojan Women*, see Battezzato 2005, Fanfani 2017 and 2018, Weiss 2018: ch. 3. In general, see Henrichs 1996.

16. The Euripides quotations are from Diggle's OCT edition. The translations are by Kovacs (with slight modifications).

17. See e.g. Panagl 1972 and Bers 1997: 23–115 (102–15 on lyrics).

18. Panagl 1972: 11 raises the problem of the interpretation of λεώς: 'people', but also 'army' (e.g. in *Tr.* 30: Θεσσαλὸς λεώς). What clarifies the meaning of the term here, however, is Euripides'

emphasis on the collective involvement of the population of Troy (e.g. 527–8). Indeed, if we wished to understand λεώς in a military sense, we would have to improperly assign it the meaning of 'watchmen'.

19. The closest parallel seems to be in the first stasimon of Aeschylus' *Suppliants* (583–8); a discussion and defence of the *oratio recta* is found in Bers 1997: 29 with n. 11. In this case, however, the idea is not that of a people acting in unison, but merely of a sort of *vox populi* proclaiming Epaphus' divine origin. In *Trojan Women*, another instance of direct speech occurs in the third stasimon (1091–9), where – at least in theory – we have again a collective speaker, the 'crowd of children' (τέκνων . . . πλῆθος, 1089): see Lee 1976: 252 against Parmentier's βοᾷ κόρα at 1091. Nevertheless, as suggested by the first-person singular, 'this is the lament of one girl' (Kovacs 2018: 298 [on lines 1091–2]) rather than the voice of an organic community.

20. See Panagl 1972: 12 and Lee 1976: 166.

21. See e.g. Higbie 1997. On Sophocles' *Ajax*, see Scodel 2006.

22. That is to say, 'under divine protection': Lee 1976: 252 with LSJ *s.v.* II.3 (frequently used for places).

23. Cf. the analysis by Athanassaki 2018: 98–9.

24. In general, see Mastronarde 2010: 143.

25. Isolated mentions of Athens in a stasimon do not count here. The two closest cases would seem to be provided by *Oedipus at Colonus* and *Medea*, where Athens is extensively praised, albeit through a single choral intervention – respectively in the first (*OC* 668–719) and third stasimon (*Med.* 824–65). Nevertheless, even in *Medea*'s case, the link with the setting is evident, since the encomium takes the previous Aegeus scene as its starting point and is consistent with the Corinthian identity of the chorus: see Mastronarde 2002: 304–5.

26. *Schol. vet.* E. *Tr.* 31 (i.349.3–6 Schwartz). *Pace* Lee 1976: 70 (on line 31), what is regarded as encomiastic is not the mere mention of the Theseids but rather their participation in the distribution of the spoils: ἔνιοι ταῦτά φασι πρὸς χάριν εἰρῆσθαι· μηδὲν γὰρ εἰληφέναι [ἐκ] τοὺς περὶ Ἀκάμαντα καὶ Δημοφῶντα ἐκ τῶν λαφύρων ἀλλὰ μόνην τὴν Αἴθραν κτλ. ('some say that these words are pronounced in order to gratify [the Athenians], for [they state that] Acamas and Demophon with their companions had taken nothing from the spoils, but only Aethra [their grandmother] . . .'). On the scholium, see Kovacs 2018: 129 (on line 31).

27. Dué 2006: 138.

28. As acknowledged by Dué 2006: 150. Cf. Kovacs 1997: 163–4 and 2018: 10–11; J. Roisman 1997: 43–4.

29. Strictly speaking, the chorus women cannot be assigned to the Athenians: the Theseids receive their prisoners (εἴληχ', 31) when the latter are still 'unallotted' (ἄκληροι, 32). This, like other information (e.g. the storm awaiting the Greek fleet), is only known to the two deities of the prologue, Poseidon and Athena. The chorus would thus have struck any spectators aware of this detail as even more pitiful.

30. It is worth noting that the Thessalians had already been mentioned alongside the Theseids in the prologue (Θεσσαλὸς λεώς 29). As pointed out by Kovacs 2018: 161 (on lines 214–7), the praise of Thessaly 'is mostly plausibly interpreted as a compliment to some of Athens' fifth-century allies'.

31. See, at least, Westlake 1953 (on the historical aspects) and Gibert 2011: 389–90, 398 (on the ideological aspects and the recent debate).

32. So, e.g., Westlake 1953: 190 (the aim of this ode would be 'to win the favour of [Euripides'] audience by echoing its current opinions').

33. E.g. Lee 1976: 102. Kovacs 2018: 161 (on lines 220–3) highlights the 'strong ties' between Athens and some Sicilian cities.

34. A similar argument may apply to the desire to take part in the rites held in honour of Artemis on Delos (*Hec.* 455–65): on the relevance of these celebrations for the civic ideology of Athens, see especially Wilson 2000: 44–6.

35. Battezzato 2016: 150–1 (cit. 151).

36. To do this, the chorus must ignore the episode of the first sack of Troy at the hands of Heracles: Battezzato 2016: 151–2.

37. On the revealing dresses of Spartan women, see Battezzato 2018: 199 (on *Hec.* 934). C. W. Marshall has suggested to me that it may not be an unmotivated or unexpected leap to associate their immodest clothing with that of Spartan women, but rather they might be thinking of the clothing of the only Spartan woman that they have ever seen, Helen.

38. Battezzato 2016: 151.

39. For the concept of ritual memory (applied to Euripides' *Children of Heracles*), see Taddei 2014.

40. In *Od.* 8.493, Epeius builds the horse 'with Athena's help' (σὺν Ἀθήνῃ), but what that help actually consists of remains dubious: Hainsworth (in Heubeck et al. 1988: 397) argues for a figurative help: cf. *Il.* 15.410–2. However, Athena offers very concrete help in *Ilias parva* (*arg.* 1.14 Bernabé: καὶ Ἐπειὸς κατ᾽ Ἀθηνᾶς προαίρεσιν τὸν δούρειον ἵππον κατασκευάζει) and Stesichorus (ἀνὴρ | θ]εᾶς ἰ[ό]τατι δαεὶς σεμν[ᾶς Ἀθάνας] | μέτ[ρα] τε καὶ σοφίαν; fr. 100.10–12 Finglass): see West 2013: 193–4 and Finglass 2013: especially 7–10, 13–14.

41. Cf. Papadopoulou 2001: 299–301, who stresses 'the double role of Athena in Troy' (cit. 299). See, e.g., *Tr.* 10 (μηχαναῖσι Παλλάδος), 46–7 (εἴ σε μὴ διώλεσεν | Παλλὰς Διὸς παῖς, ἦσθ᾽ ἂν ἐν βάθροις ἔτι), 72 (καὶ μὴν ἐπερσάν γ᾽ Ἴλιον τῶι σῶι σθένει). Hera is mentioned as co-responsible only at line 24 (συνεξεῖλον). If, at line 540, one reads with the Aldine edition φόνια (πατρί[δι), the ground of Athena's sanctuary is even called 'bloody/homicide for the fatherland'; but the dative πατρίδι remains problematic: see Diggle 1981: 63–4, who suggests φονέα ('killer,' referring to the horse), as printed in his OCT; the conjecture is approved by Kovacs 2018: 212–13.

42. On the priestess, see Kirk 1990: 200: 'certainly 300 [τὴν γὰρ Τρῶες ἔθηκαν Ἀθηναίης ἱέρειαν] appears to emphasize the idea of public choice.' The inconsistency between 6.300 and 6.89 (it is not Theano but Hecuba who is expected to lead the procession) suggests a change in religious practices: Kirk 1990: 165. On the peplos, see Karanika 2001: 285–7.

43. Cf. Kovacs 2018: 211 (on line 526): 'The Trojans thought of their goddess as Trojan Athena [...], equivalent to Athena Polias for Athenians.' The use of this epithet in connection with Athena is attested for the fifth-century Troad in Hdt. 7.43: Lee 1976: 166.

44. The horse is offered to Athena in the *Ilioupersis* epic (*arg.* 5 Bernabé: οἱ δὲ ἱερὸν αὐτὸν ἔφασαν δεῖν τῇ Ἀθηνᾷ ἀνατεθῆναι) and, presumably, in Stesichorus' *Sack of Troy* (the text of fr. 103 has many gaps): see Davies and Finglass 2014: 424 (on line 33).

45. LSJ *s.v.* I.1. The interpretation 'lift up, raise' (e.g. S. *Ph.* 866: LSJ *s.v.* I.6) is to be excluded on the basis of the dative Ἰλιάδι Διογενεῖ κόραι: the horse must not only be 'raised', but moved to the temple of Athena.

46. A comparison between the two versions is provided in Davies and Finglass 2014: 396–7, 404.

47. On the pairing, see Kovacs 2018: 211. It is difficult to determine to what extent this divergence in the narrative can be ascribed to Euripides. Even in Virgil's version the bringing in of the horse is accompanied by religious manifestations: *pueri circum innuptaeque puellae | sacra canunt funemque manu contingere gaudent* (*Aen.* 2.238–9). Horsfall 2008: 214 sees 'a touch of Eurip(ides) here'. On these images in the Roman religious tradition, see Kovacs 2018: 213–14.

48. See e.g. Mansfield 1985 and Sourvinou-Inwood 2011: 262–311.

49. Our source is Thuc. 6.57.1–3 (Hipparchus is killed when the Panathenaic procession is still outside, in the so-called Keramikos, ἔξω ἐν τῷ Κεραμεικῷ καλουμένῳ): cf. Thuc. 1.20.1 and *Ath. Pol.* 18.3, where Hipparchus is killed when the procession reaches the Leokoreion, in the agora. Exhaustive discussion in Shear 2001: 122–4 and ch. 8.

50. The passage is listed, alongside *Tr.* 512, in LSJ *s.v.* ἀνάγω, I.1.

51. See e.g. Neils 1996a, especially 182–90.

52. Slabs 7–8 (drawing by Jacques Carrey, 1674): Brommer 1979: 32 (fig. 20), 61.

53. On the epic antecedents and implications of the expression, see Sansone 2009: 198–9.

54. E.g. Sansone 2009: 200–2, who argues that Euripides is rereading the episode of the testing of the troops in *Iliad* 2. On lines 537–8, see Kovacs 2018: 212.

55. E.g. Parker 2007: 265, who quotes E. *Hec.* 466–74, *IT* 222–4; Ar. *Eq.* 566–8.

56. The use of the Panathenaic ship is dated back to the fifth century by Mansfield 1985: 68–78 (cf. Parke 1977: 39). This hypothesis is cogently ruled out by Shear 2001: 143–55 (mostly on the basis of epigraphical evidence). A balanced discussion and further bibliography can be found in Wachsmann 2012: 239.

57. Cf., e.g., Parke 1977: 40–1. On the symbolism in this scene, see especially Sourvinou-Inwood 2011: 284–307.

58. Orth 2009: 18–20; Fiorentini 2017: 1–3.

59. On the second title, see Orth 2009: 144 and Fiorentini 2017: 123–4. The other two possible candidates are Pausanias, king of the Macedonians in 394/3, and the last Thessalian lover of Lais: see the thorough discussions in Orth 2009: 145–8 and Fiorentini 2017: 125–6, who definitely accept the identification with Agathon's lover. (But even if we were to opt for one of the alternative identifications, the dating would be roughly the same.) On Agathon's date of death, see e.g. Lévêque 1955: 73–7.

60. Cf. the passages quoted in Orth 2009: 162 and Fiorentini 2017: 139.

61. Cf. Parker 2007: 262: 'the recurrent use of nautical language [. . .] is odd if the vehicle was not already a real or at least symbolic ship.'

62. An in-depth discussion of this passage is to be found in Taddei 2014: 216–22. Taddei convincingly argues that the evoking of the Panathenaic rites and the reference to the Acropolis was intended to trigger the ritual memory of the Athenian public (cit. 221).

63. E.g. Tracy 1991: 147 and Parker 2007: 257. On the inscription in general, see Rhodes and Osborne 2003: 396–402 (nr. 81) and Lambert 2012: 82–5 (nr. 7). Translations by Lambert (*Attic Inscriptions Online*).

64. Pritchett 1987, followed by Shear 2001: 83–4. Pritchett quotes, e.g., Pl. *R.* 1.328a (Bendideia) and *IG* II² 974 (cf. *SEG* 18.26) (Asklepieia). Cf. Parker 2007: 257.

65. Wilkins 1993: 151–2 (on *Heracl.* 782–3) suggests that '[t]he sequence of rites in the stanza (hecatomb, komos and choruses, pannychis) reverses the order of the Panathenaia, and lays stress on the pannychis', which ends up at the end of the stasimon.

66. The work was still to be found there at the time of Pausanias, who provides a description of it (1.23.8). The use of the Attic alphabet in the dedicatory inscription (*IG* I³ 895) suggests 403/2 as a possible *terminus ante quem*. See especially Stieber 2011: 185–92. Stieber hypothesizes that Euripides is explicitly alluding to the work of art. Her thesis, however, is not a very convincing one: (1) *Tr.* 13–14 remains dramaturgically problematic and must therefore be expunged (Lee 1976: 68 and Kovacs 2018: 126–7); (2) while ornate, the

horse described in the stasimon is never presented – either directly or indirectly – as a bronze one.

67. Cf. *Heracl.* 781 and the observations in Taddei 2014: 221.

68. This expression is borrowed from Mastronarde 2010: 143 (where it serves a different function).

69. Cf., at least, Pind. *O.* 3.13 (κόσμον ἐλαίας), 8.82–3 (λιπαρὸν | κόσμον), 11.13 (κόσμον ἐπὶ στεφάνῳ ... ἐλαίας) with Verdenius 1997: 18.

70. Pind. *N.* 4.18, *I.* 2.20, fr. 76 S-M, *O.* 13.111 (λιπαρός referred to Marathon); Ar. *Ach.* 640. See Lee 1976: 212, Olson 2002: 238, Bagordo 2003: 207–9, and Kovacs 2018: 253.

71. Cf. Lee 1976: 209: this ode 'intensifies the sympathy we feel for Troy'. For an analysis of the ode, see Burnett 1977 and Kovacs 2018: 251.

72. Plut. *Pel.* 29.9–11 (quoted and discussed by Dué 2006: 165).

73. On Euripides' *Hecuba* and *Trojan Women*, see especially Visvardi 2011. See also Easterling 1994, Taplin 1999, Rosenbloom 2011.

CHAPTER 8
CHORAL MIRRORING IN EURIPIDES' *PHAETHON*
Rosa Andújar

With a decades-long concealed paternity, a flaming flying chariot and a charred corpse, the myth of Phaethon, son of the god Helios, is among antiquity's most sensational narratives.[1] The surviving fragments of the eponymous tragedy suggest that Euripides continued to enhance the myth's ability to astound.[2] Not only does the tragedian set his drama on the very day in which Phaethon dies after steering his father's fiery chariot, but he additionally stages Phaethon's death on his wedding day, which is furthermore the same day in which the young man, the son of the nymph Clymene, learns of his true paternity: namely, Phaethon discovers that his father is not Merops, king of Ethiopia, as he had been previously raised to believe. Extraordinarily for a fragmentary fifth-century tragedy, we know a great deal about its chorus, which consists of a group of slave women, since two of the play's principal fragments feature choral lyric: one fragment contains the parodos (F 773 *TrGF*[5.2] = *Phaethon* 53–108) and another (F 781 *TrGF*[5.2]) preserves not only an astrophic ode by the chorus (*Phaethon* 270–83) but also a wedding song sung by a secondary chorus in the direct presence of the main chorus (*Phaethon* 214–51).[3]

In this chapter, I examine *Phaethon* 214–51, the extraordinary scene that is precipitated by the performance of this secondary chorus which celebrates Phaethon's nuptials in the immediate aftermath of the arrival of his smouldering body onstage. As I illustrate, their song not only interrupts and displaces the main chorus' initial reactions to Phaethon's death, but it also forces the main chorus (as well as the viewing audience) to witness a wedding song at the most inappropriate moment. Through this act of what I call 'choral mirroring', Euripides presents both the internal and external viewing audiences with an alternative and impossible reality. My discussion centres on the implications of this scene for our understanding of tragic chorality, as Euripides not only achieves this counterfactual reality by multiplying the number of choral performers onstage, but he also reveals a novel dynamic based on the juxtaposition of two collectives with opposed and incompatible ritual motives. As I furthermore contend, the counterfactual reality that is enacted by the secondary chorus and silently witnessed by the main chorus provides a compelling contrast to the extreme mourning that is typically provoked by Phaethon's death in the broader mythical tradition.

My chapter has two main parts. I first provide a brief overview of secondary choruses in extant tragedy in order to highlight the manner in which the actions of the two choruses in Euripides' *Phaethon* deviate from those found in other plays. I then offer an analysis of the scene that is presented in *Phaethon* 214–51. In both cases my larger aim is to enhance our overall understanding of tragic chorality, drawing particular attention to the versatility and dynamism of the tragic chorus in performance.[4]

Secondary choruses in Greek tragedy

In order to understand the extraordinary nature of the scene found in *Phaethon* 214–51, we must first consider the appearance and role of secondary or subsidiary choruses in extant tragedy.[5] The examples of tragic secondary collectives can generally be divided into two types: (1) a secondary chorus that is brought onstage to perform a single ritual song, typically as they accompany one of the actors,[6] and (2) a chorus that engages and interacts with the main chorus, usually speaking or singing antiphonally with them.[7] Many such moments involve a significant increase in the number of choral performers onstage.[8] This is certainly the case in the *Suppliants* of both Aeschylus and Euripides, examples of the latter type in which a subsidiary chorus interacts with the main chorus of the tragedy. In Aeschylus' play, the final lyrics consist of a dialogue between the main chorus of the Danaids and a secondary chorus whose identity is contested; the play may have also featured a third chorus of Egyptian soldiers who accompany the herald.[9] Euripides' *Suppliants* stages an impressive *thrēnos* between the main chorus of the mothers of the Seven and an additional chorus of their grandchildren in order to create a large collective of mourners.[10] Most surviving examples, including Euripides' *Phaethon*, however, typically consist of the former case, that is, a secondary chorus singing a stand-alone song without any interaction with the main chorus, usually as the attendant of an actor arriving onstage. Such an involvement might be described as fleeting at best, but, as I illustrate in the following overview, such ephemeral choruses can nevertheless have great dramatic impact.[11]

One of the most notable secondary choruses is the chorus of escorts at the end of Aeschylus' *Eumenides*. The *Eumenides* ends with a short ode consisting of two strophic pairs sung by this additional chorus of escorts (προπομποί) as they guide the main chorus of the Eumenides in a triumphant procession (*Eumenides* 1033–47). In the first strophe (lines 1033–5), this secondary collective carefully delineates the various groups that are present onstage: not only is the main chorus addressed, the Eumenides, who are referred to as 'great, proud children of the night' (μεγάλαι φιλότιμοι | Νυκτὸς παῖδες, 1033–4), but this secondary chorus also refer to themselves as escorts (πομπᾶι, 1034) and also to a *third* group consisting of the inhabitants of the land (χωρῖται, 1035).[12] The second antistrophe (1045–7) additionally encourages Athena's citizens (Παλλάδος ἀστοῖς, 1045) to join the procession and song (specifically, via the command 'to shout joyously', ὀλολύξατε, at 1047). In this manner this secondary chorus not only draws attention to the many collectives onstage, but it additionally celebrates the entire city as a joint community engaged together in song. In this scene the secondary chorus thus appears in order to direct a spectacular final procession, one involving so many performers that it can be said to replicate a large festival, perhaps even the Panatheneia.[13]

The identity of this secondary group of escorts has previously been disputed by scholars. A scholion in Laurentian manuscripts M and F at line 1032 indicates that the singers were women – as indicated by the female definite article modifying the noun 'escort' (**αἱ** προπομποί, my emphasis) – the attendants of the goddess Athena which are briefly alluded to in the text at line 1004: 'by the sacred light of these escorts' (πρὸς φῶς ἱερὸν τῶνδε προπομπῶν).[14] Oliver Taplin, however, posits that this group of escorts consisted of the (male) jurors of the Areopagus, as they were a group of extras of about the right size already present onstage.[15] His main objection to having a separate chorus of female escorts consists of the lack of introduction in the text, where the group is mentioned in a passing reference by the goddess as the torch bearers in line 1004.[16] Despite the absence of a proper introduction, and regardless of who they might have been, it is clear that a second collective was present onstage and that they were differentiated from the main chorus of the Eumenides. Rather than debating the identity of this chorus, I would like instead to accentuate the impact of this secondary chorus, whose mere presence transforms the stage into a space teeming with a large number of singing performers. When we consider the fact that other Aeschylean plays also end with large processional endings likewise involving large groups, such a crowd at the end of the *Oresteia* trilogy is not surprising.[17] In fact, the presence of such a choral multitude precisely at a play's close creates a grand musical spectacle, one that ultimately impacts our understanding of the play, and in the case of the *Oresteia*, the entire trilogy. For the end of *Eumenides*, such a celebration featuring multiple choruses (especially a secondary chorus bearing torches) stands in stark contrast to the opening of *Agamemnon,* which began with a lone figure as he desperately awaits a flame.

In the surviving work of Euripides, however, the presence of such collectives appears to be less spectacular and more transient, as typically secondary choruses appear accompanying an actor in order to sing one song, after which they promptly disappear.[18] The most prominent example of a Euripidean secondary chorus can be found in *Hippolytus* 58–71, immediately after Aphrodite's prologue, when Hippolytus appears with a chorus of attendants. Unlike the secondary group in *Eumenides* which is not properly introduced, this collective accompanying Hippolytus is prominently announced by the departing goddess:

πολὺς δ' ἅμ' αὐτῷ προσπόλων ὀπισθόπους
κῶμος λέλακεν, Ἄρτεμιν τιμῶν θεὰν
ὕμνοισιν.

A great throng of his servants treads close at his heels,
as a band they shout, joining him in singing the
praises of the goddess Artemis.

54–6[19]

The goddess draws attention to the band of attendants, a singing collective which is closely identified with Hippolytus.[20] Here, they sing a hymn to Artemis, exiting well before the entrance of the main chorus consisting of women of Troezen and thus avoiding the choral multitude that is seen in Aeschylus' *Eumenides*. Though their involvement is only momentary, their presence and, in particular, their ritual song effectively underline Hippolytus' special relationship with the goddess of hunting.

This remarkable moment, furthermore, provides testimony for two additional secondary choruses in Euripidean theatre. Commenting on the presence of this additional chorus in *Hippolytus*, a scholiast compares similar situations in the fragmentary plays *Alexander* and *Antiope*:

> (Hippolytus' entrance at *Hipp.* 58ff. seems to have been accompanied by a secondary chorus of huntsmen.) ἕτεροί εἰσι τοῦ χοροῦ, καθάπερ ἐν τῷ Ἀλεξάνδρῳ οἱ ποιμένες. ἐνταῦθα μὲν οὖν δύναται προαποχρήσασθαι τοῖς ἀπὸ τοῦ χοροῦ, ἐκεῖ δὲ συνεστῶτος τοῦ χοροῦ ἐπεισάγει τοιοῦτο ἄθροισμα, ὡς καὶ ἐν τῇ Ἀντιόπῃ δύο χοροὺς εἰσάγει, τόν τε τῶν Ἀθηναίων γερόντων διόλου καὶ τὸν μετὰ Δίρκης.

> (The huntsmen who enter with Hippolytus at *Hipp.* 58ff.) are different from the chorus, like the herdsmen in *Alexander*. Notice that here (in *Hippolytus*) Euripides can use some of the chorus-members in advance (i.e. before the entrance of the full chorus), whereas in *Alexander* he brings on this group with the (main) chorus already present, as he also introduces two choruses in *Antiope*, the one comprising the old Athenians generally and the one with Dirce.

> Schol. Eur. Hipp. 58[21]

This evidence, though clear, is hard to corroborate, given the lack of surviving text in both cases. Nevertheless, scholars have speculated about the role of these alleged secondary choruses. For *Antiope*, scholars have proposed that the secondary chorus that the scholiast claims is associated with Dirce must be a chorus of maenads, for the simple reason that Hyginus' *Fabulae* mentions that Dirce is possessed by Dionysus.[22] This brief remark suggesting a Bacchic possession leads to the assumption that the play featured a scene involving Dirce and a chorus of maenads singing a hymn to Dionysus, which would certainly add a ritual touch to the drama.[23] If we combine the evidence from the scholiast to *Hippolytus* 58 above, as well as the details revealed in Hyginus' summary, we can safely assume that the scene of Dirce's possession would have probably taken place in the presence of the main chorus, as it was unlikely that the play opened with such a scene (i.e. that it would have occurred before the parodos).

With the *Alexander*, in contrast, we are on slightly more stable ground. The discovery of the play's hypothesis in an Oxyrhynchus papyrus confirms that there was likely a second group of shepherds present in addition to the main chorus:

> οἱ δ' ἄλλοι νομεῖς διὰ [τ]ὴν ὑπερήφανον
> συμβίωσιν [δ]ήσαντες ἐπ[ὶ] Πρίαμον ἀνήγα-
> γον αὐτόν·

> The other shepherds, because of his arrogant
> behaviour towards them, bound and brought
> him before Priam.[24]

> P. Oxy. 3650, 15–17

This brief summary reveals only the identity of this secondary chorus, as well as the fact that they bring Alexander before Priam. Crucially, it does not give any particular clues as to whether they were tied to a particular ritual function, as in the previous examples.[25] The scant surviving evidence additionally does not indicate whether this supplementary chorus of shepherds actually sang, as there are no any surviving fragments from the scene in question. It would be difficult, however, to imagine a large collective which does not sing after it is summoned onstage. Nevertheless, from the hypothesis it can be assumed that this group at the very least interacted with Priam and Alexander; the contact between this subsidiary collective and the play's main characters would have, at the very least, impacted the course of the drama, if not propelled a key scene. If we therefore accept the testimony of the scholiast to *Hippolytus*, both *Antiope* and *Alexander* appear to have featured secondary choruses which shared the stage with the main chorus, a feat which would create, albeit briefly, a choral multitude. Whether they sang or not, this choral crowd would have dominated the viewing audience's visual horizon for the duration of that scene, regardless of its brevity. These multitudes previously have been seen as a sign of the presumed spectacular nature of Aeschylean theatre, lavish with extravagant stagecraft and effects, which Oliver Taplin's seminal work has partly debunked.[26] For Euripides, who employs such crowds for only single scenes, the effect appears to be more tempered. In any case, a secondary chorus, no matter how fleeting its presence, has the potential to enhance both the dramatic effect and ritual mood of a play, all while accentuating the complexity and richness of the tragic chorus which can momentarily expand in order to accommodate supplementary collectives.

The secondary chorus in Euripides' *Phaethon*

Having given a brief overview of secondary choruses in tragedy, I now wish to focus on one of the most fascinating examples of the phenomenon, one which illustrates that, despite their fleeting nature, Euripidean secondary choruses can nevertheless have a spectacular effect. As I contend, the secondary chorus found in Euripides' *Phaethon* shows that a subsidiary collective can do much more than simply heighten the ritual mood of a drama as in *Hippolytus* and potentially *Antiope*, or to bring the drama to a triumphant close as in *Eumenides*. This subsidiary collective not only shares the same dramatic space as the main chorus, creating a choral multitude, but additionally performs a counterfactual reality before them. In this scene Euripides produces a striking visual tableau: a secondary collective which enacts an impossible reality before the paralysed main chorus which is forced to witness, silently, an alternative version of itself.

In order to understand why the main chorus is stunned into silence by the performance of a subsidiary chorus, we must first consider the parodos of the play (F 773 *TrGF*[5.2] = *Phaethon* 53–108), the scene when the chorus first appears onstage.[27] Prior to their entry, Phaethon himself announces their identity as the domestic workers who labour in his father's palace:

ἀλλ᾽ ἕρπ᾽ ἐς οἴκους· καὶ γὰρ αἵδ᾽ ἔξω **δόμων**
δμῳαὶ περῶσιν, αἵ πατρὸς κατὰ σταθμὰ

σαίρουσι **δῶμα** καὶ **δόμων** κειμήλια
καθ’ ἡμέραν φοιβῶσι κἀπιχωρίοις
ὀσμαῖσι θυμιῶσιν εἰσόδους **δόμων**.

But come into the house, for here are the slave girls coming out from it, who sweep the house in my father’s palace; they cleanse the house’s laid-up things daily and fume the house-entrances with native scents.[28]

54–8

Whereas this lengthy description of the entering chorus has been previously cited in discussions of the play’s entrances and staging,[29] here I wish to emphasize the unambiguous manner in which their role and identity as domestic cleaners is described. Throughout, Phaethon additionally emphasizes the intimate connection that this female collective has to the house, as can be seen by the manner in which he repeats the word δῶμα (‘house’) and its variants (which I have highlighted above). From the outset of the play, both their social position and function are clear.

The entry song of this female servant chorus at 63–101, which follows Phaethon’s introduction, can be roughly divided into two distinct parts. To begin, the first strophic pair and second strophe (63–78 and 79–86) depict an impressive soundscape of morning activities, ranging from birdsong (67–70) to pipes (71) and the tuneful swan (78), as well as the wind (80), and the cries of crewmen embarking on a voyage (82). These musical sounds contribute to what Collard, Cropp and Lee describe as ‘small scenes collected under the title “Now it is dawn”, resembling ‘an active and idealized but still everyday landscape of the kind animating so many Renaissance and later paintings’.[30] In the second part of the song, the chorus swiftly moves away from descriptions of the soundscape of morning to a preview of the play’s actual soundscape, as the chorus articulates their particular desire to sing at their master’s wedding. Beginning in the second antistrophe, they dismiss the pastoral activities which had previously served as the focus of their song as ‘the concerns of others’ (τὰ μὲν οὖν ἑτέροισι μέριμνα πέλει, 87), and instead emphasize their own ‘duty and desire to sing in honour of their master’s wedding’ (κόσμον δ’ ὑμεναίων δεσποσύνων | ἐμὲ καὶ τὸ δίκαιον ἄγει καὶ ἔρως | ὑμνεῖν, 88–90). In the epode, they continue to accentuate both their desire for the wedding and their future crucial role as wedding singers:

ὁρίζεται δὲ τόδε φάος γάμων τέλει,   95
τὸ δή ποτ’ εὐχαῖς ἐγὼ
λισσομένα προσέβαν ὑμέναιον ἀεῖσαι
φίλον φίλων δεσποτᾶν·
θεὸς ἔδωκε, χρόνος ἔκρανε
λέχος ἐμοῖσιν ἀρχέταις.   100
ἴτω τελεία γάμων ἀοιδά.

The day is marked out for the marriage celebration, the day which I begged for long ago in my prayers; I have come forward to sing the wedding hymn for my dear master. God has willed, time fulfilled, marriage for my rulers. Let the song begin to celebrate the marriage!

95–101

The language employed implies not only the long-awaited culmination of the marriage but also the rite itself (e.g. τέλει at 95). Line 99, in particular, possesses a solemn liturgical thrust; according to the translators, the phrase 'God has willed, time fulfilled' replicates 'the "liturgical" parallelism of sense, syntax, sound and metre' of the original verse in Greek θεὸς ἔδωκε, χρόνος ἔκρανε.[31] The final line of the song (101) ends with a call to begin the song to celebrate the marriage, with τελεία echoing τέλει from the epode's opening at 95, creating an emphatic repetition of the word 'rite' (τέλος) at the very end of the epode. At the close of the chorus' opening song, it is therefore strongly suggested that the main chorus will play a role in the celebration of marriage, specifically through song.

Soon after, however, this expectation that the chorus might sing a wedding hymn vanishes as the charred corpse of Phaethon is brought onstage. Fragment 781 *TrGF*[5.2] begins with the tail end of Clymene's reactions after being confronted with the body of her son. Despite their fragmentary beginning, lines 214–16 reveal not only the nymph's distress but also the presence of Phaethon's dead body onstage.[32] Suddenly, Clymene changes the focus of her distressed reaction to her son's death as she sees her husband Merops approaching the stage with a group of virgins who will sing the wedding hymn: 'my husband, my husband is almost here leading the maiden girls in singing the wedding music' (πόσις πόσις μοι πλησίον γαμηλίους | μολπὰς ἀϋτεῖ παρθένοις ἡγούμενος, 217–18). This prompts the nymph to ask the chorus to take the body into the house (216) and to mop up any blood that might have fallen from the corpse (οὐ σταλαγμὸν ἐξομόρξετε, | εἴ πού τίς ἐστιν αἵματος χαμαὶ πεσών; 219–20). From her urgent instructions and repeated calls for haste we can assume two things: first that Merops is unaware of Phaethon's death, but also that the king still tragically believes him to be his son.

At this point, Clymene presumably leaves the stage with the body (as indicated by lines 221–3 where she states she will hide him inside)[33] before the merry crowd's arrival. The virgins then sing a type of wedding song consisting of a single strophic pair:

ΠΑΡΘΕΝΟΙ	CHORUS OF MAIDENS
στρ. Ὑμὴν Ὑμήν.	Hymen, Hymen!
τὰν Διὸς οὐρανίαν ἀείδομεν,	We sing to honour Zeus' daughter in the
τὰν ἐρώτων πότνιαν, τὰν παρθένοις	sky, mistress of loves, wedding-maker
γαμήλιον Ἀφροδίταν. 230	for maiden girls, Aphrodite.
πότνια, σοὶ τάδ' ἐγὼ νυμφεῖ' ἀείδω,	Mistress, for you I sing this bridal song,
Κύπρι θεῶν καλλίστα,	Cypris most beautiful of gods,
τῶι τε νεόζυγι σῶι	and for your boy newly-wed
πώλωι τὸν ἐν αἰθέρι κρύπτεις,	whom you hide in the heaven,
σῶν γάμων γένναν· 235	offspring of your marriage;

ἀντ. ἃ τὸν μέγαν   you who will make the marriage
       τᾶσδε πόλεως βασιλῆ νυμφεύεαι   for the great king of this city,
       ἀστερωποῖσιν δόμοισι χρυσέοις   our ruler dear to the starry golden palace!
       ἀρχὸν φίλον Ἀφροδίτα·   Aphrodite!
       ὦ μάκαρ, ὦ βασιλεὺς   Oh blessed man, oh greater still
            μείζων ἔτ' ὄλβον,   than
       ὃς θεὰν κηδεύσεις   241   king in your happiness! You will be
       καὶ μόνος ἀθανάτων   marriage-kin to a goddess and be sung
       γαμβρὸς δι' ἀπείρονα γαῖαν   throughout the boundless earth
       θνατὸς ὑμνήσηι.   as the only mortal father of a groom
                                                   for immortals.

Despite containing the 'hymenaios' tag in its opening line (227) and *makarismos* (240), this hymn does not correspond with anything in actual Greek practice, as James Diggle points out, 'neither with the *hymenaeus* sung during the procession which accompanied the bride to her husband's home nor with the *epithalamion* which was sung outside the marriage-chamber'.[34] Instead of taking place at the bride's house, this particular hymn is sung at the home of the groom.[35] Rather than attempting to determine the nature of this wedding song,[36] I am instead concerned with the larger implications of this scene if we consider the likely possibility that the main chorus stayed to witness this song. Some commentators believed that the main chorus followed Clymene inside the house while this song was taking place,[37] but I agree with Diggle and others who assert that the collective remains onstage to witness this wedding hymn sung by Merops' accompanying chorus.[38] After all, there is no indication that they leave the scene, and additionally the main chorus' panicked astrophic outburst at 270–83 only makes sense if they had remained.[39]

If they do stay, then the presence of the two choruses produces an indelible visual: the viewing audience would have been confronted by at least twenty-four individuals (assuming the chorus consisted of at least twelve members), a definite choral multitude, but one in which half of its members are presumably silent and motionless as they observe a different version of themselves sing a wedding song.[40] In this way, the secondary chorus of virgins is not only performing before the main chorus, but also in spite of them, as the ritual song that this secondary collective sings stands in strong dramatic contrast to the activity of the main chorus, who had just been wiping up the blood and helping Clymene hide the body, a chorus which had, furthermore, articulated its fervent desire precisely to sing the wedding song at the outset of the play. This secondary chorus thus allows the viewing audience to witness and experience two realities at the same time: the tragic present and a counterfactual reality in which a living Phaethon is celebrated as bridegroom. The addresses in the future tense to the dead Phaethon in lines 241 ('you will be marriage kin', κηδεύσεις) and 244 ('you will be sung', ὑμνήσηι) are particularly poignant: here, the chorus of virgins unwittingly addresses him as blessed and as the happy subject of song. In this manner Euripides utilizes the secondary chorus to present his audience with a twisted choral mirror, depicting an impossible reality.

Equally striking in this scene is the suppression of a mourning song by the main chorus precisely through the imposition of the wedding song by the secondary collective. This goes beyond the manner in which tragedians tend to juxtapose weddings and funerals, as the work of Richard Seaford and Rush Rehm has investigated.[41] With the arrival of Phaethon's body, the stage is arguably set for a ritual lament (*thrēnos*),[42] but the appearance of the ignorant Merops and the chorus of virgins automatically displaces the song of mourning which would have presumably taken place between Clymene and the main chorus had they never appeared. Laura Swift discusses how tragedians blend multiple lyric genres, each of which carries particular associations and norms, to create competing generic narratives within the same play; the result of such blending, she argues, creates significant tension between competing interpretative possibilities.[43] Here, we find a practical application of this phenomenon, as Euripides does not deliberately confuse weddings and funerals or set them up in opposition, but rather forces the viewing audience and the chorus to witness the performance of a wedding hymn for an actual corpse. In this manner, the superimposition of a wedding song when the situation demands a lament not only corrupts the wedding song but simultaneously implicates both external and internal audiences in the corruption as they are forced to witness such a travesty.

Moreover, if we consider the larger mythical tradition around Phaethon, this scene becomes even more remarkable precisely because it suppresses the expected scene of lamentation. According to various accounts, the death of Phaethon was an event that provoked extreme mourning. The accounts found in Plutarch and Polybius testify to the enormity of the grief that Phaethon's death produced.

οὐδὲ γὰρ Θρᾷκας ἐπαινοῦμεν, ὅτι στίζουσιν ἄχρι νῦν τιμωροῦντες Ὀρφεῖ τὰς αὐτῶν γυναῖκας, οὐδὲ τοὺς περὶ Ἠριδανὸν βαρβάρους μελανοφοροῦντας ἐπὶ πένθει τοῦ Φαέθοντος, ὥσπερ λέγουσιν· ἔτι δ' ἂν, οἶμαι, γελοιότερον ἦν εἰ, τῶν τότ' ἀνθρώπων ὅτε διεφθάρη Φαέθων, παραμελησάντων, οἱ πέντε γενεαῖς ἢ δέκα τοῦ πάθους ὕστερον γεγονότες ἤρξαντο τὴν ἐσθῆτα μεταβάλλειν ἐπ' αὐτῷ καὶ πενθεῖν.

Nor yet do we commend the Thracians for tattooing their own wives to this day in revenge for Orpheus, nor the barbarians on the Po for wearing black in mourning for Phaethon, as the story goes; and the absurdity, I think, would be all the greater if at the time of Phaethon's death men had neglected any observance, while those born five or ten generations after the disaster had introduced this change of attire in his honour and gone into mourning.[44]

Plutarch, Moralia [De sera numinis vindicta] *557d–e*

and

παρά γε μὴν τοῖς ἐγχωρίοις ὁ ποταμὸς προσαγορεύεται Βόδεγκος. τἄλλα δὲ τὰ περὶ τὸν ποταμὸν τοῦτον ἱστορούμενα παρὰ τοῖς Ἕλλησι, λέγω δὴ τὰ περὶ Φαέθοντα καὶ τὴν ἐκείνου πτῶσιν, ἔτι δὲ τὰ δάκρυα τῶν αἰγείρων καὶ τοὺς

μελανείμονας τοὺς περὶ τὸν ποταμὸν οἰκοῦντας, οὕς φασι τὰς ἐσθῆτας εἰσέτι νῦν
φορεῖν τοιαύτας ἀπὸ τοῦ κατὰ Φαέθοντα πένθους, καὶ πᾶσαν δὴ τὴν τραγικὴν καὶ
ταύτῃ προσεοικυῖαν ὕλην, ἐπὶ μὲν τοῦ παρόντος ὑπερθησόμεθα, διὰ τὸ μὴ λίαν
καθήκειν τῷ τῆς προκατασκευῆς γένει τὴν περὶ τῶν τοιούτων ἀκριβολογίαν.

The native name of the river is Bodencus. The other tales the Greeks tell about this
river, I mean touching Phaëthon and his fall and the weeping poplar trees and the
black clothing of the inhabitants near the river, who, they say, still dress thus in
mourning for Phaëthon, and all matter of a tragic nature and similar to this legend,
may be left aside for the present, detailed treatment of such things not suiting very
well the character of my introduction.[45]

Polybius 2.16.13

In both accounts Plutarch and Polybius indicate the practice of local inhabitants who
continue to observe his death generations later. Polybius additionally alludes to
Phaethon's famous sisters who lament him unceasingly until Zeus in pity turns them into
weeping poplar trees. These two sources additionally testify to the fact that the bulk of
the evidence for the myth of Phaethon, and especially for his sisters, can be found in
predominantly post-classical and Roman sources.

Nevertheless, some hints of the earlier accounts of the myth in the archaic and
classical periods can be gleaned. In particular, these illuminate the role of Phaethon's
sisters, the Heliades (daughters of Helios), in the tale. Hyginus' account of Hesiod's
Phaethon, which contains a summary of the myth, relates their famous unrelenting grief
as it would have appeared in the archaic didactic poet's work:

Phaethon Clymeni Solis filii et Meropes nymphae filius, quam Oceanitidem
accepimus, cum indicio patris auum Solem cognouisset, impetratis curribus male
usus est. nam cum esset propius terram uectus, uicino igni omnia conflagrarunt, et
fulmine ictus in flumen Padum cecidit; hic amnis a Graecis Eridanus dicitur, quem
Pherecydes primus uocauit. Indi autem quod calore uicini ignis sanguis in atrum
colorem uersus est, nigri sunt facti. sorores autem Phaethontis dum interitum
deflent fratris in arbores sunt populos uersae. harum lacrimae, ut Hesiodus indicat,
in electrum sunt duratae; Heliades tamen nominantur. sunt autem Merope Helie
Aegle Lampetie Phoebe Aetherie Dioxippe. Cygnus autem rex Liguriae, qui fuit
Phaethonti propinquus, dum deflet propinquum in cygnum conuersus est; is
quoque moriens flebile canit.[46]

Phaethon was the son of Clymenus (son of the Sun) and the Nymph Merope who,
as we have been told, was an Oceanid. When Phaethon learned that his grandfather
was the Sun from something his father said, he was granted use of the Sun's chariot
but grossly mishandled it. For when he flew too close to the ground, everything
was burned up by the nearby flame, and he, struck by a thunderbolt, fell into the
Po River. This river is called Eridanus by the Greeks (Pherecydes was the first to
call it this). The Indians turned black because their blood was changed into a dark

color by the heat of the nearby flame. Phaethon's sisters turned into poplar trees while they were weeping over their brother's death; their tears, Hesiod tells us, hardened into amber. They are called the Heliades. Their names were Merope, Helia, Aegle, Lampetia, Phoebe, Aetheria and Dioxippe. Cygnus the king of Liguria, and one of Phaethon's relatives, was turned into a swan (*cygnus*) while he was lamenting over his relative. The swan too, as it dies, sings a mournful dirge.[47]

Hyginus Fab. *154, Hesiod's* Phaethon [Phaethon Hesiodi]

Here, the sisters' unending grief for their brother leads to their transformation into poplar trees, and their continual tears explain the origins of amber. Pliny the Elder also cites this metamorphosis that was propelled by their extreme mourning:

Phaëthontis fulmine icti sorores luctu mutatas in arbores populos lacrimis electrum omnibus annis fundere iuxta Eridanum amnem, quem Padum vocavimus, electrum appellatum, quoniam sol vocitatus sit Elector, plurimi poetae dixere primique, ut arbitror, Aeschylus, Philoxenus, Euripides, Nicander, Satyrus.

The story how, when Phaethon was struck by the thunderbolt, his sisters through their grief were transformed into poplar trees, and how every year by the banks of the River Eridanus, which we call the Po, they shed tears of amber, known to the Greeks as 'electrum', since they call the sun 'Elector' or 'the Shining One' – this story has been told by numerous poets, the first of whom, I believe, were Aeschylus, Philoxenus, Euripides, Nicander and Satyrus.[48]

Pliny Natural History *37.31*

Pliny's account also lists earlier representations of the myth of these sisters, including ones by Aeschylus and Euripides. Both accounts indicate the prominent and dramatic role played by the sisters' lamentation in the aftermath of Phaethon's death.

This is a role that tragedians besides Euripides certainly exploited. Though we only have sparse fragments of Aeschylus' *Heliades* – a play which would have certainly been staged prior to *Phaethon* – it is very likely that the sisters were involved in the drama.[49] Two surviving fragments focus specifically on lamentation:

Ἀδριαναί τε γυναῖκες τρόπον ἕξουσι γόων
And the women of Adria shall have this manner of lamentation.

F 71

†ὄρα σε† κρήνης ἀφθονεστέραν λίβα
He/it stirred up in them/you/us (?) a flow more abundant than a fountain.

F 72[50]

If we take on board the title of the play as additional evidence for the larger mythical tradition, we can assume that Aeschylus must have featured Phaethon's sisters as the chorus, and that at some point this chorus would have expressed their famous grief for their brother in song.[51] If this is true, as I suspect it is, then the innovations of Euripides in the *Phaethon* – that is, his choice of a female chorus that is not the Heliades and the introduction of a merry secondary collective – would have shocked the viewers, in that both alterations upend the extreme grief that is typically due to Phaethon. That the grief is denied specifically by means of a wedding song compounds the shock, dramatically subverting the expectations of the audience, who might have assumed from the play's title and the larger mythical tradition that they would witness a spectacular song of mourning in the course of the drama.

By drawing our attention to the use and role of secondary collectives, in particular the manner in which they create choral multitudes, even if for brief scenes, it is my hope to enhance our understanding of the tragic genre's flexibility and variability, and in particular to expand our conceptions of choral performance beyond the singing of choral odes. As my discussion has revealed, their presence can be used to enhance the ritual impact of particular scenes, as the subsidiary collective sings hymns that emphasize existing relationships with particular deities or sings a song in a grand procession. In the case of the *Phaethon*, Euripides additionally employs a secondary chorus in order to produce a 'mirroring' effect in which the audience is invited to witness and consider contrasting realities and competing song genres. The mirror, in particular, accentuates Euripides' own innovations in his presentation of the myth, especially his ability to dramatize the story of Phaethon without his famous grieving sisters. By producing such aural, dramatic and visual eclipsing effects, secondary choruses thus allow us to witness Greek tragedy's spectacular nature.

Notes

1. Earlier versions of this chapter were presented at Bristol, Mexico City, and at Greek Drama V in Vancouver. I am grateful to those audiences for their feedback.
2. Diggle 1970; Collard, Cropp and Lee 1995: 195–239; Kannicht 2004: 798–826 [=*TrGF*[5.2]]; Collard and Cropp 2008b: 323–67. For accounts of the myth in earlier Greek poetry, see Gantz 1993: 31–4. On the myth in earlier fifth-century tragedy, see Poli Palladini 2013: 128–31.
3. Throughout this chapter I refer to the text printed by Diggle 1970.
4. For recent accounts of the tragic chorus, see, e.g., Perusino and Colantonio 2007; Gruber 2009, Swift 2010; Gagné and Hopman 2013; Andújar, Coward and Hadjimichael 2018; Weiss 2018.
5. Lammers 1931; Carrière 1977; Barrett 1964: 167; Pickard-Cambridge 1988: 236–7; Taplin 1977: 230–8; Karamanou 2017a: 134–5.
6. Besides the *Phaethon*, this is the case in Euripides' *Hippolytus* 58–71 and Aeschylus' *Eumenides* 1033–47. The scholiast to *Hippolytus* 58 suggests that this is also the case in two further tragedies: Euripides' *Alexandros* and *Antiope*. However, their fragmentary nature makes it difficult to confirm this; see my discussion below. Carrière (1977: 49–75) calls this type an 'accompanying' secondary chorus ('*chœur secondaire conjoint*').
7. This is the case in Aeschylus' *Suppliants* 825–65 and Euripides' *Suppliants* 1123–64. Carrière (1977: 5–48) refers to this type as an 'autonomous' secondary chorus ('*chœur secondaire autonome*').

8. On the number of the tragic chorus; see *Vit. Soph.* 4; Pollux *Onomasticon* IV. 108–10; Pickard-Cambridge 1988: 234–6; Taplin 1977: 323.

9. Garvie 1969: 191–7; McCall 1976; Taplin 1977: 230–8.

10. Collard 1975: 18–19, 390–406.

11. Sommerstein (2010a: 24) notes the momentary nature of such choruses in extant tragedy: 'a subsidiary chorus will normally be present, and sing, in one scene only, and (at least in tragedy) its leader will not be given words to speak.'

12. The text is that of Page 1972; the translation is adapted from Podlecki 1989.

13. Cf. Headlam 1906 and Taplin 1977: 410–15. Sommerstein (2010a: 166) counts a minimum of thirty-two performers onstage during this scene.

14. Smith 1976: 65.

15. Taplin 1977: 410–11. Cf. Sommerstein 1989: 282–3.

16. Taplin 1977: 410: 'But we might expect that a group of extras which is actually going to sing would be given a clear introduction beyond a passing deictic pronoun.'

17. This can be seen at the close of *Persians* when the chorus leads Xerxes into the palace, during the procession of two hemichoruses by opposite *eisodoi* at the end of *Seven*, and with the Argive Bodyguard which escorts the Danaids as *Suppliants* draws to an end. On the presumed 'spectacular' nature of Aeschylean theatre, see Taplin 1977: 411–14.

18. Karamanou 2017a: 134 suggests that Seneca later takes up the Euripidean practice of associating the secondary chorus with an individual character.

19. Text is that of Diggle 1984; the translation is adapted from Kovacs 1995.

20. The manuscripts assign only the first three lines to Hippolytus, where he instructs them to sing about Artemis, while the rest of the song (61–71) is given to this 'chorus of servants'. Modern editors of the text have had a problem with this assignment of roles, which suggest that Hippolytus is silent, and instead tend to list Hippolytus as singing along with the collective, thus subsuming the secondary chorus with the protagonist. Cf. Maas 1920; Barrett 1964: 169; Taplin 1977: 194 n. 3; Prauscello 2006: 100 n. 325.

21. The text and translation are those of Collard and Cropp 2008a: 42–3. Cf. Karamanou 2017: 67.

22. Hyginus *Fab.* 8.4. However, there is no mention of this in Apollodorus 3.5.5 and in the scholia to Apollonius Rhodius 4.1090, the two other main sources of the otherwise lost play. Cf. Kambitsis 1972: xiv–v, *TrGF*[5.2]: 274–6, Collard and Cropp 2008a: 170–9.

23. E.g. Karamanou 2017a: 134: 'As in the *Hippolytos*, the secondary chorus in the *Antiope* consists of followers of Dirce in a maenadic state.'

24. The text and translation are those of Collard and Cropp 2008a: 40–1, which stem from *P. Oxy.* 3650 (Coles 1974). Cf. Karamanou 2017a: 127.

25. There is very little information on the chorus in *Alexander*, despite being one of the best preserved of the fragmentary plays; see Karamanou 2017a: 17. In fact, the publication of this hypothesis debunked an earlier assumption proposed by Lanza 1963 who suggested that the secondary chorus were followers of Alexander, much like those of Hippolytus.

26. Taplin 1977.

27. Cf. Hose 1990: 122–31 and Mastronarde 2010: 129.

28. All translations of the *Phaethon* are adapted from Collard, Cropp and Lee (1995).

29. E.g. Diggle 1970: 94–5, Kannicht 1972: 5. Cf. Collard, Cropp and Lee 1995: 202.

30. Collard, Cropp and Lee 1995: 227. The discovery of this fragment also inspired Goethe to translate a reconstruction of the play; Collard, Cropp and Lee 1995: 203.

31. Collard, Cropp and Lee 1995: 229. Cf. Diggle 1970: 115.

32. Particularly telling is line 216: 'It has destroyed me! Carry the body into the house, won't you?' (ἀπωλόμην· οὐκ οἴσετ᾽ εἰς δόμους νέκυν;).

33. 'I will hide him in the dressed-stone chamber where my husband's gold is kept but where I alone command the door's seal' (κρύψω δέ νιν | ξεστοῖσι θαλάμοις, ἔνθ᾽ ἐμῶι κεῖται πόσει | χρυσός, μόνη δὲ κλῆιθρ᾽ ἐγὼ σφραγίζομαι).

34. Diggle 1970: 149. Cf. Swift 2010: 251.

35. For discussion on the possible identity of Phaethon's bride, see Diggle 1970: 155–60.

36. See e.g. Contiades-Tsitsoni 1994, who compares this hymn to those found in *Trojan Women* 308–41 and *Iphigenia at Aulis* 1036–79.

37. E.g. Ritchie 1964: 118.

38. Diggle 1970: 150. Cf. Barrett 1964: 167.

39. Lines 275–6 specifically support the notion that the chorus remained onstage: 'The wretched queen inside and her son | his hidden body' (βασίλεια τάλαινα παῖς τ᾽ ἔσω | κρυφαῖος νέκυς).

40. The sheer number of performers involved here raises the question of the date of the play, and specifically whether the *Phaethon* was performed in a trilogy with other Euripidean plays of the 420s which likewise needed additional performers (e.g. *Hippolytus* or *Suppliant Women*). On the dating of the play, see Diggle 1970 and Calder 1972.

41. Seaford 1987 and Rehm 1994.

42. On the ritual lament, see Alexiou 1974; Holst-Warhaft 1992; Foley 2001: 19–56; Swift 2010: 298–366.

43. Swift 2018.

44. The text and translation are those of De Lacy and Einarson 1959.

45. The text and translation are those of Paton 2010.

46. The text is that of Marshall 1993.

47. The translation is that of Smith and Trzaskoma 2007.

48. The text and translation are those of Eichholz 1962.

49. See Radt 1985 (=*TrGF*³): 185–9. For a comprehensive overview, see Poli Palladini 2013: 113–61.

50. The text and translation are those of Sommerstein 2008a. Cf. Radt 1985.

51. The chief evidence for this assumption are fragments 68 and 69, both of which appear to be choral fragments which contain the word 'father' in association with Helios (e.g. F 68: πατρὸς Ἡελίου). Cf. Poli Palladini 2013: 113.

CHAPTER 9
ERŌS IN PIECES (?): TRAGIC *ERŌS* IN EURIPIDES' *ANDROMEDA* AND *ANTIGONE*

Anastasia-Stavroula Valtadorou

Accounts of love in Greek tragedy have formed a consensus that *erōs* is never meant to have positive effects, but, rather, leads to misfortune.[1] These views give the impression that heterosexual *erōs* is presented in drama as a condition for trauma, an amplification of trauma or a trauma in itself.[2] One example of this trend is Thumiger's contribution to the volume *Eros in Ancient Greece* (2013). Thumiger, following the scholarly trend that focuses on the negative aspects of tragic love, claims that tragic *erōs* is never meant to be seen as an auspicious emotion and can only be fathomed as a calamity.[3] Her conclusion is ominous for all the characters who are presented as being in love:[4]

> *Eros* cannot be shared, communicated, compromised, and channelled in diverse, less harmful directions. It is not surprising that it should become the catalyst both of the isolation of the individual from the rest of the community, and of the destructiveness of other paroxysms of self-affirmation.[5]

Similar is the statement of Toohey and McClure: 'There is little evidence of strong sexual or erotic feelings [i.e. in tragedy]. Where they occur, [. . .], they appear perverse.'[6]

I argue for a more complex picture of *erōs* in tragedy, where it is possible to observe both positive and negative constructions. First, even those who concentrate on the negative representation of tragic love would recognize that in many extant plays it is the characters' disrespect towards *erōs* or the existence of an extramarital affair that proves to be catastrophic (e.g. Aeschylus' *Agamemnon*, Sophocles' *Trachiniae*,[7] Euripides' *Medea* and *Hippolytus*),[8] and not the amorous emotions between a couple.[9] Secondly, there are dramas that portray spouses' longing for each other that does not end in disaster, such as Euripides' *Helen* (412 BCE), which discusses, in a suggestive way, the joyous and erotically charged reunion of Menelaus and Helen.[10]

However, in order to paint a fair and complete picture of heterosexual *erōs* as presented in drama, I argue that it is essential for fragmentary plays to also be taken into consideration.[11] In other words, tragic *erōs* comes forth as an even more complex notion when the fragments that survive are also taken into account.[12] In particular, some fragments present us with examples of couples whose *erōs* does not end with disaster, but with a wedding. In this chapter, I focus on Euripides' *Antigone* (420–406 BCE) and *Andromeda* (412 BCE).[13] My analysis of *Antigone* will be slightly longer than that of *Andromeda*, since the latter has been more frequently discussed.[14] In both plays a young couple, after triumphing over formidable obstacles, will marry, have children and, in all likelihood, live happily together. Not only does *erōs* not destroy, but it even leads to the establishment of a new *oikos*.[15]

I would like to acknowledge that a thorough study of tragic *erōs* is not feasible within the limits of this chapter; an effective re-evaluation of *erōs* cannot be carried out without the extensive analysis of multiple (complete and fragmentary) plays of all three dramatists.[16] Rather, my goal is to show that fragmentary dramas can work as a window that allows us to perceive Euripidean *erōs*, and perhaps tragic *erōs* in general, in a new light.[17] I also acknowledge that looking for positive constructions of erotic love in tragedy may be viewed as anachronistic. Nevertheless, I think it is worth following this path of inquiry, given the surviving evidence, which suggests that there may be a place for non-destructive tragic *erōs*. With this in mind, I shall start the analysis of the two dramas that almost certainly ended with happiness and celebration.

Euripides' *Antigone*: Not a Virgin Anymore?

The *Hypothesis* of Aristophanes of Byzantium to the Sophoclean *Antigone* is one of the main ancient sources that contributes to the reconstruction of Euripides' play. His remark is rather short, but possibly constitutes one of our most reliable sources:[18]

> Κεῖται ἡ μυθοποιία καὶ παρὰ Εὐριπίδη ἐν Ἀντιγόνη. πλὴν ἐκεῖ φωραθεῖσα μετὰ τοῦ Αἵμονος δίδοται πρὸς γάμου κοινωνίαν. καὶ τέκνον τίκτει τὸν Μαίονα.

> The plot is found also in Euripides in *Antigone*, except that there Antigone is detected in company with Haemon and is joined with him in marriage; and she gives birth to a child, Maion.[19]

Aristophanes informs us that Euripides' play narrates the same mythological events as Sophocles', i.e. the interment of Polynices by Antigone and her arrest, when she was caught (φωραθεῖσα, 'caught'). If this source is reliable, then it seems likely that Euripides sets his *Antigone* during the course of, or in the aftermath of, the burial (cf. fragment 176).[20] Yet two striking differences are mentioned here. First, it seems plausible that Aristophanes uses the preposition μετά with the genitive, which could mean 'in common with' or 'along with',[21] in order to modify the participle φωραθεῖσα, thereby rendering Haemon an accomplice of the illegal act.[22] (Sadly, it is not clear whether they were caught together for the same reason, i.e. the burial of Polynices' body, or whether Antigone was the perpetrator of the deed and Haemon was caught along with her, while they were trying to conceal it.)[23] Such a role, though impossible to determine, would underline Haemon's affection towards Antigone. Secondly, we are informed by Aristophanes that, despite the exposure of their non-compliance, Haemon and Antigone will marry and have a son. The phrase πρὸς γάμου κοινωνίαν ('to a communion of marriage') along with the verb δίδοται ('is given') implies that Antigone is given to a formal marriage by her κύριος ('legal guardian'),[24] who in this case is Creon – provided that all her male relatives

are dead. Therefore, we can conclude that Creon, after discovering their defiance, decides
to set them free and marry them to each other.

The Schol. 1351 on Sophocles' *Antigone* almost repeats Aristophanes' words,[25] giving
the impression that the scholiast obtained the relevant information from Aristophanes
(NB the repetition of the participle φωραθεῖσα, the noun γάμος and the reference to
Αἵμων): Διαφέρει τῆς Εὐριπίδου Ἀντιγόνης ὅτι φωραθεῖσα ἐκείνη διὰ τὸν Αἵμονος ἔρωτα
ἐξεδόθη πρὸς γάμον. ἐνταῦθα δὲ τοὐναντίον ('This version deviates from Euripides'
Antigone on the grounds that, after being caught, she is wedded (to him) thanks to
Haemon's *erōs*. Here, though, the exact opposite occurs').[26] Here the scholiast explicitly
mentions Haemon's *erōs*. Moreover, he refers to Antigone as the only agent of the act
(φωραθεῖσα ἐκείνη), thus implying that Haemon did not collaborate with her, even though
we cannot be sure whether the scholiast did this on purpose or for the sake of brevity.

In this section I shall discuss the fragments of *Antigone* that may have to do with *erōs*.[27]
First, in fragment 160, there is a reference to a shared experience of some concealed
misfortune:[28]

νέοι νέοισι συννοσοῦσι τὰφανῆ

Youths share their invisible diseases with each other.

Collard and Cropp translate, 'Young share their faults with young . . . in their uncertainties
(?),' recognizing that this sentence does not make full sense.[29]

There are two levels of interpretation to this line. First, it probably refers to the joint
performance of burial rites for Polynices by the young (betrothed?) royals. For the word
τὰφανῆ ('hidden', 'invisible') may allude to the secretiveness that encompasses the
action,[30] while the verb συννοσοῦσι ('share an illness', 'be a fellow sufferer') may well refer
to the youths' common action. Secondly, I shall tentatively suggest that this fragment
may allude to Haemon's decision to carry on this forbidden, and thus covert, deed
because of his feelings for Antigone.[31] τὰφανῆ is something that could easily refer to an
emotion. Moreover, συννοσέω may support this line of reasoning. Although it is often
used in the literal sense to indicate physical suffering or disease,[32] it sometimes denotes
the experience of a malady that two or more loved ones suffer jointly (Euripides' *IA* 407).
Occasionally, though, it refers to the shared life of a couple and the difficulties a person
is willing to experience together with his/her significant other when he/she suffers. One
example is Pseudo-Lucian's *Erotes* (46.15), while another is fragment 545a/909N[2],
perhaps belonging to Euripides' *Oedipus*,[33] a play known for its positive representation of
marriage.[34] Returning to *Antigone*, it is not impossible for συννοσέω to be associated
with the shared calamity of two partners, who jointly commit this forbidden act, and in
particular with their emotions.[35] Unfortunately, this fragment alone does not provide
enough evidence to determine whether the involvement of Haemon in this 'disease'
comes as a result of his *erōs*.[36] However, the fragments 161, 162 and 162a may well lead
towards this conclusion.

In fragment 161, we encounter a direct reference to human *erōs*, which is equated to madness:

ἤρων· τὸ μαίνεσθαι δ᾽ ἄρ᾽ ἦν ἔρως βροτοῖς

I was [*or* 'they were'?] in love: and that showed that love is madness for mortals.

Pertinent is the verb ἐράω ('to love', 'to be in love with'), which is located at the beginning of the verse and grammatically can be construed as either the singular form of the first person or the plural form of the third person of the imperfect tense.[37] Hence, the interconnection between love and madness is articulated either by the person who talks, and thus refers to himself and his personal experience of love, or by a third person (the chorus? Creon?) who contemplates the negative outcome that *erōs* can have in human affairs.[38] In the first instance, the character who utters these words is plausibly Haemon,[39] since Antigone's motivating force must have been her brotherly love for Polynices. If we accept Aristophanes as a reliable source, then we could suppose that here Haemon admits that he was complicit in the burial of Polynices, motivated by his *erōs* for Antigone.[40] However, if ἤρων is a plural form, then this fragment provides us clear evidence of the mutual feelings between Haemon and Antigone.[41] Unfortunately, the lack of context does not allow us to determine which of the two alternatives is correct.

In all probability, fragment 162 points to the same dramatic context, as it bears a resemblance to fragment 161:

ἀνδρὸς δ᾽ ὁρῶντος εἰς Κύπριν νεανίου
ἀφύλακτος ἡ τήρησις, ὡς κἂν φαῦλος ᾖ
τἄλλ᾽, εἰς ἔρωτα πᾶς ἀνὴρ σοφώτατος.
†ἣν δ᾽ ἂν προσῆται Κύπρις ἥδιστον λαβεῖν†

When a young man looks to Aphrodite, there's no watch can be kept on him; for even if he's bad at other things, every man is very clever in the pursuit of love. † If Aphrodite approves [love? or 'allows love to come'], it is very sweet to seize it.

Here, a person who could be Creon, the chorus or a guard comments on the great power of *erōs*. The speaker almost certainly remarks upon the action undertaken by Haemon and the impossibility of keeping him under surveillance because of his *erōs*.[42] As for the text itself, I suggest that the phrase εἰς Κύπριν can be understood both as the characteristic metonymy for erotic passion and sexual matters in general,[43] and as a metaphor for a girl who arouses this passion (cf. Euripides *Trojan Women* 368–9, where Helen is called both a woman and a Cypris, that is, a woman who arouses desire: οἳ διὰ μίαν γυναῖκα καὶ μίαν Κύπριν, | θηρῶντες Ἑλένην, μυρίους ἀπώλεσαν, 'who for the sake of one woman and one passion, have lost thousands of men, while hunting for Helen'). Haemon's *erōs* for Antigone, an attractive woman, results in an ἀφύλακτος τήρησις. For he perhaps assists her because of his *erōs*, thus becoming resourceful. Last, the phrase can be interpreted as a literal reference to the goddess herself (which I find less likely).

As for fragment 162a, it probably constitutes a self-reference on Haemon's part:[44]

ἐγὼ γὰρ ἔξω λέκτρ᾽, ἅ τοι καλῶς ἔχειν
δίκαιόν ἐστιν οἷσι συγγηράσομαι

For I shall have a marriage which it is right should do well, I tell you, with a wife with whom I shall grow old.[45]

In these lines the character who speaks underscores his/her entitlement to marry a person of his/her choice with whom it is just to grow old together (συγγηράσομαι).[46] It can be assumed that here Haemon is speaking to Creon about his decision to marry the right person for him, Antigone.[47] This scene reminds us of the encounter between Creon and his son in Sophocles (631–765). Yet there are two striking deviations: in the Euripidean *Antigone* we come across an explicit reference to Haemon's desire to age together with Antigone. Moreover, significant is the verb ἔξω. The use of the future tense of the verb ἔχω ('to have') signifies that the wedding to which he aspires is going to happen in the future. This indication confirms, at one level, the reliability of Aristophanes' summary, which refers to their wedding as an event that is about to happen.

Last, I shall discuss fragment 177:

ὦ παῖ Διώνης, ὡς ἔφυς μέγας θεός,
Διόνυσε, θνητοῖς τ᾽ οὐδαμῶς ὑποστατός

O son of Dione, Dionysus,[48] how great a god you are, and in no way to be resisted by mortal men.

By reason of this fragment it has been suggested that Dionysus acts as a *deus ex machina* in this drama.[49] He is the one who intervenes, thus saving Antigone's life.[50] This assumption makes perfect sense, for Creon must have had a change of heart for good reason.[51] Therefore, we can imagine that an in-person (or through other means?)[52] divine intervention by Dionysus resulted in the deliverance of Antigone. Moreover, we can assume that Dionysus is the one who openly endorses the marriage of Antigone and Haemon and predicts the birth of Maion, and perhaps thus we find the reference to Maion in Aristophanes' summary.[53]

In the most typical versions of the myth Dionysus is the son of Semele, daughter of the founder of Thebes, Cadmus.[54] Nevertheless, Dionysus is here apostrophized as son of Dione,[55] who is traditionally the mother of Aphrodite.[56] This unusual connection between Dionysus and Dione has been left unexplained in most modern treatises,[57] a connection that, I think, is not casual at all. In a play where the theme of love must have played a notable role, Euripides presents onstage (or refers to) Dionysus as the son of Dione, thus making him a brother to Aphrodite. Accordingly, it makes perfect sense that in this *Antigone* Dionysus, the brother of the goddess of love, not only intervenes and saves this young couple from catastrophe and death, but also ensures their wedding.

All in all, it is evident from the inspection of these fragments (160, 162, 162a, 164, 177) that *erōs* must have played a significant role in Euripides' *Antigone*. It is within reason to assume that the person who speaks about himself as being in love is Haemon; his *erōs* for Antigone must have acted as a prime motivating force. As regards the mutual aspects of this relationship, the only textual element that perhaps insinuates reciprocity between Haemon and Antigone is the verb ἤρων (fragment 161), which can refer to their reciprocal love, provided that this is the plural form of the verb. What is more important, though, is the positive outcome of this relationship. As far as we know, *erōs* does not lead to destruction and death in this *Antigone*, but to a (perhaps happy?) marriage and a progeny.[58]

Erotic Passion in Euripides' *Andromeda*

Andromeda is a play that has to do with erotic desire.[59] The Ethiopian princess is meant to die near the seashore, probably because of her mother's insult against Poseidon,[60] and is saved by Perseus, who falls in love with her. Thanks to the popularity of this drama, several ancient sources either preserve some parts of it, especially its beginning,[61] or provide us with information about the plot and the final happy outcome.[62]

We are almost certain that, instead of the more traditional prologue in spoken iambics, *Andromeda* starts with the title character being bound to an arch rock and singing monodic anapaests alone in the dark (fragment 114).[63] Her complete desperation is underlined not only by her loneliness and her total immobility,[64] but also by her inability to sing without hearing her voice echoing in the cliffs (fragment 118).[65] The situation changes slightly when a chorus of consoling *parthenoi* appears and laments her fate along with her (fragments 117, 119, 120, 121, 122).[66] During the first episode Perseus enters the scene flying and falls in love with Andromeda at first sight (fragments 123, 124, 125). Subsequently, his *erōs* urges him to kill the sea monster destined to devour the princess (fragments 127, 129, 136) and is then determined to marry her.[67] Although there must have been strong opposition to this prospective wedding (most probably on the part of her parents Cepheus and Cassiopeia),[68] Andromeda remains thankful to her rescuer and follows him to Argos.[69] As with Euripides' *Antigone*, the quarrel between Perseus, Andromeda and her parents was possibly resolved by a divine agent, Athena, who acted as *dea ex machina*.[70]

In this section I shall discuss the fragments related to *erōs*. First, in fragment 125 we are witnesses to a unique scene in Greek drama: Perseus falling in love onstage.[71] Perseus arrives onstage, probably on the μηχανή (fragment 124), sees the stunning girl bound on the rocks and mistakenly takes her for a statue (fragment 125):

ἔα· τίν' ὄχθον τόνδ' ὁρῶ περίρρυτον
ἀφρῶι θαλάσσης; παρθένου δ' εἰκὼ τίνα
ἐξ αὐτομόρφων λαΐνων τυχισμάτων,
σοφῆς ἄγαλμα χειρός;

Hold – what promontory do I see here, lapped by sea foam, and what maiden's likeness, a statue carved by an expert hand to her very form in stone?[72]

This reference to Andromeda as a sensuous statue is, no doubt, 'tinged with eroticism'.[73] Equally intriguing is the reference to ἀφρὸς θαλάσσης ('sea foam') that may remind us of Aphrodite, who, according to one mythological version, was born in the sea as a result of Uranus' castration.[74]

After realizing his mistake, Perseus feels pity for Andromeda and attempts to converse with her (fragments 126, 127). Next, he offers to save her life, by asking whether she will be thankful to him (fragment 129):

ὦ παρθέν᾽, εἰ σώσαιμί σ᾽, εἴσηι μοι χάριν;

Maiden, if I should rescue you, will you show me gratitude?

Of interest is the noun χάρις ('grace', 'favour', 'gratitude').[75] Despite its broad semantic range, χάρις often has amorous undertones, since, along with its derivatives (e.g. χαρίζεσθαι), it serves to connote sexual acts.[76] I maintain that the expression χάριν εἰδέναι τινί ('to feel grateful towards someone') has erotic connotations,[77] for it possibly suggests the continuing exchange of beneficial acts and shared pleasure that is about to commence between them thanks to Perseus' initiatory χάρις.[78] Equally significant is the term παρθένος ('maiden', cf. fragment 127),[79] for it underscores the unmarried status of Andromeda and her availability as a bride (cf. her lament for not having heard the wedding paean in fragment 122, that may call to mind Antigone's grievance in Sophocles: 869, 876, 891).[80]

Thereafter, in fragment 129a, which can be considered as an answer to fragment 129,[81] Andromeda is ready to surrender herself to Perseus:

ἄγου δέ μ᾽, ὦ ξεῖν᾽ εἴτε πρόσπολον θέλεις
εἴτε ἄλοχον εἴτε δμωΐδ᾽ . . .

Take me with you, stranger, whether you want me as a servant, a wife or a slave.

Although there is no direct statement that she has amorous feelings as well,[82] her initiative to offer herself as a servant, wife or slave is straightforward and perhaps arousing to Perseus (and the viewer).[83] Furthermore, her desire to surrender to Perseus should not be regarded as forced or fully dictated by her current circumstances. Even after her rescue from the beast and release from the bonds, Andromeda chooses to live with Perseus,[84] against the will of her parents (cf. fragments 140, 141, 142, 143, 144, 149, 150, 151 for the dispute between Perseus and her parents).

The fact that Perseus is enamoured of Andromeda is also insinuated by fragment 136, where the speaker –certainly Perseus – prays to Eros in order to assist him in his effort. I hold with the majority of scholars that this invocation probably comes right before the killing of the monster.[85] Nevertheless, Klimek-Winter's suggestion, that these verses could have also been uttered before Perseus' confrontation with Andromeda's opposed parents, should not be considered totally unfounded (fragment 136):[86]

σὺ δ᾽ ὦ θεῶν τύραννε κἀνθρώπων Ἔρως,
ἢ μὴ δίδασκε τὰ καλὰ φαίνεσθαι καλά,[87]
ἢ τοῖς ἐρῶσιν, ὧν σὺ δημιουργὸς εἶ
μοχθοῦσι μόχθους, εὐτυχῶς συνεκπόνει.
καὶ ταῦτα μὲν δρῶν τίμιος + θεοῖς + ἔσηι,
μὴ δρῶν δ᾽ ὑπ᾽ αὐτοῦ τοῦ διδάσκεσθαι φιλεῖν
ἀφαιρεθήσηι χάριτας, αἷς τιμῶσί σε.

And you, Eros, tyrant over gods and men – either don't teach us to see beauty in what is beautiful, or help those who are in love to succeed in their efforts as they suffer the toils that you yourself have crafted. If you do this, you will be honoured by gods, but if you do not, even by teaching them how to love, you will be deprived of the gratitude with which they honour you.[88]

Last, fragment 138 discusses the ramifications of *erōs* on humans:[89]

ὅσοι γὰρ εἰς ἔρωτα πίπτουσιν βροτῶν,
ἐσθλῶν ὅταν τύχωσι τῶν ἐρωμένων,
οὐκ ἔσθ᾽ ὁποίας λείπεται τόδ᾽ ἡδονῆς.

Whenever mortals who have fallen in love find their loved one is virtuous, no joy exceeds the joy of it.

As Klimek-Winter argues, these verses express a general meaning (that erotic love can have tangible positive effects in people's lives), which is the dominant theme of *Andromeda*. Therefore, they can be attributed to a number of different characters (Perseus, Andromeda, chorus, Athena) and to different parts of the play.[90]

Overall, the theme of erotic love must have played a prominent role in *Andromeda* that may well have ended with celebration and marriage. It is clear that Perseus falls in love with this princess. Although we do not have enough information about the way Andromeda felt about him,[91] the longevity and the solidity of this marital bond possibly betray – by implication – its reciprocal character.[92] All the same, in *Andromeda*, just as in *Antigone*, a severe conflict arises between the lovers and her guardians. This dispute is eventually resolved by a god, a fact perhaps suggesting that there is no place for *erōs* without the more conventional bonding of families.[93]

Conclusion

One critical feature that must have characterized Euripide's *Antigone* and *Andromeda* is their favourable representation of *erōs*. Evidently, both Haemon and Perseus fall in love with their future wives. Although the fragments do not specify if the same applies to the heroines, their consent to marriage seems to be implied. Furthermore, it is of importance that – despite the various objections raised by other parties – the emergence of *erōs* does not have deleterious effects, but, on the contrary, leads to the formation of two long-lasting *oikoi*. Hence, I suggest that the study of fragmentary plays can help us redefine our standard views on tragic *erōs*, which is more complex and multifaceted than it is sometimes thought to be.

Notes

1. I am indebted to the Greek Drama V audience, and particularly to Professors Martin Cropp, Melissa Funke and Elizabeth Scharffenberger for helpful comments and constructive criticism. Furthermore, I am grateful to Professor Douglas Cairns, Dr Richard Rawles and Dr Lilah Grace Canevaro for meticulously commenting on earlier drafts, and to the editors and anonymous readers for numerous invaluable suggestions. Moreover, I thank Professors Patrick Finglass, Maarit Kaimio and Matthew Wright for sharing their papers with me. Last, I would like to express my gratitude to the AHRC, the University of Edinburgh and the A. G. Leventis Foundation for funding my overall project on *erōs* in Greek drama.

2. I thank Ian Ruffell for this formulation.

3. Seaford 1987; 1990a; 1994; Rabinowitz 1993; Rehm 1994. Thumiger's conclusion applies to heterosexual relations, given that the surviving dramas discuss sexual passion between men and women, inside or outside of marriage. As Matthew Wright suggested to me, two plays that may well have treated pederastic *erōs* are Aeschylus' *Myrmidons* and Sophocles' *Lovers of Achilles*.

4. A critique of this article can be found in Wright 2017: 221–2.

5. Thumiger 2013: 40. Cf. Thumiger 2013: 39 n. 34.

6. Toohey and McClure 2013: 1241.

7. For Deianira's catastrophic *erōs* and her decision to die as a 'female sexual partner', see Papazoglou, in this volume.

8. This is also argued by Harris 2014: 306–7. For destructive *erōs* in fragments, see e.g. Euripides' *Cretans*, *Cretan Women* and *Stheneboea*.

9. Dramas that present the disastrous effects of extramarital *erōs* often end with the re-establishment of marriage as an institution. In *Agamemnon* an extreme aberration of marriage is on display (Jenkins 1983: 138); Clytemnestra is almost portrayed as the mother of the groom, while eagerly awaiting to greet both Agamemnon and Cassandra, who come followed by an exuberant parade (783–808, cf. Eur. *Phoenissae* 344–6). Nonetheless, *Oresteia* as a trilogy ends with a proper re-establishment of marriage by Athena (*Eumenides* 834–6, cf. Lebeck 1971: 69). It can be assumed that a similar sequence was followed in Aeschylus' *Danaides* trilogy. In *Suppliant Women* the Egyptian Danaides have travelled to Argos so as to ask for help from their ancestors. The reason behind this immigration lies in their desire to avoid their wedding to their cousins. Although the Argive *demos* accepts their supplication, they are wedded to the Aegyptids by force in the trilogy's second drama. While forty-nine of them kill their spouses on their wedding night, only one daughter spares her husband's life. Again, the third drama possibly ended with an institutionalization of marriage, as fragment 44 Radt perhaps suggests.

10. Menelaus is called ποθεινός by Helen ('longed for', 540), while their long-awaited encounter and embrace is described by her as τέρψις ('delight', 626) and ἡδονάν ('pleasure', 634). Menelaus' behaviour is slightly less enthusiastic, yet he still expresses his joy for their reunion (cf. 630–2, 637–45, 652–5). Equally revealing is the reference to the bath Menelaus will receive

(1296–300): Helen's words have erotic connotations and may make the audience suspect – after so many double entendres – that she will provide him with more pleasures than just a relaxing bath. Cf. Craik 1990: 260–2; Kaimio 2002: 107–13; Fisher 2013: 50–3.

11. See Funke 2013.

12. Collard notes that the interrelation between love and marriage in Euripides' surviving and fragmentary plays manifests itself in various ways. For the contrasting representation of married women in *Cretan Women* and in *Alcestis*, two dramas produced in the same year (438 BCE), see Collard 2005: 51, 57.

13. There is common agreement concerning the production date of Andromeda due to the Σ *Frogs* 53. See Webster 1965: 29; Cropp and Fick 1985: 70, 73–4; Gibert 1999/2000: 75; Collard, Cropp and Gibert 2004: 142–3; Kannicht 2004: 233; Collard and Cropp 2008: 128; Galli 2010: 62. Regarding *Antigone*, Cropp and Fick (1984: 70, 74) and Collard and Cropp (2008: 159) believe that it was produced between 420 and 406 BCE, while Webster (1967b: 15) thinks that it was presented between 416 and 409 BCE, probably in 414 BCE.

14. Concerning *Antigone*, Zimmermann (1993: 161–88), Inglese (1992, 1998), Bañuls and Morenilla (2008) and Karamanou (2017: 138–41) constitute some of the rare modern discussions on the play, while Petersmann (1978: 93–5), Galli (2010: 67–8), Cairns (2016: 118–19) and Wright (2017: 235–6) mention it briefly. Cf. Webster 1967b: 181–4; Gantz 1993: 520–1; Jouan and Van Looy 1998: 191–212; Collard and Cropp 2008: 156–9, 203. As regards Euripides' *Andromeda*, the state of affairs is markedly better. Cf. Bubel 1991; Carrara 1993; Klimek-Winter 1993; Beverley 1997: 112–26; Gibert 1999/2000; Wright 2005; Bañuls and Morenilla 2008; Mastromarco 2008; Sfyroeras 2008; Podlecki 2009; Pagano 2010; Major 2013; Wilfred 2013; Marshall 2014: 140–87; Marshall 2015; Phillips 2015; Wright 2017.

15. Bañuls and Morenilla (2008: 101, 107–8). Their paper came to my attention after the final draft of this chapter was written. While we agree in many points, their paper did not influence my overall argument.

16. Other fragments that might have portrayed *erōs* in a more positive light are Aeschylus' *Danaids*, Sophocles' *Oenomaus*, and Euripides' *Protesilaus* and *Skyrians*.

17. I view Euripides as a representative of the tragic genre working within its norms. See Mastronarde 1999–2000; Wright 2010.

18. A different opinion is expressed by Huddilston (1899: 201) and Bates (1930: 220, 222). Regarding the synoptic nature of Aristophanes' *Hypothesis* and the confusion caused by its vagueness, see Mesk 1931: 6–10.

19. I follow the text of Kannicht 2004. All the translations are from Collard and Cropp 2008, except for fragment 160, where the translation is mine. For Aristophanes' summary, cf. Robert 1915: 386; Petersmann 1978: 93. Taplin (2007: 185) translates differently: '. . . Haimon stole Antigone away. . .'. For a different interpretation, see Zimmermann 1993: 180–1. For Maion as Haemon's son, see *Iliad* 4.394.

20. Cf. Inglese 1992: 178; Gantz 1993: 521; Zimmermann 1993: 183; Karamanou 2017: 139. Karamanou's chapter was published after this paper was submitted to the editors. While we are in broad agreement, her chapter nevertheless did not influence my argument as developed here.

21. See LSJ s.v. II. μετά and genitive.

22. Cf. Paton 1901: 268; Mesk 1931: 3; Webster 1967b: 181; Dunn 1996: 186; Kannicht 2004: 262; Collard and Cropp 2008: 157; Funke 2013: 48; Collard 2017: 359; Karamanou 2017: 139.

23. I cannot rule out another possible interpretation of Aristophanes' comment, namely that Antigone was caught (φωραθεῖσα) and then given in marriage (δίδοται πρὸς γάμου

κοινωνίαν) to Haemon (μετὰ τοῦ Αἴμονος). Either reading is possible and, by the same token, neither can be ruled out.

24. For the expression γάμου κοινωνίαν, see LSJ s.v. κοινωνία. Cf. Paton 1901: 274; Robert 1915: 388; Rosen 1930: 40; Mesk 1931: 3. On Athenian wedding rituals and the role played by the bride's father, cf. Sutton 1981; Jenkins 1983; Sutton 1997/8.

25. Cf. Huddilston 1899: 185; Paton 1901: 268; Mesk 1931: 2–3; Xanthakis-Karamanos 1980: 50 n. 5; Kannicht 2004: 262.

26. This translation is mine.

27. Scharffenberger, in this volume, suggests that *inc. fab.* fragment 1063 (Kannicht) may belong to Euripides' *Antigone*.

28. Zimmermann (1993: 163) argues that this line must have been uttered by an older person.

29. See Collard and Cropp 2008: 163.

30. LSJ s.v. ἀφανής. Cf. Blaydes (as quoted by Kannicht 2004: 264).

31. See Karamanou 2017: 139.

32. Cf. Aristotle, *Generation of Animals* 784a30; Galen, *Commentary on the Aphorisms of Hippocrates* 17b472, 17b855; Plutarch, *Precepts of Statecraft* 824a3.

33. Vaio (1964: 52) maintains that this fragment is genuine and probably refers to the marriage of Iocaste and Oedipus. Cf. Webster 1967b: 244–5, Collard, Cropp and Gibert 2004: 107, 118–19; Kannicht 2004: 577; Collard 2005: 58; Collard 2017: 360. In contrast, Stephanopoulos (2012), Liapis (2014) and Finglass (2017: 17–19) claim that the fragment is not authentic.

34. Cf. Bethe 1891: 68–9 n. 40; Robert 1915: 305–31; Vaio 1964; Stephanopoulos 2012; Funke 2013: 73–4; Liapis 2014; Collard 2017: 359; Finglass 2017.

35. Bañuls and Morenilla (2008: 99) similarly argue that this line may refer to their love.

36. For *erōs* as disease in Euripides, see *Hippolytus* 40, 394, 405, 477, 479, 512, 597, 698, 730, 766, 1306; *Cretans* fragment 472e, lines 12, 20, 35; *Stheneboea* fragment 661, lines 6, 20.

37. See Morwood 2001: 74.

38. Cf. Kannicht 2004: 265; Collard and Cropp 2008: 163. Nonetheless, it is possible that these verses were uttered by Creon in an exasperated (or ironic) way.

39. Cf. Webster 1967b: 183; Xanthakis-Karamanos 1980: 51; Kannicht 2004: 265; Collard and Cropp 2008: 163.

40. See Webster 1967b: 183.

41. Collard and Cropp 2008: 163.

42. Cf. Webster 1967b: 183; Kannicht 2004: 265; Collard and Cropp 2008: 163.

43. For example, cf. Scholia Vetera *Iliad* 5.330 Erbse; Euripides *Andromache* 179, 631; *Troades* 988; *Cretans* fragment 472e, line 7; *Dictys* fragment 331; *Hippolytus Veiled* fragment 428; Aristophanes *Assemblywomen* 722; Eubulus fragment 67; Hesychius E 2966 s.v. ἔνευνοι; [Phocylides] *Sententiae* 190.

44. Cf. Kannicht 2004: 265; Collard and Cropp 2008: 163; Funke 2013: 132–3; Karamanou 2017: 139.

45. These verses are corrupt and their translation is inevitably awkward. See Zimmermann's translation (1993: 165): 'Ich werde nämlich eine Ehe haben, von der es recht ist, dass sie schön ist, und in der ich (sc. zusammen mit meiner Frau/meinem Mann) alt werde.'

46. The verb συγγηράσκω continues to connote the simultaneous ageing of two partners in later literature. Cf. [Callisthenes] *History of Alexander the Great* Recensio b 2.20.40–3; Alciphron *Letters* 4.18.3.

47. The reference to their similar age perhaps suggests 'some type of equality' between them (Funke 2013: 59).

48. This is the second mention of the god's name in Euripides' *Antigone*. Through the fragment *178 we learn that Dionysus sent the Sphinx to Thebes. See Σ MA Euripides' *Phoenissae* 1031.

49. Cf. Sophocles' *Antigone* 1115–54.

50. This was first suggested by Boeckh in 1824 and subsequently accepted by Mesk (1931: 12), Webster (1967b: 182–3), Petersmann (1978: 94), Xanthakis-Karamanos (1980: 52), Karamanou (2017: 140). Paton (1901: 275) agrees with the idea that divine intervention is necessary for the plot, but insists that this deity 'must be left unnamed.' Cf. Huddilston 1899: 189–90; Zimmermann 1993: 185 n. 325. Robert (1915: 394) provides us with the alternative that Herakles speaks these lines, thus addressing his half-brother Dionysus, also νόθος son of Zeus.

51. Cf. Theoklymenus' change of heart after the appearance of the Dioskouroi (*Helen*, 1680–7) and the similar change of atmosphere after the appearance of Apollo in *Orestes* (1625–81). Cf. *Antigone* fragments 165, 169 and 170, where someone, certainly a mortal, is trying (unsuccessfully?) to convince the king.

52. Cf. Athena's vocal intervention in Sophocles' *Ajax* (1–13).

53. See Xanthakis-Karamanos 1980: 52.

54. Cf. *Iliad* 14.325; Hesiod *Theogony* 940–1; Bacchylides *Dithyramb* 5.48–50; Euripides' *Bacchae* 1–3; Herodotus 2.145; Theocritus *Idyll* 26.6; Pausanias 3.24.3; Diogenes Laertius 2.102.

55. As such only in adesp. fragment 204. Cf. Hesychius B 128 s.v. Βάκχου Διώνης; Collard and Cropp 2008: 169.

56. Cf. *Iliad* 5.370–1; Euripides' *Helen* 1098; [Apollodorus] *Library* 1.13.5; Plotinus *Ennead* 3.5.2.

57. Only Zimmermann (1993: 164, 171, 184) and Karamanou (2017:140) make this connection.

58. For the happy ending of *Antigone*, cf. Paton 1901: 275; Webster 1967b: 187; Inglese 1992: 178; Gantz 1993: 521; Zimmermann 1993: 185–8; Bañuls and Morenilla 2008: 106–8; Collard and Cropp 2008: 157; Funke 2013: 48; Collard 2017: 355; Karamanou 2017: 139–41. For the importance of their romance, cf., among others, Huddilston 1899: 188; Paton 1901: 275; Xanthakis-Karamanos 1980: 55–6; Zimmermann 1993: 171, 186; Bañuls and Morenilla 2008: 99–100, 106–8; Karamanou 2017: 139–41. We cannot be absolutely certain whether the outcome is positive or not, since we do not know if Antigone reciprocated Haemon's *erōs*. Is her marriage to Haemon forced, like the marriage between Iole and Hyllus in Sophocles' *Women of Trachis*? If this is the case, it would have a considerable impact on our understanding of the play and could place Antigone in the same category of other Euripidean female characters who are raped and thus subjected to bad *erōs* (Funke 2013). However, there is no textual element that could lead us to that conclusion, nor is this suggested by any other reader of the play, ancient or modern.

59. See Aristophanes *Frogs* 52–4. Cf. Müller 1907; Moorton 1987: 435; Falcetto 1998: 64; Gibert 1999/2000; Sfyroeras 2008: 303–4; Pagano 2010: 19; Funke 2013: 177; Marshall 2014: 141.

60. There is no direct reference to the boast in the fragments. See Collard, Cropp and Gibert 2004: 138–9.

61. Aristophanes' *Women at the Thesmophoria* is one of our most invaluable sources. For Aristophanes' parody, cf. Rau 1967: 65–89; Bubel 1991: 159–69; Mastromarco 2008; Funke 2013: 171–94; Major 2013.

62. For the ancient testimonia, cf. Bubel 1991: 8–23, 64–70; Klimek-Winter 1993: 60–6, 94–118.

63. Cf. Wecklein 1888: 87–8; Müller 1907: 58; Knox 1979: 242–3; Bubel 1991: 15; Klimek-Winter 1993: 58–9; Mastromarco 2008: 182; Marshall 2014: 145, 149.

64. Cf. Beverley 1997: 120–1; Marshall 2014: 153.

65. Some scholars claim that Echo is present onstage, exactly like in Aristophanes. Cf. Robert 1878: 18; Major 2013: 401. To my mind, Echo's physical absence would underline, in a more tangible manner, the loneliness of Andromeda. Cf. Petersen 1904: 100; Müller 1907: 56; Webster 1965: 29–30; Rau 1967: 68; Webster 1967b: 194; Bubel 1991: 16–17; Beverley 1997: 121–2; Falcetto 1998: 56–7; Collard and Cropp 2008: 126; Marshall 2014: 150.

66. For the complex use of choruses in Euripidean fragmentary dramas, see Rosa Andújar, in this volume.

67. Fragments related to *erōs*, marriage and the value of legitimate children: 137, 138, 141.

68. In the versions narrated by Apollodorus and Ovid (among others), Phineus, the fiancé of Andromeda, tries to thwart her union with Perseus. Some scholars endeavoured to reconstruct the plot of *Andromeda* through these texts and assumed that Phineus was present in Euripides as well. Cf. Wecklein 1888: 90–2; Petersen 1904; Arias 1962: 53; Webster 1965: 32. I do not think that the evidence is strong enough to support this claim. Cf. Robert 1878: 19; Müller 1907: 48–51; Klimek-Winter 1993: 57; Gibert 1999/2000: 85 n. 36; Collard and Cropp 2008: 127.

69. Cf. [Eratosthenes'] *Catasterisms* 17 (21.2 Olivieri = 216 b 20 Maass); Hyginus' *Astronomica* II.11; Schol. Germ. S. BP. G.

70. Cf. Wecklein 1888: 95; Müller 1907: 63; Bubel 1991: 61–3; Klimek-Winter 1993: 56; Funke 2013: 178. Marshall (2014: 179–82) maintains that Athena does not appear *ex machina*, and draws attention to the fact that the summary of *Electra* in *P.Oxy.*5284 omits reference to the god.

71. Cf. Gibert 1999/2000: 76; Collard, Cropp and Gibert 2004: 160; Bañuls and Morenilla 2008: 101; Mastromarco 2008: 178; Sfyroeras 2008: 303; Pagano 2010: 20; Marshall 2015: 136.

72. All the translations are from Collard and Cropp 2008, slightly adapted.

73. Collard, Cropp and Gibert 2004: 160. For women as ἀγάλματα, cf. Aeschylus *Agamemnon* 208, 414–19; Euripides *Alcestis* 348–54; *Hecuba* 557–65.

74. Cf. Hesiod *Theogony* 188–98; *Hymn to Aphrodite* 6.1–5; Plato *Cratylus* 406c7–d2; Pausanias 2.1.8, 5.11.8; Galen *On semen* 4.531; Athenaeus 7.126.

75. See LSJ s.v. χάρις. Cf. *Andromeda* fragment 136. For *charis* in Greek literature, cf. MacLachlan 1993; Fisher 2013.

76. Cf. *Iliad* 11.243; Aeschylus *Agamemnon* 1206; Euripides *Hecuba* 829–30; Plato *Phaedrus* 254a; Plutarch *Moralia* 751d. For *charis* as erotic delight, see Euripides *Iphigenia in Aulis* 543–57. Charites also are associated with Aphrodite in Greek literature. Cf. *Iliad* 5.338; *Odyssey* 8.362ff; *Hymn to Aphrodite* 5.61; Hesiod *Works and Days* 73; Euripides *Helen* 1338–52; Aristophanes *Acharnians* 988–9; *Peace* 40–1, 456; Pausanias 6.24.7; Athenaeus 15.30; *Greek Anthology* 9.625. Furthermore, in one manuscript of *Helen* (L), Aphrodite is called Χάρις (1006), while in later literature *charis* is also used to designate love potions. See Lucian *Alexander* 5; *On Salaried Posts in Great Houses* 40.

77. See LSJ s.v. χάρις II.2. For the erotic undertones of χάρις in *Andromeda*, cf. Bubel 1991: 132; Klimek-Winter 1993: 215; Funke 2013: 185; Marshall 2015: 136.

78. For the various kinds of erotic reciprocity, see Fisher 2013: *passim*, and especially 39–43.

79. This word refers to young unmarried women, without always denoting their physical state of virginity. See LSJ s.v. *parthenos*. Cf. Calame 1997: 27.

80. See Pagano 2010, 227. Cf. Polyxena's similar grievance in Euripides' *Hecuba* 416.

81. Diogenes Laertius 4. 29.

82. Regarding Andromeda's feelings, Klimek-Winter (1993: 220) concisely summarizes the view of many scholars: 'ob Andromedas Bereitschaft, sich von Perseus unter der Bedingung der Ehe retten zu lassen, auch von Eros motiviert war, lässt sich nicht sagen, scheint aber zumindest möglich.' Cf. Müller 1907: 52; Bubel 1991: 146; Falcetto 1998: 64, 68–9; Collard, Cropp and Gibert 2004: 140; Funke 2013: 176–8. Moreover, even if we accept that Andromeda did not experience any passionate emotions towards Perseus, we can regard her decision to follow him in terms of female agency and independence. Cf. Falcetto 1998: 64, 69; Gibert 1999/2000: 82; Collard, Cropp and Gibert 2004: 140; Funke 2013: 176 n. 430, 185.

83. For instance, see Podlecki 2009: 79.

84. See above n. 69.

85. See the list of Klimek-Winter 1993: 254.

86. See Klimek-Winter 1993: 253–4.

87. For Eros as teacher, cf. Euripides' *Hippolytus Veiled* fragment 430; *Stheneboea* fragment 663; *inc. fab.* fragment 897 (Kannicht).

88. I keep Athenaeus' θεοῖς instead of Dobree's emendation (θνητοῖς), thus the adopted translation of Collard and Cropp. For instances in tragedy where gods are pronounced as (dis)honoured by other gods, see Aeschylus *Eumenides* 721–2, Sophocles' *Oedipus Tyrannus* 214–15 (Finglass 2018a) and Euripides' *Troades* 49. Cf. Biehl 1989: 114. I also translate τοῦ διδάσκεσθαι as middle. For διδάσκομαι used as middle for gods, see LSJ s.v. διδάσκω; Plato *Menexenus* 238b. I thank Mark Huggins for pointing this out to me.

89. I shall not discuss fragment 138a, because I agree with Klimek-Winter (1993: 88) who supports its inauthenticity.

90. Klimek-Winter 1993: 267.

91. See Collard, Cropp and Gibert 2004: 140.

92. For the long history of this marriage, see Hesiod's *Catalogue* fragment 135. For the significance of its durability, cf. Collard, Cropp and Gibert 2004: 140; Ogden 2008: 82. For contrast with the doomed-to-fail romance between Ariadne and Theseus in Euripides' *Theseus*, see Collard, Cropp and Gibert 2004: 141.

93. Euripides *Orestes* 1638, 1653–5.

CHAPTER 10
THE CASE AGAINST DOMESTIC SECLUSION IN (EURIPIDES) FR. 1063

Elizabeth Scharffenberger

The sixteen iambic trimeter verses of fr. 1063 are preserved by the early-fifth-century CE anthologist Joannes Stobaeus[1] in a collection of passages that are grouped under the heading 'counsels concerning marriage' (γαμικὰ παραγγέλματα, 4.23.26a).[2] Lines 2–7 are also cited by the rhetorician Choricius of Gaza, who was active in the early sixth century CE (*Orations* 8.52):[3]

ἐκπυνθάνεσθαι γὰρ σὲ νῷν χήμᾶς σέθεν.
τὸ μὲν μέγιστον, οὔποτ' ἄνδρα χρὴ σοφόν
λίαν φυλάσσειν ἄλοχον ἐν μυχοῖς δόμων·
ἐρᾶ γὰρ ὄψις τῆς θύραθεν ἡδονῆς·
5   ἐν δ' ἀφθόνοισι τοῖσδ' ἀναστρωφωμένη
βλέπουσά τ' εἰς πᾶν καὶ παροῦσα πανταχοῦ
τὴν ὄψιν ἐμπλήσασ' ἀπήλλακται κακῶν·
[τό τ' ἄρσεν αἰεὶ τοῦ κεκρυμμένου λίχνον.]
ὅστις δὲ μοχλοῖς καὶ διὰ σφραγισμάτων
10   σῴζει δάμαρτα, δρᾶν τι δὴ δοκῶν σοφόν
μάταιός ἐστι καὶ φρονῶν οὐδὲν φρονεῖ·
ἥτις γὰρ ἡμῶν καρδίαν θύραζ' ἔχει,
θᾶσσον μὲν οἰστοῦ καὶ πτεροῦ χωρίζεται,
λάθοι δ' ἂν Ἄργου τὰς πυκνοφθάλμους κόρας·
15   καὶ πρὸς κακοῖσι τοῦτο δὴ μέγας γέλως,
ἀνήρ τ' ἀχρεῖος χἠ γυνὴ διοίχεται.[4]

For (it is right) for you to learn from us two, and for us (to learn) from you. This is most important: a wise man ought never keep watch over his wife too closely, confining her in the inner rooms of the house. For the eye[5] longs for pleasure (derived) out of doors.[6] When a woman moves freely amid this abundance[7] and gazes at everything and is present everywhere, she is delivered from evils, having satisfied her eye. The male, too, is always curious about what has been hidden.[8] Whoever secures his wife by bars on the door and through seals impressed on clay – while appearing to do something wise, this man is foolish, and though being sensible he lacks sense. If anyone of us women has a heart bound for out of doors, she takes off[9] faster than an arrow or a bird in flight, and she would elude the close-packed eyes of Argus. This is humiliation on top of troubles. The husband is inept, and his wife vanishes.[10]

The passage is plainly excerpted from a dramatic exchange in which two speakers with different views confront one another in argument. The speaker of these lines is female, as is made clear by the feminine relative pronoun (ἥτις) coupled with the first-person plural partitive genitive ἡμῶν in line 12, and her addressee is almost certainly male. The emendation in the first verse adopted by all modern editors, reading γὰρ σὲ νῷν χἠμᾶς σέθεν for the nonsensical and obviously corrupt τάρσένων δ'ἡμᾶς σέθεν found in Stobaeus, posits the speaker as one of two women involved in the action at hand, and it invites us to imagine that she speaks not only for women in general, but on behalf of another female figure who is present onstage with her. Neither Stobaeus nor Choricius names the author or title of the work from which the verses are excerpted, and Stobaeus places the fragment immediately after a pair of verses from an unknown comedy by Menander (fr. 816 K.-A.), without any indication that it is derived from a drama by a different playwright. Choricius, however, identifies lines 2–7 as a 'tragic speech' authored by 'a sensible man who hated women' (τραγικὴν ῥῆσιν ... ἀνδρὸς μισογύνου καὶ σώφρονος), and the reputation for misogyny Euripides garnered in antiquity has encouraged all modern editors to attribute the fragment to Euripides. The phrase ἐν μυχοῖς δόμων ('in the inner rooms of the house') in line 3 is very close to phrases found in Euripides' *Helen*, *Medea* and *Hecuba*, and the paradoxical expression φρονῶν οὐδὲν φρονεῖ ('though being sensible he lacks sense') in line 11 occurs almost verbatim in *Bacchae* 332.[11] In addition, the participial phrase τὴν ὄψιν ἐμπλήσασ(α) ('having satisfied her eye') in line 7 features the same vocabulary as the clause τὰν γυναικεῖον ὄψιν ὀμμάτων ὡς πλήσαιμι (literally, 'so that I might satisfy the womanly sight of my eyes') in *Iphigenia in Aulis* 233–4. These phrases might make the attribution of the fragment to Euripides seem even more secure. But let us consider more carefully the genre and author of the fragment's source-play after we have examined its content.

Fr. 1063 has received little scholarly attention. Isabelle Torrance's concise analysis stands out for its discernment of the fragment's 'important thematic emphasis on sight' and the significance of line 14's reference to the mythical hundred-eyed herdsman Argus, whose legendary ability to see all is the desired object of 'the deprived wife' (lines 5–7).[12] Otherwise, commentaries briefly note the interest the fragment shares with other passages from dramas by Athenian playwrights, notably Euripides, in the 'safeguarding' of married and marriageable women within the confines of the home.[13] David Cohen has persuasively argued that this practice, typically termed 'domestic seclusion' in modern scholarship, was not the norm in classical Athens, where women, though often separated from men and barred from participating in 'exclusively male activities such as war and politics', were 'not confined in their houses in "oriental seclusion"' and were, in fact, expected to go out.[14] Acknowledging that some in Athens may have nonetheless embraced the model of seclusion as a cultural ideal despite its detachment from 'the life of the society', Cohen helpfully suggests that playwrights such as Euripides and Aristophanes engage in a 'practice of conscious dramatic manipulation of ideologically determined stances' in the confrontations they stage concerning the public appearances of women, which exploit 'the contradiction between ... woman as men think she should be, woman as men fear she is, and the mothers, maids, wives, and widows of everyday existence'.[15]

With this in mind, it is appropriate to ask what kind of 'conscious dramatic manipulation' may be at work, and what is actually at stake, in the distinctive case fr. 1063 presents against domestic seclusion. As I see it, the speaker's argument conspicuously inverts the emphasis that the model of seclusion puts on the visibility of women to male viewers by foregrounding, instead, the ability and desire and need of women to be active viewers in their own right. As it elicits empathy for the feminine experience with its imaginative, vivid account of the hypothetical wife's desire to 'gaze at everything' and the consequences of her frustration when she is cooped up at home, it advances a fundamentally positive conception of the married woman as a competent, mature agent who is fully capable of self-regulation. This robust conception may have certainly been framed as a counterweight to general social prejudices that minimized the capabilities and contributions of women, thus entering into the competition of what Cohen terms 'ideologically determined stances'.[16] More particularly, I submit, it responds to unflattering representations of female weakness and licentiousness in drama and other poetic genres dating back to the archaic period. Though brief, the fragment perhaps presents a noteworthy instance of self-conscious reflection on the conventions of poetic representation, especially the representation of women, thus participating in the tendency toward metapoetic reflections and confrontations that became increasingly prominent in late-fifth-century drama.[17]

To get a sense of what makes fr. 1063's argument against domestic seclusion distinctive, it is instructive to compare it with the sentiments preserved in the small handful of dramatic fragments, all attributed to Euripides, in which the speakers call into question the wisdom and efficacy of efforts to seclude women.[18] François Jouan and Hermann van Looy note a particular similarity between the sentiments expressed in fr. 1063.11–16 and the resigned concession in fr. 1061, which Stobaeus explicitly attributes to Euripides (4.23.10):

μοχθοῦμεν ἄλλως θῆλυ φρουροῦντες γένος·
ἥτις γὰρ αὐτὴ μὴ πέφυκεν †εν δος†,
τί δεῖ φυλάσσειν κἀξαμαρτάνειν πλέον;

We labour in vain, keeping watch over the race of women. Any woman who is not born [with an innate sense of right and wrong[19]] – what good is there in keeping watch over her, exacerbating one's mistake?[20]

Yet there is an important difference in the perspectives of fr. 1061's male speaker and fr. 1063's female speaker. The female speaker of fr. 1063 strives to persuade her listener of not only the futility, but also the superfluity, of efforts to 'keep watch' over his wife 'in the inner rooms of the house' (line 3). Although her speech has a cautionary dimension in its claims that the man who tries too assiduously to shut his wife indoors will end up driving her away (lines 9–16), her primary aim is arguably to ease her listener's worries about the integrity of his household – worries that would appear very similar to those that inform the pronouncements in favour of domestic seclusion of women elsewhere in Athenian drama.

In support of her claim that 'a wise man ought never keep watch over his wife too closely' (line 2), fr. 1063's speaker presents a fascinating hypothesis concerning the psychological necessity of visual stimulation that has, as far as I know, no close parallel in Athenian drama or in other extant texts dating to the classical period.[21] On her argument, the desire to see things 'out of doors' is so basic and strong that, if someone tries to thwart it – for example, an overprotective husband who forbids his wife access to the outside world – the attempt will inevitably backfire in the most counterproductive and mortifying manner. Yet, as strong as this desire is, it is also harmless when satisfied and, in fact, has a salutary effect. With the assertion that a woman is 'delivered from evils, having satisfied her eye' (line 7), the speaker appears to suggest that the fulfilment of the desire for visual stimulation acts as a prophylactic against the very kind of disruptive (i.e. sexually transgressive) behaviour that might cause husbands to worry about their wives leaving the home in the first place.[22] It is worth noting that, although the argument focuses on the situation of married women, the speaker's initial claim that the eye 'longs for pleasure out of doors' (line 4) is presented in gender-neutral terms. It is possible, then, that the overall thrust of her argument is to suggest that the desires for visual stimulation experienced by women and men are very much alike, if not identical.[23]

We may wonder how credible this female speaker's argument would have seemed to Athenian spectators, and whether the playwright who brought her to life on the stage crafted her words so as to arouse suspicions about not only the soundness of her reasoning, but also her motivations for making this counterintuitive case about the steps that a husband might take to ensure his wife's fidelity.[24] The speaker does not shy away from erotically charged language, most notably in line 4 ('the eye longs for [ἐρᾷ] pleasure derived out of doors').[25] Her framing of the need to 'satisfy the eye' in terms of 'longing' (ἔρως), which is typically identified as the driving force behind illicit sexual desire, may in itself constitute a red flag for spectators, who might have listened with suspicion and assumed that 'pleasure derived out of doors' is, in fact, 'that of attractive men'.[26] Moreover, the events that unfolded in the drama could have made the speaker seem unreliable in some regard – we might think of figures like Medea in Euripides' *Medea* or Clytemnestra in Aeschylus' *Oresteia*, or Phaedra's nurse in Euripides' *Hippolytus* – leading to the conclusion that her argument should be dismissed as an effort to generate opportunities as well as pretexts for women to pursue illicit sexual liaisons.

Conversely, we cannot rule out the possibility that elements of the argument preserved in fr. 1063 could have struck a chord with members of the audience. This could have easily been the case if the speaker resembled Jocasta in Euripides' *Phoenician Women* – i.e. a wise, responsible and dignified mediator who strives to resolve problems by reasonably moderating her interlocutors' views, and whose aspirations would have seemed unquestionably innocuous.[27] And even if she was more of a Medea than a Jocasta, it is nonetheless conceivable that her argument had traction. Donald Mastronarde argues persuasively that male spectators in the Theatre of Dionysus may have been capable of 'some degree of sympathetic engagement' with the positions of threatening female figures such as Euripides' Medea and Aeschylus' Clytemnestra.[28] If it is arguable that, despite the dangers she poses, Medea's meditation on the difficulties experienced by married women (*Medea* 230–51) could have had some cogency for Euripides' audience, we might also entertain the proposition that, no matter what her disposition was, the speaker's argument in fr. 1063 and the vivid picture she paints of a hapless wife locked indoors by her jealous husband (lines 9–11) were not designed to be dismissed out of hand. In particular, the wording of lines 5–7 ('When a woman moves freely amid this abundance and gazes at everything and is present everywhere, she satisfies her eye and is delivered from evils') emphasizes the act itself of seeing, not the object seen, as the source of pleasure and satisfaction.[29] These verses may have encouraged spectators to imagine the scenario envisioned here, of a woman innocently satisfying 'her eye' out of doors and then returning home 'released from evils', in terms of their own pleasurable experiences in the very place they currently sat, watching this very drama – i.e. in the theatre.[30]

These verses appear to engage the actual experiences of spectators in other ways as well, as they invite reflection on the representations of women in the drama and other familiar forms of poetry to which spectators in the Theatre of Dionysus received regular exposure. Unlike, for example, the opening strophic pair in the first stasimon of Euripides' *Medea* (410–30), the fragment does not explicitly advertise an interest in metapoetic reflection that self-consciously calls attention to traditional treatments of female conduct in song and in the theatre. Nonetheless, its conceptualization of the woman as an active and engaged viewer, whose powers of discernment and self-control match those of men, appears to push back against two basic perceptions of women, especially as women relate to the act of seeing, which were popularized in drama and other forms of poetry. First, the reference to 'the close-packed eyes of Argus' (line 14) arguably gestures towards the conventional image of the female as the 'thing seen' by male viewers, such as the gorgeous Helen whose beauty dazzles the old men of Troy when she first appears in *Iliad* 3.154–60.[31] But in contrast to the hapless Io, who cannot escape Argus' watchful eyes, the frustrated wife in the fragment's hypothetical scenario ultimately eludes her overzealous husband's surveillance; this is the humiliating outcome of his failure to recognize her need to see in her own right.[32] At the same time, by emphasizing the pleasure derived from the activity of seeing and then claiming that the woman who 'gazes at everything' ends up being released from 'evils', the speaker addresses worries about the vulnerability of women as viewers – the sorts of worries that might have been entrenched by the image of Helen inflamed by lust at the mere sight of the handsome Paris, as in Euripides' *Trojan Women* 987–91.[33] On this speaker's argument, the woman who 'satisfies her eye' is not distracted from her domestic responsibilities. She voluntarily keeps her place in the home as a loyal wife and does not attempt to arrogate the political, social or sexual privileges of men. It is, rather, the overprotected woman whose frustration impels her to desert her home and assume masculine prerogatives of independence and self-gratification.

Put in other terms, the argument preserved in this fragment seems to reposition the married woman as a 'subject' rather than an 'object', insofar as it casts her as a mature, responsible agent who desires to see, but is capable of managing her desires and, in particular, of regulating her responses to what she sees in an appropriate fashion that ensures conformity with the demands imposed by her social and familial obligations.[34]

As it counters unflattering images in drama and other forms of poetry, this repositioning would also seem to confront broader cultural prejudices about the intellectual and ethical capacities of women. Rendering this confrontation particularly potent is the scenario described in lines 9–10, which vividly imagines the fruitless measures taken by the misguidedly zealous man who 'secures his wife by bars on the door and through seals impressed on clay' (ὅστις δὲ μοχλοῖς καὶ διὰ σφραγισμάτων | σῴζει δάμαρτα ...), presumably as he locks her in the women's quarter of his house.[35] The image of the husband trying to 'secure' his wife 'with door bars and (clay) seals' (μοχλοῖς καὶ διὰ σφραγισμάτων), the very means that one would use to secure goods like wine, oil and grain in a dark and isolated storeroom, plainly locates his mistake in his treatment of his wife as an inanimate thing, rather than as a mature and responsible person who is unable to bear the extreme sensory deprivation entailed by 'being secured' in the home. The expression σῴζει δάμαρτα reinforces the impression that the husband trips himself up by objectifying his wife. Whereas the verb φυλάσσειν ('keep watch over', used in line 3) is the usual verb to describe the act of watching over an adult so as to keep him or her out of harm's way, the verb σῴζειν, used in line 9, typically means 'save from death' when its object is an adult and takes on the significance of 'safeguard' or 'secure' only when applied to inanimate objects or children.[36] Using domestic seclusion as its explicit target, the infelicitous scenario imagined in these verses arguably presents an implicit challenge to a more extensive, and more socially significant, complex of attitudes, assumptions and practices that objectify and infantilize women.

We are now well positioned to return to the questions we left open concerning the genre and author of fr. 1063's source-drama. Certain aspects of the fragment's content and its handling of metre dispose me to put credence in Choricius' attribution to a tragedy, and to think that the apparent attribution to Menander in the manuscripts of Stobaeus resulted from an error, by Stobaeus himself or one of the sources that transmitted the fragment to him, or from the omission in later copies of the proper attribution made in Stobaeus' original text. Porson's Law is strictly observed in these sixteen verses as they are conventionally edited, which reflects the practice in tragedy but not in comedy.[37] Whereas we would expect to see free use of resolved short syllables in a passage of this length by Menander or Aristophanes,[38] the first two syllables of line 3's ἄλοχον present the only instance of a long element resolved into two short syllables, and this conservative use of resolution also suggests a tragic source. Apart from the extraordinary image of the jealous husband in lines 9–11, the fragment presents a straightforward appeal devoid of the jokes and humorous flourishes that tend to crop up in comic efforts at persuasion, and this feature might further recommend a tragedy as the fragment's source. It is true that *Lysistrata* 1124–35 could be adduced as a parallel in comedy for the sort of earnest appeal to good sense presented in fr. 1063. Like the fragment, this prelude to Lysistrata's critique of the conduct of Athenian and Spartan men does not feature the kinds of jokes and funny images we find in, for example, *Acharnians* 496–556. We should note that *Lysistrata* 1124 and its immediately following verses clearly have a tragic pedigree, echoing the protagonist's words in Euripides' *Melanippe the Wise*. Nonetheless, comic licence quickly asserts itself in the handling of the trimeters, with violations of Porson's

Law in both 1128 and 1130; in contrast, there is no encroachment in fr. 1063 of comic metrical licence that creates tension with its tragic phraseology and the speaker's earnest tone.[39] The short phrases in fr. 1063 with close resemblances to wording found in extant Euripidean tragedies – ἐν μυχοῖς δόμων ('in the inner rooms of the house') in line 3 and φρονῶν οὐδὲν φρονεῖ ('though being sensible he lacks sense') in line 11 – do not offer solid evidence that the fragment is derived from a comedy that parodied Euripides, because they are not framed by the sort of commentary or cheeky distortions that typically flag the quotations of tragic phrases in comedies.[40] Rather, the phrases suggest that the author was Euripides himself, who comfortably recycled his own turns of phrase, or another tragedian who may have aimed to have his work sound Euripidean.

In this context, the vocabulary in fr. 1063.9 merits special attention. The word used here for the imprinted clay seal around the door frame, σφράγισμα, and its source-word, the noun σφραγίς, occur infrequently in drama. When they are used in dramatic texts, both words almost always denote either a signet ring presented as a token of identity or the impression made by such a ring on the wax seal of a letter.[41] The important exceptions are in this verse and in *Thesmophorizusae* 414–17, at the midpoint of the speech delivered by the first speaker at the women's assembly that has been convened in order to determine how best to punish Euripides for the unflattering representations of female figures in his tragedies.[42] As she details the ways, she claims, Euripides' dramas have adversely affected the lives of Athenian women because of the suspicions they arouse in men concerning the misbehaviour of the females in their households, Aristophanes' speaker asserts:

εἶτα διὰ τοῦτον ταῖς γυναικωνίτισιν
σφραγῖδας ἐπιβάλλουσιν ἤδη καὶ μοχλοὺς
τηροῦντες ἡμᾶς, καὶ προσέτι Μολοττικοὺς
τρέφουσι μορμολυκεῖα τοῖς μοιχοῖς κύνας.

And then, because of this man [i.e. Euripides], they now place seals and bars on the women's quarters, trying to keep watch over us, and on top of this they keep Molossian dogs as bogey wolf-monsters for our boyfriends.[43]

In *Thesmophoriazusae* 415, σφραγῖδας and μοχλούς refer to the very same objects – imprints of seals pressed on clay caulked around a door (typically a door of a storeroom) and crosspieces used to secure doors – as the μοχλοῖς and σφραγισμάτων in fr. 1063.9. The conjunction of μοχλός and σφραγίς/σφράγισμα in the two verses is unparalleled elsewhere in extant Athenian dramas and fragments. Moreover, the action described by Aristophanes' speaker – of men shutting their wives in the women's quarters by means of the hardware conventionally used to secure a storeroom – is identical to the scenario envisioned in the fragment. These affinities are remarkable and will presently receive more attention. For the moment, let us note, by way of an important difference, how quickly the complaint of Aristophanes' speaker about hypervigilant husbands segues into a joke that capitalizes on the familiar comic stereotype of female libidinousness, thereby humorously disrupting her logic and undercutting the notion that there is something wrong with husbands 'trying to keep watch over' their wives. There is no such humorous disruption in fr. 1063, and this should make us hesitate to construe the affinities in the two passages as evidence that the fragment derives from a comedy. Rather, I submit, the absence of humorous disruption in the verses following the image of the overzealous husband in fr. 1063.9–10 corroborates what we noted above: despite its deployment of a hyperbolic image that is plainly at home in Aristophanes, the fragment sustains an evenness in argument and a restraint in tone and metre that are in keeping with the style of tragedy rather than that of comedy.

There remains the intriguing fact that fr. 1063.9–10 and *Thesmophorizusae* 414–16 use virtually identical vocabulary to envision identical scenarios. The almost exact correspondences between the two passages could be products of coincidence, but they could also point to a relationship between Aristophanes' comedy and the drama – the tragic drama, as I would have it – that contained the verses preserved in the fragment. Any argument for such a relationship is admittedly of a highly speculative nature. Nonetheless, given the striking similarities of the two passages and their unique points of contact, I think that it is at least worth entertaining the possibility that one of the dramas is indebted to the other.

Which drama is most likely to have been the source of inspiration? We might naturally assume that the comedian Aristophanes, ever eager to exploit tragic drama for humorous ends, derived his general inspiration for the allegation in *Thesmophoriazusae* 414–16, as well as the specific collocation of σφραγῖδας and μοχλούς, from the tragedy that contained fr. 1063.[44] If the fragment is indeed excerpted from a tragedy by Euripides, we might suppose that the incentive for Aristophanes to appropriate its vivid image of the anxious husband, caulking clay and signet and door bars at the ready, would have been considerable, given that Euripides and Euripidean tragedy are central to *Thesmophoriazusae*'s plot. But, if Aristophanes was borrowing from a tragedy – especially from a tragedy by Euripides and in a speech where his character is in the process of detailing all of Euripides' alleged failings – he might reasonably be expected to mine the humour of the appropriation more extensively, and to exploit the opportunity for a joke by flagging it with an obvious comic distortion or signpost, as he does with the immediately preceding Euripidean paraphrases in lines 403–4, 406 and 414. Passing up opportunities for jokes is not something Aristophanes typically does, and this suggests to me that *Thesmophoriazusae* 414–16 is not an appropriation of fr. 1063.9–10.

Rather, my suspicion is that the author of the tragedy that contained fr. 1063 took his cue from Aristophanes, which means that the tragedy in question would have post-dated *Thesmophoriazusae*. Scholars today are comfortable with the proposition that Athenian tragedies, especially in the last decade of the fifth century, appropriated material from comedy with a variety of effects,[45] and it is therefore not unthinkable that the author of the fragment's source-drama may have co-opted Aristophanes' vivid comic scenario and vocabulary to capture his spectators' attention. The author may not have necessarily expected his spectators to recognize *Thesmophoriazusae* as his specific source of inspiration, but the distinctive conjunction of σφράγισμα and μοχλός in fr. 1063's description of the worried husband could be construed as an allusive reference to Aristophanes that was designed to trigger recollection of *Thesmophoriazusae*.[46] The conservative handling of resolution in the fragment's trimeters, however, might be taken as an indication that its source-tragedy was composed before *Thesmophoriazusae*'s production in 411 BCE, especially if we suppose that the fragment derives from a tragedy by Euripides.[47] On the other hand, the absence of resolutions in these sixteen verses could result from a deliberate stylistic choice, perhaps contingent on the author's desire to make the speaker sound measured, calm and self-controlled, and it may not necessarily indicate that the fragment comes from a tragedy composed before 411. The unique adjective πυκνοφθάλμους ('with close-packed eyes') in fr. 1063.14 possibly corroborates a date of composition after 411, since the adjectival compounds that it most closely resembles, πυκνόπτερος ('many-feathered') and πυκνόστικτος ('dappled'), occur only in Sophocles' *Oedipus at Colonus*, which was composed in the last decade of the fifth century.[48]

This speculation brings us back to the fragment's authorship. Features of its style, principally the seemingly awkward string of feminine nominative singular participles in lines 5–7 (ἀναστρωφωμένη ... βλέπουσά ... παροῦσα ... ἐμπλήσασ(α)) might make us hesitate to attribute it to an accomplished poet like Euripides.[49] But this concentration of participles can itself be viewed as a deliberate stylistic choice, whereby the speaker focuses attention on the moment-to-moment experiences of the hypothetical woman she envisions exploring the world out of doors. Nothing else in the fragment speaks strongly against assuming, as all modern editors have, that it is from a tragedy by Euripides. Moreover, the fragment's interest in using the practice of domestic seclusion as a means for probing attitudes towards women corresponds closely to what we find in tragedies and other fragments securely attributed to Euripides.[50] If we are comfortable with the proposition that even in his later tragedies Euripides could temper his use of resolutions in iambic trimeter, and if we hold to the notion that the fragment borrows from *Thesmophoriazusae*, we can readily imagine that *Thesmophoriazusae*'s plot – and the specific allegations made by the first woman who speaks against Aristophanes' fictive Euripides – could have given the actual Euripides a singular motivation to repurpose the very words and image used by his comic accuser in *Thesmophoriazusae* 414–16 in the service of crafting a truly robust conceptualization of female agency.

The task awaits to identify a Euripidean tragedy, dating to the few years between the comedy's performance in 411 BCE and Euripides' death in early 406, that could have featured the kind of exchange to which the fragment clearly belongs. With its focus on the romantic relationship of Antigone and Haemon, Euripides' fragmentary *Antigone* seems a plausible candidate.[51] Uncertainties attend this suggestion, because we cannot be sure beyond doubt that *Antigone* post-dates *Thesmophoriazusae*,[52] and because the extant fragments do not confirm that another female figure aside from Antigone herself had a speaking role in the tragedy. Aristophanes of Byzantium remarks in his hypothesis to Sophocles' *Antigone* that Euripides' treatment of the myth matches the earlier treatment of Sophocles, except for the denouement that happily leads, in Euripides' version, to the marriage of Haemon and Antigone.[53] This remark makes it legitimate to wonder whether Euripides, like Sophocles, could have developed a significant role for Eurydice, wife of Creon and mother of Haemon, who commits suicide in Sophocles' version but may have survived in Euripides' drama along with her son and his bride-to-be. If we speculate along these lines, we might find a place for fr. 1063 in Euripides' *Antigone* by assigning it to Eurydice, and by conjecturing that some anxiety, perhaps stirred by long experience with the overly rigid and protective ways of Creon, prompted her to confront her son and urge him to exercise restraint in his relationship with Antigone.

Attractive as this possibility is to me, I want to remain open to an alternative conjecture concerning the authorship of fr. 1063: that it was excerpted from a tragedy composed by another Athenian tragedian who sought to emulate Euripides. As Ralph Rosen has argued, Euripides was well on his way to becoming a 'classic' author in his own lifetime,[54] and his dramas seem to have remained very popular in the years immediately after his death, if the comic quotations by Strattis, Sannyrion and Theopompus (all active at this time) can be relied on as evidence.[55] It is conceivable, then, that at least one tragedian composing in the very last years of the fifth century or the first decade of the fourth century, if not several, was eager to ride the early coat-tails of Euripides' posthumous popularity, and that this eagerness could have inspired him to embrace Euripides' interest in women (and in the possibilities afforded by domestic seclusion for exploring competing views of women) and, moreover, to incorporate phrases echoing Euripidean locutions as a means of establishing himself as the recently deceased tragedian's artistic heir. If we entertain this proposition alongside the suggestion that fr. 1063 responds to *Thesmophoriazusae*, we can imagine that our would-be emulator crafted his sophisticated vision of the responsible female agent as a tribute to Euripides that also gives a sly nod to Aristophanes – just as Euripides himself might have done.[56]

Notes

1. I owe many thanks to the editors of this volume, Professor C. W. Marshall and Professor Hallie R. Marshall, the referees of Bloomsbury Academic UK and Anastasia-Stavroula Valtadorou; their careful reading of this paper's final drafts led to several significant improvements. I am also indebted to the audiences of earlier versions of the paper at the Comparative Drama Conference (April 2013), the Department of Classics at the CUNY Graduate Center (September 2014), Feminism and Classics VII (May 2016) and Greek Drama V (July 2017), whose thoughtful questions and suggestions inspired me to rethink and revise many aspects of my argument. All remaining errors in fact and interpretation are my own.

2. Wachsmuth and Hense 1958 (vol. 4): 578–9; cf. Meineke 1856 (vol. 3): 56.

3. Foerster and Richtsteig 1929: 355–6.

4. For his text of fr. 1063 (cited here), Kannicht 2004:1003–4 adopts most of the emendations accepted in other major editions of Euripides' fragments, such as Nauck 1889: 696–7, Jouan and van Looy 2003 (vol. 8.4) 96–7, and Collard and Cropp 2008 (vol. 8.2): 598–9, and in the editions of Stobaeus and Choricius cited above in n. 2 and n. 3. The *apparatus critici* of Nauck, Wachsmuth and Hense, Foerster and Richtsteig and Kannicht present full accounts of the fragment's textual issues and the proposed emendations.

5. Kannicht (on line 4) notes that ὄψις (literally, 'sight' or 'sense of sight') is used as a synonym for ὄμμα ('eye') in Euripides, *Cyclops* 458–9, 462–3, 486 and 595. See also Euripides, *Iphigenia*

in Aulis 233, for the phrase τὰν γυναικεῖον ὄψιν ὀμμάτων (literally, 'the womanly sight of (my) eyes').

6. In Choricius, line 4 is followed by an additional verse, ἐρᾷ δ'ἀκούειν ὧν φυλάττεται κλύειν ('and (she) longs to hear things she is guarded from hearing'), which Collard and Cropp suggest was included to ease 'the awkward transition' between line 4 (with ὄψις as the subject) and line 5 (with the wife as the subject). The possibility of a lacuna of a verse or two after line 4 cannot be ruled out.

7. Cf. the use of the phrase ἐν ἀφθόνοις (literally, 'amid abundant things') in Xenophon, *Anabasis* 3.2.25 (ἐν ἀφθόνοις βιοτεύειν, 'to live in luxury'), and Demosthenes, *On the Crown* 256 (ἐν ἀφθόνοις τραφείς, 'having been raised in affluence').

8. Kannicht as well as Collard and Cropp bracket line 8 as an interpolation, following Nicolaus Wecklein, who suggested as well that fr. 1063 may be two fragments (i.e. lines 1–7 and 9–16) cobbled together from two different sources; cf. Jouan and van Looy. But, in defending the unity of the fragment, Headlam 1901: 108 makes the attractive suggestion that there is a lacuna after line 7, in which a verse linking the train of thought in lines 1–7 and 8–16 has dropped out. Headlam suggests that the verse could have been something like τὸ θῆλυ γὰρ πέφυκεν ἐξ ἴσου γένος which, coupled with line 8 (τό τ' ἄρσεν αἰεὶ τοῦ κεκρυμμένου λίχνον), would yield sense along the lines of 'The female race is by nature, equally as is the male, curious about what is hidden.'

9. Nauck and Jouan and van Looy read χαρίζεται instead of χωρίζεται in line 13 ('She gratifies her desire faster than an arrow . . .'), but do not comment on the source of the variant.

10. Text Kannicht 2004: 1003–4; my translation.

11. As noted by Jouan and van Looy, who compare line 3's ἐν μυχοῖς δόμων to οἴκων ἐν μυχοῖς (also meaning 'in the inner rooms of the house', *Helen* 820), μυχοῖς . . . ἑστίας ἐμῆς, ('in the recesses of my hearth', *Medea* 397) and οἴκων τῶνδ' . . . μυχούς ('the inner rooms of this dwelling', *Hecuba* 1040).

12. Torrance 2013: 118.

13. E.g. Jouan and van Looy and Collard and Cropp. Notable passages in Athenian tragedy concerning the desirability of keeping women inside the home and away from public view include Aeschylus, *Seven Against Thebes* 200–1 and 230–2, Euripides, *Andromache* 876–8 and 929–53, *Children of Heracles* 476–7 and *Bacchae* 215–25. Also relevant to this theme are Euripides, *Hippolytus* 645–50 and *Phoenician Women* 88–91. Aristophanes, *Thesmophoriazusae* 395–418 and 785–99 supply the most extensive comic treatment of the topic. Important discussions of Athenian attitudes concerning the domestic seclusion of women, especially as reflected in fifth-century drama, are Shaw 1975, Gould 1980, Foley 1982b and 2001: 61–87, Walcot 1984, Gardner 1989, Katz 1992, Humphreys 1993: 58–78, Moreau 1994/5, McClure 1999: 142–6 and 196–8 and Rabinowitz 2013.

14. Cohen 1990: 157; cf. Cohen 1989 and Olson and Austin 2004: 184 (on *Thesm.* 414).

15. Cohen 1989: 4–5.

16. Cohen 1989: 5. The fragment's positive conception of the active female viewer may present a complication for the argument of Rabinowitz 2013, who suggests that '. . . a seeming cause of feminist celebration – the representation [in tragedy] of women's active gaze – negates neither the relegation of women to the domestic interior nor the prescription of downcast eyes. Rather, women outside and women looking are intertwined with allusions to the norms prohibiting those very locations and actions' (196–7).

17. For a comprehensive discussion of metapoetry in Euripides' tragedies, see Torrance 2013.

18. I.e. *Alope*, fr. 8; *Danaë*, fr. 320 and fr. 1061 (from an unknown play).

19. Most editors accept ἔνδικος ('innately just'), J. M. Gesner's emendation for the manuscripts' nonsensical εν δος in line 2.

20. Text Kannicht 2004: 1003; my translation.

21. The overview in Caston 2015: 29–37 of the theories of sense perception articulated in pre-Socratic writings underscores the interest of early thinkers in the mechanics, rather than the psychological effects, of sense perception. Gorgias' *Encomium of Helen* 15–19 closely links ἔρως and ὄψις, as it theorizes about the impact of different kinds of visual experiences on the human soul (e.g. the sight of an enemy's army, which inspires panic, and the sight of a beautiful person, which inspires lust). But Gorgias' attribution to 'sight' (ὄψις) of an overwhelming power that 'disturbs the soul' (ἐτάραξε τὴν ψυχήν, 16) and inspires uncontrollable emotions seems diametrically opposed to the argument in fr. 1063.

22. On this point, comparison of fr. 1063's argument with the attitudes expressed by the sightseeing chorus of Chalcidean women in the parodos of *Iphigenia in Aulis* (163–302) is illuminating. The chorus acknowledges that satisfying the desire to see the Greek army is a source of pleasure († μείλινον † ἀδονάν, 234); nonetheless, as Rabinowitz 2013: 203 observes, 'they corroborate the norm of women's *aidôs* by saying they are embarrassed to be looking (187–8).' In contrast, the speaker of fr. 1063 appears to challenge the norm that equates feminine modesty with 'not looking'.

23. If line 8 is accepted as part of the fragment, the suggestion of similarities in the experiences of men and women is explicit. See the discussion of this verse in n. 8 above.

24. McClure 1999: 71 argues that the speech of certain female figures in tragedy, such as Clytemnestra in Aeschylus' *Oresteia*, 'harks back to the archaic topos of women's seductive persuasiveness', and that in particular Clytemnestra's 'vacillations' between 'masculine and feminine verbal genres . . . destabilize gender roles' in a disturbing fashion. Moreover, Griffith 2001: 123 observes that 'female speech [in tragedy] is more likely . . . to talk positively about the effects of erotic desire . . .'. This observation, coupled with McClure's argument concerning the problematization of the 'deceptive, figurative, and erotic speech' deployed by Aeschylus' Clytemnestra (1999: 110), might dispose us to conclude that the case articulated by fr. 1063's female speaker, which is tantamount to a defence of ἔρως, would have seemed instantly suspect, especially if we assume for Athenian tragedy a general tendency to emphasize the destructive consequences of erotic passion – see, for example, Thumiger 2013. Wright 2017 and Valtadorou (in this volume), however, have challenged assumptions concerning the uniform negativity in tragic perspectives on ἔρως, and their analyses give cause for considering that fr. 1063's account of the benefits stemming from satisfying 'the eye's longing' could have seemed credible rather than off-putting.

25. Images of sexual availability and self-indulgence might also be conjured by the participial phrases in line 5, 'moving freely amid this abundance' (if this is an acceptable interpretation of ἐν δ' ἀφθόνοισι . . . ἀναστρωφωμένη, which is the emendation adopted by all modern editors of the unmetrical ἀναστροφωμένη and ἀναστρεφωμένη transmitted in Stobaeus and Choricius – cf. ἐν νέοις στρωφωμένη ('freely moving among young men') in Euripides, *Alcestis* 1052), and in line 7, 'having satisfied her eye' (τὴν ὄψιν ἐμπλήσασα). Such images could be further reinforced by line 13, if χαρίζεται is read instead of χωρίζεται ('She gratifies her desire faster than an arrow or a bird in flight'), and by the adjective λίχνον ('curious', but also possibly with negative connotations of self-indulgent 'gluttony') in line 8, if the verse is retained as part of the fragment.

26. Collard and Cropp 2008: 599.

27. As Hall 2010: 136 astutely observes, 'the understandable fascination with women who come into conflict with men in Greek tragedy has perhaps tended to obscure the variety and impact of the women who conduct themselves uncontroversially and with dignity in many plays.'

28. Mastronarde 2002: 26–8.

29. Moreover, the use of erotically suggestive language in these verses can be construed as a component of the speaker's strategy for drawing attention to and denaturalizing prejudices concerning unruly female desire.

30. See Rehm 2002: 35–7 on the opportunities that the Theatre of Dionysus afforded for taking pleasure in 'gazing' at spectacles, not only of the dramas performed onstage, but also of 'the sky … the beaten earth of the orchestra, the city, its plains, hills, and out toward the sea'. As Rehm goes on to note, 'the spectators also looked at one another because the slope where they sat and the common light of the sun forced them to survey themselves even as they watched performances'. See also Rabinowitz 2013: 197–200.

31. On *Iliad* 3.154–60, see Finglass 2018b: 140–2. More generally, Rabinowitz 2013: 200 notes that women 'are prominently represented as objects of the gaze in Greek art and literature'.

32. Cf. Torrance 2013: 118.

33. See also Euripides' *Medea* 1156–62, which describes how Creon's daughter cannot resist the sight of the beautiful gifts brought by Medea and Jason's children. As Rabinowitz 2013: 204 observes, 'the effects of the desiring female gaze' are typically presented as 'deadly'; moreover, a 'powerful look' is what marks aggressive women such as Clytemnestra as 'problematic'.

34. This conception of the 'subject', as an individual capable of autonomous regulation and also cognizant of the role external (social) forces play in ordering her existence and shaping her desires, has roots in the philosophy of G. W. F. Hegel. For influential articulations of the conception, see e.g. Foucault 1982 and Butler 1997. Rabinowitz 2013: 209–10 draws attention to the 'performance of subjectivity' in Polyxena's declaration to Odysseus, 'I see you' (ὁρῶ σε), in Euripides, *Hecuba* 342, but argues that the power Polyxena momentarily exerts over Odysseus is 'transformed into self-sacrifice', whereby 'she makes herself the object of the male gaze'. In contrast, fr. 1063's speaker appears to envision scenarios in which females can meaningfully sustain their 'performances of subjectivity'.

35. See Austin and Olson 2004: 183–4 (on *Thesm.* 414) for a concise description of the layout of the typical Athenian house and its women's quarters (γυναικωνῖτις), typically on the upper floor, which were supposed to be inaccessible to men outside the family. Lysias 1.13 and Xenophon, *Oeconomicus* 9.5 show that, at least in some (wealthy?) homes, the door to the women's quarters could be secured by a bolt, and in Lysias it seems that the door could be so secured from the outside by means of a key. But the sealing up of such a 'bedroom' door with clay caulking imprinted by the homeowner's signet seal (σφράγισμα or σφραγίς) is plainly the stuff of fantasy. As Austin and Olson 184–5 (on *Thesm.* 415) note, this kind of caulking technique was used to secure the entrances either to storerooms in private houses or to treasuries in public buildings. Hermione's injunction, in *Andromache* 950–1, that men should 'guard the gates of your houses with bolts and bars' (εὖ φυλάσσετε | κλήθροισι καὶ μοχλοῖσι δωμάτων πύλας) in order to keep other women from visiting their wives provides the closest parallel in extant tragedy for the scenario envisioned in fr. 1063.9–10. Conspicuously lacking is any reference to σφραγίσματα.

36. See LSJ A2 σῴζω for the uses of σῴζειν in Aristophanes, *Peace* 730 (with τάδε τὰ σκεύη ('these tools') as the object), *Birds* 380 (with παῖδας οἶκον χρήματα ('children, house, property' as the object), *Birds* 1062 (with εὐθαλεῖς καρπούς 'flourishing crops' as the object) and *Thesmophoriazusae* 819–20 (with τὰ πατρῷα 'their fathers' possessions' as object). The choice of σῴζει in fr. 1063.9 can also be contrasted with, for example, the imperative φυλάσσετε in *Andromache* 950 and the infinitive φυλάττειν in *Thesmophoriazusae* 791.

37. Goodwin 1977: 358 (§1660).

38. White 1909: 139–40; West 1982: 84–5.

39. Henderson 1987: 197 (on *Lys.* 1124) notes, 'The line is a quotation from Euripides' *Melanippe the Wise* (fr. 483), but the following lines (though they are quasi-tragic in diction and language) cannot continue the quotation ...'. The tension between comic licence and (quasi-) tragic diction is perhaps heightened by the exuberant alliterations of λ, β and μ in line 1128: λαβοῦσα δ᾽ ὑμᾶς λοιδορῆσαι βούλομαι.

40. Examples of comically offset quotations abound in Aristophanes (*Acharnians* 893–4, *Thesmophoriazusae* 855–7 and *Frogs* 100–2, to name just three); see also Strattis, *Phoenician Women* fr. 47 K.-A., Sannyrion, *Danaë* fr. 8, Theopompus, *Odysseus(es)* fr. 35, Nicostratus fr. 29, Philippides, *Philadelphoi* fr. 18 and Diphilus, *The Parasite* fr. 60.

41. Euripides, *Hippolytus* 864, *Electra* 1223 and *Iphigenia in Aulis* 155; also Sophocles, *Women of Trachis* 615. The dative plural of σφραγίς (σφραγῖσι), apparently with the sense of 'seal on a door frame', is found in a fragment that purports to be from Euripides' *Danae* (fr. 1132.59), but is most likely the work of a Byzantine imitator. See Kannicht 2004: 1030.

42. Cf. Kannicht 2004: 1004.

43. Text Austin and Olson 2004: 19; my translation.

44. Olson and Austin 2004: 183 (note on *Thesm.* 414–17) suggest that the verses possibly allude to the plot of Euripides' *Danaë*, in which the protagonist may have been locked away in the παρθενών (the bedroom of an unmarried girl inside the women's quarters) by her worried father Acrisius.

45. For discussions (with bibliographies) concerning the appropriations from comedy by Athenian tragedians, especially Euripides, and the competitive relationship that developed in the late fifth century between the genres of tragedy and comedy, see Foley 2008: 28–33, Walton 2009: 62–78, and Torrance 2013: 267–98.

46. It is worth noting that the concern about the treatment of women as objects to be kept out of sight resurfaces in the first part of *Thesmophoriazusae*'s parabasis (786–99), as the chorus leader details the hypocrisy of the typical male attitude that relegates women to the status of things. (The neuter (τὸ) κακόν ('awful thing') is pointedly used seven times in 787, 789, 791, 794, 796, 797, 799, along with the neuter diminutive τὸ γύναιον ('wife-y') and the pronominal αὐτό ('it') in 792, the neuter adjective φροῦδον ('gone') in 794 and neuter participle παρακύψαν ('peeping out') in 799.) Aristophanes' parabasis, then, shares fr. 1063's interest in the (misguided) objectification of women and even acknowledges the desire of women to get a look at the world outside, as they 'peep out' of their homes (797–9). Yet the passage as a whole remains focused on men's reactions to women, and it does not significantly move past envisioning women as passive objects of men's regard. In contrast, the speaker of fr. 1063 brings about a literal shift of perspective, as she switches the gender of the spectator from male to female and asks her listener to imagine the range of emotions that a woman might feel when she is permitted access to, or deprived of, the rich variety of visual experiences that await her out of doors. If we entertain the prospect that fr. 1063 self-consciously refers back to *Thesmophoriazusae*, we might consider how the fragment's robust conceptualization of female agency capitalizes on ideas and images nascent in the comedy, but also surpasses them in a gesture that is simultaneously appreciative and competitive.

47. Cropp and Fick 1985.

48. πυκνόπτερος ('many-feathered') occurs in *Oedipus at Colonus* 17, and πυκνόστικτος ('dappled') in *Oedipus at Colonus* 1092.

49. In conversation, Martin Cropp has expressed doubts about the Euripidean authorship of this fragment, centring on what he views as the awkward aggregation of participles in lines 5–7. Cf. Mastronarde 1994: 140–1 on the 'odd heaping of participles' in Euripides, *Phoenician Women* 1–3, which has contributed to the doubts of some (but not all) commentators about the authenticity of the first two verses.

50. Cf. Cohen 1989: 4–5.

51. See Paton 1901, Jouan and van Looy 1998 (vol. 8.1): 200–1, and Valtadorou (in this volume), and Foley (forthcoming) on the likelihood that Haemon and Antigone's relationship was a central concern in Euripides' *Antigone*.

52. See Jouan and van Looy 1998 (vol. 8.1): 192–3 for an overview of the proposed ranges of dates. Inglese 1992: 188–90 suggests that *Antigone* may have been performed in 410 BCE.

53. Jouan and van Looy 1998 (vol. 8.1): 194–200 discuss the usefulness of the remark in the Sophoclean hypothesis for determining the contours of Euripides' plot.

54. Rosen 2006.

55. Cited above in n. 40.

56. See Scharffenberger 1995 and 1996 for arguments that Euripides' *Phoenician Women* and *Antiope* responded to (respectively) Aristophanes' *Lysistrata* and *Thesmophoriazusae*.

CHAPTER 11
AESCHYLUS AND THE ICONOGRAPHY OF THE ERINYES

Anna Simas

The language that Aeschylus uses in the *Oresteia* to describe the Erinyes paints a vivid picture of them.[1] Indeed, because of the specificity of Aeschylus' descriptions of the Erinyes, we are able to envision them before our very eyes. Aeschylus was clearly familiar with trends in visual art, since he uses the language of visual arts, and specifically of vase-painting, to describe the Erinyes. In this chapter, I will show that Aeschylus was aware of trends in vase-painting and uses language evocative of visual art in order to prepare his audience for the unprecedented appearance of the Erinyes onstage. I will argue that the language surrounding the materialization of the Erinyes evokes depictions of female monsters such as Gorgons and Harpies that would have been familiar to the audience, and situates Orestes and the Erinyes within a stock scene common in vase-painting: the pursuit scene. By comparing the Erinyes to Gorgons and Harpies and by having Orestes say that he is being chased from his homeland, Aeschylus both foreshadows the physical materialization of the Erinyes and places Orestes within his own, onstage version of the pursuit scene which is so common in vase-painting.

Before I turn to my argument about Aeschylus' engagement with vase-painting in the *Oresteia*, I will discuss his influence on visual art. Scholars generally agree that Aeschylus was the first tragedian to bring the Erinyes onstage, and that he adhered to existing conventions of depicting female monsters in order to prepare his audience for the physical materialization of the Erinyes.[2] However, scholars disagree about whether the Erinyes appeared in visual art prior to the original production of the *Oresteia* in 458 BCE. A. J. N. W. Prag holds that Aeschylus did not introduce the possibility of depicting the Erinyes in visual art, but simply changed the existing conventions of representing them. Prag argues that early representations of the Erinyes depict them as anguiform, and Orestes' flight from them is meant to emulate mythological scenes in which a hero fights a serpent, as with Apollo and Python or Cadmus and the serpent.[3] However, as Haiganuch Sarian shows, the pre-Aeschylean visual depictions that Prag argues are Erinyes cannot be conclusively identified, and there is nothing in extant literary sources to suggest that the Erinyes ever had any form that was not anthropomorphic.[4] Indeed, in no pre-Aeschylean source that discusses them are the Erinyes described in significant physical detail.[5] Therefore, it is likely that Aeschylus introduced the possibility of visually depicting the Erinyes; the first production of the *Oresteia* sparked a new trend in Attic vase-painting of portraying the Erinyes pursuing Orestes. However, as I will discuss, vase-painters do not simply transfer Aeschylus' physical portrayal of the Erinyes from the stage to their pottery. Instead, Attic vase-painters in the period just after the *Oresteia* was produced reformat the Erinyes in a way that adheres to the conventions of depicting female monsters in vase-painting.

There are six extant Attic red-figure vases depicting Orestes in flight from the Erinyes; four of these have been attributed to Late Mannerist painters.[6] The Late Mannerists, so identified by Sir John Beazley and active between about 450 and 425 BCE, 'decorated chiefly column-kraters, hydriai, and pelikai.'[7] Figures painted by the Late Mannerists are generally characterized by 'triangular and wide open' eyes, one or two lines above the eye to represent the upper eyelid, relatively 'few anatomical details', and intricate pleating and movement of their garments.[8] Standard chronology of red-figure vase-painting conservatively dates the four Late Mannerist vases depicting the flight of Orestes to between 475 and 425 BCE; several scholars, including A. D. Trendall and T. B. L. Webster, have proposed an even narrower range of dates, arguing that these vases were produced in the decade between 450 and 440 BCE. Trendall and Webster maintain that these vases were produced after the original performance of the *Oresteia* in 458 BCE, since the depicted scenes strongly suggest features of the Oresteia-mythos likely invented by Aeschylus, such as the roles of Apollo and Athena as, respectively, witness in and presider over Orestes' trial.[9] Trendall and Webster also believe that certain elements in painted depictions of Orestes and the Erinyes reflect the realities of stage decoration, such as the 'altar … on which Orestes takes refuge', which they assert must have been visually reminiscent of the *ekkuklēma* used in the production of *Eumenides*, or the snaky hair of the Erinyes, which is believed to have been part of their original costuming.[10] Additionally, since revivals of the *Oresteia* likely did not occur until the mid 420s BCE, it is reasonable to assume that these vases are a response to the trilogy's original production in 458 BCE.[11] Thus the dating of these four vases follows the chronology of Late Mannerist vase-painting and of productions of the *Oresteia*.

The stylistic similarity of these vases to one another has led scholars to believe that they may have originally comprised part of a now-lost group of bespoke vases: Trendall and Webster argue that these vases were commissioned as prizes for members of the Association of the Educated (θίασος ἐκ τῶν πεπαιδευμένων), a guild of actors allegedly founded by Sophocles around 450 BCE.[12] Prag likewise subscribes to the theory that these four vases were part of a larger group of commissioned vases, since the painters seem to have been working from a common template.[13] Indeed, the stylistic uniformity of these four vases is readily observable: Orestes, nude except for a cloak and hat and with sword drawn, kneels on a pile of stones.[14] He is protected by Apollo, who holds a forked staff. In two of these vases, Apollo is accompanied by Athena (Louvre K343) or by Artemis (Berlin F2380). Orestes is pursued by either a single Erinys or a pair of Erinyes, who wear chitons. Some are winged, while others are not; some brandish snakes or have snakes in their hair, while others do not. Despite these relatively small differences, the scene's composition and the poses of the figures are fairly standardized among these four vases.

In each of these vases, the supernatural status of the Erinyes is indicated either by the presence of snakes or by the addition of wings to their backs – a detail which is noticeably contrary to Aeschylus' portrayal of them, in which they are wingless.[15] Despite the fact

Figure 11.1 Orestes at Delphi, Athenian red-figure column krater attributed to the Orestes Painter, 475–425 BCE. London, British Museum: 1923, 10–16.1. © The Trustees of the British Museum.

Figure 11.2 Orestes and the Erinyes, Athenian red-figure hydria by an unknown Late Mannerist, 475–425 BCE. Berlin, Antikensammlung: F2380. Photo credit: bpk Bildagentur/Antikensammlung/Jutta Tietz-Glagow/Art Resource, NY.

147

Figure 11.3 Orestes with Athena, Apollo and Erinyes, Athenian red-figure column krater attributed to the Duomos Painter, 475–425 BCE. Paris, Musée du Louvre: K343. Photo: Hervé Lewandowski. © RMN-Grand Palais/Art Resource, NY.

that it surely would have been possible to visually depict the terrifying characteristics of Erinyes in the *Oresteia*, like their bleeding eyes, in vase-painting they have none of these aside from their wings and snakes.[16] The disparity between the iconography of the Erinyes in vase-painting and in *Eumenides* invites us to question whether these vases convey significant information about the staging of the *Oresteia*. While it is difficult to posit a direct connection between stage productions and the ceramic arts, scholars agree that vase-painters were often inspired by the theatre, adapting scenes from the stage for their own medium. This kind of adaptation usually required the vase-painters to 'reformat' dramatic scenes for their own audience, adhering to the iconographical conventions of their own time and medium. To this point, Emily Vermeule notes:

> 'Illustrations' in vase painting are not, of course, straight transcriptions from poem or stage to the vase surface. They necessarily contaminate the literary images with stock motifs forming the artistic repertory of the period, because the artist had to

move inside the framework of his trade and could not often go free to create new compositions direct from a literary experience.[17]

Although vase-paintings are not 'straight transcriptions' of dramatic performances, they often do contain details inspired by such performances. Vermeule notes that, especially in the case of particularly popular plays, visual artists incorporate elements drawn from dramatic productions while still adhering to contemporary artistic conventions. Such vases do not usually depict a single dramatic moment, but rather compress multiple dramatic moments into a single painted scene; as Prag notes, this reminds the viewer of 'the most important incidents' in a play.[18] We might therefore expect the vases depicting the pursuit of Orestes by the Erinyes to summarize *Eumenides*, and each figure therein to represent a central plot point: the figure of Apollo reminds the viewer both of Delphi, where Orestes is purified, and of his role as witness in the trial of Orestes; the figure of Athena calls to mind both her role as presider over Orestes' trial and the city of Athens, where Orestes is ultimately exculpated;[19] Orestes' cloak and travelling hat evoke his wanderings; the short chitons and wings of the Erinyes represent their pursuit of Orestes; and the snakes and wings of the Erinyes denote their monstrousness, and thus explain Orestes' apparent terror. These visual cues remind the viewer of the entire plot of *Eumenides*, rather than of a singular scene in the play, since these vases clearly incorporate elements from throughout the play in their presentation of the flight of Orestes.

Upon first glance at any of these vases, there is nothing about the Erinyes that makes them particularly terrifying – in fact, without their wings and snakes, they might even look beautiful.[20] Nonetheless, Orestes is clearly afraid of them, which is indicated by the fact that he is drawing or has drawn his sword in an attempt to protect himself from them. Scholars like Oliver Taplin and R. R. Dyer have argued that the 'beautiful' Erinyes of vase-painting are a response to Aeschylus' innovative linking of the Erinyes with the Semnai Theai, protective goddesses worshipped at Athens.[21] However, though the Erinyes in these vases have none of the terrifying facial features that Aeschylus gives them in the *Oresteia*, Orestes is still clearly terrified of them. Whereas Dyer and Taplin argue for the conflation of these 'beautiful' Erinyes with the Semnai Theai, Susan B. Matheson interprets the 'beautiful' Erinyes as monstrous within the conventions of fifth-century Attic vase-painting.[22] The vase-painters certainly meant to depict these Erinyes as terrifying, especially given the fact that Orestes is clearly distressed in each instance. These Erinyes are frightening, not peaceful; these vases depict the Erinyes before their transition from monstrous to benevolent. Moreover, Orestes seems to be frightened because the Erinyes in each vase are pursuing him; this assertion is supported by the visual depiction of the Erinyes who wear short chitons, which allow their legs to move freely as they run. As I will show, these Erinyes fit into the type of pursuit scene in which a female monster pursues a male quarry.

A fair amount of work has been done on the typical pursuit scene, in which a male figure pursues either a female or a young male sexual partner.[23] However, the conventions of depicting a female who pursues a male quarry are different. According to Robin Osborne, in female-driven pursuit scenes, the female pursuer's body must be 'necessarily different from the human body' in order to indicate that pursuit is not an action appropriate for mortal women.[24] The female pursuer in vase-painting is always marked by attributes that act as a visual shorthand to indicate her non-human status. In the case of monstrous females, their status as monsters is identified by snakes, wings or sometimes both wings and snakes.[25] It is important to note that, aside from the wings and snakes which denote the monstrous female body, female monsters are often depicted in vase-painting as otherwise normal-looking, or even beautiful, women.[26] Despite the fact that their wings (and sometimes snakes) are the only attributes that mark these female figures as non-human, the men in these scenes are clearly afraid of them; this is because (1) their wings and snakes are shorthand symbols that indicate to the external viewer that these are fearsome creatures, and (2) these monstrous females are specifically pursuing the male figures in these scenes.

Now I return to the matter of Aeschylus' use of the language of visual art to describe the Erinyes. By inviting his audience to picture the Erinyes as iconographically similar to Gorgons or Harpies, Aeschylus evokes familiar scenes in vase-painting in which these female monsters terrorize a male quarry.[27] In order to make the argument that Aeschylus is creating an onstage pursuit scene modelled after earlier scenes in which the Harpies and the Gorgons pursue male quarries, I will examine the textual instances in which the Erinyes are compared to Gorgons and Harpies. The Erinyes first appear at the end of *Libation Bearers* just after Orestes has killed Clytemnestra; here, though, they are only visible to Orestes, whose lines prime the audience for their onstage apparition. When he sees them for the first time, Orestes describes them to the chorus in this passage from *Libation Bearers*:

Ὀρ. ἂ ἄ·
δμοιαὶ γυναῖκες αἵδε Γοργόνων δίκην
φαιοχίτωνες καὶ πεπλεκτανημέναι
πυκνοῖς δράκουσιν· οὐκέτ' ἂν μείναιμ' ἐγώ.   1050
Χο. τίνες σε δόξαι, φίλτατ' ἀνθρώπων πατρί,
στροβοῦσιν; ἴσχε, μὴ φοβοῦ, νικῶν πολύ.
Ὀρ. οὐκ εἰσὶ δόξαι τῶνδε πημάτων ἐμοί,
σαφῶς γὰρ αἵδε μητρὸς ἔγκοτοι κύνες.
Χο. ποταίνιον γὰρ αἷμά σοι χεροῖν ἔτι·   1055
ἐκ τῶνδέ τοι ταραγμὸς ἐς φρένας πίτνει.
Ὀρ. ἄναξ Ἄπολλον, αἵδε πληθύουσι δή,
κἀξ ὀμμάτων στάζουσιν αἷμα δυσφιλές.
Χο. εἷς σοὶ καθαρμός· Λοξίας δὲ προσθιγὼν
ἐλεύθερόν σε τῶνδε πημάτων κτίσει.   1060
Ὀρ. ὑμεῖς μὲν οὐχ ὁρᾶτε τάσδ', ἐγὼ δ' ὁρῶ·
ἐλαύνομαι δὲ κοὐκέτ' ἂν μείναιμ' ἐγώ.

Or.:   Ah! Ah! Look – foul women like Gorgons, dark-robed and entwined with close-packed serpents! I can no longer remain.

Ch.:   What visions beset you, dearest of men to your father? Bear up, do not fear, since you are very victorious.

Or.:   These are not visions of troubles for me, for they are clearly the grudge-bearing hounds of my mother.

Ch.:   Yes, for there is still fresh blood on your hands: because of this, madness falls upon your wits.

Or.:   Lord Apollo, they multiply even as I look at them! And they drip hateful blood from their eyes.

Ch.:   There is one way of purifying you. Loxias will touch you and make you free of these pains.

Or.:   You do not see them, but I do. I am driven out and can no longer remain.

Libation Bearers 1048–62.

He cannot identify what kind of creatures the Erinyes are, exactly, and draws upon characteristics of female monsters that are more familiar to him in order to classify them. The Erinyes look like Gorgons (Γοργόνων δίκην) because they are 'foul women' (δμοιαὶ γυναῖκες) who are 'dark robed' (φαιοχίτωνες) and 'entwined with close-packed serpents' (πεπλεκτανημέναι πυκνοῖς δράκουσιν). The Erinyes are also terrifying because they drip blood from their eyes, as we see in line 1058. Blood upon the eye often connotes the Gorgon, a detail that is not surprising given the deadliness of the Gorgon's gaze.[28] In this scene, Aeschylus connects the Erinyes with the Gorgons whose iconography is already standardized in vase-painting.[29]

The pursuit of Orestes by the Erinyes is also introduced in this passage. In line 1050, when Orestes says that he 'can no longer remain' (οὐκέτ' ἂν μείναιμ' ἐγώ), he means that he must flee to Delphi to seek purification; this claim is repeated with an important extra detail at line 1062, when Orestes says that he is 'driven out and can no longer remain' (ἐλαύνομαι δὲ κοὐκέτ' ἂν μείναιμ' ἐγώ). The verb ἐλαύνομαι, 'I am driven out', is a verbal representation of the pursuit scene which is so common in vase-painting; the phrase as a whole indicates that Orestes cannot remain because the Erinyes will chase him from his homeland. More specifically, in this scene Aeschylus invites the audience to liken Orestes' pursuit by the Erinyes to those in which the Gorgons Stheno and Euryale chase Perseus following the decapitation of their sister Medusa. As Erich Neumann notes, painted depictions of Perseus and the Gorgons tend to focus not on the act of decapitating Medusa, but on his flight from her avenging sisters.[30] In depictions of this scene, the Gorgons are usually winged, running with arms extended toward Perseus, and often with head turned directly towards the external viewer; Perseus is often accoutred in typical fashion, with his sickle, winged sandals and the satchel containing the head of Medusa.[31] Despite the fact that in vase-paintings Perseus usually appears in active flight, while Orestes is stationary, depictions of the Gorgons and the Erinyes both adhere to conventions of painting female monsters: that is, winged, and clearly terrorizing the male hero. Aeschylus evokes this iconographical similarity in the *Oresteia* by repeatedly likening Orestes' murder of Clytemnestra to Perseus' beheading of Medusa, drawing correspondences between Clytemnestra and Medusa, the Erinyes and Medusa's sisters, and Orestes and Perseus.[32] The full effect of these correspondences is achieved when Aeschylus concludes the description of the Gorgonesque Erinyes with the detail that Orestes is being driven out of his homeland, pursued by these horrifying female monsters.

In *Eumenides*, the Pythia describes the Erinyes in great detail, and with good reason, for in this play the Erinyes will be visible to all the characters onstage as well as to the audience for the first time:

πρόσθεν δὲ τἀνδρὸς τοῦδε θαυμαστὸς λόχος
εὕδει γυναικῶν ἐν θρόνοισιν ἥμενος.
οὔτοι γυναῖκας, ἀλλὰ Γοργόνας λέγω·
οὐδ' αὖτε Γοργείοισιν εἰκάσω τύποις.
εἶδόν ποτ' ἤδη Φινέως γεγραμμένας   50
δεῖπνον φερούσας· ἄπτεροί γε μὴν ἰδεῖν
αὗται, μέλαιναι δ', ἐς τὸ πᾶν βδελύκτροποι,
ῥέγκουσι δ' οὐ πλατοῖσι φυσιάμασιν,
ἐκ δ' ὀμμάτων λείβουσι δυσφιλῆ λίβα·
καὶ κόσμος οὔτε πρὸς θεῶν ἀγάλματα   55
φέρειν δίκαιος οὔτ' ἐς ἀνθρώπων στέγας.

And in front of this man sleeps a wondrous band of women sitting on chairs. But no – they aren't women, but I call them Gorgons. Then again, I cannot liken them to the forms of Gorgons. I once saw some female creatures like these in a painting, carrying off the feast of Phineus – but these are wingless, and black-robed, completely disgusting to behold, and they snore with unapproachable blasts, and from their eyes they drip hateful drops; their attire is not fit to bring either before the statues of the gods or into the houses of men.

Eumenides 46–56

In this passage, the Erinyes are described in the language of vase-painting. When the Pythia struggles to identify the Erinyes in line 49, she says that she 'cannot liken them to the forms of Gorgons' (οὐδ' αὖτε Γοργείοισιν εἰκάσω τύποις). τύπος is a word that can be used to describe the reliefs on temple pediments; as Mary Stieber notes, Gorgons were popular decorations for temple exteriors, especially in the archaic period.[33] This is a particularly interesting detail, given that the beginning of *Eumenides* is set in the temple of Apollo at Delphi; the audience might reasonably wonder whether the temple decorations had come to life and fallen asleep inside the temple.[34] However, Stieber argues that, in this passage, Aeschylus carefully directs his audience to connect the onstage Erinyes with a very specific artistic representation of the Gorgon. Aeschylus is careful not to have the Pythia liken the Erinyes to a Gorgon that they might see on a temple pediment; by not 'liken[ing] them to the forms [τύποις] of Gorgons', the Pythia instructs the audience not to envision the Erinyes like the 'gape-mouthed and lolling-tongued' carved Gorgons that appear on, for example, the temple of Artemis at Corfu.[35] The Pythia discounts this interpretation, and instead likens these creatures to ones that she has seen 'in a painting' (γεγραμμένας, 50).[36] As Stieber notes, the verb γράφω, 'write, draw, paint', is commonly used to reference vase-painting: it was common for vase-painters to sign their work with their name followed by ἔγραψεν, 'painted this'.[37] According to the Pythia, these creatures are more physically similar to painted female monsters than to sculpted or carved ones; Aeschylus' use of the verb γράφω, 'write, draw, paint', to describe the Erinyes indicates that he intends to evoke depictions of creatures who appear on vases rather than creatures who appear in temple carvings.

As the *Oresteia* progresses, the role of the Erinyes as pursuers is referenced a number of times; in several instances, the Erinyes are likened to hunting dogs pursuing their prey.[38] When the Erinyes are likened to hunting dogs, Orestes is the prey they pursue, and Clytemnestra acts as a *kunagos*, or hunt leader, who commands the Erinyes to action.[39] The comparison of the Erinyes with hunting dogs first appears in *Libation Bearers*, when Clytemnestra threatens Orestes in an attempt to persuade him not to kill her:

Κλ. ὅρα, φύλαξαι μητρὸς ἐγκότους κύνας.
Ὀρ. τὰς τοῦ πατρὸς δὲ πῶς φύγω, παρεὶς τάδε;

Cl.: Take care; beware the grudge-bearing hounds of your mother.
Or.: How shall I escape the hounds of my father, if I disregard this?

Libation Bearers 922–5

Orestes uses the same language when he describes the Erinyes as 'grudge-bearing hounds' (ἔγκοτοι κύνες) at *Libation Bearers* 1054. As Cristiana Franco has shown, the doggishness of the Erinyes reflects both their loyalty to their master (Clytemnestra) and their penchant for hunting human prey, in this case, Orestes.[40]

The *eidōlon* ('ghost') of Clytemnestra compares the Erinyes to hunting dogs twice more in *Eumenides*, when she reproaches them for sleeping. In the first instance, Clytemnestra's *eidōlon* describes Orestes as a fawn who has escaped the snare of the Erinyes (*Eum.* 111–13). In the second instance, Clytemnestra's *eidōlon* compares the Erinyes to hunting dogs who only pursue their prey in a dream, letting their real prey escape. Like a *kunagos*, Clytemnestra's *eidōlon* gives commands to the Erinyes, urging them onward to track Orestes. Her commands – 'listen' (ἀκούσαθ', 114), 'take heed' (φρονήσατ', 115) and 'follow' (ἕπου, 139) – are reminiscent of those that a *kunagos* might give to her hounds. Further, the Erinyes themselves take on the role of dogs in their vocalizations in this scene: the stage direction indicated by μυγμός in lines 117, 120 and 129 can be used to describe the whimpering of dogs.[41] Additionally, in line 130, the sleeping Erinyes chant 'Get him, get him, get him, get him! See there!' (λαβὲ λαβὲ λαβὲ λαβέ· φράζου), a line which recalls the hunt. Alan H. Sommerstein argues that this line represents 'probably not the calls of huntsmen, but the vocalizations of hounds on the trail, made articulate and meaningful. The rapid, repeated λαβέ suggests the panting of the hounds as they pursue their quarry ... then suddenly the leader gives a loud double bark, interpreted linguistically as φράζου'.[42] The Erinyes here are treated by and respond to Clytemnestra like hunting dogs.

The Erinyes also describe themselves like hunting dogs tracking their prey and Orestes as the fawn they hunt:

εἶεν· τόδ' ἐστὶ τἀνδρὸς ἐκφανὲς τέκμαρ·
ἕπου δὲ μηνυτῆρος ἀφθέγκτου φραδαῖς·   245
τετραυματισμένον γὰρ ὡς κύων νεβρὸν
πρὸς αἷμα καὶ σταλαγμὸν ἐκματεύομεν.
πολλοῖς δὲ μόχθοις ἀνδροκμῆσι φυσιᾷ
σπλάγχνον· χθονὸς γὰρ πᾶς πεποίμανται τόπος,
ὑπέρ τε πόντον ἀπτέροις ποτήμασιν   250
ἦλθον διώκουσ' οὐδὲν ὑστέρα νεώς.
καὶ νῦν ὅδ' ἐνθάδ' ἐστί που καταπτακών.
ὀσμὴ βροτείων αἱμάτων με προσγελᾷ.

Good; this is a clear sign of the man. Follow the hints of a voiceless guide. For just as a dog tracks a wounded fawn, we track him by the drip of blood. My lungs pant from many toils that would exhaust a mortal, for every country of the earth has been traversed by our flock, and I have come over the sea in wingless flight, pursuing him no slower than a ship. And now he is here, cowering somewhere. The smell of mortal blood smiles upon me like the face of a friend.

Eumenides 244–53

In this passage, the Erinyes themselves use the language of tracking: 'follow' (ἕπου, 245), 'we track' (ἐκματεύομεν, 247) and 'pursuing' (διώκουσ', 251). Significantly, the fawn is wounded and the hunting dogs track it by the scent of its blood; this imagery is particularly apt to Orestes' situation, since the Erinyes are pursuing him because of the blood he has shed. They have pursued him in his flight, tracking him by the scent of the blood droplets left in his wake.

The image of the young male as prey for a pack of dogs is reminiscent of another story from Greek myth – that of Actaeon, who is torn apart by his own hunting dogs.[43] As Franco notes, the Actaeon myth is emblematic of the 'grave suspicions' that the Greeks felt towards hunting dogs: that the dog, in the heat of the moment during a hunt, might forget his domestication and 'turn into a fierce wolf and unleash indiscriminate aggression against the wrong prey'.[44] Further, comparison of the images of Orestes pursued by the Erinyes with images in which Actaeon is torn apart by his hunting dogs confirms that the link between hunting and pursuit existed in the visual tradition. For example, in this depiction of the Actaeon myth, Lyssa, the personification of madness, is dressed as a huntress who urges the dogs onward to attack Actaeon.

Consideration of the vases in Figures 11.1–3 and Figure 11.4 together makes apparent that hunting and pursuit are connected not only in the conceptual sense evident in the text of the *Oresteia*, but also in the visual tradition of the Aeschylean period.[45] The male central figure kneels on his right knee with his left leg extended; he is nearly nude, and holding a weapon in his right hand. In both, a female figure dressed in hunting gear pursues the central male figure, as we can see by the position of her legs and the fact that her skirt is swinging backward to indicate her forward motion. Further, as Franco has argued, the Erinyes and Lyssa are similar to each other in that they are both 'divine agents of madness and mental blindness'; their connection to dogs becomes apparent when we

Figure 11.4 Actaeon pursued by Lyssa and hunting dogs, Athenian red-figure bell krater, *c.* 440 BCE, Museum of Fine Arts, Boston: 00.346. Photograph © 2020 Museum of Fine Arts, Boston.

consider what Franco calls the 'congenital weakness' of dogs that sometimes drives them to attack human men.[46] In this way, hunting dogs, with their 'lurking madness', are similar to, and dangerous like, women: they could turn on their male masters at any moment.

In Greek culture, the figure of the dog is linked with the negative aspects of women; this is certainly true of the Erinyes, who are by nature monstrous females dangerous to men. Therefore, it is not insignificant that when the Erinyes are changed into the Eumenides, goddesses who protect Athens and ensure its fertility, their transformation includes the loss of their function as pursuers.[47] Instead of roaming the earth in pursuit of a quarry, the Eumenides are now stationary and permanently occupy the cave below the Acropolis which represents the successful subjugation of the monstrous female whose power exists outside of the patriarchal structure of Athens.[48] The Erinyes are tamed, losing their function as hunting dogs who pursue parricides, as their power is appropriated for Athens.

As I have shown, the visual portrayal of the Erinyes is consistent with the conventional depiction of monstrous females, even though, as we have already seen, Aeschylus provides ample physical descriptors for the Erinyes that a vase-painter could easily have chosen to represent. Instead, vase-paintings depicting the Erinyes follow the conventions of depicting female monsters, using visual shorthand cues to represent the monstrousness of the Erinyes. In the same way, Aeschylus himself adapts the language of vase-painting in the *Oresteia* for the stage, painting his own version of the pursuit scene onstage, as a means of indicating the danger that Orestes faces. Aeschylus and the Attic vase-painters who depict the pursuit of Orestes were clearly in dialogue with each other, and referenced each other in their work.

Notes

1. I would like to thank the following people for their help and support during various stages of this chapter's development: C. W. Marshall, Hallie Marshall, Ruby Blondell, Kathryn Topper, Olga Levaniouk, Alexander Hollmann, Nektaria Klapaki and Bloomsbury's anonymous referees. Thank you also to the audience of the Greek Drama V '*Oresteia* reception' panel at which this was presented, as well as to my fellow panellists, Brett M. Rogers and Paul G. Johnston. My research for this chapter was funded by the 2018 Eleftherios and Mary Rouvelas Endowed Writing Prize in Hellenic Studies and a 2018 Jim Greenfield Dissertation Fellowship; I currently hold an American Fellowship from AAUW (2019–20). The texts I have used in preparing this chapter were Garvie 1986 (*Libation Bearers*) and Sommerstein 1989 (*Eumenides*). All translations are my own, unless otherwise noted.

2. For discussion of the argument that Aeschylus was the first to bring the Erinyes onstage, see Frontisi-Ducroux 2007: 166, Prag 1985: 48, Harrison 1922: 231, and Goldman 1910: 139–41.

3. Prag 1985: 44.

4. See Sarian's entry in the *Lexicon Iconographicum Mythologiae Classicae*, s.v. *Erinys* (1981) and Sarian 1986.

5. Although the Erinyes are mentioned several times in both Homer and Hesiod, their physical characteristics are never described in detail prior to Aeschylus. In Homer and Hesiod, the adjectives used of the Erinyes are στυγερός, 'hateful' (*Iliad* 9.454; *Odyssey* 2.135, 20.78), ἠεροφοῖτις, 'walking in darkness' (*Iliad* 9.571, 19.87) and κρατερός, 'strong' (*Theogony* 185). The most detail given about the Erinyes prior to Aeschylus is at *Odyssey* 15.234, in which an Erinys is called θεὰ δασπλῆτις, 'frightful goddess' (*Odyssey* 15.234).

6. Images of three of these vases are included below; my argument also takes into consideration a fourth vase depicting Orestes, Apollo and the Erinyes, which is attributed to the Hephaestus Painter and housed in the Museo Archeologico Regionale Paolo Orsi Siracusa (41621; Beazley 214757). I exclude from consideration a column-krater attributed to the Naples Painter (Italian market Finarte) and a column krater by the Painter of Brussels (Bologna 221), although they seem to follow a similar template as the other four vases. However, scholars disagree on whether these are creations of Late Mannerists, or whether they were created just after the period in which the Late Mannerists were active. See Prag 1985: 50–1 on the relationship of the Naples Painter and the Painter of Brussels to the Late Mannerists.

7. Mannack 2001: 115 and Beazley 1963: 1106–25. On the name and definition of 'Mannerist', see Mannack 2001: 3–11.

8. Mannack 2001: 24–41.

9. Trendall and Webster 1971: 5–6. For more on Aeschylean innovations to the existing Oresteia-mythos, see Sommerstein 1989: 1–6.

10. Trendall and Webster 1971: 5–6. On the snaky hair of the Erinyes as particularly Aeschylean, see Mannack 2001: 90 and Pausanias 1.28.6.

11. For a summary of the relevant scholarship, see Radding 2015: 836 n. 8. For discussions of such revivals, see Paul G. Johnston and Brett M. Rogers, both in this volume.

12. Trendall and Webster 1971: 5 and Jacoby 1950: sec. 334.36. Despite the claim that the Association of the Educated was active beginning in 450, Mannack notes that almost nothing is known about the prize-vases commissioned for them (Mannack 2001: 90).

13. Prag argues that the painters of these four vases 'can be assumed to have had connections with each other in any case: one can readily imagine that if one of them was approached with a commission at short notice for more pots than he could produce in the available time ... he would turn to his friends for assistance. The Naples Painter was not normally an associate of theirs, but he was presumably called in on this occasion because he was available' (Prag 1985: 50).

14. Scholars disagree about the meaning of the stones upon which Orestes kneels. They have proposed numerous theories about these stones, including that they are a reference to the omphalos at Delphi, that they represent a stone altar or that they denote the Stone of Injury, upon which the defendant in a case heard at the Areopagus stood. On these theories, see Prag 1985: 49–50 and Mannack 2001: 90. For more on the Stone of Injury, the corresponding Stone of Ruthlessness upon which the prosecutor stood, and their relationship to Orestes' trial, see Pausanias 1.28.5.

15. See *Eumenides* lines 51 and 250. Scholars disagree on the true meaning of ἄπτερος: some argue that it means 'wingless', while others believe that it means 'featherless'. P. G. Maxwell-Stuart argues that the Erinyes must be winged, since they cannot pursue Orestes over the sea if they are wingless (Maxwell-Stuart 1973: 83). Rather, argues Maxwell-Stuart, ἄπτερος refers to the featherless wings of the Erinyes, which are 'membraned' like the wings of bats (Maxwell-Stuart 1973: 83–4). He maintains that the Erinyes are, in fact, human-sized bats belonging to the family *Vespertilionidae* (Maxwell-Stuart 1973: 84). However, he does not account for Athena, who also flies without wings and is decidedly anthropomorphic. In her speech at *Eumenides* 397–414, Athena tells us that she has arrived from Troy by means of wingless flight: ἔνθεν διώκους' ἦλθον ἄτρυτον πόδα, | πτερῶν ἄτερ ῥοιβδοῦσα κόλπον αἰγίδος ('From there I have come on rapid and unwearied foot, not flying on wings but flapping the folds of my aegis', (trans. Sommerstein 2008b). Athena's wingless flight suggests the possibility that the Erinyes are likewise wingless. For a full summary and analysis of the various arguments about ἄπτερος, see Fraenkel 1950 on *Agamemnon* 276.

16. See *Libation Bearers* 1048–62 and *Eumenides* 34–63 for the most thorough physical descriptions of the Erinyes.

17. Vermeule 1966: 6. Vermeule argues that the original performance of the *Oresteia* in 458 BCE constituted a 'literary experience', effects of which can be detected in subsequent literary and visual art (1966: 6). By 'literary experience', Vermeule seems to refer to the way in which a dramatic text was 'experienced' via its performance in the theatre.

18. Prag 1985: 50.

19. The hydria in Figure 2 replaces Athena with Artemis. On this replacement, see Prag 1985: 50.

20. Pausanias reports that 'on the images neither of these [the Erinyes] nor on any of the underworld deities is there anything terrible (οὔτε ... ἔπεστιν οὐδὲν φοβερόν)' (1.28.6, trans. Jones, slightly adapted).

21. Sommerstein believes that Aeschylus was the 'first to identify the Semnai with the Erinyes' (1989: 11). He notes that the shrine of the Semnai Theai 'was an especially inviolable place of refuge for persons fleeing from enemies' (1989:10–11); the Semnai were also thought to ensure the continued fertility of Athens (Harrison 1922: 252). For more on the function of the Semnai Theai at Athens, see Harrison 1922: 239–53 and Lardinois 1992. For the argument

that the vase-painters depict the Erinyes as beautiful as a reaction to Aeschylus' conflation of the Erinyes with the Semnai Theai, see Taplin 2007: 59 and Dyer 1969: 53.

22. Matheson 1997: 23.

23. For discussion of the erotic pursuit scene, see especially Zeitlin 1986, Cohen 1996, Frontisi-Ducroux 1996 and Topper 2007. Topper also gives a comprehensive list of scholarship that discusses the erotic pursuit scene (Topper 2007: 82–3).

24. Osborne 1996: 67.

25. Osborne (1996: 67) also notes that in male-driven pursuit scenes, the male pursuers often carry 'add-ons', items external to the pursuer's body, which indicate their identity or their power over the pursued figures. These 'add-ons' are usually sceptres, tridents or thyrsoi, which Osborne argues can easily be 'left out or left behind'.

26. Consider, for example, the 'beautiful Gorgons' discussed by Topper (2007). For an example in vase-painting of beautiful Gorgons, consider the red-figure kantharos which depicts a Gorgon pursuing Perseus (c. 420–400 BCE, Class of Bonn 94. Strasbourg, Institut d'archéologie classique 1574). For an example in vase-painting of beautiful Harpies, consider the Athenian red-figure hydria in which the Harpies attack Phineus (500–450 BCE, Rome, Mus. Naz. Etrusco di Villa Giulia), and see also Trendall and Webster 1971: 58–61 on the possible relationship of Aeschylus' *Phineus* with vases depicting Phineus and the Harpies.

27. Prag notes that 'from a theatrical point of view, it was natural that Aeschylus should adopt the traditional artist's idea of female monsters in its late archaic form for his Furies, not just because he was clearly very conscious of what was going on in the visual world, but also for the simple reason that it was only in this fashion that he could bring them on stage within the conventions of the period . . . making them immediately recognizable to his audience' (Prag 1985: 48).

28. Wilk 2000: 186. On the connection between bleeding eye imagery and Gorgon imagery in the *Oresteia*, see Simas 2016.

29. Furtwängler divides the iconography of Gorgons into three phases and argues that it follows a predictable linear progression (Furtwängler 1884: 1886–90). Topper finds Furtwängler's classification system 'fraught with difficulties' because of the 'resistance' of the images to such precise classification (Topper 2007: 75).

30. Neumann 1954: 214–15. See also Woodward 1937 and Slater 2014: 326–7. Woodward notes that, in some cases, Medusa's headless body joins her sisters in their pursuit of Perseus (Woodward 1937: 67).

31. Woodward 1937.

32. See *Agamemnon* 1426–30 and *Libation Bearers* 523–34, 831–7, 896–8, 1048–50 and 1057–8 for instances of Gorgon imagery. For the argument that Clytemnestra is associated with Medusa and Orestes with Perseus, see DeForest 1993, Doyle 2010, Slater 2014 and Simas 2016.

33. LSJ s.v. τύπος; Stieber 1994: 96.

34. Sommerstein argues that the first scene of *Eumenides*, until line 234, 'is before the temple of Apollo at Delphi' (1989: 79).

35. Stieber 1994: 96.

36. Sommerstein notes that we are meant to understand these 'creatures in a painting' as the Harpies, though the Erinyes lack the wings required to classify them as Harpies (1989: 90).

37. For discussion of examples, see Petrovic 2013: 886–7. On the question of how literate the vase-painters were, see Immerwahr 2008.

38. In addition to the instances of hunting imagery discussed below, the language of pursuit is used of the Erinyes at *Eumenides* 334–40, 354–9, 372–6, 421–4 and 604–5.

39. On Euripides' reception of Clytemnestra as *kunagos* in *Bacchae*, see Paul G. Johnston, in this volume. Johnston argues that Agave and her band of Theban women are modelled on Aeschylus' Clytemnestra and her band of Erinyes, a point which is supported by the hunting language in both *Eumenides* and *Bacchae*.

40. Franco 2014: 96.

41. LSJ s.v. μυγμός.

42. Sommerstein 1989: 106.

43. 'The story made famous by Ovid . . . that Artemis was angry with Actaeon because he had seen her bathing is not attested before Callimachus . . . in Euripides he had boasted that he was a better hunter than the goddess' (Sommerstein 2008: 247). See Frontisi-Ducroux 1997 for a summary of the various iterations of the Actaeon myth.

44. Franco 2014: 30.

45. For more on the iconographical similarities of Lyssa to the Erinyes, see Aguirre 2010: 136.

46. Franco 2014: 145.

47. For discussion of the Erinyes as fertility goddesses in relation to Aristophanes' *Clouds*, see Brett M. Rogers, in this volume.

48. For discussion of the conversion of the 'parthenic'-type female monster into a protector of the city, see Hopman 2012.

CHAPTER 12
THE WOMEN OF THEBES AS AESCHYLEAN ERINYES: THE FIRST MESSENGER SPEECH OF EURIPIDES' *BACCHAE*

Paul G. Johnston

Aeschylus' *Eumenides* opens with a catalogue of the deities honoured by the Pythian priestess.[1] Included among these is Dionysus. She explains her worship of Dionysus by reference to the specific event that first established his power in central Greece, the very same event which would later provide the plot of Euripides' *Bacchae* – namely, the god's revelation at Thebes and his destruction of its king, and his own cousin, Pentheus (24–6):[2]

> Βρόμιος δ' ἔχει τὸν χῶρον, οὐδ' ἀμνημονῶ,
> ἐξ οὗτε Βάκχαις ἐστρατήγησεν θεὸς
> λαγὼ δίκην Πενθεῖ καταρράψας μόρον.

> Bromius has held this region – I do not forget him – ever since the god led the bacchants into battle and stitched up a death like a hare for Pentheus.

24–6

This brief allusion might make us notice some similarities between the myths of the pursuit of Pentheus by the bacchants and the pursuit of Orestes by the Erinyes that is the focus of *Eumenides*. Both stories involve pursuit by a group of women, divinely possessed in the first case, truly divine in the second.[3] More pointedly, the mother of the man being pursued plays a central role in both groups: the women who pursued Pentheus included his mother, Agave, while the Erinyes who are in pursuit of Orestes are roused and spurred on by his mother, Clytemnestra. In *Eumenides*, hunting imagery also connects these stories and makes their similarities more obvious: Pentheus was killed like a hunted hare, while the Erinyes are regularly depicted as hunters and Orestes as their prey in the *Oresteia*.[4] The key difference between the two myths is that, while Pentheus is caught and killed, Orestes will ultimately escape the Erinyes. It is not unreasonable to suggest, as Sommerstein does in his commentary on *Eumenides*, that this mythic allusion acts as a foreboding reminder of the fate that awaits Orestes if the Erinyes should, in fact, successfully capture him.[5]

It is my contention that Euripides' *Bacchae*, written around fifty years after the *Oresteia* was first staged, also manipulates this similarity between the myths of Pentheus and Orestes, and, moreover, that this connection is developed with particular reference to the specific version of the pursuit of Orestes by the Erinyes presented in Aeschylus' *Eumenides*. Quite simply, I suggest that the first messenger speech of *Bacchae* presents the women of Thebes in the manner of Aeschylus' Erinyes. This has some important dramatic effects in contributing to the sense of foreboding that the audience feels about Pentheus' transgressions against Dionysus, as well as foreshadowing the particular version of the myth that Euripides will present, where Agave is the main aggressor against Pentheus. In addition, the allusions to *Eumenides* contribute a further dimension to *Bacchae*'s well-established metatheatrical themes. Dionysus as the god of theatre does not merely act as the director of the play that he happens to be in, but he also inserts elements of the *Oresteia*, in many ways the archetypical tragic tetralogy, and this has significant implications for understanding this highly metatheatrical play's perspective on the state of tragedy at the end of the fifth century.

Euripides' interest in his poetic relationship to Aeschylus, his most prominent predecessor, and especially to Aeschylus' magnum opus, the *Oresteia*, is well known and commonly expressed in his extant works. We can often detect in Euripides a certain degree of what Harold Bloom called the 'anxiety of influence' about his relationship to Aeschylus.[6] Nowhere is this clearer than in the infamous recognition scene in Euripides' *Electra* (518–44), which adapts and implicitly comments upon the corresponding scene in Aeschylus' *Choephori*, and is usually read as a highly self-conscious reflection on Euripides' relationship to his tragic forebear.[7] But the shadow of Aeschylus, and especially his *Oresteia*, hangs over all of Euripides' work. This is particularly true of his plays about the house of Atreus (*Electra*, *Iphigenia among the Taurians*, *Orestes*, *Iphigenia at Aulis*).[8] *Bacchae* itself is generally thought to be inspired by, and draw its basic plot from, plays by Aeschylus about Dionysian theoxeny.[9] Many of the plot details and much of the imagery of Euripides' play resemble what we know of Aeschylus' plays treating the myths of Dionysus' visits to Pentheus and Lycurgus. It is, of course, hard to say very much about the specifics of *Bacchae*'s relationship to the Aeschylean Dionysus plays because of the extremely limited evidence for those plays.

Nevertheless, there are good reasons to believe that theatrical audiences of the late fifth century could be reasonably expected have some knowledge of Aeschylean tragedy. It is impossible to know *exactly* how familiar the audience who watched the first performance of *Bacchae* would have been with Aeschylus' works, but we can safely assume that theatre-going Athenians of the end of the fifth century could be relied upon to have at least some degree of familiarity with Aeschylus' major works – and especially the *Oresteia*. Indeed, it is likely that the *Oresteia* was reperformed at least once towards the end of the fifth century after a state decree was passed permitting the production of Aeschylus' plays at the dramatic festivals.[10] The repeated use of lines from the *Oresteia* in Aristophanes' *Frogs*, first performed in the very same year as *Bacchae*, stands as a particularly clear attestation of the fame of the *Oresteia*, and of playwrights' (in this case comic) ability to take advantage of Athenians' familiarity with it at the end of the fifth century.[11] In this context, an intertextual connection between Euripides' *Bacchae* and Aeschylus' *Eumenides* is hardly surprising; such an intertext is very plausibly within the capability of a late-fifth-century audience to recognize.[12]

When the first messenger in *Bacchae* begins to narrate his encounter with the women of Thebes on Mount Cithaeron, therefore, we ought to notice the striking similarity of the sequence of events he describes to the opening scenes of *Eumenides*. In the messenger speech, the Theban women are first encountered asleep (677–88). Similarly, the chorus of Erinyes in *Eumenides* are sleeping when they first appear onstage. But neither the women nor the Erinyes stay asleep for long: they are soon awoken by Agave (689–91) and the ghost of Clytemnestra, respectively. These two are, of course, each the mother of the central character of their play,[13] and both will turn out to have a hostile relationship to their son: Agave ends up killing Pentheus by the end of *Bacchae*, while the exact inverse of this situation was enacted in *Choephori*, the play which preceded *Eumenides* in its tetralogy, when Orestes killed Clytemnestra. Moreover, in *Eumenides* itself, Clytemnestra's only appearance onstage is to awaken and encourage the Erinyes to pursue her son in revenge for her death; this is closely mirrored by Agave's role spurring on the women to pursue and catch the men who stumble upon them.

Explicit hunting and animal imagery in the messenger speech serves to further connect the Theban women with the Erinyes. Perhaps most strikingly, Agave addresses the Theban women as her hunting dogs (ὦ δρομάδες ἐμαὶ κύνες, 731).[14] In the opening scenes of *Eumenides*, Aeschylus' Clytemnestra compares the noises of the Erinyes to a dog (κύων) barking (131–2), and beyond this the Erinyes have a general association with dogs and hunting in the *Oresteia*.[15] The messenger in *Bacchae* also tells us that the Theban women girdled their garments with snakes (δορὰς ὄφεσι κατεζώσαντο, 697–8) and that snakes cleaned the women's faces after they attacked the men (σταγόνα δ᾽ ἐκ παρηίδων γλώσσῃ δράκοντες ἐξεφαίδρυνον χροός, 767–8). This recalls a general association of snakes with the Erinyes in contemporaneous literary and visual depictions, including of course the *Oresteia*, as well as other fifth-century tragedies.[16] It is true that both dogs and snakes also have traditional Dionysian associations,[17] but in this context, where other factors encourage us to make comparisons with the Erinyes of *Eumenides*, this imagery must be understood as performing a kind of double duty.

This scheme may even extend to a direct verbal allusion to *Eumenides*. This occurs in a passage where the Theban women are described as they wake up:

αἳ δ᾽ ἀποβαλοῦσαι θαλερὸν ὀμμάτων ὕπνον
ἀνῇξαν ὀρθαί, θαῦμ᾽ ἰδεῖν εὐκοσμίας,
νέαι παλαιαὶ παρθένοι τ᾽ ἔτ᾽ ἄζυγες.

The women threw deep sleep from their eyes and stood up straight (a wonder of orderliness to behold): young, old and girls yet unmarried.

692–4

The bold oxymoronic sequence νέαι παλαιαὶ παρθένοι recalls a strikingly similar oxymoron in *Eumenides*, which occurs in Apollo's description of the sleeping Erinyes:[18]

ὕπνωι πεσοῦσαι δ᾽ αἱ κατάπτυστοι, κόραι
γραῖαι, παλαιαὶ παῖδες, αἷς οὐ μείγνυται
θεῶν τις οὐδ᾽ ἄνθρωπος οὐδὲ θὴρ ποτε.

Those detested women have fallen to sleep, aged maidens, ancient children, with whom none of the gods nor any human nor beast ever mingles.

68–70

Again we see a sequence of contradictory nouns and adjectives: κόραι γραῖαι παλαιαὶ παῖδες. The similarity is obvious, although the sequence must be understood grammatically differently in each case: the words must be taken in apposition in *Eumenides* but conjunctively in *Bacchae*. Although there is only one shared vocabulary item (παλαιαί), it falls in the exact same position in each line, while the words surrounding it are effective synonyms, and the overall scheme of alternating words for young and old women (in the nominative plural) is identical.[19] The immediate contexts of both oxymorons also have some other similarities that strengthen the case for making a connection: in *Bacchae* the women cast off sleep (ἀποβαλοῦσαι ὕπνον), while in *Eumenides* the Erinyes have fallen to sleep (ὕπνωι πεσοῦσαι); in *Bacchae* (some of) the women are unmarried (ἔτ᾽ ἄζυγες), while in *Eumenides* the Erinyes are unmarriable (69–70).[20] Given the other resemblances of the messenger's description of events to the beginning of *Eumenides*, it seems plausible that this may be a deliberate allusion to that play.[21]

There are a substantial number of factors that should encourage us to view the first messenger speech of *Bacchae* as echoing the first part of *Eumenides*: the broad shape of the events described, the imagery used, and, perhaps, a direct textual allusion. The most obvious implication that this has is in enhancing the terrifying effect of the messenger's speech by suggesting that the Theban women have a certain resemblance to Erinyes, quite literally embodiments of vengeance. The otherworldliness and unnaturalness of the women's behaviour are reinforced, and Pentheus' foolishness in disregarding the power of Dionysus is underscored. The women's behaviour is not merely strange, but akin to the monstrous Erinyes. However, the tone of the description of the Theban women never shades into the physical grotesqueness and outright horror that characterize the true Erinyes. The women may be behaving like the Erinyes, but visually and otherwise they remain the human women of Thebes. The effect is one of incongruity and uncanniness but there remains a distinctive kind of terror in this inversion of norms, and the latent potential for human women to be bewitched by a god into behaving like the terrifying female monsters of myth.[22]

In *Bacchae*, Euripides has chosen to portray a particular version of the myth of Pentheus which more closely resembles the story of the *Oresteia* than other variants. While Pentheus' death at the hands of the Theban women is the inevitable and unavoidable mythological outcome of his shunning of Dionysus,[23] the specific detail that his own mother Agave was his killer is far from universal in treatments of the myth: *Bacchae* is actually the first extant version of the myth in which she is.[24] What is more, there seem to be allusions elsewhere in the play to alternative versions of the myth, in which the women of Thebes are led into battle by Dionysus, perhaps in order to enhance the play's dramatic tension, since this is not how events will, in fact, turn out.[25] Yet in this messenger speech, Agave is presented in a way which makes her resemble Clytemnestra in *Eumenides*, hinting that *Bacchae* could conclude with intergenerational familial violence. This is balanced, though, against allusions elsewhere in the play to conflicting versions of the myth. Agave's role as a Clytemnestra figure among the Theban women is a detail which will help make her eventual murder of her son more comprehensible. Later in the play, at its most viscerally shocking moment, when Agave appears onstage carrying her son's head, this scene helps ensure that, for the audience, surprise does not shade into incredulity. The audience is subtly prepared, if not to expect, at least to consider the potential for savage mother–son violence of the kind explored in the *Oresteia*.[26]

But perhaps the most interesting aspect to this allusion is its self-consciousness.[27] A passing reference to the myth of Pentheus in *Eumenides* implying parallels between the pursuits of Orestes and Pentheus is here extended into an entire messenger speech which develops the resemblance between the women of Thebes and the Erinyes at length. Importantly, the speech frames the events in a way which does not recall the Erinyes in general, but rather the Erinyes specifically as they are depicted by Aeschylus: and indeed as they are depicted in that play's memorable, formally daring opening scenes.

This is metatheatre: the messenger reports seeing the women acting as if they are Aeschylus' *chorus* of Erinyes; and indeed he explicitly mentions seeing 'three *choruses* of women' (τρεῖς γυναικείων χορῶν, 680; cf. 682). Moreover, the Dionysian context of the messenger's report and the representation of the women of Thebes as possessed by Dionysus resembles the performance context of the Athenian theatre, at festivals of Dionysus, and in which the actors could be considered to be possessed by Dionysus in their performance.[28] It is as if the messenger stumbled upon a rudimentary theatrical festival, at which an embryonic version of *Eumenides* was being performed.[29] Indeed, this whole scene is focalized through the perspective of a tragic messenger, which is, as others have noted, implicitly metatheatrical because it is a spectator's perspective, and therefore analogous to the perspective of an audience member.[30] This tableau on the mountain can be understood as a kind of mini-play, with the god of theatre himself, Dionysus, as the writer-director,[31] Agave cast as Clytemnestra and the women of Thebes playing the Erinyes. Pentheus thus becomes the Orestes figure, soon to be hunted by his mother and her 'wrathful hounds'.[32]

This moment, of course, reflects a wider scheme of metatheatrical effects that pervade the play. As is widely agreed, and articulated at length by a number of scholars,[33] the entire main action of *Bacchae* can be profitably viewed as a kind of play-within-a-play, directed by the god Dionysus and with Pentheus taking a prominent role as both protagonist and would-be spectator.[34] Dionysus controls the action, directing, manipulating and even costuming the characters to ensure events occur as he wishes.[35] These events on the mountain are only a single scene in the drama directed by Dionysus.

But in this case the metatheatre takes on another dimension, because Dionysus is not merely controlling the play's action, but actually making it explicitly resemble one of the most famous real-life Athenian tragedies. Dionysus engineers a scene which comprises an innovative twist on the traditional repertoire of tragedy as represented by Aeschylus and his most famous tetralogy.[36] In this sense Dionysus is a tragedian after Euripides' own heart, composing a highly self-conscious style of tragedy where events unfold in ways which explicitly and implicitly recall and reinterpret the tragic tradition. And indeed, as the god of theatre, Dionysus is a symbol of the creative process of theatre production in general, but also, significantly, a more specific image of Euripides' own creative ability and potential.[37] Dionysus seems aware of Aeschylus as his predecessor, and of the models for tragic action that Aeschylus' plays provide, just as Euripides is. Insofar as the first messenger speech is a 'microcosm of the dramatic action of the play,'[38] we might see Euripides' process in creating *Bacchae* as a whole as analogous to Dionysus' in choreographing the events of the first messenger speech: like Dionysus, Euripides takes an Aeschylean framework as the basis for his play.[39]

The speech's immediate context provides further support for understanding Dionysus as a representative of a 'Euripidean' style of tragedy. Torrance has argued that the adjective καινός ('new') functions throughout Euripides' works as a metapoetic signal of the novelty of his approach, and as one of the defining characteristics of his tragic style as he himself represents it.[40] In this context, Pentheus' complaint, shortly before the messenger speech, that Dionysus is 'always introducing new (καινός) stories' (τοὺς λόγους γὰρ ἐσφέρεις καινοὺς ἀεί, 650) becomes significant. Dionysus will indeed do precisely what he is accused of by enacting a καινός (in Euripides' metapoetic sense of the word) mini-drama in the messenger speech which begins only ten lines later. Dionysus and Euripides, it seems, are both creators of tragic stories, speeches, plays, turns of events (λόγοι) which are characterized by 'newness' (καινότης).

For tragedians at the end of the fifth century this issue of originality and contemporary tragedy's relationship to its tradition seems to have been a significant one: consider the bold adversarial manipulation of traditional mythology in the 'Helen never went to Troy' storyline of Euripides' *Helen* (and similarly inventive mythology in other plays like *Ion* and *Orestes*),[41] and the deliberate and emphatic differentiation of Euripides' *Electra* from Aeschylus' canonical version in *Choephori*.[42] Euripides' younger contemporary Agathon provides particularly striking evidence of the strength of desire for novelty among late-fifth-century tragedians, with his unconventional play titled *Anthus* or *Antheus* which, according to Aristotle, jettisoned traditional myth entirely for completely invented characters and storyline.[43]

Euripides' Dionysus arguably embodies and enacts the paradox of this obsession with novelty: by the late fifth century, tragedy, for all its interest in 'newness', was inherently and deeply reliant on the tradition of tragedy that preceded it, and it tended to a large extent to restage stories and story patterns which had already been represented in the tragic theatre. Even the god of theatre himself cannot help but make action occur in a way which resembles another very well-known play. The adjective καινός takes on a very specific meaning: not 'new' in the sense of never-before-seen, but 'novel' in the sense of an innovative take on the existing tradition. Dionysus' καινός version of *Eumenides* is hardly any different in this respect from Euripides' καινός version of *Choephori* in *Electra*. The tableau on the mountain can therefore be viewed as a kind of microscopic model of exactly how and in what way tragedy can be successful at the end of the fifth century and at the end of a century of tradition, and that is precisely in a self-conscious Euripidean mode.

Of course, the events of *Bacchae* take place in the mythical past, and indeed in mythological chronology (murky as it is) before the events of the *Oresteia*. It is possible, therefore, to view Dionysus as also, in a certain sense, foreshadowing Aeschylus' depiction of the Erinyes. As befits his role as the god of tragedy, Dionysus acts as a kind of theatrical pioneer, shaping the conventions of tragedy before tragedy even exists.[44] One of the boldest moments of tragic stagecraft turns out to originate with Dionysus himself (naturally).[45] Read in this light, Dionysus' role as the divine source of inspiration behind Athenian tragedy becomes abundantly clear.

The allusions to *Eumenides* are best understood to suggest both of these perspectives: Dionysus as the self-conscious tragedian in the manner of Euripides, and Dionysus as the ultimate source of all tragedy. Dionysus thus becomes a representative of tragedy as a whole: the source of inspiration for (relatively) early tragedians like Aeschylus, but also himself a relentlessly modern tragedian like Euripides. Dionysus' tableau on the mountain seems to embody and therefore encapsulate all of tragic history in a single scene, from Aeschylean tradition to Euripidean innovation.[46] Adopting the framework of Jaussian reception theory,[47] we can say that the *Oresteia* is received and interpreted in this messenger speech as an emblem for the genre of tragedy as a whole: the tragic canon embodied in a single tetralogy and its reception and reinterpretation by other playwrights, caught in its moment of genesis directly from the god of tragedy on his arrival to Greece. But to canonize a literary tradition is inevitably to enclose it and place a limit upon it: indeed, perhaps Segal had the right idea when he suggested that *Bacchae* '[a]rguably ... embodies a *fin-de-siècle* self-awareness about a literary form that was now nearing the end of its creative life'.[48] To these metatheatrical and metapoetic implications must be added the more immediate effects of the allusions in enhancing the terror of the scene depicted, and foreshadowing Agave's particular role in the death of Pentheus. The intertextual presence of *Eumenides* in the first messenger speech of *Bacchae*, therefore, has multivalent effects: it enhances the emotional effects of the play's action, but simultaneously encourages the audience to step back and reflect on what these allusions suggest about the nature of tragedy, its status at the end of the fifth century and Dionysus' role in creating, inspiring and performing it.

Notes

1. I am grateful to the audience at Greek Drama V, the anonymous referee, the editors and Suzanne Paszkowski for advice and criticism on earlier versions of this paper.

2. There is particular emphasis given to line 26 by its metrical features: it is the only trimeter in all of Aeschylus with a medial caesura but without an elision at its midpoint; this is perhaps a metrical image of the violent death by *sparagmos* that befell Pentheus. See Sommerstein 1989: 84 *ad loc*.

3. It is intriguing that the only time Aeschylus ever uses the word μαινάς (literally 'mad woman' but much more commonly 'maenad/female follower of Dionysus'), aside from in a one-line fragment which seems to be the beginning of a prayer addressed to Dionysus (fr. 382), is later

in *Eumenides*, where the Erinyes are described as 'mortal-watching maenads' (βροτοσκόπων μαινάδων, 499–500).

4. See *Choephori* 924, 1054; *Eumenides* 111, 147–8, 231, 246. For discussion of the hunting imagery in these lines, see Simas in this volume.

5. Cf. Sommerstein 1989: 85.

6. Bloom 1973; and cf. Torrance 2013: 9–11 on the applicability of (some of) Bloom's notions in Euripides' literary-historical context.

7. The authenticity of this passage has, however, sometimes been doubted, largely because of its irreverent tone and the overtness of its intertextuality: see Bain 1977; West 1980: 17–22; Kovacs 1989. In defence of its authenticity, see Lloyd-Jones 1961: 177–81; Bond 1974; Basta Donzelli 1980; Cropp 1988: 137–8; Davies 1998; Gallagher 2003.

8. See Aélion 1983; Garner 1990: 49–177 for extended accounts of Aeschylus' influence on Euripides. On Euripides' Orestes plays and the *Oresteia* in particular, see Davies 1999; Easterling 2005: 30–3; Zeitlin 2005; and especially Torrance 2011 and 2013: 13–62 as well as the works in n. 6 above.

9. See Dodds 1960: xxviii–xxxiii; Aélion 1983: 1.251–9; Seaford 1996: 26–7. On Aeschylus' Dionysus plays generally, see Jouan 1992.

10. See *Life of Aeschylus* 12; Quintillian 10.1.66; Philostr. *VA* 6.11; Aristophanes *Acharnians* 10, *Frogs* 868; with Newiger 1961: 427–30; Dover 1993: 23; Sommerstein 1996: 232–3 *ad* 868 (who suggests that Aeschylus may have even been a school text in the late fifth century); Revermann 2006: 66–87; Scodel 2007: 130–3; Griffith 2013: 116. Biles 2007 has, however, questioned whether such reperformances did in fact occur. On the reception of the *Oresteia* in fifth-century Athens more generally, see Podlecki 1989: 22–3; Easterling 2005.

11. *Agamemnon* 104, 109, 111, 1345 ~ *Frogs* 1276, 1285, 1289, 1214; *Choephori* 1–5 ~ *Frogs* 1126–8, 1138, 1152–3, 1172–3; *Eumenides* 1012–13 ~ *Frogs* 1530. Lines from *Choephori* are also referenced in other Aristophanic plays: *Choephori* 164–94 ~ *Clouds* 534–6; *Choephori* 750 ~ *Acharnians* 478; *Choephori* 826 ~ *Birds* 313. See Rau 1967 for further instances of borrowing from Aeschylus in comedy; cf. also Rogers, in this volume. Note especially that when Euripides tells Aeschylus to 'recite the [prologue] from the *Oresteia*' (τὸν ἐξ Ὀρεστείας λέγε, 1124), this turns out (1126–8) to refer not, as we might expect, to the memorable prologue of the tetralogy's first play, *Agamemnon*, but to that of its second play, *Choephori*, implying that the Athenians were familiar enough with the tetralogy that this specific prologue was well known enough for such a shorthand reference to be meaningful. It is unlikely that Ὀρέστεια was used in the later fifth century as a name for *Choephori* specifically: Sommerstein 1996: 257 *ad* 1124; Dover 1993: 332 *ad* 1124.

12. In invoking the concept of intertextuality, I use the term in its common, largely structuralist sense, as influentially theorized for classical literature by Hinds 1998 and Edmunds 2001. Cf. Torrance 2013: 3–6 for reflections on the applicability of the concept to Euripidean tragedy. Cf. Garner 1990: 161–2 for a few further potential echoes of Aeschylus in *Bacchae*.

13. A point made emphatically at *Bacchae* 682 and 689.

14. Cf. also the messenger's report that the Theban women were suckling wolf cubs at *Bacchae* 699–700. See Seaford 1996: 230 *ad* 1020–3; Thumiger 2006: 196–202 for the Theban women as hunters in *Bacchae* generally.

15. Aeschylus *Choephori* 924; *Eumenides* 111–13, 147, 246–7; cf. Euripides *Electra* 1253.

16. See Prag 1985: 48–51; Scott 1975: 334–9; Harrison 1922: 232–9; see also Simas, in this volume, on the imagery and iconography of the Erinyes. In tragedy cf. Aeschylus *Choephori* 924; *Eumenides* 128; Euripides *Electra* 1255–6; 1345; *Iphigenia among the Taurians* 286; *Orestes* 256.

17. See Dodds 1951: 275–6; Bremmer 1984: 268–9; Seaford 1996: 160 *ad* 101–3 on snakes in Dionysian religion.

18. Some editors have preferred the conjecture παλαιόπαιδες at 69 (first suggested in Wilamowitz-Moellendorff 1914) for reasons of balancing nouns and epithets (Sommerstein 1989: 95 *ad* 69) or because it is more semantically vague than the bold oxymoron (Rose 1958: 2.235–6 *ad* 69: but the oxymoron is presumably precisely the point) or without any real justification except the vague assertion that the manuscript reading is 'scarcely tolerable' (W. Headlam *apud* Thomson 1966: 2.193 *ad* 68–9). This emendation would, of course, make the resemblance to *Bacchae* less clear; in any case I find the manuscript reading more convincing: I print the text and punctuation of West 1990a, which retains the manuscript reading, balancing nouns and epithets more elegantly by taking κατάπτυστοι as a substantive and adjusting the punctuation accordingly: see West 1990b: 273 for a defence of this.

19. The intertext may also help to explain the grammatically unusual asyndeton between νέαι and παλαιαὶ in *Bacchae* (as Dodds (1960: 163) writes, 'in an enumeration it is against normal usage to attach a connective to the last item only'), which elicits extended explanations by commentators: see Dodds 1960: 163; Roux 1972: 463–4; Seaford 1996: 206 *ad* 694. See Seaford 1988: 126 on the significance of the mixing of married and unmarried women in Dionysian religion in general.

20. Cf. Sommerstein 1989: 95 *ad* 69: the sexual connotations of μείγνυται 'cannot but be present after κόραι and -παιδες' (*sic*).

21. Note, too, that as Garner (1990: 189) has observed, intertextual allusion is especially common in messenger speeches.

22. In terms of the impact of this upon the audience, comparison might usefully be made to the paradoxical enjoyment viewers take from modern horror films (and similar texts in other media). Carroll (1990: 158–95) argues, in his insightful discussion of the appeal of narrative horror, that this appeal largely extends from a sense of curiosity about a monster, and the satisfaction of that curiosity in the gradual revelation that takes place over the course of the narrative. Just as in a horror film, we can be more or less certain that Pentheus will eventually meet with Dionysus' wrath (since the myth demands it), and the appeal is in the suspense awaiting the particular route, that is to say the particular monster, that the narrative will employ to reach its preordained ending. Cf. Lamari's (2010, 119–22) comments: 'in [Greek] tragedy suspense relates to *how*, i.e. the way in which the narrative will proceed to usually an already well-known result' (119).

23. This much is suggested by treatments of the myth in earlier tragedy and representations of the myth (most commonly of the death of Pentheus, in particular) on vases: see Philippart 1930; Dodds 1960: xxviii–xxxvi; March 1989; Seaford 1996: 25–8.

24. Of course, Euripides was not necessarily the first to present this version of the myth, as Seaford (1996: 27) rightly stresses; cf. Dodds 1961: xxxiv; Seaford 1993: 123 n. 38; against March 1989 and others.

25. Cf. March 1989; Macleod 2006.

26. As Foley (1980: 125; 1985: 244) writes, '[t]he first messenger speech gives Pentheus the precise scenario for his own death and a chance – by learning through presentation – to avoid it.' It is widely recognized that the first messenger speech foreshadows the play's second messenger speech which describes Pentheus being savaged by his mother: cf. Perris 2011: 42; Macleod 2006: 578; Buxton 1991: 43; March 1989: 40; Taplin 1977: 57. Cf. also Garner 1990: 161 who identifies a different allusion to the *Oresteia* in the fourth stasimon of *Bacchae*, where the chorus calls for justice to strike down Pentheus, applying to the figure of justice the distinctive epithet 'sword-bearing' (ξιφηφόρος, *Bacchae* 991) which was perhaps first coined by Aeschylus

to describe the justice Orestes delivered upon Clytemnestra (*Choephori* 584). He suggests that it 'implies both by allusion and collusion . . . that the justice called for in this stasimon may well be the savage familial sort found in *Choephori*'.

27. On Euripides' self-consciousness in general, see Winnington-Ingram 1969; Bain 1988; Torrance 2013.

28. See Segal 1982: 240–2 on the significance of Mt Cithaeron, the setting of the events described in this speech, as a second, unseen stage in *Bacchae* generally. Cf. Plato *Ion* esp. 533d–6d for the idea of poetic performance as possession by a god.

29. Cf. Foley 1985: 215: 'the festival, or protofestival, introduced by Dionysus can also be read as a primitive version of his own theatrical festival in Athens'; cf. Foley 1980: 118 n. 16.

30. Jong 1991: 9–10 esp. n. 21; Zeitlin 1994: 143; and esp. Barrett 2002: 102–31 on the messengers of *Bacchae* specifically.

31. This sense is made even more acute by the fact that Dionysus effectively predicts the content of the messenger's speech before he actually says a word (657–8): cf. Foley 1980: 113 n. 10.

32. Cf. Sommerstein 1989: 85 and *Choephori* 924, 1054.

33. Foley 1980; 1985: 205–58; Segal 1982: 215–71; Goldhill 1986: 259–86; Bierl 1991: 177–226; Barrett 2002: 102–31.

34. Cf. Segal 1982: 263; Foley 1985: 212; Bierl 1991: 212–14; Barrett 2002: 104–18 on Pentheus' 'failed' spectatorship.

35. Cf. too, of course, the metatheatrical portrayal of Euripides, and Agathon, as directors and costume designers of a series of miniature reperformances of Euripidean plays in Aristophanes' *Thesmophoriazusae* (on which, see e.g. Zeitlin 1996: 375–416; Bobrick 1997).

36. On Aeschylus as the representative of traditional (i.e. pre-Euripidean) tragedy in fifth- and fourth-century Athens, see esp. Scodel 2007: 130–3.

37. Cf. Segal 1982: 233; Foley 1985: 220.

38. Macleod 2006: 578.

39. Cf. n. 8 above.

40. Torrance 2013: 218–37.

41. The idea that the 'real' Helen went to Egypt is not Euripides' own invention, being already discussed in Herodotus (2.113–20), but his engagement with the mythology of the Trojan War in *Helen* is undeniably innovative and often somewhat contradictory to traditional accounts of the story (especially Homeric epic); the play was tellingly described one year after its first performance by Aristophanes as 'the new *Helen*' (τὴν καινὴν Ἑλένην, *Thesmophoriazusae* 850); and cf. also Arnott's (1990) insightful analysis of the role of surprise and novelty in the play's dramatic action.

42. Cf. Gellie 1981; Hammond 1984.

43. Aristotle *Poetics* 1451b.

44. The effect is perhaps enhanced by the archaizing features that characterize *Bacchae* as a whole: see Dodds 1960: xxxvi–xxxviii, Winnington-Ingram 1948: 2; cf. Goldhill 1985: 267–8.

45. The theatrical spectacle of *Eumenides* and especially its presentation of the Erinyes is not to be underestimated. The impact of the terrifying presentation of the Erinyes became legendary in antiquity: the ancient *Life of Aeschylus* 9 reports (almost certainly apocryphally) that children fainted and women miscarried upon the chorus' arrival onstage at the play's first performance.

46. It is perhaps not just a coincidence that Aristophanes in *Frogs* from the very same year also presents Aeschylus and Euripides as the representatives of tradition and innovation, respectively, in the tragic theatre.

47. As articulated in Jauss 1982 and refined and applied to classical literature in Martindale 1993.

48. Segal 1982: 216. The *fin de siècle* here is, of course, a purely metaphorical one; *Bacchae* had its first performance close to the end of a century (405 BCE) only according to a dating system first used many hundreds of years later.

CHAPTER 13
ELECTRA-STYLE: RECEPTION(S) OF AESCHYLUS' *ORESTEIA* IN ARISTOPHANES' *CLOUDS*

Brett M. Rogers

In the parabasis of our received text of Aristophanes' *Clouds*, the poet evokes the mythic figure of Electra (lines 534–6):

νῦν οὖν Ἠλέκτραν κατ' ἐκείνην ἥδ' ἡ κωμῳδία
ζητοῦσ' ἦλθ', ἤν που 'πιτύχῃ θεαταῖς οὕτω σοφοῖς·
γνώσεται γάρ, ἤνπερ ἴδῃ, τἀδελφοῦ τὸν βόστρυχον.

> So now, just like that famous Electra, this comedy has come searching, in the hope of chancing upon clever spectators somewhere; for if she should see it, she will recognize her brother's lock.[1]

534–6

This chapter starts from a simple question about these lines: why does Aristophanes want his audience to see this comedy as proceeding Ἠλέκτραν κατ' ἐκείνην 'like that famous Electra' or 'Electra-style'?

To make sense of Aristophanes' self-identification with this *parthenos*, we face several difficulties: (i) the (im)precise nature of the analogy; (ii) the relationship of this passage to the rest of the parabasis and *Clouds* as a whole; (iii) the date and performance context for this version of *Clouds*; (iv) the play's relationship to the (re)performance of other Electra-narratives that an audience – or, at least, a clever audience (θεαταῖς οὕτω σοφοῖς, 535) – may have in mind; (v) the play's relationship to comedy, if not also tragedy; and (vi) the play's relationship to Athens of the time period. Each of these difficulties is formidable and, given the nature of our evidence, may never be fully addressed or understood. Nevertheless, I want to argue for this short Electra passage and this version of Aristophanes' *Clouds* as a reception of Aeschylus' *Oresteia*. I am not the first to make such an argument: half a century ago Hans-Joachim Newiger suggested there are several Oresteian resonances in *Clouds*; and Mario Telò has pressed the case for seeing Aeschylus' *Oresteia* as key to Aristophanes' poetic self-representation in *Clouds*.[2] I suggest here that *Clouds* is not only a reception of the *Oresteia* – perhaps the earliest surviving complete text that 'receives' Aeschylus' famous drama – but a more thorough re-envisioning of the *Oresteia* than has been previously understood. In what follows, I address what I have labelled difficulties (iii) and (iv) in the first section, then (i) and (ii) in the second section, then (v) and (vi) in the conclusion.

1. *Clouds* and Other Oresteian Narratives

The reference to 'that famous Electra' (Ἠλέκτραν ... ἐκείνην) requires Aristophanes' intended audience to have a particular Electra in mind. This raises the question of which narratives featuring Electra were available to Aristophanes' audience prior to seeing or reading this parabasis. Nested in this consideration is a second, more fundamental question: what is the date of our surviving text of *Clouds*? In this section I address questions of the dates for both this version of *Clouds* and other Oresteian narratives, returning to the Electra analogy in the next section. As Hallie Marshall has demonstrated, there are only two secure facts about *Clouds*. First, didascalic records show that *Clouds* was produced at the City Dionysia in spring 423 BCE and took third place: this is *Clouds I*, and there was no entry for a subsequent performance at the Lenaia or City Dionysia. Second, two texts of *Clouds* circulated in antiquity, one of them a revised version of the earlier play: this is *Clouds II*, and is the script that survives and contains the Electra passage. Anything else we think we know about *Clouds* has come from sources that we hope are reliable.[3]

Most scholars argue that the parabasis of *Clouds II* – at least lines 518–62 – was composed sometime between 420 and 416.[4] In the parabasis, Aristophanes criticizes several of his competitors for stealing and reusing derivative material, and he focuses on comedies that attack the politician Hyperbolus. Aristophanes begins with a critique of Eupolis' *Marikas* (*Clouds* 553–4), performed at the Lenaia in 421; he then mentions a subsequent comedy by Hermippus (believed to be *Breadsellers*, performed in 420 or 419) and 'the others now all piling on Hyperbolus' (*Clouds* 557–8).[5] Since there is no reference to Hyperbolus' ostracism, which took place in 416 or 415, 415 provides a *terminus ante quem* for lines 518–62 of *Clouds II*.[6] If *Clouds II* was ever performed, it did not compete at the City Dionysia or Lenaia but somewhere else for which we have no record.[7]

The revised parabasis belongs to a number of revisions 'affecting virtually every part of [the script]', as we learn from *Clouds*'s Hypothesis I.[8] Three places in particular contain material 'which happens to be entirely new in [the play's] arrangement' (ἃ δὲ ὁλοσχερῆ τῆς διασκευῆς τοιαῦτα ὄντα τετύχηκεν, Hypothesis I.6–7): (1) the parabasis (including the Electra passage); (2) the scene in which Stronger Logos chatters against Weaker Logos; and (3) the scene in which Socrates' school is burned down. It is tempting to accept the scholiast's claim at face value – except that other bits of evidence complicate what constitutes 'entirely new' material. Kenneth Dover points to a scholion on line 889 claiming that 'the Logoi [we]re shown on stage in wicker cages fighting like birds'. There is no reference to such a staging in *Clouds II*, and Dover subsequently argues that, if the scholiast has preserved a real staging, this must refer to a scene from *Clouds I*. In turn, this would mean both plays featured the two Logoi in some way and Hypothesis I cannot mean the scene with the Logoi was entirely new so much as significantly different.[9] Likewise, 'Hypothesis I neither excludes nor fortifies the possibility that the first version ended with some act of violence against Socrates and his school'.[10] Judgments about any changes must be made by each timely reference and personal joke. The reference to Eupolis' *Marikas* obviously belongs to *Clouds II*, since it could not have appeared in the

423 performance; in contrast, for all we know, the parabasis of *Clouds I* also evoked the figure of Electra, though it would have been for different purposes or effect, since *Clouds* had not yet lost in competition and Aristophanes' analogy would not have made sense.

Which Electra narratives might Aristophanes be drawing upon? Some scholars have assumed that Aristophanes means older narratives about Electra – for example, Sommerstein's translation of Ἠλέκτραν ... ἐκείνην as 'Electra of old' encourages this interpretation.[11] Electra appears in neither Homeric epic nor Pindar's mini-Oresteia in *Pythian* 11 (474 or 454) but does appear in Hesiod's *Catalogue of Women* (line 16, fr. 19 Most = 23a M-W).[12] The only known narratives prior to *Clouds II* that (might) include Electra are Stesichorus' *Oresteia* and Aeschylus' *Oresteia* (first performed in 458), in whose second play, *Choephori*, Electra appears as a character.[13] Notably, Aristophanes draws on both sources in the late 420s. He appears to parody Aeschylus' *Oresteia* in *Wasps*, produced in 422 (discussed below). Aristophanes also quotes and interweaves Stesichorus' *Oresteia* (frr. 210–2 Campbell) into the parabasis in *Peace* (775–818), produced in 421. A papyrus commentary (fr. 217 Campbell) relates that Stesichorus' *Oresteia* included the recognition by means of Orestes' lock of hair but does not explicitly refer to the presence of Electra; this same commentary also notes that Aeschylus drew material for his *Oresteia* from Stesichorus' poem.[14] Further, Strepsiades refers to his fondness for Aeschylus (*Clouds* 1363–73), although he does not explicitly refer to the *Oresteia*. These references confirm that Aristophanes was actively thinking about and playing with the Oresteia myth in the period 423–421.

In contrast, if Ἠλέκτραν ... ἐκείνην means something more akin to 'that famous Electra', then we might search for more recent antecedents. There are three known possibilities: Sophocles' *Electra*, Euripides' *Electra*, and a possible reperformance of Aeschylus' *Oresteia*. Scholarly opinion on the dates of Euripides' and Sophocles' *Electra* tragedies varies widely. Since Sophocles' *Electra* omits Orestes' lock of hair, which is crucial to the vehicle of the Electra analogy in *Clouds II*, it cannot be the referent. Euripides' *Electra* poses a trickier problem, since its plot includes the discovery of Orestes' lock; moreover, the proposed dates for its performance range from as early as 421 to as late as 413.[15] However, other considerations make Euripides' *Electra* an unlikely antecedent: unlike Aeschylus' character, Euripides' Electra does not 'come seeking' help at the altar of her father.[16] Further, Aristophanes uses the lock as a legitimate form of evidence, unlike Euripides' Electra (487–584): the analogy does not make sense if the audience has the Euripidean Electra in mind, since it would require Aristophanes to be saying his comedy will fail to recognize whatever it seeks. All this suggests that *Clouds II* either predates Euripides' *Electra* or Aristophanes chooses to ignore it.[17]

Indeed, *Clouds II* and *Electra* both presuppose an audience already familiar with Aeschylus' *Choephori*. Aristophanes is not the only comic poet to assume such knowledge: as Emmanuela Bakola has shown, Cratinus also draws extensively on Aeschylus' *Oresteia* in *Eumenides* (frr. 69–70), *Runaways* (*Drapetides*, fr. 59), and *Wealth Gods* (*Ploutoi*, frr. 171–7), produced *c.* 429.[18] David Rosenbloom has demonstrated the lively competition onstage among several comic poets who sought to align their personas with Aeschylus, including Cratinus and Pherecrates.[19] Both tragedy and comedy, then, point to an audience with sufficient knowledge to recognize references to the *Oresteia*.

Yet the *Oresteia* was first performed in 458, thirty-five years before *Clouds I*. How would an audience have encountered Aeschylus so as to have specific knowledge of *Choephori* and get the reference? In *Frogs* (first produced in 405), Aristophanes has Aeschylus claim that his poetry did not die with him (868). C. W. Marshall suggests that audiences in the late fifth century encountered Aeschylus's dramas through three conduits: reperformances, the reading of texts (by those few people who were literate), or having learned them as school children.[20] Newiger proposes that there must have been a reperformance of the *Oresteia* not long before the composition of *Clouds*.[21] Based on specific moments and visual cues from the *Oresteia* that we find in Aristophanes' *Acharnians* (9–12), Euripides' *Hecuba* (424) and continuing into subsequent tragedies, Marshall argues for a reperformance of the *Oresteia* at the City Dionysia sometime in the mid-420s, while Rosenbloom suggests that reperformances would have taken place in the 420s at the Rural Dionysia.[22]

The suggestion of a mid-420s date for reperformance(s) of the *Oresteia* is supported by Telò's reading of Aristophanes' *Wasps* (produced in 422). When Philocleon appears onstage drunk with wine, waving both his limp 'rope' and a torch (*Wasps* 1322–44), in Telò's view Philocleon is evoking the Erinyes (though he is not drunk with blood, as Cassandra tells us the Erinyes are at *Ag.* 1188–90). Philocleon's words may even include a sly nod to the *Eumenides* trial as he rants about hating to hear lawsuits and wanting to throw out all the voting urns (*Wasps* 1335–41). We might have some reservations about this identification in light of Wilson and Taplin's argument that 'the Erinyes seem to have become, after the *Oresteia*, something of a symbol of tragedy', although visual representations of the Erinyes seem to have been strongly associated with the *Oresteia* (which may have provided the first visual depiction of the Furies).[23] Moreover, Marshall argues that parodic scenes such as those in *Hecuba* and *Wasps* cannot merely evoke an Aeschylean 'feel' (as it were), but 'require the source to be identifiable' for the parody to work, especially in the context of a single performance in competition.[24]

I will not pretend there are definitive solutions to these questions about the date of the revisions to *Clouds* and the precise chronology with respect to the two *Electra* tragedies. There is good evidence, nevertheless, for the following claims: (i) Aristophanes is thinking about the *Oresteia* in his comedies in the late 420s; (ii) other comic poets are also doing so at the same time (and perhaps earlier in the decade); (iii) Aristophanes does not know (or deliberately ignores) the two *Electra* tragedies. This points to *Clouds II* as a response to likely reperformance(s) of the *Oresteia* in the 420s and makes a strong case for *Choephori* as the source for 'that famous *Electra*'. Proceeding cautiously from these assumptions, let us return to the passage itself.

2. Electra-style and the *Oresteia* in *Clouds II*

The logic of Aristophanes' Electra passage works as follows: just as Electra came in search of . . . well, something . . . and recognized the lock of Orestes, so, too, has this comedy

Table 13.1 The analogy of the Electra passage in Aristophanes' *Clouds II*

Electra (Ἠλέκτραν κατ' ἐκείνην)	this comedy (ἥδ' ἡ κωμῳδία)
seeks X	seeks spectators so wise (θεαταῖς οὕτω σοφοῖς)
and finds brother's lock (τἀδελφοῦ τὸν βόστρυχον)	and finds Y

come searching, hoping to encounter wise spectators; the comedy will know ... well, something ... when it sees it. In other words, Aristophanes omits two crucial terms in the analogy, as we see in Table 13.1: first, what Electra has come in search of (represented in the table as 'X'), and, second, what 'this comedy' *Clouds* hopes to find (represented as 'Y'). Drawing on the conclusions from the previous section, let us turn to Aeschylus' *Oresteia* to complete the logic of this analogy.

Linking Aristophanes' analogy to *Choephori* is not without its problems. As Dover observes, Aristophanes' analogy is an imprecise one: neither in *Choephori* nor in the extant mythos does Electra 'go seeking' Orestes. Rather, Electra and the chorus of libation bearers have been sent by Clytemnestra to Agamemnon's tomb in order to offer a sacrifice and prayer on Clytemnestra's behalf (*Cho.* 22–3, 87–90). Dover writes this off as 'mythological imprecision', while Alan Sommerstein asserts that 'Ar[istophanes]'s memory of *Choephori* may be hazy'.[25] Sommerstein nevertheless suggests that the crucial point for Aristophanes is 'the sight of the lock [a]s a complete surprise', and thus the comic poet emphasizes the visual and dramatic value of the scene.[26] Second, Dover observes that Electra never states she is searching for Orestes per se, though Electra and the chorus do pray for 'someone bringing justice' (δικηφόρον, *Cho.* 120), an 'avenger' (τιμάορον, 142) and for Orestes' return (138–41). Telò sidesteps Dover's concern by describing the scene in different terms: Electra approaches the tomb of Agamemnon in search of support (his interpretation of 'X') against Clytemnestra and Aegisthus (*Cho.* 119–21, 143–4); her discovery of 'Orestes's lock is a concrete expression of such support'.[27] Telò's reframing emphasizes the importance of visual cues for Aristophanes' analogy: Electra enters, Electra discovers the locks of hair, then 'concrete support' (i.e. Orestes) dramatically appears. Thus Aristophanes' analogy depends heavily on a visual understanding of the *Choephori*, which is, I argue, characteristic of how Aristophanes evokes the *Oresteia* throughout *Clouds*.

With Telò's argument, it is not difficult to reconcile the events staged in *Choephori* with the meaning of the Electra analogy in *Clouds II*. As Telò observes, following Hackforth, one scholiast (R) on *Clouds* argues that the token (τι σύμβολον) the comedy hopes to find ('Y') is the praise (τὸν ἔπαινον) of the audience.[28] In other words, the analogy asserts that *Clouds II* comes 'like that famous Electra' in search of wise spectators and that it will recognize support, whatever form it takes, when it sees it. In Telò's reading, this support is not only the audience's applause but also – crucially – a dramatic victory, such that the Electra passage fits precisely with the explicit concern in the parabasis (esp. *Clouds* 520–5) about the third-place finish for *Clouds I*. I would further argue that, in depicting *Clouds* as the maiden Electra and evoking two other male characters, the Prudent Boy and Buggered Boy (ὁ σώφρων τε χὠ καταπύγων, 529) from his earlier play *Banqueters* (427), Aristophanes evokes a trio of children. It is tempting to suggest Aristophanes does this in the *Clouds* parabasis to connote the visual centerpiece in the middle of *Choephori* – the trio of Electra, Orestes and Pylades gathered together seeking revenge.[29]

Telò interprets the parabasis as alluding to Electra's portrayal in *Choephori* and Aristophanes' search for support and victory in competition. Electra defends paternal authority and exhibits female restraint in the face of matriarchy. She 'displays a compulsive concern with choosing the best words to please her father': Electra expresses concern with speaking in a manner that will be well received and gain support (*Cho.* 87), and she prays that Agamemnon grant her both greater self-control than her mother possesses and a more pious hand (140–1). Aristophanes uses this particular Electra as his 'alter-ego' in order to contrast himself with his poetic opponents, whom he refers to earlier in the parabasis as 'vulgar men' (ἀνδρῶν φορτικῶν, *Clouds* 524) and lowbrow, plagiarizing hacks (537–62).[30] The choice of Electra, the pious daughter, also provides a contrast in the intradiegetic narrative of *Clouds II* to Pheidippides, who defies paternal authority, follows his mother's lavish habits and bankrupts his father in the process. In contrasting Electra with both Pheidippides and his comic rivals, Aristophanes tactily aligns Pheidippides with Eupolis and Hermippus, and undercuts any attempt on their parts to claim for themselves *sōphrosynē* or a properly Aeschylean persona.

There are strong indications beyond the parabasis in *Clouds II* of verbal and visual resonances with Aeschylus' *Oresteia*, and this is reinforced with no fewer than nine allusions to, or evocations of, the *Oresteia*, including the Electra passage (see Table 13.2). These come from Telò, Newiger and H. N. Couch, as well as three new suggestions; I discuss each in turn.

Table 13.2 Scenes in *Clouds II* with receptions of the *Oresteia*

Clouds	*Oresteia*
i. Strepsiades laments in middle of the night, tosses and turns (ἰοὺ ἰού!) (1–24)	Watchman laments in middle of the night, tosses and turns (ἰοὺ ἰού!) (*Ag.* 1–39)
ii. Socrates makes Strepsiades remove clothes and shoes before entering Thinkery (498–9)	Clytemnestra makes Agamemnon remove boots and tread on tapestries (*Ag.* 905–74)
iii. Parabasis: This comedy comes like Electra, will know brother's lock when she sees it (534–6). Trio of Prudent Boy, Buggered Boy and *Clouds II* qua Electra.	Electra discovers Orestes' lock (*Cho.* 164–211). Trio of Orestes, Pylades and Electra.
iv. Logoi debate definitions of *dikē*, with reference to Zeus binding his father (900–7)	Trial scene includes debate over *dikē*, with reference to Zeus binding his father (*Eum.* 614–44)

v. Cloud-chorus demands judges' vote in exchange for fertility of the land and dry weddings (1115–30)	Erinyes demand *timē* from Athena in exchange for fertility of the land and people (*Eum.* 778–995)
vi. Strepsiades welcomes back Pheidippides 'gleaming with double-edged tongue' (1161–2)	Clytemnestra welcomes back Agamemnon to Argos (*Ag.* 607–8, 896–901 and 966–72)
vii. Strepsiades defends himself against Pheidippides, with reference to rearing son (1380–90)	Clytemnestra defends herself against Orestes, with reference to rearing son (*Cho.* 750–62)
viii. Strepsiades' *pathei mathos* (1462–4)	Argive Elders declare principle of *pathei mathos* (*Ag.* 160–83, esp. 177), referred to *passim* in *Oresteia*
ix. Strepsiades brandishes torch to burn down the Thinkery, chaotic *exodos* (1476–511)	Procession with torches, then celebratory *exodos* (*Eum.* 1032–47)

i. Tossing and turning (Clouds 1–24)

I suggest Aristophanes alludes to the *Oresteia* at the opening of *Clouds II* by offering a recognizable visual parody of the beginning of *Agamemnon*. Strepsiades – 'Mr. Twisty' – first demonstrates his twisty nature when he tosses and turns in bed, lamenting (ἰοὺ ἰού, *Clouds* 1) the darkness and interminable night (2–3) as well as the current war (6–7); while son dreams of horses (14–16), father sleeplessly watches the moonlight indicating the coming need to pay debts (12–13, 16–17).[31] The language and physical movement required of Strepsiades here is strikingly similar to that of the Watchman in the opening lines of *Agamemnon*, who also laments (ἰοὺ ἰού, *Ag.* 25) anxious nights in bed without dreams (12–19). The evocation of *Agamemnon* also lends comic force to Strepsiades' complaint that 'the household slaves are snoring, but would not have in the old days' (οἱ δ' οἰκέται ῥέγκουσιν. ἀλλ' οὐκ ἂν πρὸ τοῦ, 5), since it is no longer the Aeschylean *oiketēs* (the Watchman) who stays up all night but now the master of the household (Strepsiades).

This comic inversion is reinforced by the scene's staging and use of imagery. Unlike the Watchman atop the *skēnē*, Aristophanes here uses what Martin Revermann calls an '"indoor scene staged outside" scenario', distinct from the use of the *skēnē* in the *Oresteia* to demarcate spaces as clearly 'inside' or 'outside'.[32] Instead of the household slave tossing and turning outside the house, now the master tosses and turns inside the house, but for all the audience to see. The scene also comically plays with the symbolic meaning of light and dark, so prominently part of the *Oresteia*'s visual and poetic imagery.[33] Aeschylus' Watchman patiently awaits the signal fire symbolic of the sack of Troy and Agamemnon's return (8–10), whereas the light of the moon indicates the return of Strepsiades' troubles and creditors seeking the repayment of debt. The repeated comic play with the lamp (*Clouds* 18–20, 56–9) may also evoke the Watchman's repeated references to torches (*Ag.* 8–9, 22–3, 28). Aristophanes again plays on imagery of light and darkness, I argue, at the comedy's end (see ix. below).

179

ii. Shoeless Strepsiades and the Carpet Scene *(Clouds* 498–9)

When Socrates invites Strepsiades to enter the Thinkery, he forces Strepsiades to remove his clothes (*Clouds* 498–9); as lines 856–8 indicate later in the script, Strepsiades has notably removed his shoes. While this bit may refer to how Socrates and his followers went about unshod (e.g. Plato *Symposium* 173b, 220b), Telò argues that Aristophanes here 'remakes *Agamemnon*'s carpet scene' – the prop of the sandals generating 'an intense inter-theatrical echo, causing Agamemnon's tragic shoe-shedding to haunt the comic father's initiation'.[34] Socrates becomes a Clytemnestra-like figure who employs verbal deceit, speaks impiously, threatens Strepsiades' age and masculinity, and controls the physical entrance to the Thinkery (just as Clytemnestra famously controls the entrance to the palace in *Agamemnon*). This Oresteian reading works, too, at the metatheatrical level and plays into the concern in the parabasis with dutiful daughters and immoral rivals. As Telò puts it:

> If . . . Strepsiades' interactions with Socrates reflect the comic audience's experience of a deceitful comedian resembling Eupolis, the final image of the old father as a shoeless and helpless Agamemnon sets up Aristophanes' parabatic self-assimilation to Electra as a child rescuing a paternal audience from Clytemnestra-like rivals. In other words, the miniature reperformance of *Agamemnon* that comes just before the parabasis supplies the backdrop against which, in the parabasis, Aristophanes constructs his comic practice as a reenactment of *Libation Bearers*.[35]

Telò thus posits that *Clouds II* offers an early allusion to *Agamemnon*'s tapestry scene, anticipating the direct reference to Electra of the *Choephori* in the parabasis at the halfway mark. If I am correct that the opening scene (i.) has already evoked *Agamemnon* and prepared audiences for Oresteian allusions, then shoeless Strepsiades further intensifies or confirms the 'intense inter-theatrical echo'.

iii. The Electra analogy *(Clouds* 534–6)

This has been discussed earlier in this section.

iv. Debates about justice and sons overthrowing fathers *(Clouds* 900–7)

In addition to his central argument for a reperformance of the *Oresteia* in the 420s, Newiger identifies three sets of 'reminiscences' (*Reminiszenzen*) of the *Oresteia* in *Clouds*.[36] In the first of these passages, Newiger links the scene in which the Logoi squabble over whether justice exists (τὰ δίκαια, *Clouds* 900; Δίκην, 902) and debate the justice of Zeus binding his own father (904–6) to the comparable debate in the trial scene of *Eumenides* (614–43) about the nature of justice (τὸ δίκαιον, *Eum.* 619) and what the Erinyes identify as Zeus' hypocrisy in honouring the father but binding his own father Cronus (640–3). Aristophanes places the argument of the Erinyes – who lose their case

– in the mouth of Weaker Logos; as Dover observes, the arguments of both the Erinyes and Weaker Logos are in response 'to an emotional outburst' by their respective opponents (Apollo and Stronger Logos).[37] However, in an inversion of *Eumenides*, Weaker Logos both wins his debate and is entrusted with the task of teaching Pheidippides his style of argumentation (*Clouds* 1105–12, 1146–51).

Through this allusion, Aristophanes creates the expectation that Weaker Logos aligns with the Erinyes, although it leads to actions that Aeschylus' Erinyes would object to – namely, violence against one's own kin. I argue that Aristophanes deliberately misleads his audience here, in anticipation of the next scene, in which the Cloud-chorus itself takes on the role of the Erinyes (see v. below), and the later scene when Pheidippides beats Strepsiades, arguing that it is indeed just to beat one's own father, then threatens violence against his mother (see vii. below). If Aristophanes wants the audience to view him as an Electra figure, then it is a curious development that he aligns Pheidippides with an Orestes gone bad.

v. The Chorus demands *timē* from the judge(s) *(Clouds 1115–30)*

In the second parabasis of *Clouds II*, the Cloud-chorus demands that the judges award first prize to them, offering in exchange wet fertility for the judges' crops and claiming that any slight in *timē* will result in the infertility of that judge's land or rain on a friend's wedding night (*Clouds* 1115–30). The terms of this negotiation, I argue, resonate strongly with the last third of *Eumenides* (778–995), where the Erinyes, in their anger at the trial's ruling in favour of Orestes and the slight to their own *timē* (ἐγὼ δ' ἄτιμος, 780, 810; ἀτιμοπενθεῖς, 792, 822; cf. 845–6, 879–80), threaten to pollute the Athenian land (780–7, 810–17). Since Athena grants the Erinyes control over fertility of the Athenian land and people, the analogy produced through this allusion suggests that to defy the Cloud-chorus and the comic poet would be to act in a most unAthenian manner.

If I am correct to identify this allusion, there is a shift in Aristophanes' poetic persona across the two parabases, from the dutiful daughter Electra to the destructive Erinyes seeking vengeance for a previous *timē* slight. In other words, Aristophanes does not halt his poetic persona mid-*Oresteia*, but follows the logic of the trilogy through, from *Choephori* to *Eumenides*, from the heroine seeking vengeance in the second drama to the chorus of goddesses seeking vengeance in the final play. Telò's argument thus requires modification, since the second parabasis implies that the heroic rhetoric of the first parabasis will be insufficient to win over the judges and secure a dramatic victory.

vi. A murderous child *(Clouds 1161–2)*

Nearly a century ago, H. N. Couch suggested that Strepsiades' shout of exultation (*Clouds* 1154–65) upon Pheidippides finishing his education includes, at 1161–2, a 'composite reminiscence' of three of Clytemnestra's speeches (*Ag.* 607–8, 896–901 and 966–72) about welcoming Agamemnon home from Troy.[38] These reminiscences are, moreover, prefaced by Strepsiades referring to Pheidippides as 'shining with double-edged tongue' (ἀμφήκει γλώττῃ λάμπων, *Clouds* 1160), which, Couch suggests, 'would assuredly suggest ἀμφήκει φασγάνῳ (or ξίφει) λάμπων' – that is, Clytemnestra's murder weapon.[39] In a shift from the earlier carpet scene, in which Socrates evoked the deceitful Clytemnestra, now Strepsiades plays the role of Clytemnestra as he welcomes Pheidippides onstage. However, contrary to expectation, it is the newly trained Pheidippides who is transformed via Aeschylean allusion into both Clytemnestra's double-edged murder weapon and, fittingly, the son Orestes about to murder his parent.

vii. A parent's defence *(Clouds 1380–90)*

The second set of 'reminiscences' that Newiger identifies links the scene where Pheidippides assaults his father and Strepsiades defends himself (*Clouds* 1380–90) on the grounds that he himself raised his son (σ' ἐξέθρεψα, 1380) with two scenes in the *Oresteia*: the Nurse's description of raising Orestes (*Cho.* 750–62, esp. ὅν ἐξέθρεψα, 750) and Clytemnestra's defence that she herself raised Orestes (σ' ἔθρεψα, 908) just before Orestes kills her. By the time Clytemnestra offers this defence in *Choephori*, the audience has already heard the Nurse's speech and has been primed not to trust Clytemnestra's claim.[40] Aristophanes relies here on a similar technique, insofar as Strepsiades has already aligned himself via allusion with Clytemnestra (see vi. above). Strepsiades' defence thus makes him seem more Clytemnestra than Cilissa, leading him to his moment of 'learning through suffering'.

viii. pathei mathos *(Clouds 1462–4)*

Pheidippides escalates the *Oresteia* plot by threatening to beat not only Strepsiades qua Clytemnestra but also his actual mother (1442, 1444–6). Strepsiades blames the Cloud-chorus for this turn of events, to which the chorus replies punningly that Strepsiades has himself to blame since he 'twisted himself towards evil affairs' (στρέψας σεαυτὸν εἰς πονηρὰ πράγματα, *Clouds* 1455). Strepsiades responds 'Ah, Clouds, a lesson hard but just! I shouldn't have tried to get out of repaying the money I borrowed' (ὤμοι, πονηρά γ', ὦ Νεφέλαι, δίκαια δέ· οὐ γάρ με χρῆν τὰ χρήμαθ' ἀδανεισάμην ἀποστερεῖν, 1462–4). Commentators typically refer to this moment when they describe *Clouds II* as having an Aeschylean 'feel': the Clouds are 'distinctly Aeschylean moralizers';[41] it is an 'almost Aeschylean admission of *hybris*';[42] Strepsides' lament evokes the principle of *pathei mathos* expressed throughout the *Oresteia*.[43] The notion of *pathei mathos* or 'learning by suffering' is first formulated by the Argive Elders (*Ag.* 160–83, esp. 177), though what this means is not without complication.[44] For our purposes, Newiger's suggested 'reminiscences' from the *Oresteia* align the Cloud-chorus with the choruses from *Agamemnon* and *Choephori*, and Protean Strepsiades with Orestes, even though just moments before Pheidippides had been playing the role of Orestes.

These surprising pairings indicate a change in *Clouds II*'s reception of the *Oresteia* after Pheidippides completes his education (see vi.–vii. above). In the first five allusions to the *Oresteia* in *Clouds II*, the allusions follow their respective narrative sequence in the

Oresteia, such that *Clouds II* appears to be a 'Strepsiadeia' (as it were). However, once Pheidippides is educated in Weaker Logos, those previous alignments become destabilized; Strepsiades twists and turns from Clytemnestra in *Agamemnon* to her role in *Choephori* to Orestes the matricide. It is only once Strepsiades decides to take matters back into his own hands that the Strepsiadeia narrative is reasserted.

ix. Burning down the house *(Clouds* 1476–511*)*

Strepsiades aligns his cause with that of the Cloud-chorus and seeks to burn down the Thinkery. Telò argues that 'in wielding the flame ... [he] appropriates the manic, Erinys-like appearance of the Cratinean Philocleon in the final scenes of *Wasps* and thereby makes lowbrow comedy a victim of its own weapon.'[45] Since Telò is focused on *Wasps*, he does not see that Aristophanes may be alluding not to *Wasps* but to *Eumenides,* or to *Eumenides* via *Wasps.* I suggest that the burning of the Thinkery and the final chaotic *exodos* (*Clouds* 1476–511) is indeed a visual allusion to, and inversion of, the final celebratory torch procession in *Eumenides* (1032–47).

This reading, I think, has several advantages. For one, it restores the narrative sequence of the Strepsiadeia, which had been disrupted by the re-education of Pheidippides, and thus allows Aristophanes' full-scale transformation of Aeschylus' *Oresteia* to reach completion in *Clouds II*. Second, it dovetails with my reading of the opening scene in *Clouds II* as an allusion to, and inversion of, the Watchman's speech in *Agamemnon*: 'Strepsiades' kindled torch, a brilliant substitute for the bridal torch which ends other plays, finally clears away the darkness of the opening lines.'[46] This resonates in particular with the *Oresteia*'s own play around imagery of light and darkness, as Aristophanes cleverly transforms the image of the final celebratory torch procession in *Eumenides* into a final celebratory torching of the Thinkery, an act of destruction that puts an end to the Thinkery's effect of rendering young Athenian men pale, infertile and effeminate parent-beaters. This act of destruction raises questions not only about its possible staging, but also whether Aristophanes intends this scene as an act of destruction against the theatre that awarded him third place, against the failed *Clouds I* or against *Clouds II* itself and its Oresteian project.[47]

3. Conclusions: Why Electra-style?

Aristophanes makes no fewer than nine allusions to, or evocations of, Aeschylus' *Oresteia* in *Clouds II*. Several of these allusions (i.–v., ix.) run in the same narrative sequence in *Clouds II* as they do in the *Oresteia*, especially when they pertain to Strepsiades and the Cloud-chorus, such that they suggest reading *Clouds II* as a kind of Strepsiadeia. There is a disruption of this sequence once Pheidippides emerges from the Thinkery (vi.–viii.). In the two parabases, Aristophanes' poetic persona first takes on the appearance of Electra who seeks to please her father, then transforms into the destructive Erinyes who threaten to destroy Athens if they do not receive their due. There remains, of course, the question of whether all the passages I identify as allusions to the *Oresteia* belong only to *Clouds II*, or whether any of this material may have been present in the production of 423.

We might draw further conclusions from this Oresteian reading of *Clouds II*. For several readers of *Clouds*, there are pressing questions about its generic filiation, whether we ought to read the comedy as textual hybrid or 'tragicomedy' or the like.[48] Rather than think in generic terms, it is important to consider the presence of tragic *Oresteia* in comic *Clouds II* through the shared lens of education and the figure of the *didaskalos*. In the diction of both tragedy and comedy, the dramatic poet is quite literally a *didaskalos* in both senses of the word ('dramatist' and 'teacher'), which meant that any investigation into the nature of wisdom or *paideia* or educating the polis could easily become both dramatic and metatheatrical. It had become a topos on the comic stage for the dramatist to represent his poetic persona as a *didaskalos*.[49] Since the *Oresteia* is particularly concerned with notions of teaching and learning and their effects on the polis, it should come as no surprise that Aristophanes was drawn to the *Oresteia* as a narrative frame for *Clouds II*, a comedy composed by a dissed *didaskalos* about *didaskaloi* dangerous to the demos.[50]

In this light, Aristophanes' 'Electra-style' poetic persona seems surprising. In *Choephori*, Electra is not a *didaskalos*, but a young maiden who seeks instruction from libation bearers. We might expect Aristophanes to align his persona with Orestes, but instead he aligns Orestes with Pheidippides. In relocating Aeschylus' Orestes of 458 into the intellectual climate of the late 420s, Aristophanes estimates that, under the guiding hand of sophistic education, Orestes would become an amoral gadabout who violates fundamental social norms. Since Orestes no longer afforded Aristophanes a viable model for a comic poetic persona, we can see why Electra may have become the preferable figure for Aristophanes. As Telò suggests, Aristophanes' adoption of the persona of Electra allows Aristophanes to assert his own *sōphrosynē*, while simultaneously delegitimating his comic rivals' own claims to being Aeschylean and thus allows Aristophanes to place himself in the Aeschylean tradition.[51] This move anticipates not only the later valorization of Aeschylus as the wisest tragedian in *Frogs* (wherein Aristophanes returns to *Choephori* at 1124–76), but also looks ahead thoughtfully to Aristophanes' status in the comic canon and legacy. But we might go further still: Aristophanes' choice to represent himself as Electra—and also as the Erinyes— emphasizes that the restrained comic poet nevertheless seeks revenge, whether on his opponents or Athenian audiences. This glimpse of Electra as a figure of vengeance not only strengthens the argument that Aristophanes' Electra belongs to *Clouds II*, but also anticipates the recurrent use of Electra as a prominent figure for revenge in Sophocles' and Euripides' Electra plays (as well as, perhaps, the female-driven revenge plot of *Thesmophoriazusae*). In presenting himself 'Electra-style', Aristophanes in *Clouds II* may not only offer our earliest surviving play-length reception of the *Oresteia*, just one generation after its first performance, but may also have provided the key figure – Electra – with whom other dramatic poets would soon explore the effects of new habits of intellect and new models of education on the polis.

Notes

1. Text: Dover 1968: 35. Unless otherwise noted, all translations are mine. I offer my deepest gratitude to the editors, Hallie Marshall and C. W. Marshall, for hosting Greek Drama V, for their many useful and supportive suggestions on this paper since its inception, and for their generous patience. Thanks also to Mike Lippman for insightful comments. I dedicate this paper to Thompson Marshall, the highlight of GDV (with the *ekkyklēma* taking a close second). All errors are mine alone.

2. Newiger 1961 and Telò 2016: 125–56.

3. Marshall 2012: 57.

4. The critical consensus that *Clouds II* belongs to the early 410s points to the potential problem of the reliability of the scholia. For example, Hypothesis II in Dover 1968: 1–2 = test. i in Henderson 2007: 294–5 claims that Aristophanes revised *Clouds*, attempting and failing to restage it during the archonship of Ameinias (422). Since our surviving script must date after 421, this means that either Hypothesis II is wrong or there is another stage of revision prior to *Clouds II*.

5. See Dover 1968: 170–1.

6. Thus Major 2006: 131 n. 3 offers the catch-all range 420–415. Dover 1968: lxxx–lxxxi places the parabasis of *Clouds II* between spring 420 and winter 417 (though lines 575–94 likely belong to *Clouds I*, since they attack Cleon, who died in 422). Storey 1993 argues for 418 for *Clouds II*, based on Eupolis' *Baptai* belonging to the period 417–415. Sidwell 2009: 5–30 argues for 415, Kopff 1990: esp. p. 327, for 414 or 413.

7. Sidwell 2009: 10–13, Marshall 2012: esp. 59–64. On staging *Clouds II*, see Revermann 2006: 326–32 and Biles 2011: 167–210. Csapo 2010b: 103 notes that 'some think it [*Clouds II*] unperformable', but without citation.

8. Dover 1968: 1 = test. ii in Henderson 2007: 294–7. Sommerstein 2010b: 402 with n. 11 suggests Aristophanes 'had to write out the script again from scratch. This is clearly what was done when *Clouds* was revised' (this revises Sommerstein 1982: 2–4).

9. Dover 1968: xc–xciii; cf. Revermann 2006: 213–17. The vase formerly at the Getty (and known as the 'Getty Birds', Malibu 82.AE.83) may depict this scene. Green 1985 proposed the scene was from *Birds*; Taplin 1987: 95–6 suggested *Clouds I*, followed by Csapo 1993. Taplin then recanted the position (1993: 103) based on costuming and the lack of wicker cages; cf. Hubbard 1991: 93 n. 1. Revermann 2006: 217–19 suggests it depicts a satyr drama or an appropriation of satyr drama into comedy. Experts now date it to *c.* 425 or earlier; see Gaunt in Dobrov 2010: xi and Csapo 2014: 102–4, who compares the Getty vase to the 'Emory vase' (Atlanta 2008.4.1) depicting a single figure in a similarly styled cock costume.

10. Dover 1968: xciii–xciv.

11. Sommerstein 1982: 61, 188; cf. 'like the legendary Electra' in Henderson 1998: 83. Sidwell 2009: 13 rejects this position on the grounds that the referent is Aristophanes' earlier play *Banqueters*. Neither interpretation takes into sufficient account an *Oresteia* reperformance, on which see below.

12. See Swift 2015: 127–8. According to Aelian (*VH* 4.26) the lyric poet Xanthus, who antedates Stesichorus, claims Electra was originally named Laodice (mentioned in Homer *Iliad* 9.145), then was called 'Electra' after Agamemnon's murder when she became a perpetual virgin; cf. Campbell 1991: 26 n. 2.

13. Sommerstein 1982: 188: 'it is probably of Aeschylus that Ar[istophanes] is thinking here.'

14. Swift 2015: 127–8 infers that Stesichorus included Electra.

15. Prior to Zielinski 1925, general consensus was that Euripides' *Electra* dates to 413; see, e.g., Denniston 1939: xxxiii–xxxiv, who supposes that Sophocles' *Electra* is earlier (xxxiv–xxxix). Once scholars accepted the conclusions of Zielinski, consensus has tended to favour 420–419 for Euripides' *Electra*; see, e.g., Dale 1967: xxiv–xxv, Storey and Allan 2005: 265 and Cropp 2013: 31–3, the last of whom suggests 422–417 represents the most likely range. Scholars now generally place Sophocles' *Electra* after Euripides' *Electra*: the precise date for Sophocles' version 'is a matter of great uncertainty, but 418–410 seems most likely', as Storey and Allan 2005: 255 note; cf. Dale 1967: 134, who places it before *Helen*, produced in 412, followed by Kells 1973: 1–2 n. 2. Nevertheless, there are still those who hold to the older dating of Euripides' *Electra*, such as Gallagher 2003: 415.

16. The adjective ἐκείνην implies the particular version of Electra that Aristophanes intends is 'well known' and not 'new-fangled' (καινήν), a term Aristophanes applies to Euripides' *Helen* at *Thesmophoriazusae* 850 (Arnott 1990). That Aristophanes makes this distinction rebuts the suggestion of Leitao 2012: 127 with n. 72 that *Clouds II* could refer to Euripides' *Electra* (which Leitao dates to *c.* 420).

17. So also concludes Sommerstein 1982: 188.

18. See Bakola 2013 (on *Wealth Gods*) and 2009: 122–79, esp. 135–8 on *Wealth Gods*, 150–2 with n. 52 on *Runaways*, and 174–7 on Cratinus' *Eumenides*. For discussion of the date of *Wealth Gods*, see, e.g., Storey 2011: i.346–7. Bakola does not address whether or not Cratinus is drawing on reperformances of the *Oresteia*, but suggests that Cratinus depends on an Aeschylean poetics – itself linked to an older Solonian-Hesiodic concept.

19. Rosenbloom 2017: 54 points not only to *Wealth Gods* but also to an anecdote from *de Comoedia* (= test. iii Storey 2011: i.238–9) that Cratinus 'fashion[ed] himself in the character of Aeschylus' (κατασκευάζων εἰς τὸν Αἰσχύλου χαρακτῆρα) and a fragment from Pherecrates' *Tiddlers* (Grk. *Krapataloi*, fr. 100).

20. Marshall 1996: 83.

21. Newiger 1961: esp. 427–8. In a reading of Euripides' *Electra*, Davies 1998: 392–3 argues for '*a revival of Aeschylus*' Oresteia *that was still fresh in his audience's memory*' (his italics), accepting Newiger's argument on the parabasis of *Clouds II*.

22. See Marshall 1996: esp. 82–4, 94, Rosenbloom 2017: 61–4, esp. nn. 27 and 32.

23. Wilson and Taplin 1993: 176, cf. 175. Cf. Telò 2016: 96–101. On the *Oresteia* and visual representations of the Furies, see Simas in this volume.

24. Marshall 1996: 84.

25. Dover 1968: 168; Sommerstein 1982: 188, asserting that Aristophanes also exhibits 'hazy' memory 'of Aeschylus' *Persians* . . . in *Frogs* 1028–9'.

26. Both commentators overlook that one of the key themes in this scene is how characters exploit the gap between the public performance of an obligation and a character's hidden personal feeling. (Cf. Clytemnestra's welcome of Agamemnon at *Ag.* 855–942; Orestes' deception of Clytemnestra at *Cho.* 658–706.) The chorus may dress and act as slaves, but they weep with hidden grief (δακρύω δ᾽ ὑφ᾽ εἱμάτων | ματαίοισι δεσποτᾶν | τύχαις, κρυφαίοις πένθεσιν παχνουμένη, *Cho.* 82–4); cf. Garvie 1986: 67 on the ambiguity of δεσποτᾶν. Electra feels conflicted emotion when she asks the chorus how to pray (84–123), and both she and the chorus offer libations with a prayer tailored to their own purposes. It is easy to see how a spectator could read the scene 'imprecisely' since Electra's journey to Agamemnon's tomb changes as her inner feelings emerge and she gradually asserts her will.

27. Telò 2016: 130–1.

28. Hackforth 1938: 5.

29. This word picture may aim to evoke *Choephori* 476–8, whose concluding stanza takes on new meaning when read through Aristophanes' poetic persona in the parabasis and his desire to attain a dramatic victory; cf. Kitto 1956: 147, who sees *nikē* as a key term in *Choephori*, with Telò 2016: 130.

30. Telò 2016: 125–54, esp 126–7.

31. Toph Marshall further suggests that Strespsiades' name may also work to evoke the eponymous character in the *Oresteia*'s satyr drama, *Proteus*. Indeed, *Clouds II* is full of Protean characters – not only Strepsiades but also the shape-shifting Cloud-chorus; cf. Segal 1969: 163 and Park 2017: 76.

32. Revermann 2006: 180, who also suggests that the opening of *Clouds II* shares more in common with the use of space in Euripides' *Electra*.

33. See Lebeck 1971.

34. Telò 2016: 141.

35. Telò 2016: 142.

36. Newiger 1961: 428.

37. Dover 1968: 211; cf. Sommerstein 1982: 205.

38. Couch 1933. Cf. Segal's observation that these lines of Strepsiades are evocative of 'tragedy and perhaps Aeschylean tragedy' (2002 (1967): 176, esp. n. 29). Following Couch, Sommerstein 1982: 217 observes that the other tragic sources in this speech include a lost tragedy called *Peleus* and Euripides' *Hecuba* (171–4).

39. Couch 1933: 59. Marshall 2001 argues that, in the reperformance of *Agamemnon* to which Euripides refers in *Electra*, Clytemnestra uses not a sword (as Couch assumes here) but an axe (πέλεκυς).

40. Cf. Garvie 1986: 248: 'her [the Nurse's] sincerity contrasts with the hypocrisy of Clytemnestra.' Garvie notes here (*ad Cho*. 750) a possible parody of the Nurse's speech in *Acharnians* (μητρόθεν δεδεγμένος, 478), which might reinforce my argument that Aristophanes is thinking with the *Oresteia* in particular in the mid to late 420s. On *Acharnians* and the *Oresteia*, see Nelson 2016: 106–40.

41. Segal 2002 (1967): 162, comparing the Cloud-chorus (at 1454–62, esp. 1458–61) to the ghost of Darius in *Persians* (742), 'who takes a hand in punishing a man bent on evil ways in order to teach him fear of the gods'.

42. Storey in Meineck 2000: 118. The translation here is from Henderson 1998: 205. Cf. the description in Segal 2002 (1967): 175 of Strepsiades as exhibiting an Aeschylean 'rash confidence before disaster'.

43. Newiger 1961: 428 points to the Argive elders' declaration at *Ag.* 1564 and 1568, as well as similar declarations by the libation bearers (*Cho.* 308–14) and Orestes (1010–17).

44. Different views are found at Dörrie 1956: 324–6, Lebeck 1971: 25–6, Gagarin 1976: 139–50, Smith 1980: ix, 21–3, Ewans 1975: 23–4 and Clinton 1979, and see especially Fraenkel 1950: ii.99–114 and Bollack 1981: ii.197–248, esp. 223–8, 245–7.

45. Telò 2016: 153.

46. Segal 2002 (1967): 179, and see 162 and 167.

47. See Anderson 2018.

48. Silk 2013: 38 suggests the play may not have been staged because of its generic indeterminacy.

49. Bakola 2008, Biles 2011.

50. The scholarship on teaching and learning in the *Oresteia* is vast: see, e.g., Rogers 2005: 126–93 and 2013.

51. Telò 2016: 131.

CHAPTER 14
MAKING TERMINOLOGY: GENRE DESIGNATIONS IN OLD COMEDY
A. Novokhatko

Athenian Old Comedy, and particularly the comedies of Aristophanes, are the most important sources for our knowledge of the development of scholarship in fifth-century BCE Greece.[1] This material serves as a useful reflection of the main trends in philological thought at that time. It also actively contributed to the development of the vocabulary of scholarship. In the present paper, passages of Attic Old Comedy where generic terminology and specific terms indicating self-referentiality are employed will be discussed. In particular, the development of four generic terms connected to the Dionysiac festival and dramatic performance will be analysed: τραγῳδία, 'tragedy', but originally a processional goat-song leading a goat to sacrifice; κωμῳδία, 'comedy', with an etymology suggesting a 'village revel-song'; τρυγῳδία, 'trygedy', a humorous alternative to 'comedy' that sounds like 'tragedy' but with an etymology suggesting a 'wine-lees song'; and finally δρᾶμα 'drama', but literally 'act' or 'deed'. The use of these terms in other fifth-century BCE authors will place the origins of genre classification in the more general literary context.

The focus here is the development and coinage of terms that contributed to the scholarly terminology of dramatic genres. As argued below, most of the dramatic terms and concepts that were to become standard in later critical thought were created in comedy. All literature is aware of its genre: 'Authors, consumers, critics, producers, middlemen, and original geniuses cannot move without acknowledging the conventions within which or against which they wish to work.'[2] Comedy displays these terms, and provides the opportunity to coin new ones. Terms that otherwise would have been known to us from scarce epigraphical evidence (such as the τραγῳδοί and κωμῳδοί in fifth-century inscriptions) come alive through comic voices. As the fifth-century evidence reveals, Attic Old Comedy is our main source for the use and meanings of the terms 'tragedy', 'comedy' and 'drama'. The terms are almost never mentioned in other fifth-century texts.[3] The use of genre terms in comedy is crucial for the establishment of scholarly terminology. This use is dynamic, not static, and reveals the development of the notions and terms of dramatic genre during the thirty years *c.* 430–400 BCE. For convenience, this paper will group texts by decade, to the 420s, the 410s and the 400s BCE.

1. 420s BCE

Four terms denoting dramatic performance at the Dionysiac festival – τραγῳδία, κωμῳδία, τρυγῳδία and δρᾶμα – occur for the first time in the 430s BCE, or just before.

This begins with an unassigned fragment by Ecphantides (*fl.* 458–430 BCE) quoted in an anonymous commentary on Aristotle:[4] Μεγαρικῆς κωμῳδίας †ᾆσμα δίειμαι† (fr. 3 PCG: '†I dismiss the song† of Megarian comedy'). The authenticity of the fragment has been questioned. Here it is only relevant to say that, if it is authentic, then it is the first attestation for the word κωμῳδία in Greek, and that it shows Megarian comedy deliberately distinguished from Attic comedy.[5]

There is some evidence for the term τραγῳδία in early comic playwrights as well. Crates (*fl.* 450–430 BCE) mentions the term in his *Paidiai*, probably in the parabasis: τοῖς δὲ τραγῳδοῖς ἕτερος σεμνὸς πᾶσιν λόγος ἄλλος ὅδ᾽ ἔστιν (fr. 28 PCG: '[However] all the tragic performers have a diverse solemn plot, this is different').[6] The new genre onstage is characterized by its style, with the term σεμνὸς λόγος, which will become a part of the standard terminology of literary criticism.[7] The use of τραγῳδοί should mean 'tragic performers' here, framing the subject as fundamentally a performer.[8] This is clear in the much-discussed choregic dedication from Anagyrous (IG I³ 969, dated to between *c.* 440 and 431 BCE): Σωκράτης ἀνέθηκεν. Εὐριπίδης ἐδίδασκε. τραγωιδοί Ἀμφίδημος, Πύθων, Εὐθύδικος, etc. ('Socrates dedicated. Euripides directed. Tragic performers: Amphidemus, Python, Euthydicus …'). Fourteen names are listed for τραγῳδοί in this inscription instead of the expected fifteen, perhaps because the *chorēgos* excluded the chorus leader (*koryphaios*).[9] Both τραγῳδοί and κωμῳδοί also occur in epigraphical evidence from the second half of the fifth century BCE.[10] However, the terms might refer to various activities connected to play production such as composer, performer, actor, member of the chorus, which seem not to be distinguished from one another.[11] From the very beginnings, genre terms are used in comedy, and stylistic peculiarities such as the tragic solemn style or Megarian humour are identified, with the audience of the theatre apparently capable of following this discussion.

Cratinus (*fl.* 453–423 BCE) mentions τραγῳδία in his *Hōrai* (fr. 276 PCG, date unknown):

Ἴτω δὲ καὶ τραγῳδίας
ὁ Κλεομάχου διδάσκαλος, παρατιλτριῶν
ἔχων χορὸν Λυδιστὶ τιλλουσῶν μέλη
πονηρά.

Let the son of Cleomachus go as well, the trainer of the chorus of tragedy, who has a chorus of hair-plucking women, who pluck the songs/limbs in the Lydian mode in an ugly way.

The meaning here should be performative: τραγῳδία denotes the performance at a Dionysiac festival and is supported by further theatrical vocabulary, such as the terms διδάσκαλος ('director') and χορός ('chorus').[12] The director is called by name (Gnesippus, the son of Cleomachus) and profession (τραγῳδίας διδάσκαλος). Often only a name is sufficient, as with this same Gnesippus in Cratinus' *Boukoloi* (fr. 17 PCG). Elsewhere, Cratinus coined a term by which two genres meet: εὐριπιδαριστοφανίζων (fr. 342 PCG, literally 'Euripid-Aristophanizing'). These identifications of authors with the genres, combined with the function of ὀνομαστὶ κωμῳδεῖν ('to mock by name'), helped identify and classify genres.

Further evidence for both terms τραγῳδία and κωμῳδία is to be found in Aristophanes' comedy *Acharnians* (425 BCE). The protagonist Dicaeopolis is speaking in the name of the author of the comedy and declaring that he suffered 'because of the last year's comedy' (διὰ τὴν πέρυσι κωμῳδίαν, 378). Again, κωμῳδία points to a performance at the City Dionysia festival, in all probability the performance of Aristophanes' *Babylonioi* in 426 BCE.[13] In the same play, Aristophanes uses the term τραγῳδία to refer to the work of Euripides: in the earliest extant use of the word, Euripides is said to be at home 'creating tragedy' (ποιεῖ τραγῳδίαν, 399–400).[14] In the prologue, Diaceopolis says (9–11):

ἀλλ᾽ ὠδυνήθην ἕτερον αὖ τραγῳδικόν,
ὅτε δὴ ᾽κεχήνη προσδοκῶν τὸν Αἰσχύλον,
ὁ δ᾽ ἀνεῖπεν, 'εἴσαγ᾽, ὦ Θέογνι, τὸν χορόν.'

However, I had on the other side grief referring to tragedy, when I was open-mouthed waiting for Aeschylus, and the guy proclaimed 'Bring on your chorus, Theognis!'

The adjective τραγῳδικός (9), here employed ironically, surrounded by the two 'tragic' names of Aeschylus and Theognis, may have been an Aristophanic creation, as it is used exclusively by Aristophanes (*Frogs* 769, 1495 and *Plutos* 424).[15]

In *Acharnians* τραγῳδία is connected exclusively with Euripides. Returning to the scene where the slave describes Euripides' activities, Dicaeopolis uses the word with his question whether Euripides wears 'these rags from tragedy' (τὰ ῥάκι᾽ ἐκ τραγῳδίας ἔχεις, 412). Here τραγῳδία is used in its primary meaning of theatrical performance, as Euripides literally wears theatrical costumes, rags from his own pieces.[16] τὰ ῥάκι᾽ ἐκ τραγῳδίας emphasizes stage requisites rather than a written literary text, although it might have been accorded this secondary metaphorical meaning as well. The character Euripides uses the term τραγῳδία when referring to his own work (464). Dicaeopolis took the requisites from Euripides' 'beggar-plays' and Euripides claims that 'none remained' (470).[17] We can conclude that in 425 BCE τραγῳδία indicates both a script being composed (as in 398–400) and a piece to be performed, the materialization of the authorial work onstage with the necessary theatrical requisites (as in 412 and 464).

Finally, the paradigmatic pun τρυγῳδία ('new-wine-song') was coined in Aristophanes' *Acharnians*. It refers to the close connection between both performative genres, τραγῳδία on the one hand, and κωμῳδία with τρύξ ('wine-lees'), its pure Dionysian constituent, on the other (498–500):[18]

εἰ πτωχὸς ὢν ἔπειτ᾽ ἐν Ἀθηναίοις λέγειν
μέλλω περὶ τῆς πόλεως, τρυγῳδίαν ποιῶν.
τὸ γὰρ δίκαιον οἶδε καὶ τρυγῳδία.

Although being poor I am going to speak before the Athenians about the city while composing a 'trygedy'. For what is just knows 'trygedy' as well.

Dicaeopolis plays here both with his name – which means 'just-city' – and at the same time with the fresh terminology, emphatically proclaiming a manifesto for the genre, of his own impending comedic performance in which he will parody tragedy, and immediately juxtaposing it to its sibling genre 'tragedy'.[19] The process of term creation is significant here, as this close link and juxtaposition of two genres and the use of their names together will be transferred to Plato, and through him to later times.[20]

This emphatic use of the new vocabulary of making comedy continues in the parabasis where Aristophanes explains his role as a comic playwright and the function of his genre (628–32):[21]

ἐξ οὗ γε χοροῖσιν ἐφέστηκεν τρυγικοῖς ὁ διδάσκαλος ἡμῶν,
οὔπω παρέβη πρὸς τὸ θέατρον λέξων ὡς δεξιός ἐστιν·
διαβαλλόμενος δ' ὑπὸ τῶν ἐχθρῶν ἐν Ἀθηναίοις ταχυβούλοις,
ὡς κωμῳδεῖ τὴν πόλιν ἡμῶν καὶ τὸν δῆμον καθυβρίζει,
ἀποκρίνασθαι δεῖται νυνὶ πρὸς Ἀθηναίους μεταβούλους.

Since our director has taken charge of comic ['trygic'] choruses, he has never come forward to the audience saying that he is clever. But slandered by the enemies among the swiftly-making-up-their-mind Athenians with the charge that he is the one who composes a comedy about our city and insults the people, he now begs for permission to reply to the changing-their-mind Athenians.

The terms 'comic choruses' (χοροῖσιν τρυγικοῖς), 'director' (ὁ διδάσκαλος), 'composes a comedy' (κωμῳδεῖ) are used in a purely performative context here. Comic choruses are also called 'trygic' (τρυγῳδικός), as a metaphor for a peaceful entertainment, as Dicaeopolis speaks to an eel: ἦλθες ποθεινὴ μὲν τρυγῳδικοῖς χοροῖς (886: 'you came longing for comic ["trygic"] choruses'). The transitive verb κωμῳδεῖν is in active use from the very beginning (κωμῳδήσει τὰ δίκαια, 655), used as a generic term. The repeated use of 'justice' linked to the serious material of tragedy emphasizes the poet's awareness of the serious function of comedy. Through this repeated self-affirmation Aristophanes introduces genre terminology and renders it meaningful.

The word δρᾶμα, which is applied as a theatrical term in the fifth century BCE exclusively to tragedy, also seems to have been in use from the 420s BCE. Herodotus 6.21.2 mentions it referring to Phrynichus' tragedy *Milētou halōsis* (490s BCE?):

Ἀθηναῖοι μὲν γὰρ δῆλον ἐποίησαν ὑπεραχθεσθέντες τῇ Μιλήτου ἁλώσι τῇ τε ἄλλῃ πολλαχῇ καὶ δὴ καὶ ποιήσαντι Φρυνίχῳ δρᾶμα Μιλήτου ἅλωσιν καὶ διδάξαντι ἐς δάκρυά τε ἔπεσε τὸ θέητρον καὶ ἐζημίωσάν μιν ὡς ἀναμνήσαντα οἰκήια κακὰ χιλίῃσι δραχμῇσι, καὶ ἐπέταξαν μηκέτι μηδένα χρᾶσθαι τούτῳ τῷ δράματι.

For the Athenians made it clear – as they were feeling deep grief for the taking of Miletus – in various ways, and towards Phrynichus as well who composed and directed the play 'The Taking of Miletus'; and the audience broke into tears, and they [the Athenians] fined him a thousand drachmae for reminding them about home calamities and forbade anyone from reusing this play, forever.[22]

It is possible that δρᾶμα might simply mean 'deed, act' here, but the combination with both verbs engaged with the production of tragedy, ποιεῖν and διδάσκειν, as well as the earliest attested use of the noun θέατρον here (translated as 'audience'), renders it likely that we are here observing the establishment of the term. The almost complete absence of the term τραγῳδία from Herodotus indicates that it was not yet in common use.[23]

In Aristophanes' *Acharnians,* δρᾶμα occurs twice, both referring to Euripides' tragedies (414–415 and 470). Approximately at the same time the term is also used in an unassigned fragment of Telecleides, with someone 'roasting a new play for Euripides' (φρύγει τι δρᾶμα καινόν Εὐριπίδῃ, fr. 41 PCG).[24] An enigmatic work of Ion of Chios is *Mega drāma* from before 421 BCE.[25] Ion is said to have composed different kinds of poetry, but was known mainly for his tragedies and dithyrambs. Three fragments of *Mega drāma* survive, though nothing can be judged concerning the meaning of the title from them.

The chorus in Aristophanes' *Knights* (424 BCE) swears to the Paphlagonian that if it doesn't hate him, 'may I be taught to sing an accompaniment to a tragedy by Morsimus!' (διδασκοίμην προσᾴδειν Μορσίμου τραγῳδίᾳ, 401). Here τραγῳδία is regarded from the perspective of a chorus member: the chorus considers it a punishment to be engaged in the stage production of a bad playwright. The vocabulary of chorus activities is also used (διδάσκειν and προσᾴδειν). Further, in the parabasis the chorus leader presents the history of the performance of comedy in Greece from early on, and discusses κωμῳδοδιδασκαλία, 'the production/direction of comedy' (507–17):[26]

εἰ μέν τις ἀνὴρ τῶν ἀρχαίων κωμῳδοδιδάσκαλος ἡμᾶς
ἠνάγκαζεν λέξοντας ἔπη πρὸς τὸ θέατρον παραβῆναι,
οὐκ ἂν φαύλως ἔτυχεν τούτου ...
ἃ δὲ θαυμάζειν ὑμῶν φησιν πολλοὺς αὐτῷ προσιόντας
καὶ βασανίζειν, ὡς οὐχὶ πάλαι χορὸν αἰτοίη καθ᾽ ἑαυτόν,
ἡμᾶς ὑμῖν ἐκέλευε φράσαι περὶ τούτου. φησὶ γὰρ ἀνὴρ
οὐχ ὑπ᾽ ἀνοίας τοῦτο πεπονθὼς διατρίβειν, ἀλλὰ νομίζων
κωμῳδοδιδασκαλίαν εἶναι χαλεπώτατον ἔργον ἀπάντων·
πολλῶν γὰρ δὴ πειρασάντων αὐτὴν ὀλίγοις χαρίσασθαι·

If any of the old directors of comedy compelled us to come forward to the audience and to say words, he would not have gained this easily ... he says that many of you come to him and wonder and question him about why he did not ask for a chorus in his own name long ago, and he asked us to speak to you about this. For the man says that he had remained in this situation not from stupidity, but thinking that comic production/direction is the most difficult labour of all; for from those many who have tried her, she has favoured only a few.

The noun κωμῳδοδιδασκαλία (516) is personified here, the metaphor of sexual contact between a comic director/playwright with his production (a female figure) being employed for the process of creation of comedy. The word occurs only here; the profession of the director κωμῳδοδιδάσκαλος (507) is a more common term.[27]

In *Clouds* (originally produced in 423, but revised in the next decade), several puns are made against both comic and tragic playwrights. Socrates uses a comic coinage τρυγοδαίμονες (literally, 'men inspired by wine-lees', 296) to refer to comic poets/ performers and their activities. Further tragic poets/performers (1091 τραγῳδοῦσι) are attacked together with advocates (1089 συνηγοροῦσι) and politicians (1093 δημηγοροῦσι) as passive homosexuals. In the parabasis the chorus leader refers to the first version of the *Clouds*. The play onstage in performance is the first meaning of 'comedy' here, the author explicitly speaking to the spectators (ὑμᾶς θεατάς, 521), who receive the best of his comedies (τῶν ἐμῶν κωμῳδιῶν, 523). At *Clouds* 534–6, the use of a simile casts Electra as the genre of tragedy:[28]

νῦν οὖν Ἠλέκτραν κατ' ἐκείνην ἥδ' ἡ κωμῳδία
ζητοῦσ' ἦλθ', ἥν που 'πιτύχῃ θεαταῖς οὕτω σοφοῖς·
γνώσεται γάρ, ἤνπερ ἴδῃ, τἀδελφοῦ τὸν βόστρυχον.

But now like the famous Electra, this comedy has come searching if she would find so clever spectators; for she will recognize, if she sees it, the lock of her brother.

A personified comedy is thus juxtaposed with a personification of tragedy. The generic link of comedy to tragedy points to the closeness of the two genres.

Even more personified and allegorized is κωμῳδία in Cratinus' comedy *Pytine,* which defeated *Clouds* at the City Dionysia of 423 BCE. According to a scholion, Cratinus' wife Κωμῳδία was the protagonist (*Schol. Ar. Eq.* 400a = Cratin. *Pytine* test. ii PCG):

ὅπερ μοι δοκεῖ παροξυνθεὶς ἐκεῖνος, καίτοι τοῦ ἀγωνίζεσθαι ἀποστὰς καὶ συγγράφειν, πάλιν γράφει δρᾶμα, τὴν Πυτίνην, εἰς αὐτόν τε καὶ τὴν μέθην, οἰκονομίᾳ τε κεχρημένον τοιαύτῃ. τὴν Κωμῳδίαν ὁ Κρατῖνος ἐπλάσατο αὑτοῦ εἶναι γυναῖκα καὶ ἀφίστασθαι τοῦ συνοικεσίου τοῦ σὺν αὐτῷ θέλειν, καὶ κακώσεως αὐτῷ δίκην λαγχάνειν, φίλους δὲ παρατυχόντας τοῦ Κρατίνου δεῖσθαι μηδὲν προπετὲς ποιῆσαι καὶ τῆς ἔχθρας ἀνερωτᾶν τὴν αἰτίαν, τὴν δὲ μέμφεσθαι αὐτῷ ὅτι μὴ κωμῳδοίη μηκέτι, σχολάζοι δὲ τῇ μέθῃ.

Stimulated by this, it seems to me, although having withdrawn from competing and composing, he wrote a play again, the Pytine, attacking himself and the drunkenness, using the following plan. Cratinus imagined Comedy to be his wife; she wanted to divorce him and claimed against him for ill treatment. Cratinus' friends happened along there begging him not to do anything reckless and to ask her about the reason of her hatred. And she blamed him that he did not compose comedies any more, but had leisure for Drunkenness.

'Comedy' wanted to divorce him because he did not compose comedies anymore (ὅτι μὴ κωμῳδοίη μηκέτι), but devoted himself to 'Drunkenness'.[29] Such personification and incorporation of comedy onstage must have shaped the acceptance of the genre by the audience, and thus accorded key characteristics to it.[30] Evidence from painting points to the personification of Comedy in this play as part of an artistic trend. A female figure named Τραγωιδία ('Tragōidia'), appears on vases approximately during this period, from the 440s BCE, while the first female figure named Κωμωιδία ('Kōmōidia') appears on vases in the mid fifth century BCE.[31] This evidence is crucial to support the argument that the designations for tragedy and comedy start being in active use at this time, both on sympotic vessels and onstage. Hall argues that visualization becomes one of the factors in the development of the genre. The images of tragedy and comedy are auxiliary to the establishment of genres, and the changes in the imagery correspond to gradual multimedia conceptualizations of them.

Aristophanes' *Wasps* (422 BCE) develops an interactive dialogue between comedy and tragedy onstage.[32] In the prologue, the term κωμῳδία is used for a number of other playwrights' 'bad comedy' (κωμῳδίας δὲ φορτικῆς, 66).[33] Xanthias thus announces in the prologue the coming 'cleverer' play (66). This motif of others' 'bad comedy' is developed in the *Wasps*. The protagonist Bdelycleon says: 'It is hard, and appropriate for a clever disposition, and far beyond what comic performers/poets ['πὶ τρυγῳδοῖς] do, to cure an ancient illness inborn in the city' (650–1). Other τρυγῳδοί are not able to do what the author intends to achieve. The use of self-referential terminology recurs in the parabasis. The adjective κωμῳδικός (1020), used here for the first time, and meaning 'relating to comedy', recalls τραγῳδικός at *Acharnians* 9. Surprisingly, κωμῳδικός is being linked to the literary text (κωμῳδικὰ πολλὰ χέασθαι 'to pour many verses of comedy').[34] It reappears, more explicitly related to 'verses', in the same monologue, referring to the performative context with ἀκοῦσαι ('to have heard', 1047), and the written script with ἔπη κωμῳδικά ('verses from comedy', 1047).

The text of the *Wasps* also has a number of references to comedy and tragedy. A lover upset with his boy-love asks the poet to write a comedy about him (κωμῳδεῖσθαι παιδίχ' ἑαυτοῦ, 1026), and a hapax created out of the root κωμῳδεῖν and λείχειν ('to lick') results in the verb κωμῳδολοιχεῖν ('to play the parasite', 1318).[35] Turning back to tragedy's roots, the 'inventor' of tragedy and first actor, Thespis, is mentioned in the play's finale (1479). The old man Philocleon is said by the slave Xanthias to have danced all night long, and to have claimed that he would compete against contemporary τραγῳδοί (1480–1). The old-fashioned Philocleon threatens to beat the modern tragic performance with a tragic performance à la Thespis. The generic challenge is expressed explicitly as the comic character invokes the genre of tragedy.[36] Three tragic poets/performers (three sons of Carcinus) enter the orchestra to accept Philocleon's challenge, and so represent contemporary tragedy. Xanthias announces their appearance on stage using the appropriate terminology (1497–511). It seems reasonable to conclude from this passage that the term τραγῳδός is used here as a hypernym for both arts of tragic activity, performing and composing. All three brothers are supposed to be performers. The first two are called τραγῳδοί (1498 and 1505); the youngest one is said to compose tragedy (1511: ὃς τὴν τραγῳδίαν ποιεῖ). The final scene ends with a *sphragis* (a 'seal' of authorial self-reference), in which the term χορὸν τρυγῳδῶν ('chorus of comic performers') speaks about itself (1535–7):[37]

ἀλλ' ἐξάγετ', εἴ τι φιλεῖτ', ὀρχούμενοι, θύραζε
ἡμᾶς ταχύ· τοῦτο γὰρ οὐδείς πω πάρος δέδρακεν,
ὀρχούμενον ὅστις ἀπήλλαξεν χορὸν τρυγῳδῶν.

But now lead out, please, dancing out of the theatre quickly; for none has ever done this before, to discharge a dancing chorus of comic performers.

At the same festival of Lenaea in 422 BCE, *Proagon*, written by Aristophanes, was directed by Philonides. The surviving fragments do not exhibit the use of the terminology of either tragedy or comedy, but one might expect that specific vocabulary referring to tragedy was used beyond the title.[38]

Finally, in *Peace* (421 BCE), Aristophanes zooms in and out, so to speak, emphasizing the range of perspectives from which tragedy and comedy may be viewed. The verb κωμῳδεῖν is used in the parabasis (751).[39] Melanthios and his chorus are mentioned (803–8, especially 806–7: τῶν τραγῳδῶν τὸν χορόν). Tragedy as 'the chorus of tragic performers' stands for the performative side here, and is shown from the perspective of the chorus members. Furthermore, an audience-oriented attitude of the term τραγικός occurs when Trygaeus' daughter advises her father how to take on a 'more tragic' air (135–6);[40] τραγικώτερος evokes Crates' reference to the solemn style (σεμνός).[41] The word is also emphasized acoustically, at the end of the verse and requiring a resolution after a series of unresolved trimeters, something 'certainly intended to be humorous'.[42] Another audience-oriented use of the 'tragic' is found when Trygaeus lists the things Eirene smells of (530–1), such as harvest time (ὀπώρας), the festivals of Dionysus (Διονυσίων) and the tragic performance (τραγῳδῶν). Finally, τραγῳδία can embody an author-oriented perspective, the process of the creation of tragedy being referred to (147–8):

εἶτα χωλὸς ὢν Εὐριπίδῃ
λόγον παράσχῃς καὶ τραγῳδία γένῃ

and then being lame you would provide a plot for Euripides, and a tragedy would be born

Here 'tragedy' is the product of its creator, highlighting the process of dramatic composition. τραγῳδία is juxtaposed to λόγος (*logos*, 'plot'), as the plot comes first, and might derive from an external feature, such as lameness. Yet it takes a Euripides to make a tragedy of it.[43] In the parabasis, Aristophanes returns to the production of comedy

(734–8). Two functions of the process are emphasized separately, though they both refer to the same person (these two functions were often but not always combined). The word κωμῳδοποιητής ('comic poet', 734) highlights the composition of comedy, placing the author at the centre, while κωμῳδοδιδάσκαλος ('comic director', 737) refers to the function of the director.[44]

Aristophanic comedy of the 420s is overflowing with dramatic vocabulary. Though terms may have been coined some decades earlier, they become established in this decade. The genre terms τραγῳδία, κωμῳδία, τρυγῳδία and δρᾶμα are used intensively in extant comic texts from the very beginning: 'In the theatrical milieu of the fifth century, where the focus of dramatic activities was the single public performance of a play, it is misguided to imagine the text and the production as two quite separate things.'[45] If anything, Halliwell's statement could be made more forcefully. Text and production were two parts of the same activity. In these early plays of Aristophanes, one can see a shift in the meaning of the terminology from the primacy of production towards the primacy of text.

2. 410s

The 410s provide less evidence for the use of dramatic terminology. This may be due to the smaller number of plays surviving from this decade, but another factor might be that the initial boom created by the self-reflection of comedy had fizzled out. Eupolis in *Demoi* (mid 410s BCE) provides one example of the use of dramatic terminology. In a long papyrus fragment, the word τρυγῳδο[('trygi[c]', fr. 99.29 PCG) stands isolated. It is unclear which form exactly is at the end of the line, but a link to an Aristophanic coinage is plausible.[46]

No reference to comedy but several attestations of tragedy are found in Aristophanes' *Birds* (414 BCE). For the further shift in the term 'tragedy' here it is worth noting that this example incorporates a scholarly use of the term with the reference to the corpus of Sophocles' work and more specifically to his tragedy *Tereus* (100–1): 'This is how Sophocles mistreats me, Tereus, in his tragedies.'[47] A tragedy with the appearance of a Priam (512) is also mentioned. The technical term ἐξέλθοι, meaning the actor 'coming out of the *skēnē* building onto the stage', belongs to the performative context, while ἐν τοῖσι τραγῳδοῖς could be used in the literate sense as well. The chorus of birds mocks the heavy and boring tragic chorus (τοῖς χοροῖσι τῶν τραγῳδῶν, 789) in the parabasis. Peisetaerus refers to tragedy from the perspective of a spectator, a young man obsessed with tragedy (ἐπὶ τραγῳδίᾳ ἀνεπτερῶσθαι, 1444–5). From the context, we can conclude that the generic term τραγῳδία is now fixed and that the audience is expected to understand any reference to it.

In the same year, the parabasis of Aristophanes' *Amphiaraus* (414 BCE) mentions a comic-frightening theatrical mask (κωμῳδικὸν μορμολυκεῖον, fr. 31 PCG).[48] The adjective κωμῳδικός ('comedic'), attested for the first time in the *Wasps*, is used in the performative context of stage properties. A rare noun μορμολυκεῖον, otherwise attested twice in Aristophanes and once in Plato for 'fright', combined with the adjective κωμῳδικός, might apply here to the genre of comedy.⁴⁹ Similarly Aristotle, juxtaposing tragedy and comedy, mentions a comic theatrical mask (τὸ γελοῖον πρόσωπον) as a material manifestation of the genre of comedy in *Poetics* 5 (1149a33–6):

> τὸ γὰρ γελοῖόν ἐστιν ἁμάρτημά τι καὶ αἶσχος ἀνώδυνον καὶ οὐ φθαρτικόν, οἷον εὐθὺς <u>τὸ γελοῖον πρόσωπον</u> αἰσχρόν τι καὶ διεστραμμένον ἄνευ ὀδύνης.

> for the laughable is a fault or shame which is free from pain or destruction; like most obviously <u>the laughable/comic mask</u> which is something ugly and distorted but without pain.

In Aristophanes' *Thesmophoriazusae* (411 BCE) Euripides is once more a protagonist, and thus the interaction with tragedy and the use of the relevant vocabulary is more prevalent than in other plays.⁵⁰ The women of Athens plot against Euripides 'because I compose tragedies and abuse them' (ὁτιὴ τραγῳδῶ καὶ κακῶς αὐτὰς λέγω, 85).⁵¹ With the verb τραγῳδῶ, built on the κωμῳδῶ-model, the character-author's declaration – 'I compose/perform tragedies' – embodies both the performative and the literary dimensions. The performative use of the term 'tragedy' is highlighted, listing spectators, tragic performers and choruses (θεαταὶ καὶ τραγῳδοὶ καὶ χοροί, 391) as being engaged with Euripides' slander of women. Later, a woman attacks Euripides for writing atheistic tragedies (450–1), with the emphatic use of the verb ποιεῖν emphasizing the poet's craftsmanship (ἐν ταῖσιν τραγῳδίαις ποιῶν, 450). Two other terms first attested in Aristophanes' *Thesmophoriazusae* refer to Agathon, ὁ τραγῳδοποιός (maker of tragedy) and ὁ τραγῳδοδιδάσκαλος (director of tragedy).⁵² As at *Peace* 734–8, where the terms κωμῳδοποιητής (734) and κωμῳδοδιδάσκαλος (737) were juxtaposed, here τραγῳδοποιός (*Thes.* 30) distinguishes the function of poet from the performer, while τραγῳδοδιδάσκαλος (88) emphasizes Agathon's function as the director of his own chorus.

Finally, δρᾶμα occurs five times in the *Thesmophoriazusae*, always referring to tragedy: to Euripides (849), Carcinus, Agathon and Phyrynichus (52 and 166), and to the tragic playwright in general (149 and 151). The same can be seen in Aristophanes' *Dramata e Kentauros* (frs. 278–88 PCG), *Dramata e Niobos* (frs. 289–98) and *Dramata* (frs. 299–304 PCG). As is often the case with double titles, the title has perhaps been given to the work by a scribe or a bookseller, and not by the author himself. What is intended here by the word *Dramata* remains unclear.⁵³

Thesmophoriazusae also provides the first extant use of *satyroi* to refer to satyr-drama: ὅταν σατύρους τοίνυν ποιῇς (157: 'whenever you create satyrs/write a satyr-drama'). Olson has argued that 'in the classical period the word never means anything other than "satyrs"'.⁵⁴ However, the emphatic use of the verb ποιεῖν with the 'satyrs' creates a literate connotation, as in ποιεῖ τραγῳδίαν (*Ach.* 399–400).⁵⁵ Vase-painting from the 430s on proves that there was an ongoing artistic engagement with the relationship of tragedy and satyrs.⁵⁶ In a fragment from Aristophanes' *Thesmophoriazusae II* (between 415 and 406?) a further pun coinage τρυγῳδοποιομουσική (fr. 347.1 PCG) for 'the composition of comedy' reveals that the literate use of terminology related to literary production continues to be developed. While mocking Crates' bombastic language (fr. 347.2–3 PCG: Κράτητί τε τάριχος ἐλεφάντινον λαμπρὸν ἐνομίζετ᾽, 'Crates considered the saltfish to be ivoried, shining'), Aristophanes nevertheless creates an elevated term for Crates' poetic register.

The evidence from the decade 420–410 BCE suggests a reduced use of the comic dramatic terminology (κωμῳδικός appearing only once in Aristophanes' *Amphiaraus*, and τρυγῳδο[once in Eupolis' *Demoi*). This may be due to the fact that the boom of discovery and self-referentiality of comedy had passed. Tragedy remains a focus for comic playwrights, particularly in Aristophanes' *Thesmophoriazusae*, where a vocabulary denoting tragedy is actively used.

3. 400s

The next decade shows a renewal in the generation of genre terminology, seen first in comic fragments. Aristophanes' *Gerytades* (408/07 BCE?) includes one of the first classifications of genre, as three poets, representative of three genres, were elected and sent to the underworld (fr. 156.8–10 PCG):

Α. καὶ τίνες ἂν εἶεν; Β. πρῶτα μὲν Σαννυρίων
ἀπὸ τῶν τρυγῳδῶν, ἀπὸ δὲ τῶν τραγικῶν χορῶν
Μέλητος, ἀπὸ δὲ τῶν κυκλίων Κινησίας.

A. And who could they be? B. First, Sannyrion from the trygic performers/poets, then Melitus from the tragic choruses, then Cinesias from the dithyrambs.

Terms for comic performers (τρυγῳδοί) and tragic choruses (τραγικοὶ χοροί) denote categories of performative poetry.[57] The deliberate contrast of genres is crucial for this period. Three fragments survive from Alcaeus' comedy *Kōmōdotragōdia* ('comedotragedy'), produced after 408 BCE, where two distinct genres are juxtaposed and brought together.[58] The adjective τραγικός is also attested as a noun meaning tragic actor when Hegelochus[59] is ridiculed (fr. 8.3–4 PCG) in Sannyrion's comedy *Danae* (after 408 BCE).[60]

By 405 BCE, 'tragedy' and 'comedy' are fixed terms for the literary genres, and the performative connotation is gradually giving way to the literary, and the written becoming dominant. In Aristophanes' *Frogs*, Euripides is referred to as the tragic poet who is supposed to be creative and procreative (89–100):

Ηρ. οὔκουν ἕτερ᾽ ἔστ᾽ ἐνταῦθα μειρακύλλια
τραγῳδίας ποιοῦντα πλεῖν ἢ μύρια,
Εὐριπίδου πλεῖν ἢ σταδίῳ λαλίστερα;
Δι. ἐπιφυλλίδες ταῦτ᾽ ἐστὶ καὶ στωμύλματα,
χελιδόνων μουσεῖα, λωβηταὶ τέχνης,

ἃ φροῦδα θᾶττον, ἢν ἅπαξ χορὸν λάβῃ,
μόνον προσουρήσαντα τῇ τραγῳδίᾳ.
γόνιμον δὲ ποιητὴν ἂν οὐχ εὕροις ἔτι
ζητῶν ἄν, ὅστις ῥῆμα γενναῖον λάκοι.
Ηρ. πῶς γόνιμον;
Δι.   ὡδὶ γόνιμον, ὅστις φθέγξεται
τοιουτονί τι παρακεκινδυνευμένον,
'αἰθέρα Διὸς δωμάτιον' ἢ 'χρόνου πόδα'. . .

Heracles: And are not there more than countless young boys here composing tragedies, who are over a stadion more talkative than Euripides?
Dionysus: They are small grapes and chatterboxes, 'shrines of swallows', disgracers of their skill, who disappear again rapidly, as soon as they get a chorus, having just pissed over tragedy. You could not find a fertile poet if you searched for one, who could shout a noble word.
Heracles: How fertile?
Dionysus: So fertile that one would say something risky such as 'Aither, the room of Zeus' or 'the foot of time'. . .[61]

The genre is personified through the metaphor of an act of sex between the poet Euripides and tragedy.[62] The term κωμῳδία, used at the very beginning of the prologue (15), specifies the genre, with reference to repeated scenes in three other comic playwrights, Phrynichus, Lycis and Ameipsias (12–15). The verb κωμῳδεῖν occurs in the parabasis, referring to a speaker who has become a subject of comedy at the Dionysia (368: κωμῳδηθείς).[63] Aeschylus is considered the best tragic playwright (769: εἶχε τὸν τραγῳδικὸν θρόνον, 'he had the Chair of Tragedy') until Euripides arrived in the underworld. Euripides describes Aeschylus' manner of composing tragōdiai (833–4, 911–13, 935–7): strikingly, the term τραγῳδία is used exclusively by the character of Euripides in the Frogs, suggesting the novelty of such technical vocabulary, and placing it firmly in the second half of the fifth century.

On two occasions in Frogs the term δρᾶμα denotes action onstage: τὸ δρᾶμα δ᾽ ἂν διῄει ('and the play proceeded', 920), καὶ τὸ δρᾶμα ἤδη μεσοίη ('and the play was already at the middle', 923). Euripides' description of his tragedy overlaps with a critic's review: ἀλλ᾽ οὑξιὼν πρώτιστα μέν μοι τὸ γένος εἶπ᾽ ἂν εὐθὺς τοῦ δράματος ('but coming onstage my character at the very beginning immediately explained the origin of the play', 946–7). δρᾶμα also refers to Aeschylus' authorial product: δρᾶμα ποιήσας Ἄρεως μεστόν ('having composed a play full of Ares', 1021).

The famous scene of literary criticism in Aristophanes' Frogs (757–1471) scrutinizes tragedy metaphorically (798: μειαγωγήσουσι τὴν τραγῳδίαν, 'they will bring the tragedy to the scale as a sacrificial lamb'; 802: κατ᾽ ἔπος βασανιεῖν φησι τὰς τραγῳδίας, 'says he would scrutinize the tragedies, every word').[64] Specific parts of individual tragedies are examined, and four specific plays by Euripides are named by their title (860–4). The prologues of tragedies are also examined (1119–97), tragedy being clearly understood with the connotation of a literary genre (1119–21).[65] The chorus in the finale refers to

Euripides who lost the competition as one who τά τε μέγιστα παραλιπόντα τῆς τραγῳδικῆς τέχνης ('ignored the most important things of the tragedic skill', 1494–9).

Also in 405, Phrynichus' *Mousai* speaks about Sophocles who 'composed many good tragedies' (fr. 32.3 PCG, πολλὰς ποιήσας καὶ καλὰς τραγῳδίας) in a quite similar manner to Aristophanes in the *Frogs*.[66] Phrynichus also composed a comedy titled *Tragōdoi e Apeleutheroi*[67] in which tragic poets or performers were probably the chorus. A similar title is ascribed to a play by Callias, who may have composed a *Grammatikē Tragōidia/ Theōria* in the last years of the fifth century BCE.[68] Despite the persistence of debates on the chronology and genre of the play, the confrontation of genres is reflected in both of these plays. In Strattis' *Anthrōporestēs*, the playwright critizes an archon for selecting the wrong actor for the main role, and thus destroying Euripides' great tragedy *Orestes* (fr. 1 PCG). The audience is expected to analyse the quality of both author and actor, the Euripidean tragedy (Εὐριπίδου δὲ δρᾶμα, 2) being described with the superlative δεξιώτατον (2) and the actor's performance deprecated with the verb διακναίειν (3, lit. 'to scrape away').

Literary texts serve as a reflection of various processes of their time, developing terminology that is useful and relevant to technical discussion. The genre that most effectively reproduces the discourses of society is Attic Old Comedy. These plays provide important evidence for the growth and self-formation of a vocabulary of dramatic genres. Certainly, comedy operates within its cultural and intellectual context, but, to develop this discourse, comedy was obliged to develop specific language, which in turn was destined to become technical terminology employed by literary criticism. Comedy reflected both the literate and performative discourse of its time. Attic Old Comedy is a crucial source for examining genre classification as it developed in pre-Platonic Greece.

Notes

1. I wish to thank Toph and Hallie Marshall for their kind assistance and many useful suggestions.

2. Rosenmeyer 2006: 423.

3. Exceptions include Her. 5.67 and 6.21; Gorg. fr. 24 DK (cf. Ar. *Frogs* 1021).

4. Anon. in Arist. *Eth. Nic.* 4, 6, 1123a23 = CAG XX 186, 12–20 Heylbut. In PCG the fragment consists of two verses. I believe that the second verse does not belong to this fragment, but to the cover text: see Bagordo 2014: 89–93, with bibliography.

5. On Megarian humour and Attic distance from it, cf. Ar. *Ach.* 729–817, *Wasps* 57 and Biles and Olson 2015: 102–3, Eup. fr. 261 PCG and Olson 2016: 349–52 and Wright 2012: 109. See also Arist. *Poet.* 3, 1448a29–35.

6. This verse is not clear. Various translations are possible; cf. Storey 2011: 225 ('This is a different sort of story, a serious one, for all the tragic poets'), Farmer 2017: 28 n. 49 ('all the tragedians have this whole other solemn *logos*'), Perrone 2019: 150 ('ma tutt'altra storia, da rappresentazioni tragiche, per tutti veneranda è questa qui'). On the obscurity of the term λόγος here, see Farmer 2017: 28 n. 49 with further bibliography.

7. Cf. Arist. *Poet.* 4, 1449a19. See Ar. *Frogs* 833–4, 1004. See Perrone 2019: 152.

8. On the terms τραγῳδοί and κωμῳδοί, see Pickard-Cambridge 1988: 129–32 and, especially on their frequent use of the plural, see Ghiron-Bistagne 1976: 119–25.

9. Csapo 2010a: 110. On the inscription IG³ 969 see further Ghiron-Bistagne 1976: 119–21, Wilson 2000: 131–4, Csapo 2010a: 91–2 and Wilson 2015: 120 n. 90.

10. IG I³ 254, ll. 9, 21, 34 (a decree from the Rural Dionysia in Ikarion, c. 440–415? BCE with Wilson 2015 on it in detail, contains only τραγοιδός, three times), IG I³ 258bis, lines 2, 5, 6 (from the theatre at Thorikos, c. 420? BCE), IG I³ 970 (a choregic dedication from the Dionysia at Eleusis, c. 425–406? BCE with Csapo 2010a: 90–1).

11. Halliwell 1980: 41–2.

12. On the diachronical development of the terms, see Ghiron-Bistagne 1976: 125–34.

13. On Cleon and the political context of the *Babylonians* and the *Acharnians*, see Halliwell 1980 and Olson 2002: xl–lii.

14. On the use of the verb ποιεῖν and its cognates ποίησις, ποίημα and ποιητής developed during the fifth century BCE with reference to composer's individual skills, see Ford 1981: 296–368.

15. The adjective appears once more in Lucian, *Jup. trag.* 11. The adjective in *-ikos* is considered to be a typical late-fifth-century pattern of formation, see Willi 2003: 139–45 and Labiano Illundain 2004. On the adjective κωμῳδικός, see below.

16. On Aristophanes' repeated joke that Euripides' tragedies contain beggars, see Ar. *Peace* 146–8, *Frogs* 842, 846, 1063–4; cf. Sommerstein 1980: 174.

17. Rosen 2006: 28–9 n 4.

18. Taplin 1983. For more on the competitive contrast of tragedy and comedy and on τρυγῳδία, see Taplin 1986, Edwards 1991: 157–63 and Hall 2006: 328–33.

19. Olson 2002: 200–1 and Mastronarde 1999–2000.

20. Cf. numerous parallels in Plato where comedy and tragedy are listed together, such as *Theaetetus* 152e, *Philebus* 50b, *Symp.* 223d, *Laws* 658b–d, *Republic* 3, 394c–d, 395a–b.

21. On the function of the parabasis and the self-referential motives used in the *Acharnians*, see Hubbard 1991: 41–59.

22. Hornblower and Pelling 2017: 110–13.

23. The only exception is in Herodotus 5.67.5, on tragic institutions at Sicyon in the early sixth century BCE ('they celebrated with tragic choruses', τραγικοῖσι χοροῖσι ἐγέραινον): see Hornblower 2013: 204. On the contribution of early Peloponnesian tragic performances to the establishment of Attic festivals, see Stewart 2017: 94–5.

24. Bagordo 2013: 195–205.

25. Jennings and Katsaros 2007: 5, Bagordo 2014: 114–15.

26. On the parabasis of the *Knights*, see Hubbard 1991: 60–87. On this particular passage and on the question of producing/directing versus composing comedy, see Halliwell 1980.

27. Cf. Isocr. 8.14; Lys. 85, fr. 195.11; 86, fr. 196.3; Arist. *De an.* 406b17; *Eth. Eud.* 1230b19.

28. Aeschylus' *Choephori* is intended: see Dover 1968: 168, Sommerstein 1982: 188 and Rogers in this volume.

29. Rosen 2000: 26 and Hall 2000: 410–12. On the possible dialogue of Cratinus with the same metaphor in Aristophanes' *Knights* 515–17, see Biles 2011: 149–51.

30. Cf. Ar. *Peace* 794–5 containing an unclear reference to Carcinus' tragedy 'throttled by a weasel an evening before': τὸ δρᾶμα γαλῆν τῆς ἑσπέρας ἀπάγξαι. See Sommerstein 1985: 171.

31. The earliest image of Τραγωιδία is on the Athenian red-figure crater (Polygnotus group), *c.* 440–430 BCE. She is a maenad, holding a thyrsus in her right hand and a leveret in her left hand. The earliest female image named Κωμωιδία is on a red-figure crater of Hektor painter, *c.* 450 BCE. She is a maenad accompanying Hephaestus back to Olympus. See Hall 2007: 225–8.

32. Biles 2011: 154–66; Farmer 2017: 117–53; Telò 2016: 25–121.

33. Telò 2016: 58–9 and Platter 2007: 86–90.

34. On the archaic poetic imagery of the verb χεῖσθαι, see Nünlist 1998: 180–5.

35. Telò 2016: 91–2.

36. Biles and Olson 2015: 501 and Farmer 2017: 148. On Philocleon's contest in the finale, and on the more general challenge of Aristophanes' comedy to tragedy in the final scene of the *Wasps*, see Farmer 2017: 147–53 with detailed bibliography.

37. Biles 2011: 166 and Telò 2016: 115–20.

38. *Schol. Vesp.* 61c (PCG iii, 2, 158, test. iv). On Euripides in other Aristophanic fragments, see Nelson 2016: 271 n. 95.

39. Telò 2016: 4–6.

40. On the name Trygaeus and its connection to τρυγῳδία, see Hall 2006: 328–35.

41. See fr. 28 PCG above.

42. Olson 1998: 95 and Farmer 2017: 119.

43. On the vocabulary of these two verses, see Crates fr. 28 PCG above. Compare the situation in Aristophanes' *Lysistrata* (411 BCE), which alludes to Sophocles' lost tragedy *Tyro* when Lysistrata speaks about the race of women who are 'nothing but Poseidon and a tub' (138–9; having had intercourse with Poseidon, Tyro gave birth to twin boys and exposed them in a tub by the river). The author-oriented perspective is maintained as the content itself speaks, using a feminine plural: we provide the plot [*logos*], and 'the tragedy is made out of us' (οὐκ ἐτὸς ἀφ' ἡμῶν εἰσιν αἱ τραγῳδίαι, 138).

44. Olson 1998: 217–18.

45. Halliwell 1980: 42.

46. Telò 2007: 380–6 and Olson 2017: 340–1.

47. For the plural ἐν ταῖς τραγῳδίαισιν, see Dunbar 1995: 164–5; cf. Ar. *Thesm.* 450.

48. Orth 2017: 182–6 and Hedreen 2016: 126–7.

49. Ar. fr. 130, 2 PCG, *Thesm.* 417 and Pl. *Phd.* 77e. Cf. μορμολύττεσθαι ('to frighten') in Crat. fr. 10, 1 PCG and Ar. *Birds* 1245 and μορμολυ in Sophron (fr. 4b, 27 PCG) and Hordern 2004: 137–8.

50. Nelson 2016: 248–61 and Farmer 2017: 155–94.

51. Sommerstein 1994: 163 and Austin and Olson 2004: 80. Cf. Xen. *Ath. Pol.* 2.18.

52. Cf. similar compounds ἐποποιός Her. 2.120.3 and 7.161.20; μελοποιός Ar. *Frogs* 1250, Eur. *Rh.* 550 (the verb μελοποιεῖν Ar. *Thesm.* 42, *Frogs* 1328). On the function of *-poios* suffix, see Ford 1981: 341–3.

53. Sommerstein 2002: 5–6.

54. Austin and Olson 2004: 108.

55. Her. 6, 21; Ar. *Ach.* 499; *Clouds I* 392 PCG; *Thesm.* 450; *Frogs* 90; Phryn. *Muses* fr. 32 PCG.

56. Hall 2007: 231–7.

57. Farmer 2017: 197–204.

58. Pl. *Symp.* 223d; on Alcaeus' title and plot, see Orth 2013: 86–9.

59. Orth 2015: 405–6 with further bibliography.

60. On the term ὑποκριτής for 'actor' in tragedy and comedy from the last quarter of the fifth century BCE onwards, see Pickard-Cambridge 1988: 126–7 and Ghiron-Bistagne 1976: 115–19.

61. Sommerstein 1996: 164–5 and Dover 1993: 201–3.

62. The metaphor appears in Aristophanes' *Knights* 515–17 where *Kōmōdodidaskalia* does not want to have sex with all those who try; further Cratinus puts onstage his wife *Kōmōdia* (see above). On the sexual relationship of a playwright with his play, see Biles 2011: 149–51.

63. Dover 1993: 242.

64. Hunter 2009: 10–52.

65. Segal 1970.

66. Stama 2014: 204–5.

67. Stama 2014: 270–3.

68. = test. *7 PCG. See Smith 2003 and Bagordo 2014: 129–32.

CHAPTER 15
STRATOPHANES THE EPHEBE? THE HERO'S JOURNEYS IN MENANDER'S *SIKYONIOI*
Niall W. Slater

'To lose one parent, Mr. Worthing, may be regarded as a misfortune; to lose both looks like carelessness.'

Lady Bracknell in Oscar Wilde's *The Importance of Being Earnest*

Menander's *Sikyonioi* had an unusually complicated plot, many key twists of which are still discernible despite its seriously fragmentary state.[1] That plot centres around the mercenary soldier Stratophanes, who discovers not only his own true parentage in the course of the play but that of the girl with whom he is in love and can therefore marry at play's end. His story comprises long journeys both actual and metaphorical; the latter include strong resonances with civic and ritual progress, which deserve further attention.

The title of the play comes down to us in at least three forms, including both masculine and feminine singular as well as plural. The plural *Sikyonioi* seems to be the *titulus difficilior*, and Geoffrey Arnott's defense of it as 'an original didascalic title Σικυώνιοι, authenticated in the Sorbonne papyrus' has persuaded most.[2] The plural title, however, has seemed intriguingly inconsistent with an audience's experience of the play (although lost parts of the prologue may have smoothed the inconsistency away): only one (apparent) Sicyonian initially appears in the play, Stratophanes, and he ceases to be Sicyonian almost as soon as we meet him. Federico Favi has now offered the appealing suggestion that the plural title refers to Stratophanes and his love Philoumena, both originally accepted by others as Sicyonian but both finally revealed as Athenians.[3] The plural title *Sikyonioi* might create an intriguing hermeneutic challenge for the audience, looking for more than one Sicyonian—until we find there are none.

Stratophanes' journey of self-discovery had an obvious and civically flattering interest for the original Athenian audience. The plot in broad outline began with a divine prologue that would have given the audience some idea of how Stratophanes, born of Athenian parentage, was given to a Sicyonian couple who raised him as their own son. His Sicyonian foster-father was likely a mercenary soldier, as Stratophanes himself certainly is. The foster-father purchased a very young girl named Philoumena as a slave but raised her as a member of the family, and Stratophanes eventually fell in love with her.[4] At some point the Sicyonian foster-parents moved (back) to Athens, while Stratophanes pursued his mercenary career in Caria. At the play's opening Stratophanes has returned to Athens, having learned of the death of his supposed father. After his arrival he is greeted not only with the news that his supposed mother has meanwhile died but also that she has left a deathbed message, revealing that Stratophanes was adopted and supplying tokens that will allow him to find and recognize his real Athenian parents. During Stratophanes' absence, however, another young man named Moschion has taken a keen interest in Philoumena as a prospective concubine. Philoumena knows herself to have been born free, but there is no evidence that Moschion is aware of this.

The losses especially from earlier parts of the play leave some elements of the background story simply unknowable. Why was Stratophanes given to the Sicyonian couple to raise as their child?[5] His Athenian parents may have been so desperately poor when he was born that they could not raise a child. Alternatively, he may have been the product of the rape of his mother by his unknown or unrecognized father before the marriage and thus given away to protect this secret. He was nonetheless given away with tokens of clothing, which will enable his later recognition. Philoumena's origins as a child stolen by pirates along with another slave and eventually sold to Stratophanes' foster-father are clear. What is by no means clear, however, is the proximate cause for Philoumena's flight, probably from Stratophanes' house in Athens, to the sanctuary at Eleusis. There are at least three possibilities, none of them mutually exclusive. Since Philoumena knows she is freeborn, she may be seeking to avoid being forced into concubinage by Stratophanes.[6] Excessive interest from Moschion during Stratophanes' absence might yield the same result. A third possibility involves the legal complications following the death of Stratophanes' foster-father. He has died in debt to a Boeotian due to a lost legal judgment,[7] and since Philoumena is apparently a slave in his household, the creditor may be seeking to seize her along with other goods in satisfaction of the debt. It is possible that these debts are what sent Stratophanes abroad as a mercenary in the first place. In an unplaced book fragment from this play, someone reminds him of his earlier poverty:

> Στρατοφάνη,
> λιτόν ποτ' εἶχες χλαμύδιον καὶ παῖδ' ἕνα.

> Stratophanes,
> You once owned one plain cloak and one male slave!

fr.6 [375 K–A] (tr. Arnott)[8]

The actions of Stratophanes' dying foster-mother are a key impetus for the rest of the plot. Apparently neither of his foster-parents ever intended to tell Stratophanes that he was adopted. The foster-mother only does so by writing a letter on her deathbed because, if Stratophanes can assert his claim to Athenians citizenship, he will have legal protection both for his own (apparently considerable) property won in war and property inherited from his foster-parents. Stratophanes learns this when his slave Pyrrhias reports his foster-mother's death in what was originally the play's third act:[9]

> ὄντ' ἀγώγιμόν σε τούτῳ πυθομένη τῶν τοὺς νόμους
> εἰδότων τήν τ' οὐσίαν σου, τοῦτο προὐνοεῖτό σου
> καὶ τελευτῶσ' ἀπεδίδου σε τοῖς σεαυτῶν γ' εὐλόγως

When she learnt from legal experts that this man
could distrain you and your goods, she planned ahead for you, and tried
shrewdly at her death to give you back to your own family.

138–40

The sequence is clear: the mother acts after taking legal advice and out of forethought (προὐνοεῖτό) for Stratophanes' subsequent situation. Legal reasons may suffice to explain her insistence on creating a written record (γραμματεῖδιον, something suitable to stand up in court?[10]), but there may be a further resonance:

]ο τελευτῶσ' ἐνθαδὶ τὸ σὸν γένος
ἔ]γραψεν,

[ ] here's where she wrote down details of your family
on her deathbed [ ].

130–1

As the deictic ἐνθαδὶ indicates, Pyrrhias must have this written statement in his hands onstage, just as he carries (although presumably in some container) the physical tokens (γνωρίσματα)[11] necessary for the later recognition:

καὶ ταδὶ χωρὶς φέρω
τῶν γεγραμμένων ἐκείνοις, Στρατοφάνη, γνωρίσματα
καὶ τεκμήρι,

And I've these here from them, Stratophanes, in addition
to what's written down – evidence and tokens of identity.

141–3 (tr. Arnott, modified)

Despite the damage to the text, it seems perfectly clear that the feminine participle τελευτῶσ' (130) agrees with the quite certainly restored main verb ἔγραψεν. Arnott and others assume that this means she dictated the message, perhaps doubting that we are meant to imagine a woman having the skills to write her own letter,[12] but the potential evidence for female literacy here may not be as important as the symbolic import for the plot as a whole. In sending this letter, Stratophanes' foster-mother is writing a new script for his life: from the moment he learns of it, he is no longer a Sicyonian but an Athenian, although he will have to fight to establish himself as such.[13]

At this point let us recall the broad outlines of Stratophanes' physical journeys up to the actual opening of the play. He is born in Athens but given to the Sicyonian couple to raise. It is, in fact, unclear whether they ever take him to Sicyon, although the majority of scholars seem to assume such a move, which then requires the foster-parents to move back to Athens later. Stratophanes himself, however, clearly embarks on a mercenary career in the East once he reaches adulthood. He thus journeys from the place of his birth to the borders of Athens and beyond in order to engage in his first military service. We meet him only on his return to Athens, entailing his almost simultaneous discovery of his Athenian origins and citizenship. The immediate crisis that confronts him involves not only protecting his own property and his inheritance but also attempting to secure the welfare and future of Philoumena. We cannot be sure when this became clear to the audience, but Stratophanes knows that she is freeborn. Once he discerns that her parents were Athenian, he determines to find them and prove her citizenship.[14] The third act ends as Stratophanes and the parasite Theron leave the stage, presumably in pursuit of Philoumena. We later learn that he and his rival Moschion both follow her to Eleusis and end up speaking in competition before the deme assembly.

The fourth act opens with an intriguing twist: a political argument between an old man, almost certainly named Smicrines and an oligarchic supporter, and an unnamed democrat. While politics are not unknown in Menander, the exchange is sharper than usual – and focuses on Smicrines' contempt for the play-acting of democratic leaders:

ΣΜ. (?) ὄχλος εἶ, φλυάρου μεστός, ὦ πονηρὲ σύ,   150
δίκαια τὸν κλάοντα προσδοκῶν λέγειν
καὶ τὸν δεόμενον· τοῦ δὲ μηδὲ ἓν ποεῖν
ὑγιὲς σχεδὸν ταῦτ' ἐστὶ νῦν τεκμήριον.
οὐ κρίνεθ' ἀλήθεια τοῦτον τὸν τρόπον,
ἀλλ' ἐν ὀλίγῳ πολλῷ γε μᾶ[λλον συνεδρίῳ.   155
ΔΗΜ. ὀλιγαρχικός γ' εἶ καὶ πονηρός, Σμ[ικρίνη,
νὴ τὸν Δία τὸν μέγιστον.

Smik. (?) Riff-raff – that's what you are, stuffed full of drivel,
You rogue, expecting that a man who weeps
And begs will tell the truth! Today that's normally
A sign of total lack of probity.
That's not the way that truth's decided – no,
It's reached far [better] in a small [committee].
Democrat. You're an elitist, Sm[ikrines], upon
My oath – a rogue, too!

                                                                        (155–7)

The argument ends inconclusively with the exit of the democratic supporter but functions as a metatheatrical prologue to the ensuing messenger speech, which reports the offstage events at the critical deme assembly.[15]

Nothing in the preserved text tells us why the deme assembly of Eleusis was meeting that day.[16] What the audience learns about that assembly comes from a lengthy messenger speech of a man apparently himself named Eleusinios, reporting to Smicrines. As was recognized early on, this speech contains a number of paratragic echoes of the messenger speech about Orestes' trial in Euripides' *Orestes*,[17] as Eleusinios tells how Stratophanes appealed to the crowd at the sanctuary to care for Philoumena until he can find her real

Athenian father and ask for her hand. He establishes his generous treatment of her by, among other things, promising to give back to her possession the old slave Dromon,[18] kidnapped with her:

> οἰκέτης ἦν τοῦ πα]τρὸς
> αὐτῆς, ἐμὸν δ' ὄντ' ἀποδίδωμι τῇ κόρῃ.

> [He was her fa]ther's [slave].[19]
> He's mine now, but I give him back to her.

> 235–6

Stratophanes thus shows himself to be both a generous and just steward of what he inherited from his foster-father.

Stratophanes' closing appeal to the assembly, as reported by Eleusinios, is both powerful and honourable:

> τὴν ἐλπίδα
> μήπω μ' ἀφέλησθ', ἀλλ', ἂν φανῶ τῆς παρθένου
> κἀγὼ πολίτης, ἣν ἔσῳσα τῷ πατρί,
> ἐάσατ' αἰτῆσαί με τοῦτον καὶ λαβεῖν.

> Don't dash
> My hopes now, but if I as well am shown
> To share my citizenship with this girl,
> Whom I protected for her father, let me ask
> Him for her hand in marriage.

> 251–4

Unlike his tragic predecessor Orestes, Stratophanes acquits himself very well before the throng.

Moschion speaks, too, but makes a far less favourable impression.[20] He tries to accuse Stratophanes of deceptive play-acting:

> καί φησι 'ταυτὶ συμπέπεισθ', ὡς οὑτοσὶ
> νῦν ἐξαπίνης εἴληφε διαθήκας ποθέ[ν,
> ἐστί τε πολίτης ὑμέτερος, τραγῳδίᾳ
> κενῇ τ' ἀγόμενος τὴν κόρην ἀφήσε[ται;'

> and said 'Do you believe that suddenly
> He's found a will from somewhere, and is now
> Your fellow citizen? That he will take the girl
> With this empty tragic performance, then release her?'

> 260–3 (tr. Arnott, modified)

Whether the audience knows of the relationship yet or not, here is a case of like father, like son: Moschion echoes his father Smicrines' derision for speaking in the public assembly as an 'empty tragic performance' (τραγῳδία κενῇ),[21] but, unlike Orestes, Stratophanes' contemporary version proves to be both authentic and effective. The Eleusinians agree to shelter Philoumena while Stratophanes goes in search of both her and his own real Athenian parents.

The events may be a little out of order here, but I think many in the Athenian theatre audience would have perceived strong resonances between Stratophanes' journeys and actions and the peculiarly Athenian institution of the ephebeia. The perhaps now too familiar elements of rites of passage in the Athenian ephebeia involved separating adolescent males from their birth families, stationing them for military service in the liminal areas of the Athenian state and returning them to full adult citizenship at the end of their years of service.[22] Embarking on the ephebate required appearing before the deme assembly to prove both parentage and sufficient age. Normally a young man's father would have appeared to speak for him, as he had done when originally presenting his infant son for enrolment in the deme. Given mortality rates, however, many adolescent males must have lacked a living father when they themselves reached the age of 18, and, while other males from the family could have appeared to speak for them, undoubtedly some young men must have been prepared to speak for themselves. It may not simply be general praise for Stratophanes when the messenger specifically notes that in his speech before the Eleusinians he seemed 'someone very manly' (τις ἀνδρικὸς πάνυ, 215). By granting his request to protect Philoumena while he goes in search of proof, they are implicitly and corporately recognizing his claim to adult citizenship.[23]

Our text becomes much more damaged here, and we can only be sure that Stratophanes located his Athenian parents, who prove to be Smicrines and his wife. In a full-blown recognition scene, the parents recognize and identify the birth tokens that prove him to be their son.[24] Smicrines says to Stratophanes:

ἤ]δη καὐτὸς ἐμβλέπω σε, παῖ,
]ηται καιρὸς ὡς παρ' ἐλπίδας

] now I myself look at you, son
] opportunity has [ ] beyond our hopes.

(286–7)

Given that the messenger speech preceding this scene contained so many echoes of that in Euripides' *Orestes*, it may just be possible that a very alert spectator might hear a specific echo in ὡς παρ' ἐλπίδας of the same phrase at line end in *Orestes* 977,[25] where that play's chorus lamented the imminent disaster looming over Orestes and Electra. Here, however, the καιρὸς with its tragic associations nonetheless suggests the right or fated time that brings everything to fulfilment has come, and the tonality is the opposite of despairing.[26] The father rejoices to recover the son he had lost, given up through poverty or otherwise, and it looks like his wife remembers her own hopes, too, although the text is very fragmentary:

] ἐλπίσασά τε
]ν ἡ τύχη

] having hoped
] fortune

293–4

We have here just the feminine participle ἐλπίσασά and the reference to τύχη, but Arnott thinks it very likely that the participle must be the mother's avowal of her own hopes and likely thanks to τύχη for bringing about their fulfilment.

The recognition includes many details of the clothes the infant Stratophanes was wearing when given away:

πτέρυξ χιτωνίσκου γυναικείου διπλῆ·
ἔ]κρυπ[τε γὰ]ρ σῶμ' ἡνίκ' ἐξεπέμπομεν
πρὸς τὴν] ξένην σε τὴν τότ' αἰτοῦσαν τέκνα.
[ ].νεστιν ἀλλὰ τῷ βεβαμμένῳ
[ ]τ' ἔχουσα χρώματος φύσιν
πέριξ ἰώ]δους τοὐν μέσῳ δὲ πορφύρας,

Half of a woman's dress that's folded double –
It cloaked your body when we sent you [to]
[That] foreign lady who then wanted children.
] is [ ], but with the dyed
] having a shade (?) [of green]
[Around each side,] and crimson in between.

280–5

As Arnott notes, the language here is distinctly tragic in both verse rhythms and style.[27] The use of the verb κρύπτω for covering the child's body suggests both protection and also a symbolic death, as the child is lost from its natal family – but now reborn by rediscovery. The details of colour and other particulars suggest to me (as apparently to Arnott) that the mother is speaking here.

Menander may be playing here with tragic precedent in other ways as well. In a very interesting dissertation on Menander's use of offstage action, Mitchell Brown has pointed out that the principal device for introducing tragic offstage action, the messenger speech, is relatively rare in Menander.[28] Two such speeches appear in this play, however – that of Eleusinios and the earlier one in which the slave informed Stratophanes of his mother's death and his own Athenian origins. Antonis Petrides suggests that Pyrrhias thus also acts like a tragic messenger, indeed specifically like the messenger in Sophocles' *Oedipus Tyrannus*, 'who arrives suddenly and unexpectedly, [to break] the news to a son that one of his parents is no longer alive, but that he was not his/her child after all.'[29]

In this play Stratophanes negotiates the ephebe's journey to successful adulthood and full citizenship. Having lost two Sicyonian parents, though hardly through carelessness, he finds his way to his real Athenian parents. In the process he may prove himself a comic Oedipus with a happy ending, one whose quasi-incestuous desire to make a foster-sister into his concubine is transformed via the recognition of both as citizens into a legitimate Athenian marriage.

Notes

1. See Blume 2010: 24–5 for a brief account of its recovery and initial reconstruction; more fully, Blanchard and Bataille 1965 and Blanchard 2009.

2. Arnott 1997a: 3; cf. Arnott 2000. 196–8.

3. Favi 2019. His suggestion is the best explanation for why anyone might have called the play Σικυωνία, thinking the center of interest was Philoumena.

4. Even this part of the reconstruction is debatable. Some think Stratophanes himself bought the girl (so Martina 2016a: 95–7), in which case he has spent more than ten years raising her to become his concubine (so Traill 2008: 17 and n. 7), but this would be unparalleled and would make him an older bridegroom at the end even by Athenian standards. Lape 2010: 57 suggests: 'Comedy, however, regularly unites couples who seemed to be relatively close in age – or at any rate closer in age than scholars have argued was [the] norm for Athens. A character in Menander's *Aspis* specifically argues that the best marriages are those in which the partners are roughly the same age.'

5. When someone, most likely Stratophanes' birth mother, in the recognition scene describes giving him away as a baby, she says: ἐξεπέμπομεν | πρὸς τὴν] ξένην σε τὴν τότ' αἰτοῦσαν τέκνα (282–3). Describing the recipient as 'the foreign lady who then wanted children' seems to imply that this was primarily a transaction between the women, the birth mother and the adoptive mother, although we should not assume that the latter was in any way trying to deceive her husband, especially as she says 'we sent you away'. An anonymous referee suggests the intriguing, though of course speculative, possibility that the couple may have lost a child of their own soon before undertaking this arrangement. C. W. Marshall notes (pers. comm.) we need not assume Stratophanes was a newborn at the time.

6. The English term 'concubine' for Philoumena's possible future situation (with either man) seems the least unsatisfactory designation, given the opacity of both circumstances and law in this play. When Stratophanes' interest in a relationship with Philoumena develops, he still believes himself to be a Sicyonian: marriage to a freed former slave woman might be possible under Sicyonian law, or she might be treated as what Athenian law called a παλλακή. A supposedly Solonian law, cited by Demosthenes 23 *Aristoc.* 53, specified that at Athens offspring of such a union were free, though after the Periclean citizenship law they were certainly not eligible for citizenship. See brief discussions in Harrison 1968: 2, 33 n. 1 and 164 n. 2. On the other hand, in comedy a long-term relationship with a παλλακή is usually in addition to or subsequent to marriage – and we have no grounds to assume that Moschion conceives a relationship with Philoumena in these terms.

7. The one clear reference here is a statement by Pyrrhias: πολλῶν ταλάντων, Στρατοφάνη, κατὰ σύμβολα, 135 ('Stratophanes, by interstate agreements his debt was many talents').

8. Greek text and translations from the Loeb edition of Arnott 2000, unless otherwise noted.

9. Pyrrhias acts much like a tragic messenger here, as Petrides 2014: 136 notes: 'It is interesting to note that there is a distinctive similarity of situation between *Sik.* 120ff. and Sophocles'

Oedipus Tyrannus, 924ff. This is the locus classicus of a messenger speech eliciting a roller-coaster of sorrow and delight.' See further, below.

10. Compare the 'stacks of notes' (ὁρμαθοὺς γραμματιδίων) that the shameless man brings to court in Theophrastus, *Characters* 6.8.

11. Furley 2014: 112 suggests 'Menander makes conscious references to what we might call the theory of recognition' and points out 'The word γνωρίσματα, denoting the tokens by which recognition is effected, is used repeatedly.'

12. The ἐκείνοις (142) in the papyrus has been seen as problematic. Lloyd Jones 1966: 134–5 wished to read ἐκείνῃ, but, as Gomme and Sandbach say, such a corruption would be hard to explain. They accept ἐκείνοις, saying (1973: 645 *ad loc.*): 'This word can be explained as denoting the same persons as are referred to by the phrase τοῖς ἑαυτῶν in 140' [a different text from Arnott's] and thus take it as an indirect object, the birth parents being the intended recipients of the letter and tokens. Arnott 1997b: 24 argues for the reading ἐκείνοις as dative of agent with the participle γεγραμμένων 'interpreted correctly [as] ... those who attended the old woman on her death-bed, then wrote down the words that she dictated, and finally handed the tablet to Pyrrhias' (cf. the translations of Arnott 2000 and Balme 2001: 186 ('quite apart from what they wrote')). This then must be a rather loose usage – are we really to imagine multiple simultaneous transcribers at the deathbed? As Arnott 1997b: 24 continues 'Presumably Menander wrote ἐκείνοις in 142 originally without realising its vagueness, and then added the explanatory ὡς [ἐκείνην ἔφασαν οἱ δόντες λέγειν ζῶσαν] clause in 143–144 as clarification.' Perhaps ἐκείνοις might rather be dative of origin, indicating more generally that the tokens and text come from those in the household who have kept them awaiting Stratophanes' return (a second stage in the process, after the mother wrote the letter).

13. The theme of writing was probably important in lost portions of the play as well. If Stratophanes speaks line 54 in a badly damaged bit of dialogue with Theron, he is there citing things]γεγραμμένων ἄλλως ἐκεῖ ('written there in vain (?)'). This may be in reference to the tangled affairs of his foster-father's estate, since Theron already seems to be plotting to find a false witness for some plot to aid Stratophanes. Later, Theron cites the lack of a written record (διαλογισμὸν οὐθενός, 116) as an element that somehow helps the case.

14. It does seem unlikely, as Traill 2008: 19 suggests, that either Stratophanes or his foster-father would have brought Philoumena back to Athens while specifically knowing that she was Athenian, else why would they not have made efforts to find her family before this? This implies that there was a moment during the play at which Stratophanes learned her parents were Athenian, but we have no evidence for that moment.

15. It also offers ironic preparation for another plot element to come: Theron will recruit an old man named Kichesias in hopes of having him pretend to be the father of Philoumena – only to discover that he is indeed her long-lost father. For a suggestion of *color tragicus* in this passage itself, see Martina 2016b:151–2.

16. Although Theron seems to know of it in advance:'Ελευσίς ἐστι, καὶ | πανήγ]υρίς που (57–8, 'This is Eleusis, and I think there's a town meeting').

17. Lape 2004: 221 n. 47 cites the particular parallels: *Sic.* 176–7, cf. *Or.* 866–7; *Sic.* 182, cf. *Or.* 920; *Sic.* 188, cf. *Or.* 871. Similarly, however, as Furley 2014: 110 says in comparing the brother-sister recognition in the *Iphigenia in Tauris* with that in the *Perikeiromene*, 'the effect is not so much parody as contrapuntal.' (Cf. a fuller discussion in Furley 2009: 2–8), For an extensive discussion of the parallels, see Martina 2016b: 152–73, who also makes the intriguing suggestion (158): 'Non è da escludere che la vivace descrizione di questa scena abbia contribuito ad accrescere la popolarità dell'Oreste nel IV secolo e poi anche dopo.' Brief discussion of narrative style in the speech in Nünlist 2004: 303, and of characterization in

Brown 2018: 400–1. Goldberg 1993: 338 uses this scene as a key part of his argument that 'Menander's . . . *Sicyonian* therefore reshapes the human inadequacies of Euripides' *Orestes*, turning the memory of a tragic failure into a comic success.'

18. Dromon has, of course, watched over Philoumena throughout. The divine prologue describes the scene of him guarding her as they are both being sold in the slave market in Caria: καθῆτό τ' ἐπὶ τῆς ἀγκ[άλης | ἔ]χων ὁ θεράπων τὴν τροφίμην, 7–8 ('the slave sat holding his young mistress on one arm'). Cf. Lape 2010: 54 on the gender norm that 'male slaves protect the female citizens in their care from potentially predatory males.' Dromon even contributes (most exceptionally) to the discussion in the deme assembly, assuring the demesmen that she will cooperate if they agree to protect her: ὁ θερά[πων | 'ὑμῶν κελευόντων βαδιεῖται' φη[σί, 267–8 ('The slave cut in: "She'll come, if you all tell her to"').

19. This line is, of course, substantially supplemented by Handley 1965, but the sense seems very likely.

20. According to Eleusinios, the crowd judges him badly for his pallor (μειράκιον . . . λευκόχρω[ν, 200; λευκόχρω[ς, 258) and diffidence. MacCary 1970: 288–9 argues that characters in Menander named Moschion are 'weak [and] . . . manipulated by circumstances, slaves and fathers', and this view is much more richly developed by Witzke 2016: 58–60.

21. Cf., very briefly, Gutzwiller 2000: 113 n. 29, with further references.

22. Many details of the ephebate changed or developed over a nearly 700-year history, but the broad pattern of taking young men in military training about age 18, deploying them especially in border duties and then reintegrating them into adult society at the end seems persistent: see briefly Reinmuth's entry s.v. 'Ephebia' in the *Kleine Pauly* (Ziegler and Sontheimer 1967: 287–96).

23. See also the discussion by Wilfred Major in this volume of the Menandrean pattern of reintegrating soldiers into married civilian lives in their home communities. Where Orestes, of ephebic age in the *Orestes*, comes tragically close to failing to negotiate his transition to adulthood altogether (see again Goldberg 1993), Stratophanes succeeds.

24. Arnott 2000: 265 *ad loc.* notes of this scene: 'the rhythms and style approximate closely to those of tragedy, just as in the recognition scene of *Perikeiromene*.'

25. Euripides, *Orestes* 976–8:

ἰώ, ὦ πανδάκρυτ' ἐφαμέρων
ἔθνη πολύπονα, λεύσσεθ' ὡς παρ' ἐλπίδας
μοῖρα βαίνει.

Ah, ah, you race of mortals, full of tears,
trouble-laden, see how fate defeats
your expectations!

trans. Kovacs

No other instance of ὡς παρ' ἐλπίδας at line end occurs in fully preserved drama.

26. Compare the guard who returns with the captured Antigone and expresses his ἡ γὰρ εὐκτὸς καὶ παρ' ἐλπίδας χαρὰ (Sophocles, *Antigone* 392, 'delight that one has prayed for beyond hope', trans. Lloyd-Jones).

27. Arnott 2000: 265.

28. Brown 2016: 10–11 and *passim*.

29. Petrides 2014: 136.

CHAPTER 16
THE PRE-HISTORY OF THE *MILES GLORIOSUS* IN GREEK DRAMA
Wilfred E. Major

The term *miles gloriosus* has been shorthand for a braggart soldier character on the comic stage as far back as Plautus' *Captivi*, where the absence of such a character separates the play from the norm (*nec miles gloriosus*, 58; cf. Terence *Eun*. 38 for a comparable reference).[1] Modern scholars, knowing that Plautus reworked existing comic scripts composed in Greek, have logically reasoned that the braggart soldier character was an established stock figure prior to Plautus. The recovery of substantial portions of the leading practitioner of Greek 'New Comedy' as Plautus knew it, Menander, has yielded challenges to this logic, since Menander's scripts that feature or refer to soldiers have not proved comfortable fits for this model. Still, scholars have retained the basic idea that the 'stock' character of the braggart soldier was established in Greek comedy prior to Plautus. On occasion, scholars have acknowledged that this type of character is preserved primarily in the Latin tradition of New Comedy[2] but they have typically resorted to the caveat that Menander's soldier characters demonstrate creative variation and departure from the stock expectation.[3] This conceptual acrobatic should lead to fresh investigation of just what the experience and expectations of Menander and his spectators would have been. Evidence is frightfully fragmentary, but it is still fair to ask whether the available fragments are at a minimum consistent with the literary historical narrative that scholars are promulgating. Instead, this study argues, the fragments are consistent with soldier characters appearing onstage without there being a central expectation of them being braggarts, and that the centrality of the *miles gloriosus* is a post-Menander development. The final section of this paper will suggest more plausible antecedents for soldier characters in Menander as a result of this new delineation of the development of the soldier character.

Antecedents for the *miles gloriosus* on the comic stage in the fifth century BCE are scarce, and in practice the episode featuring the general Lamachus in Aristophanes' *Acharnians* (572–622, 1072–141, 1190–226) ends up carrying the weight of the idea of a tradition. These episodes do feature a comic protagonist squaring off successfully against a military figure who blusters ineffectively. Rather than a stock character, however, Lamachus belongs to a gallery of historical figures that Aristophanes caricatured onstage, ranging from Cleon to Socrates to a variety of specialists in *Birds*, and more.[4] The only other potential antecedent from this era for braggart soldiers is Phormio, attested among the fragments of Eupolis' *Taxioarchoi*.[5] Again, this is a caricature of an historical figure, but there is little testimony about the characterization. Moreover, there is no evidence that Lamachus or hypothetical other bragging soldiers were reference points for playwrights of subsequent comedy, as no specific parallels or ancient testimony link later soldier characters to fifth-century forebears. In general, Aristophanes and fifth-century comedy do not seem to have been meaningful reference points for Menander and his brethren. While an argument from silence requires due caution, in contrast, the legacy of tragedy, especially Euripides, has left substantial imprints on New Comedy and links among later comic poets are also evident.[6]

This leaves the murky era of fourth-century comedy for the development of the character. In assorted surveys of the braggart soldier, several of some two dozen or so fragments are cited as glimpses into the development of the stereotype in the decades prior to Menander and contemporary with his career.[7] Upon inspection, these examples suffer from one of two problems: either the role or presence of a soldier goes beyond the evidence or a reference to a soldier does not corroborate his character as a braggart.

As an example of the first problem, consider Ephippus fr. 5.18–21:

περιαγγέλλειν τί οὐχ ὑποκαίεις,
Λυκίων πρύτανι· ψυχρὸν τουτί·
παύου φυσῶν, Μακεδὼν ἄρχων·
σβέννυ, Κελθ'ὡς μὴ προσκαύσῃς.

... and they gave orders: 'Why aren't you kindling the fire,
O Lycian leader? This part is cold.
Stop fanning the fire, leader of Macedon.
Quench the fire, O Celt, so you don't burn it.'

trans. Slater

Athenaeus quotes this fragment from *Geryones* because of its account of an extraordinary fish dish prepared for the mythical creature Geryon. Among those called upon to help out with the cooking are a Lycian and Macedonian leader, as well as a Celt. Arnott puts this passage in the mouth of a braggart soldier, who boasts of his exotic experiences in faraway lands, reasoning from what Athenaeus says next, that the same lines were repeated in another play of Ephippus, *Peltast*, with an additional five lines (fr. 19). There is nothing, however, in the context, the text itself or other information about these fragments or plays to indicate that a peltast or any soldier character is involved. Rather, as Konstantakos proposes, *Geryones* and this scene have more to with recontextualizing mythology to the world of an Athenian cook.[8] Another dozen or so fragments that have been cited as involving braggart soldiers likewise lack any evidence of soldiers. Like the Ephippus fragments, Alexis fr. 63 and Antiphanes fr. 200 describe a marvellous event, this time an elaborate pigeon shower, but nothing of their content or context indicates that a soldier is bragging about it.[9] The same is true of the elaborate meals of Alexis frs. 135–7 and Eriphus fr. 6, where cooks are more likely candidates for speakers than soldiers. Alexis fr. 96 comes from his *Thrason*, the title character of which could well be a soldier, but the fragment itself, in which someone complains to a woman of her garrulousness, gives no indication of any involvement of a soldier. While it is sensible to expect that Alexis' Στρατιώτης (*Soldier*) included soldiers, fr. 212 from the play, a dialogue about a baby foundling, does not indicate what role the one or more soldiers played nor any indication about their character. Philemon also wrote a play titled Στρατιώτης (*Soldier*), but fr. 82, about the successful cooking of fish, gives no indication of what role or character any soldier might have had (and again a cook is a more plausible candidate as speaker). Another fragment of Philemon (fr. 124) charges someone with cowardice, which could be spoken to or by a soldier, but there is no context to help.[10] The story that Philemon insulted Magas, half-brother to Ptolemy II, in a play (fr. 132) hints at a political or even military dimension rarely found in New Comedy, but nothing about soldiers. Finally, the term ἀλαζών can refer to a braggart soldier,[11] but it also applies to other types of characters, as in Theopompus fr. 44, which applies a synonym ῥαχίστης ('boaster, braggart') to a Demophon, who, based on his name, was most likely an old man.

Other fragments do involve soldiers but not braggarts. A line from Apollodorus (fr. 10), for example, says to someone that they are a soldier rather than a free man, but this is an isolated quote from Stobaeus, so it comes with no context and does not provide evidence that a soldier or any other character was a braggart. Another fragment, ascribed to Diphilus (fr. 55), says a character does not look like a soldier, because he's equipped with household implements. Perhaps this is someone trying to look like a soldier, or who was a soldier, but in his attempt to make some sort of domestic siege fails.[12] This reference can suggest parody of a soldier, but nothing requires a bragging soldier character. Another intriguing fragment is Alexis fr. 236 (*Wounded Man*):

τίς οὐχὶ φήσει τοὺς ἐρῶντας ζῆν μόνους;
εἰ δεῖ γε πρῶτον μὲν στρατευτικωτάτους
εἶναι, πονεῖν τε δυναμένους τοῖς σώμασιν
μάλιστα, προσεδρεύειν τ᾽ ἀρίστους τῷ πόθῳ,
ποιητικούς, ἰταμούς, προθύμους, εὐπόρους
ἐν τοῖς ἀπόροις, βλέποντας ἀθλιωτάτους.

Who wouldn't say that lovers alone are really alive?
First, they have to be soldiers through and through,
Able to endure great bodily suffering,
The best at persevering in their desire,
Clever, hasty, eager, inventive
When there's no way out, looking utterly wretched.

trans. Slater

Here someone, very likely a desperate lover, says that lovers are very much like soldiers when measured by their endurance, resourcefulness and so on.[13] I want to highlight here that this equation of lover and soldier resonates broadly in Greek New Comedy. Whereas in Plautus and Terence the soldier is consistently a blocking figure, a rival lover to the civilian aristocrat lover who is the protagonist (as in Plautus' *Curculio*, *Miles Gloriosus*, *Pseudolus*, *Truculentus*, Terence's *Eunuch*), in Menander as far as recovered scripts go, the soldier is himself the protagonist lover (*Samia*, *Perikeiromene*, *Misoumenos*, *Aspis*, *Sikyonioi*). Even in the later scheme of characters and masks preserved in Pollux, the soldier is but a variation of the young man in love.[14] This can easily make the soldier a focus of comedy and ridicule but not, without additional evidence, a braggart.

Once again, a number of other fragments have been cited as examples of the braggart soldier, passages that have something to do with soldiers but nothing that requires or is in anyway predicated on them being arrogant braggarts. In Alexis fr. 120, someone sees a character drinking in a bar, with his στρωματέα ('bedding') and γύλιον ('knapsack') near him, and he may be a soldier, but this gives no hint about his character. In Adesp. fr. 1018, a slave jokes about a soldier's life to the annoyance of the soldier, but nothing indicates that the soldier is a braggart. Another bit from Alexis (fr. 181) mentions a type of cup possibly linked to soldiers, but, even so, this gives no hint about the soldier's character. A line from Antiphanes (fr. 136) says to a character, κεστρεῖς ἔχων, ἀλλ'οὐ στρατιώτας, τυγχάνεις νήστεις ('You have fasting grey mullets [= honest people] but not soldiers'), but the context is unknown and there need not even be any soldier character in the play. Antiphanes' play Στρατιώτης (Soldier), aka Tychon, likely involved at least one soldier, but the fragments – fr. 200 (a soldier asked to tell about doves fanning a king of Cyprus = Olson C13), fr. 202 (about the transience of possessions) and fr. 203 (peacocks reproduce but honest men do not) – do not indicate any characteristics of the soldier. Diphilus wrote a play Airesiteiches which sometimes included Στρατιώτης (Soldier) in the title (Airesiteiches; Eunochos or Stratiotes) but the remains (fr. 5 refers to drinking, fr. 6 to a useless torch and three other fragments are even more meagre) do not explain how soldiers might have played a role or what character they had. The speaker of Hipparchus fr. 1 asks if the listener is paying attention to a soldier, but the corrupt sequence to follow lists luxuries, and the relationship of this snatch of dialogue to the soldier mentioned is obscure. Two sententious remarks from Philemon involve soldiers but do not even mean that the plays had soldier characters (fr. 122 says doctors do not want to see their friends healthy and soldiers do not want to see a city without smoke; fr. 142 likens a soldier to a beast to be sacrificed). Apollodorus (either the one from Carystus or the one from Gela) fr. 2 Aphanizomenos is an aphorism from Stobaeus about a soldier's lot, but, yet again, with no context. Theopompus fr. 56 contrasts a soldier's pay with what it costs to support a wife or woman, and the play, based on its title (Στρατιωτίδης [Little Soldier]) likely involved one or more soldiers, but, again, nothing about a soldier's role or character is known. Adesp. fr. 1096[15] has a character whose name is abbreviated Thras- (=Thrasyleon?), presumably a soldier, but there is nothing helpful beyond his name. Plutarch (Mor. 62E [How to Discern a Flatterer 22] = Adesp. fr. 712) quotes a snatch of dialogue where someone brags about being able to fight a soldier, but Plutarch himself contextualizes the quotation such that the bragging flatterer is making a promise to someone else about the soldier, who, at least in the section quoted, does not participate in the conversation.

There is but a single fragment from Greek Middle or New Comedy that is predicated on a braggart soldier character, Phoenicides fr. 4.4–11:

εὐθὺς ἐπιχειρήσασα φίλον ἔσχον τινὰ
στρατιωτικόν· διαπαντὸς οὗτος τὰς μάχας
ἔλεγεν, ἐδείκνυ' ἅμα λέγων τὰ τραύματα,

εἰσέφερε δ' οὐδέν. δωρεὰν ἔφη τινὰ
παρὰ τοῦ βασιλέως λαμβάνειν, καὶ ταῦτ' ἀεὶ
ἔλεγεν· διὰ ταύτην ἣν λέγω τὴν δωρεὰν
ἐνιαυτὸν ἔσχε μ' ὁ κακοδαίμων δωρεάν.
ἀφῆκα τοῦτον …

… I had a lover who was a soldier. He was constantly talking about his battles and showing off his scars as he talked. But he didn't produce any income. He claimed he was getting a grant of some sort from the king, and he was always talking about it. And because of this grant I'm describing, the bastard was granted me as a gift for a year. I got rid of him …

trans. Olson

Here a hetaira complains about her life and the miserable clients she has endured. The first of these clients was a soldier who kept talking about his battle exploits, showing his wounds and had some sort of stipend from a king. The hetaira says that this stipend was what bound her to him, but he in fact produced no income and she moved on to her next client, a doctor. This image of the bragging but fraudulent soldier comes closest to the character found in Plautus and Terence: the soldier shacked up with a prostitute drawn to his wealth, and who is vaguely attached to a distant Hellenistic monarch.[16]

Although the precise date of this crucial fragment cannot be determined, all available evidence points to it falling later than Menander. Only five fragments of Phoenicides are preserved, and this one is not attributed to a particular play. One fragment (fr. 1) is preserved by Hesychius, who says that Phoenicides was from Megara but competed in Athens at the City Dionysia. The fragment quoted by Hesychius alludes to a treaty between Antigonus and Pyrrhus, which would have been in the mid-280s. Inscriptions indicate that Phoenicides did compete in Athens, as Hesychius says, at the Lenaea in the 280s (IG II² 2319.56, IG II² 2319.65 = T4–5 PCG) and won victories at the Dionysia in the 270s (IG II² 2325.76 = T3 PCG). All this puts his known career later than that of Menander, whose death was at the end of the 290s.[17] Whether Phoenicides' career extended earlier into the 290s or later beyond the 270s cannot now be determined, but broadly he seems to have been a playwright a half generation or full generation later than Menander, and in turn two to three generations earlier than Plautus, thus squarely in the pool of the authors of Greek New Comedy whose plays early Roman comic playwrights adapted, although no specific testimony says that they used Phoenicides' plays.[18] Last and least, Athenaeus, quoting a Nicostratus (fr. 8), says a braggart soldier (ἀλαζὼν στρατιώτης) boasts about his dishes, a passage that probably post-dates Menander, for the better-known Nicostratus was a son of Aristophanes, but this is more likely a later playwright of the same name (see Nicostratus II and III in PCG and IG II² 2325.4.13).

To be clear, the evidence does not indicate that there were absolutely no pompous soldiers on the Greek stage prior to or contemporary with Menander. Even the minimal evidence among the fragments allows for the type to exist. Compared to the ample evidence even among fragments for truly pompous characters, most obviously cooks but also parasites, the available testimony suggests that, in Menander's day, pompous bragging was just one of multiple options for a performance characteristic with which a soldier character could be imbued. Nonetheless, soldiers are prevalent in extant Menander, although, as it happens, there are no soldiers in the only complete play, *Dyskolos*; but they play some role in most of the other scripts with substantial remains: *Samia, Perikeiromene, Misoumenos, Aspis, Sikyonioi* and *Kolax*.

With the *miles gloriosus* thus pushed to the margins, other dynamics of Menander's soldiers derived from his scripts can take centre stage, as it were.[19] A crucial characteristic of these soldiers that has been neglected because of the assumption that they are braggarts is their mercenary service. All of Menander's soldiers are returning mercenaries. In military history, it is well established that there was an explosion of Greek mercenary service in the fourth and third centuries BCE, i.e. before and during the lifetime and career of Menander.[20] Providing a contemporary perspective on the phenomenon, Isocrates could suggest that in Greece it was easier to build an army from exiled mercenaries than from citizens (5.96). Menander's focus on mercenaries thus suggests that his soldier characters, in fact, respond to the cultural anxieties of his era. It accordingly makes sense to pursue the dynamics in his soldier characters in the context of how Greek cultural traditions, and especially theatrical traditions, addressed such anxieties, to provide context and precedent for Menander's distinct work within and continuing these traditions. Other scholarly approaches should move to the fore to contextualize the soldiers that do appear in Menander, sketching the drives and restrictions that shape and propel Menander's soldier characters in his plays.

In recent years, multiple strands of scholarship have increasingly recognized culturally driven patterns in accounting for soldiers' behaviour on the battlefield and, more directly relevant for the current discussion, as they reintegrate into civilian life. As Kurt Raaflaub demonstrates in a brief but powerful survey, the vicious consequences of war played out broadly and deeply not just on the battlefields themselves but in Greek communities throughout antiquity.[21] Rural or civic life, without the disruption of war and its consequences, appears only as a utopian vision, one articulated in large part explicitly by the absence of war's effects, but even then only sporadically.[22] Otherwise, any analysis of communal life had to reckon war not in isolation but as the intersection of battlefield consequences and ongoing communal life.

In this context, in Menander's day, no soldier was more of a concern than those who put their military skills out for pay and whose allegiances consequently could not be counted upon to remain bound to their civilian community. For example, Menander's soldiers in *Perikeiromene* and *Misoumenos* are men militarized and initially incapable or unwilling to commit to a settled domestic life. The resolution of these comedies involves these characters foregoing their military skills and devoting themselves to civilian lives as responsible husbands in their local communities. In ways relevant for this context also, I have previously argued that the political priorities of Menander's plays were most consistent with that of stable, imperial control of Athens and the broader Greek world by Macedon.[23] The testimony of Isocrates and others hinges on the perception that rootless and dangerous mercenaries were so numerous in Menander's day that a mercenary army was easier to raise than a politically loyal one. Although Macedonian leaders made extensive use of mercenaries, Menander's concern would have been the threat that such soldiers presented to stable Macedonian rule, since they did not necessarily have loyalties to any community or empire. Menander's ideological drive, then, and one that he would have shared with a crucial segment of his spectators in the theatre, was to defuse this anxiety in the moments he held the stage.

These motives and goals led Menander to capitalize on cultural patterns and tools of performance art to dramatize his narratives. Performance art in the Greek world had long articulated the intersection of soldiers' commitment with a community's values. The performance art that loomed largest in Greek antiquity as a meditation on the consequences of battle on an individual and in turn on the health of their community is, to be sure, the *Odyssey*. Although originating centuries earlier, the patterns of this epic narrative remained an easy reference point in the fourth century BCE. As an exiled mercenary trapped in non-Greek territory, for example, Xenophon naturally elided the disaffection of his soldiers to those of Odysseus in the land of the lotus eaters (*Anab.* 3.2.25[24]). And, no doubt, the *Odyssey* looms somewhere in the background of any soldier Menander depicts as moving towards domestic life.[25] Closer to Menander's immediate points of reference as a playwright were not buffoons on the comic stage but the haunted figures on the tragic stage. As Johanna Hanink has surveyed and analysed, tragedy and, in particular, Aeschylus, Sophocles and Euripides, were being valorized and canonized during Menander's lifetime.[26]

Relevant here, then, are the ways scholars explore how Greeks in antiquity probed dynamics of soldiers' lives on and off the battlefield. These scholars have been devoting ever more attention to tragedy as a community's occasion and mechanism for identifying and articulating for Greeks themselves how soldiers' battlefield traumas could or should play out. Peter Meineck has broadly outlined how Athenian tragedy offered 'cultural therapy' for combat veterans, their families and the society to which they belong.[27] Following the lead of Jonathan Shay, much scholarly exploration of soldiers on the tragic stage involves merging the experiences and perspectives in the ancient scripts with the experiences and accounts of combat veterans in modern times.[28] Nancy Sherman finds Sophocles' *Philoctetes* showcasing the difficulties of building trust for victims of moral injury in warfare in terms immediate and modern in the twenty-first century.[29] Using not just *Philoctetes* but also Sophocles' *Ajax* and Euripides' *Herakles*, the Theater of War project has been probing how the Athenian tragic stage dramatized actions and places where the combat veteran no longer fits into his community, with catastrophic results.[30]

Accordingly, Menander recasts a dangerous tragic figure as an ideologically fraught young mercenary, and then transforms him into a domesticated husband. In *Perikeiromene Misoumenos* and *Sikyonioi*, these soldiers are lovers struggling to align their domestic relationships and behaviour with the matrix of sociopolitical and erotic norms of their local communities. Eventually these young men succeed in doing so. In *Aspis*, the young man's mercenary service has disrupted his household and domestic responsibilities, and the resolution involves his restabilizing his household. In *Samia*, the young protagonist flirts with using a soldier's prerogative to avoid his looming conjugal responsibilities (618–728). In every case, Menander sets the potential ideological and political threat of a former mercenary, that his military skill could trump his allegiances to his local community – and this community that in the larger political realm is stable within the context of Macedonian rule – against the erotic and personal drive of a young male lover. In every case, the young male comes to assume his responsibilities and support a locally politically stable household as a husband and expectant father, abandoning his former military life and future prerogatives as such.

It is after the early Hellenistic period, during the third century, and especially in Latin renditions of Greek New Comedy, that the braggart soldier became the dominant iteration on the comic stage. The Plautine examples of a true *miles gloriosus*, from *Curculio*, *Epidicus*, *Truculentus* and the *Miles Gloriosus* itself, have no known links to Menander, and indeed evidence for Greek predecessors to these plays is minimal. By contrast, Menander's *Synaristosai* is adapted as Plautus' *Cistellaria*, which vestigially preserves dynamics of the sort of soldier's experience familiar from Menander, when the young man Alcesimarchus asks for military equipment and subsequently threatens a warrior's suicide.[31] In *Poenulus*, Plautus deploys a *miles gloriosus* but also refracts the various associations of a soldier character. The *miles* himself is Antamynides, who in his first appearance onstage engages in boastful banter that marks him as a classic *miles gloriosus* (471–503). Shortly afterwards, however, the young protagonist Agorastacles recruits a slave Collybiscus to pretend to be Antamynides (578–721), thus adding an actor pretending to be a *miles gloriosus* in a play which already features one.[32] More influential is Menander's *Kolax*, which featured the soldier Bias, who is an example of the *miles gloriosus* only because he is fuelled by a flatterer, and who is interpolated as Thraso into Terence's adaptation of Menander's *Eunuch*. The reputation of Menander's soldiers being arrogant braggarts rests primarily on this single instance. Consequently, the Roman playwrights deserve credit for originating and propelling the legacy of braggart soldiers on later stages in Europe and elsewhere. With the loss of Menander's own scripts, the Roman adaptations and skewed access made for the logical inference that Menander's soldiers had been exemplars of the *miles gloriosus*.[33] Fortunately, the ongoing recovery of substantial remains of Menander's scripts allows us to glimpse a more complex, diverse and fascinating development, one that allows scholars now to trace Menander's techniques with greater nuance and chart his reception in later generations, indeed centuries, with ever slightly more clarity.

Notes

1. Bountiful thanks must go to Toph and Hallie Marshall for hosting a conference experience fruitful and collegial from beginning to end, with additional thanks to Niall Slater and Simon Perris, whose presentations at our panel blended fortuitously and collegially with this paper.

2. Petrides 2014: 213.

3. See, e.g., MacCarey 1972, Ruffell 2014: 153–6.

4. Storey 2010: 221–5.

5. Storey 2003: 246–60, esp. 257–60; cf. Bowie 1988 and Olson 2015.

6. For Menander's links with other fourth-century comedy, especially Alexis, see Arnott 2004. On the Menander's absorption of tragedy, Petrides nicely summarizes, 'Tragedy ... can be anywhere and everywhere in Menander, even behind the most mundane, that is, seemingly "realistic" situations' (2014: 79).

7. Arnott 2010: 324–5, Ruffell 2014: 147–56, Blume 2001: 175–95.

8. Konstantakos 2011.

9. Note especially that the soldier of fr. 200 is asked to tell about the marvel of another king, not that the soldier is bragging about himself.

10. Adesp. fr. 152, another fragment about someone's cowardice, likewise lacks context.

11. The inspiration for Plautus' *Miles Gloriosus* was a Greek play titled ἀλάζων (*Mil. Gl.* 86), but the title cannot be matched up with any known Greek playwright. For the evolution of the term *alazon*, see MacDowell 1990, and in Aristophanes, see Major 2006.

12. See Barsby 1999: 228–39 on such scenes in Menander's *Perikeiromene* and *Kolax*.

13. Alexis' lengthy career began before Menander was even born and continued on after his death, and no information indicates where this play or passage might belong chronologically. Cf. Arnott 1996 *ad loc.*

14. Petrides 2014: 213–16.

15. Adesp. fr. 1096 = Arnott 2000 *Fabula Incerta* 7; lines 10–27 + 83–8 = Sandbach pp. 354–5.

16. As the passage is preserved only among a concatenation of quotes in Stobaeus, there is no context for it. Adesp fr. 934 might provide a Greek parallel. Syrianus quotes a reference to commanders under whom a soldier in comedy served, but he is interested mostly in the Doric pronunciation of the names and leaves his source vague (τῶν κομικῶν τις περὶ τινος ἀλάζονος στρατιώτου φησί ...), so the source, date and even accuracy of the citation are obscure.

17. Olson 2007: 415.

18. Among Phoenicides' titles is Μισουμένη (*A Hated Woman*), which could suggest a response to Menander's Μισούμενος (*A Hated Man*), but there is nothing known of the play to indicate its content or characters.

19. Niall Slater's contribution to this volume on Stratophanes in *Sikyonioi*, in fact, shows yet another example of productive ways to understand a soldier character in Menander other than as a braggart.

20. While scholarship on ancient Greek mercenaries overwhelmingly concentrates on the classical period and earlier, see Trundle 2013 for a basic survey and Bettali 2013 for a more extensive look down to the end of the classical era. For the Hellenistic era, Griffith 1935 remains the most extensive survey.

21. Raaflaub 2014: esp. 30–2 on mercenaries.

22. Race 2014 nicely supplements the survey of this idea in Lauriola 2009.

23. Major 1997; see Owens 2011 for a review of the subsequent debate.

24. Cf. Ma 2004: 330–45 and more broadly Roy 2004.

25. Shay 2002, Race 2014.

26. See Hanink 2014b, Arnott 1986 and Petrides 2014: 49–79.

27. Meineck 2012 and 2016.

28. Shay 1994 and 2002.

29. Sherman 2014.

30. Doerries 2015.

31. Cf. Charinus in *Mercator* 830–84 (derived from Philemon), except the metaphor there is sailing.

32. Manuwald 2004: 222 consequently finds Antamynides an unorthodox *miles gloriosus*, since he is not boastful nor a customary client of pimps. The relationship of *Poenulus* to its Greek antecedents is also unusually complex, for the principal model seems to have been Alexis' *Karchedonios*, but scholars have noted several passages where Plautus echoes Menander. See Arnott 2004: 67–70 for analysis, including a focus on Collybiscus pretending to be a *miles gloriosus* in a play with a real one.

33. The interplay of controversies about Menander's characters and the availability of Menander's scripts in late antiquity remains unclear, but see Choricius 42, *Decl.* 12.509 Foerster-Richtisteig (= *Misoumenos* fr. 1 Koerte = fr. 1 Sandbach) for hints at a debate in the sixth century CE about the morality of Menander's soldier characters. See Nervegna 2013: 221 for Menander's reputation in this era and Blanchard 2014: 238–40 for a survey of when and why Menander's scripts became lost.

BIBLIOGRAPHY

Aélion, R. (1983), *Euripide: Héritier d'Eschyle*. 2 vols. (Paris: Les Belles Lettres).

Aguirre, M. (2010), 'Erinyes as Creatures of Darkness', in M. Christopoulos, E. D. Karakantza and O. Levaniouk (eds.) 2010, 133–41.

Alexiou, M. (1974), *The Ritual Lament in Greek Tradition* (Lanham MD: Rowman & Littlefield). 2nd ed., 2002.

Allan, A. L. (2011), '"Am I Not the One. . .?" (Sophokles' *Phil.* 114): Neoptolemus and the Allure of Kleos', *CJ* 107: 1–26.

Allan, W. (2001), 'Euripides in Megale Hellas: Some Aspects of the Early Reception of Tragedy', *G&R* 48: 67–86.

Allen-Hornblower, A. (2014), 'The κομμός in Euripides' *Electra*', in C. Pepe and G. Moretti (eds.) 2014, 37–58.

Anderson, D. (2018), 'Burning Down the Fifth-Century Stage', Society for Classical Studies Meetings. Boston MA: Conference abstract. https://classicalstudies.org/annual-meeting/149/abstract/burning-down-fifth-century-stage (accessed 19 September 2019).

Anderson, M. J. (1997), *The Fall of Troy in Early Greek Poetry and Art* (Oxford: Clarendon Press).

Andújar, R. (2016), 'Uncles Ex Machina: Familial Epiphany in Euripides' *Electra*', *Ramus* 45: 165–91.

Andújar, R., T. Coward and Th. Hadjimichael, eds. (2018), *Paths of Song: The Lyric Dimension of Greek Tragedy* (Berlin and Boston: de Gruyter).

Arbel, V. D., P. C. Burns, J. R. C. Cousland, R. Menkis and D. Neufeld, eds. (2015), *Not Sparing the Child: Human Sacrifice in the Ancient World and Beyond* (London: Bloomsbury).

Archontidou Argyri, A. and M. Kokkinophorou, eds. (2004), *Αρχαίο Θέατρο Ηφαιστίας* (Lemnos: Υπουργείο Πολιτισμού / Κ´ Εφορεία Προιστρορικών & Κλασσικών Αρχαιοτήτων).

Arias, P. E. (1962), 'Una nuova scena del mito di Perseo e di Andromeda', *Dionisio* 36: 50–7.

Armstrong, D. (1986), 'Sophocles' *Trachiniae* 559ff.', *BICS* 33: 101–2.

Arnott, W. G. (1973), 'Euripides and the Unexpected', *G&R* 20: 49–64.

Arnott, W. G. (1979, 1996, 2000), *Menander*. 3 vols. (Cambridge MA: Harvard University Press).

Arnott, W. G. (1981), 'Double the Vision: A Reading of Euripides' *Electra*', *G&R* 28: 179–92.

Arnott, W. G. (1986), 'Menander and Earlier Drama', in J. H. Betts, J. T. Hooker and J. R. Green (eds.) 1986, 1–9.

Arnott, W. G. (1990), 'Euripides' Newfangled *Helen*', *Antichthon* 24: 1–18.

Arnott, W. G. (1996), *Alexis: The Fragments. A Commentary* (Cambridge: Cambridge University Press).

Arnott, W. G. (1997), 'First Notes on Menander's *Sikyonioi*', *ZPE* 116: 1–10.

Arnott, W. G. (2004), 'Alexis, New Comedy and Plautus' *Poenulus*', in T. Bair (ed.) 2004, 61–91.

Arnott, W. G. (2010), 'Middle Comedy', in G. W. Dobrov (ed.) 2010, 279–331.

Arweiler A. and M. Möller, eds. (2008), *Vom Selbst-Verständnis in Antike und Neuzeit / Notions of the Self in Antiquity and Beyond* (Berlin: de Gruyter).

Athanassaki, L. (2018), 'Talking Thalassocracy in Fifth-century Athens: From Bacchylides' "Theseus' Odes" (17 & 18) and Cimonian Monuments to Euripides' *Troades*', in R. Andújar, T. Coward and Th. Hadjimichael (eds.) 2018, 87–116.

Austin, C. and S. D. Olson, eds. (2004). *Aristophanes: Thesmophoriazusae* (Oxford: Oxford University Press).

Bibliography

Austin J. L. (1975), *How to Do Things with Words* (Cambridge MA: Harvard University Press).

Bagordo, A. (2003), *Reminiszenzen früher Lyrik bei den attischen Tragikern: Beiträge zur Anspielungstechnik und poetischen Tradition* (Munich: Beck).

Bagordo, A. (2013), *Telekleides. Einleitung, Übersetzung, Kommentar* (Heidelberg: Verlag Antike).

Bagordo, A. (2014), *Alkimenes – Kantharos. Einleitung, Übersetzung, Kommentar* (Heidelberg: Verlag Antike).

Bain, D. (1977), '[Euripides], *Electra* 518–44', *BICS* 24: 104–16.

Bain, D. (1988), 'Some Reflections on the Illusion in Greek tragedy', *BICS* 34: 1–14.

Bair, T., ed. (2004), *Studien zu Plautus' Poenulus* (Tübingen: Gunter Narr).

Bakola, E. (2008), 'The Drunk, the Reformer, and the Teacher: Agonistic Poetics and the Construction of Persona in the Comic Poets of the Fifth Century', *Proceedings of the Cambridge Philological Society* 54: 1–29.

Bakola, E. (2009), *Cratinus and the Art of Comedy* (Oxford: Oxford University Press).

Bakola, E. (2013), 'Crime and Punishment: Cratinus, Aeschylus' *Oresteia*, and the Metaphysics and Politics of Wealth', in Bakola, Prauscello, Mario Telò (eds.) 2013, 226–55.

Bakola, E., L. Prauscello, and M. Telò, eds. (2013), *Greek Comedy and the Discourse of Genres* (Cambridge: Cambridge University Press).

Balme, M., tr. (2001), *Menander: The Plays and Fragments* (Oxford: Oxford University Press).

Bañuls, J. V. and C. Morenilla (2008), '*Andrómeda* en el conjunto de las tragedias de Eurípides', *CFC* 18: 89–110.

Barker, E. T. E. (2009), *Entering the Agon: Dissent and Authority in Homer, Historiography and Tragedy* (Oxford: Oxford University Press).

Barker, E. T. E. and J. P. Christensen (2006), 'Flight Club: The New Archilochus Fragment and Its Resonance with Homeric Epic', *MD* 57: 9–41.

Barrett, J. (2002), *Staged Narrative: Poetics and the Messenger in Greek Tragedy* (Berkeley: University of California Press).

Barrett, W. S. (1964), *Euripides: Hippolytos* (Oxford: Clarendon Press).

Barsby, J. (1999), *Terence: Eunuchus* (Cambridge: Cambridge University Press).

Basile, C. and A. Di Natale, eds. (2001), *La Sicilia antica nei rapporti con l'Egitto: atti del Convegno internazionale, Siracusa, 17–18 settembre 1999* (Syracuse: Instituto internazionale del papiro).

Basta Donzelli, G. (1978), 'Euripide, *Elettra* 518–44', *BICS* 27: 109–19.

Bates, W. N. (1930), *Euripides. A Student of Human Nature* (London: Milford).

Battezzato, L. (2005), 'The New Music of the Trojan Women', *Lexis* 23: 73–104.

Battezzato, L. (2016), '"Shall I Sing with the Delian Maidens?" Trojan and Greek Identities in the Songs of Euripides' *Hecuba*', *MD* 76: 139–55.

Battezzato, L. (2018), *Euripides: Hecuba* (Cambridge: Cambridge University Press).

Beazley, J. D. (1963), *Attic Red-Figure Vase-Painters*, 2nd ed. 3 vols. (Oxford: Oxford University Press).

Beer, J. (2004), *Sophocles and the Tragedy of Athenian Democracy* (Westport CT: Praeger).

Belardinelli, A. M. and G. Greco, eds. (2010), *Antigone e le Antigoni. Storia forme fortuna di un mito* (Milan: Mondadori Education).

Belfiore, E. S. (2000), *Murder Among Friends. Violation of Philia in Greek Tragedy* (New York and Oxford: Oxford University Press).

Bers, V. (1997), *Speech in Speech: Studies in Incorporated Oratio Recta in Attic Drama and Oratory* (Lanham, MD: Rowman & Littlefield).

Bethe, E. (1891), *Thebanische Heldenlieder: Untersuchungen über die Epen des thebanisch-argivischen Sagenkreises* (Leipzig: Hirzel).

Bettali, M. (2013), *Mercenari: Il mestiere delle armi nel mondo Greco antico* (Saggi: Carocci).

Betts, J. H., J. T. Hooker, and J. R. Green, eds. (1986), *Studies in Honour of T. B. L. Webster. Vol. I* (Bristol: Bristol Classical Press).

Beverley, E. J. (1997), *The Dramatic Function of Actors' Monody in Later Euripides* (PhD Diss.: University of Oxford).

Biehl, W. (1989), *Euripides Troades* (Heidelberg: Carl Winter).

Bierl, A. F. H. (1991), *Dionysos und die griechische Tragödie: Politische und 'metatheatralische' Aspekte im Text* (Tübingen: Gunter Narr).

Bierl, A. F. H. (2009), *Ritual and Performativity: The Chorus in Old Comedy* (Cambridge, MA: Harvard University Press). German edn, 2001.

Bierl, A. F. H., P. von Möllendorff, and S. Vogt, eds. (1994), *Orchestra. Drama, Mythos, Bühne. Festschrift für Hellmut Flashar anlässlich seines 65. Geburtstages* (Stuttgart and Leipzig: Teubner).

Biles, Z. P. (2007), 'Aeschylus' Afterlife: Reperformance by Decree in 5th C. Athens?', *ICS* 31-2: 206-42.

Biles, Z. P. (2011), *Aristophanes and the Poetics of Competition* (Cambridge: Cambridge University Press).

Biles, Z. P. and S. D. Olson (2015), *Aristophanes' Wasps* (Oxford: Oxford University Press).

Blanchard, A. (2009), *Menandre Tome 4: Les Sicyoniens* (Paris: Les Belles Lettres).

Blanchard, A. (2014), 'Reconstructing Menander', in M. Fontaine and A. C. Scafuro (eds.) 2014, 239-57.

Blanchard, A. and A. Bataille (1965), 'Fragments sur papyrus du Σικυώνιος de Ménandre', *Recherches de Papyrologie* 3, 103-76, plates vi-xii.

Blondell, R. (2002), *Sophocles: The Theban Plays* (Newburyport, MA: Focus Publishing).

Bloom, H. (1973), *The Anxiety of Influence: A Theory of Poetry* (New York: Oxford University Press).

Blume, H. D. (2001), 'Komische Soldaten: Entwicklung und Wandlung einer typischen Bühnenfigur in der Antike', in B. Zimmermann (ed.) 2001, 175-95.

Blume, H. D. (2010), 'Menander: The Text and Its Restoration', in A. K. Petrides and S. Papaioannou (eds.) 2010, 14-30.

Blundell, M. W. (1998), *Sophocles' Antigone* (Newburyport, MA: Focus Publishing).

Bobrick, E. (1997), 'The Tyranny of Roles: Playacting and Privilege in Aristophanes' *Thesmophoriazusae*', in G. W. Dobrov (ed.) 1997, 177-97.

Bollack, J. (1981), *L'Agamemnon d'Eschyle: Agamemnon I*. 2 vols. (Lille: Presses Universitaires de Lille).

Bond, G. W. (1974), 'Euripides' Parody of Aeschylus', *Hermathena* 118: 1-14.

Bosher, K., ed. (2012), *Drama Outside Athens: Drama in Greek Sicily and South Italy* (Cambridge: Cambridge University Press).

Bowie, E. L. (1986), 'Early Greek Elegy, Symposium and Public Festivals', *JHS* 106: 13-35.

Bowie, E. L. (1988), 'Who Is Diceaopolis?', *JHS* 108: 183-5.

Bowie, E. L. (1990), '*Miles Ludens*? The Problem of Martial Exhortation in Early Greek Elegy', in O. Murray (ed.) 1990, 221-9.

Bowie, E. L. (2016), 'Cultic Contexts for Elegiac Performance', in L. Swift and C. Carey (eds.) 2016, 15-32.

Braund, D. and E. Hall (2014), 'Theatre in the Fourth-Century Black Sea Region', in E. Csapo, H. R. Goette, J. R. Green and P. Wilson (eds.) 2014, 371-90.

Braund, D., E. Hall, and R. Wyles, eds. (2020), *Greek Theatre and Performance Culture around the Ancient Black Sea* (Cambridge: Cambridge University Press).

Bremmer, J.M. (1984), 'Greek Maenadism Reconsidered', *ZPE* 55: 267-86.

Brommer, F. (1979), *Die Parthenon-Skulpturen: Metopen, Fries, Giebel, Kultbild* (Mainz: von Zabern) [= *The Sculptures of the Parthenon: Metopes, Frieze, Pediments, Cult-Statue* (London: Thames & Hudson 1979)].

Brown, M. (2016), *Menander Offstage* (PhD Diss.: University of Cincinnati).

Brown, P. (2018), 'Menander', in K. De Temmerman and E. Van Emde Boas (eds.) 2018, 391-406.

Bibliography

Bubel, F. (1991), *Euripides, Andromeda* (Stuttgart: Steiner).

Burian, P. (1972), 'Supplication and Hero Cult in Sophocles' *Ajax*', *GRBS* 13: 151–6.

Burian, P., ed. (1985), *Directions in Euripidean Criticism* (Durham, NC: Duke University Press).

Burkert, W. (1994), 'Orpheus, Dionysos und die Euneiden in Athen: Das Zeugnis von Euripides' *Hyspipyle*', in A. Bierl, P. von Möllendorff and S. Vogt (eds.) 1994, 44–9.

Burnett, A. P. (1977), '*Trojan Women* and the Ganymede Ode', *YCS* 25: 291–316.

Burnett, A. P. (1983), *Three Archaic Poets. Archilochus, Alcaeus, Sappho* (London: Duckworth).

Burnett, A. P. (1994), 'Hekabe the Dog', *Arethusa* 27: 151–63.

Burnett, A. P. (1998), *Revenge in Attic and Later Tragedy* (Berkeley and Los Angeles: University of California Press).

Burnett, A. P. (2005), *Pindar's Songs for the Young Athletes of Aigina* (Oxford: Oxford University Press).

Butler, J. (1997), *The Psychic Life of Power: Theories in Subjection* (Stanford: Stanford University Press).

Butler, J. (2005), *Giving an Account of Oneself* (New York: Fordham University Press).

Cairns, D. L. (2006), 'Virtue and Viccisitude: The Paradoxes of the *Ajax*', in D. Cairns and V. Liapis (eds), 2006, 99–131.

Cairns, D. L. (2016), *Sophocles: Antigone* (London: Bloomsbury).

Cairns, D. L. and V. Liapis, eds. (2006), *Dionysalexandros: Essays on Aeschylus And His Fellow Tragedians in Honour of Alexander F. Garvie* (Swansea: The Classical Press of Wales).

Calame, C. (1997), *Choruses of Young Women in Ancient Greece. Their Morphology, Religious Role, and Social Functions* (Lanham, MD: Rowman & Littlefield).

Calder, W. (1972), 'A Note on the Dating of Euripides' *Phaethon*', *CP* 67.4: 291–3.

Campbell, B. and A. Tritle, eds. (2013), *The Oxford Handbook of Warfare in the Classical World* (Oxford: Oxford University Press).

Campbell, D. (1991), *Greek Lyric III* (Cambridge, MA: Harvard University Press).

Carawan, E. (2000), 'Deianira's Guilt', *TAPA* 130: 189–237.

Cargill, J. (1995), *Athenian Settlements of the Fourth Century B.C.* (Leiden: Brill).

Carpenter, T. A. and C. A. Faraone, eds. (1993), *Masks of Dionysus* (Ithaca, NY: Cornell University Press).

Carrière, J. (1977), *Le Choeur secondaire dans le drame grec* (Paris: C. Klincksieck).

Carrithers, M., S. Collins and S. Lukes, eds. (1985), *The Category of the Person: Anthropology, Philosophy, History* (Cambridge and New York: Cambridge University Press).

Carroll, N. (1990), *The Philosophy of Horror or Paradoxes of the Heart* (London: Routledge).

Carter, D. M. (2004), 'Was Attic Tragedy Democratic?', *Polis* 21: 1–25.

Carter, D. M., ed. (2011), *Why Athens? A Reappraisal of Tragic Politics* (Oxford: Oxford University Press).

Cartledge, P., P. Millett and S. Todd, eds. (1990), *Nomos: Essays in Athenian Law, Politics and Culture* (Cambridge: Cambridge University Press). Reprinted 2003.

Cassin, B. and J.-L. Labarrière, eds. (1997), *L'animal dans l'antiquité* (Paris: Librairie Philosophique J. VRIN).

Caston, V. (2015), 'Perception in Ancient Greek Philosophy', in M. Matthen (ed.) 2015, 19–50.

Caston, V. and S.-M. Weineck, eds. (2016), *Our Ancient Wars: Rethinking War through the Classics* (Ann Arbor: University of Michigan Press).

Ceccarelli, P. (2004), '"Autour de Dionysos": Remarques sur la dénomination des artistes dionysiaques', in C. Hugoniot, F. Hurlet and S. Milanezi (eds.) 2004, 109–42.

Ceccarelli, P. (2010), 'Changing Contexts: Tragedy in the Civic and Cultural Life of Hellenistic City-States', in I. Gildenhard and M. Revermann (eds.) 2010, 99–150.

Chaniotis, A. (1997), 'Theatricality Beyond the Theatre: Staging Public Life in the Hellenistic World', *Pallas* 47: 219–59.

Chatman, S. (2009), 'On the Formalist-Structuralist Theory of Character', *Journal of Literary Semantics* 1.1: 57–79.

Christensen, J. P. (2018), 'Eris and Epos: Composition, Competition, and the Domestication of Strife', YAGE 2: 1–39.

Christopoulos, M., E. D. Karakantza and O. Levaniouk, eds. (2010), Light and Darkness in Ancient Greek Myth and Religion (Lanham, MD: Lexington Books).

Citti, A., A. Iannucci, and A. Ziosi, eds. (2017), Troiane classiche e contemporanee (Zurich and New York: Georg Olms Verlag).

Clinton, K. (1979), 'The "Hymn to Zeus," πάθει μάθος, and the End of the Parodos of "Agamemnon"', Traditio 35: 1–19.

Coarelli, F. (1997), Campo Marzio: dalle origini alla fine della Repubblica (Rome: Quasar).

Cohen, A. (1996), 'Portrayals of Abduction in Greek Art: Rape or Metaphor?', in N. Kampen (ed.) 1996, 117–35.

Cohen, D. (1978), 'The Imagery of Sophocles: A Study of Ajax' Suicide', G&R 25: 24–36.

Cohen, D. (1989), 'Seclusion, Separation, and the Status of Women', G&R 36: 3–15.

Cohen, D. (1990), 'The Social Context of Adultery in Athens', in P. Cartledge, P. Millett, and S. Todd (eds.) 1990, 147–66.

Coles, R. A. (1974), A New Oxyrhynchus Papyrus: The Hypothesis of Euripides' Alexandros. BICS Supp. 32 (London: Institute of Classical Studies).

Collard, C. (1975), Euripides: Supplices. 2 vols. (Groningen: Bouma).

Collard, C. (1991), Euripides: Hecuba (Warminster: Aris & Phillips).

Collard, C. (2005), 'Euripidean Fragmentary Plays: The Nature of Sources and Their Effect on Reconstruction', in F. McHardy, J. Robson and D. Harvey (eds.) 2005, 49–62.

Collard, C. (2017), 'Fragments and Fragmentary Plays', in L. McClure (ed.) 2017, 347–64.

Collard, C. and M. J. Cropp (2008a), Euripides VII: Fragments. Aegeus–Meleager (Cambridge, MA: Harvard University Press).

Collard, C. and M. J. Cropp (2008b), Euripides VIII: Fragments. Oedipus–Chrysippus. Other Fragments (Cambridge, MA: Harvard University Press).

Collard, C., M. J. Cropp and J. Gibert (2004), Euripides: Selected Fragmentary Plays. Vol. II (Oxford: Aris & Phillips).

Collard, C., M. J. Cropp, and K. H. Lee (1995), Euripides: Selected Fragmentary Plays. Vol. I (Warminster: Aris & Phillips).

Conacher, D. J. (1997), 'Sophocles' Trachiniae: Some Observations', AJP 118.1: 21–34.

Connor, W. (1989), 'City Dionysia and Athenian Democracy', C&M 40: 7–32.

Contiades–Tsitsoni, E. (1994), 'Euripides Pha. 227–244, Tro. 308–341, Iph. Aul. 1036–1079', ZPE 102: 52–60.

Cooper, C. R., ed. (2007), Politics of Orality: Orality and Literacy in Ancient Greece (Leiden: Brill).

Couch, H. N. (1933), 'On Aristoph. Nub. 1161–1162', American Journal of Philology 54: 59–62.

Cousland, J. R. C. and J. R Hume, eds. (2009), The Play of Texts and Fragments: Essays in Honour of Martin Cropp (Leiden: Brill).

Craik, E., ed. (1990), 'Owls to Athens': Essays on Classical Subjects Presented to Sir Kenneth Dover (Oxford: Oxford University Press).

Craik, E. (1993), 'Tragic Love, Comic Sex?', in A. H. Sommerstein, S. Halliwell, J. Henderson and B. Zimmermann (eds.) 1993, 253–62.

Croally, N. T. (1994), Euripidean Polemic: The Trojan Women and the Function of Tragedy (Cambridge: Cambridge University Press).

Cropp, M. J. (1988), Euripides: Electra (Warminster: Aris & Phillips).

Cropp, M. J. (2013), Euripides, Electra, 2nd ed. (Oxford: Oxbow Books).

Cropp, M. and G. Fick (1985), Resolutions and Chronology in Euripides: The Fragmentary Tragedies. BICS Supp. 43 (London: Institute of Classical Studies).

Cropp, M. J., K. Lee and D. Sansone, eds. (1999/2000), Euripides and Tragic Theater in the Late Fifth Century (Urbana-Champaign: Stipes Publishing) [=ICS 24–25].

Bibliography

Csapo, Eric. (1993), 'Deep Ambivalence: Notes on a Greek Cockfight (Part I)', *Phoenix* 47, 1–28; '(Parts II–IV)', *Phoenix* 47: 115–24.

Csapo, E. (2004), 'Some Social and Economic Conditions behind the Rise of the Acting Profession in the Fifth and Fourth Centuries B.C', in C. Hugoniot, F. Hurlet and S. Milanezi (eds.) 2004, 53–76.

Csapo, E. (2010a), *Actors and Icons of the Ancient Theater* (Chichester: Wiley-Blackwell).

Csapo, E. (2010b), 'The Production and Performance of Comedy in Antiquity', in Dobrov 2010, 103–142.

Csapo, E. (2014), 'The Iconography of Comedy', in Revermann 2014, 95–127.

Csapo, E. (2017), 'Imagining the Shape of Choral Dance and Inventing the Cultic in Euripides' Later Tragedies', in L. Gianvittorio (ed.) 2017, 119–56.

Csapo, E. (forthcoming), 'Crowns, Garlands and Ribbons for Tony Podlecki: Official and Unofficial Victory Rituals at the Athenian Dionysian Festivals', *Mouseion*.

Csapo, E., H. R. Goette, J. R. Green, and P. Wilson, eds. (2014), *Greek Theatre in the Fourth Century B.C.* (Berlin and Boston: de Gruyter).

Csapo, E. and M. Miller, eds. (2007), *The Origins of Theater in Ancient Greece and Beyond: From Ritual to Drama* (Cambridge: Cambridge University Press).

Csapo, E. and P. Wilson (2014), 'The Finance and Organisation of the Athenian Theatre in the Time of Eubulus and Lycurgus', in E. Csapo, H. R. Goette, J. R. Green and P. Wilson (eds.) 2014, 393–424.

Csapo, E. and P. Wilson (2015), 'Drama Outside Athens in the Fifth and Fourth Centuries BC', in A. A. Lamari (ed.) 2015, 316–95.

Csapo, E. and P. Wilson (2019), *A Social and Economic History of the Theatre to 300 BC. Vol. II: Theatre Beyond Athens* (Cambridge: Cambridge University Press).

Csordas, T. J. (1994), *Embodiment and Experience: The Existential Ground of Culture and Self* (Cambridge: Cambridge University Press).

Culpeper, J. (^{2}2014 [2001]) *Language and Characterisation: People in Plays and Other Texts.* (London: Routledge).

Culpeper, J. (2002), 'A Cognitive Stylistic Approach to Characterisation' in E. Semino and J. Culpeper (eds.), *Cognitive Stylistics: Language and Cognition in Text Analysis*, 251–76 (Amsterdam: John Benjamins).

Culpeper, J. and D. McIntyre (2010), 'Activity Types and Characterisation in Dramatic Discourse' in F. Jannidis, J. Eder and R. Schneider (eds.), *Characters in Fictional Worlds: Understanding Imaginary Beings in Literature, Film, and Other Media*, 176–207 (Berlin: de Gruyter).

Currie, B. (2002), 'Euthymos of Locri: A Case Study in Heroization in the Classical Period', *JHS* 122: 24–44.

Currie, B. (2012), 'Sophocles and Hero Cult', in Ormand (ed.) 2012, 331–48.

Dale, A. M. (1967), *Euripides: Helen* (Oxford: Clarendon Press).

Dalfern, J., G. Petersmann and F. G. Schwarz, eds. (1993), *Religio Graeco-Romana: Festschrift für Walter Pötscher* (Graz: Horn).

Davidson, J. (1995), 'Homer and Sophocles' *Philoctetes*', in A. Griffiths (ed.) 1995, 25–35.

Davidson, J., F. Muecke and P. Wilson, eds. (2006), *Greek Drama III. Essays in Honour of Kevin Lee* (London: Institute of Classical Studies).

Davies, M. (1998), 'Euripides' *Electra*: The Recognition Scene Again', *CQ* 48: 389–403.

Davies, M. (1999), 'Speaking and Silence: Euripides *Orestes* 1591–2', *Prometheus* 25: 227–30.

Davies, M. and P. J. Finglass (2014), *Stesichorus: The Poems* (Cambridge: Cambridge University Press).

Deacy, S. and A. Villing, eds. (2001) *Athena in the Classical World* (Leiden: Brill).

De Jong, I. J. F. (1991), *Narrative in Drama: The Art of the Euripidean Messenger-Speech* (Leiden: Brill).

De Lacy, P. H. and Einarson, B. (1959), *Plutarch Moralia. Vol. VII* (Cambridge, MA: Harvard University Press).

De Temmerman, K. and E. Van Emde Boas, eds. (2018), *Characterization in Ancient Greek Literature. Studies in Ancient Greek Narrative. Vol. IV* (Leiden: Brill).

DeForest, M. (1993a), 'Clytemnestra's Breast and the Evil Eye', in M. DeForest (ed.) 1993, 129–48.

DeForest, M., ed. (1993b), *Woman's Power, Man's Game: Essays on Classical Antiquity in Honor of Joy K. King* (Waconda: Bolchazy-Carducci Publishers).

Delebecque, E. (1951), *Euripide et la guerre du Péloponnèse* (Paris: C. Klincksieck).

Denniston, J. D. (1939), *Euripides, Electra* (Oxford: Oxford University Press).

Dickie, M. W. (2000), 'Who Practised Love-Magic in Classical Antiquity and in the Late Roman World?', *CQ* 50 (2): 563–83.

Diggle, J. (1970), *Euripides. Phaethon* (Cambridge: Cambridge University Press).

Diggle, J. (1981), *Studies on the Text of Euripides* (Oxford: Clarendon Press).

Diggle, J. (1984), *Euripides Fabulae. Vol. I: Cyclops, Alcestis, Medea, Heracliadae, Hippolytus, Andromacha & Hecuba* (Oxford: Oxford University Press).

Diller, H. (1962), 'Erwartung, Enttäuschung und Erfüllung in der griechischen Tragödie', in R. Muth (ed.) 1962, 93–115.

Dobrov, G. W., ed. (1997) *The City as Comedy: Society and Representation in Athenian Drama* (Chapel Hill: University of North Carolina Press).

Dobrov, G. W., ed. (2010), *Brill's Companion to the Study of Greek Comedy* (Leiden: Brill).

Dodds, E. R. (1951), *The Greeks and the Irrational* (Berkeley: University of California Press).

Dodds, E. R. (1960), *Euripides: Bacchae*, 2nd ed. (Oxford: Clarendon Press).

Doerries, B. (2015), *The Theater of War: What Ancient Greek Tragedies Can Teach Us Today* (New York: Knopf).

Dörrie, H. (1956), 'Leid und Erfahrung: Die Wort- und Sinn-Verbindung παθεῖν-μαθεῖν im griechischen Denken', *Akademie der Wissenschaften und der Literatur: Abhandlungen der Geistes- und Sozialwissenschaftlichen Klasse* 5.

Dover, K. J. (1964), 'The Poetry of Archilochus', in J. Poilloux, N. M. Kontoleon, A. Scherer, D. Page, K. J. Dover, W. Bühler, E. K. H. Wistrand, B. Snell, O. Reverdin and M. Treu (eds.) 1964, 183–222.

Dover, K. J. (1968), *Aristophanes: Clouds* (Oxford: Clarendon Press).

Dover, K. J. (1993), *Aristophanes: Frogs* (Oxford: Clarendon Press).

Doyle, A. (2010), 'Monstrous Motherhood and Its Mythological Antecedents: Clytemnestra in *Libation Bearers*', *Ekklesiastikos Pharos* 92.1: 143–60.

DuBois, P. (1988), *Sowing the Body: Psychoanalysis and Ancient Representations of Women* (Chicago: University of Chicago Press).

DuBois, P. (1991), *Centaurs and Amazons: Women and the Pre-History of the Great Chain of Being* (Ann Arbor: University of Michigan Press).

Dué, C. (2006), *The Captive Woman's Lament in Greek Tragedy* (Austin: University of Texas Press).

Dunbar, N. (1995), *Aristophanes: Birds* (Oxford: Clarendon Press).

Duncan, A. (2012), 'A Theseus Outside Athens: Dionysius I of Syracuse and Tragic Self-Presentation', in K. Bosher (ed.) 2012, 137–55.

Dunn, F. M. (1996), *Tragedy's End. Closure and Innovation in Euripidean Drama* (Oxford: Oxford University Press).

Dyer, R. R. (1969), 'The Evidence for Apolline Purification Rituals at Delphi and Athens', *JHS* 89: 38–56.

Easterling, P. E. (1968), 'Sophocles, *Trachiniae*', *BICS* 15 (1): 58–69.

Easterling, P. E. (1973), 'Presentation of Character in Aeschylus', *G&R* 20 (1): 3–19.

Easterling, P. E. (1977 [repr. 1983]), 'Character in Sophocles', *G&R* 24 (2): 121–29. Reprinted in E. Segal (ed.) 1983, 138–45.

Easterling, P. E. (1978), 'Philoctetes and Modern Criticism', *ICS* 3: 27–39.

Easterling, P. E. (1982), *Sophocles: Trachiniae* (Cambridge: Cambridge University Press).

Easterling, P. E. (1984), 'The Tragic Homer', *BICS* 31, 1–8.

Easterling, P. E. (1987), 'Women in Tragic Space', *BICS* 34 (1): 15–26.

Easterling, P. E. (1988), 'Tragedy and Ritual: "Cry 'woe, woe,' but may the good prevail!"', *Métis* 3: 87–109.

Easterling, P. E. (1990), 'Constructing Character in Greek Tragedy', in C. B. R. Pelling (ed.) 1990, 83–99.

Easterling, P. E. (1993), 'Gods on Stage in Greek Drama', in J. Dalfern, G. Petersmann and F.G. Schwarz (eds.) 1993, 77–86.

Easterling, P. E. (1994), 'Euripides Outside Athens: A Speculative Note', *ICS* 19:, 73–80.

Easterling, P. E. (2005), '*Agamemnon* for the Ancients', in F. Macintosh, P. Michelakis, E. Hall and O. Taplin (eds.) 2005, 23–36.

Edmunds, L. (2001), *Intertextuality and the Reading of Roman Poetry* (Baltimore: Johns Hopkins University Press).

Edwards, A. T. (1991), 'Aristophanes' Comic Poetics: τρύξ, Scatology, σκῶμμα', *TAPA* 121, 157–79.

Eichholz, D. E. (1962), *Pliny. Natural History. Vol. X: Books 36–37* (Cambridge MA: Harvard University Press).

van Emde Boas, E. (2017), *Language and Character in Euripides' Electra* (Oxford: Oxford University Press).

Ensoli, S., ed. (2012a), *For the Preservation of the Cultural Heritage in Libya: A Dialogue among Institutions* (Pisa and Rome: Fabrizio Serra Editore).

Ensoli, S. (2012b), 'L'attività della Missione Archeologica Italiana a Cirene (MAIC) della Seconda Università degli Studi di Napoli (SUN). Le ricerche svolte nel 2009 e 2010 in collaborazione con il Dipartimento alle Antichità (DoA) di Cirene: strategie e prospettive future', in S. Ensoli (ed.) 2012a, 111–38.

van Erp Taalman Kip, A. M. (1987), 'Euripides and Melos', *Mnemosyne* 40: 414–9.

van Erp Talmaan Kip, A. M. (2007), 'Athena's One-Day Limit in Sophocles' "Aias"', *Mnemosyne* 60: 464–71.

Errandonea I. (1927), 'Deianira vere *ΔHI-ANEIPA*', *Mnemosyne* 55: 145–64.

Ewans, M. (1975), 'Agamemnon at Aulis: A Study in the *Oresteia*', *Ramus* 4: 17–32.

Falcetto, R. (1998), 'L'*Andromeda* di Euripide: proposta di ricostruzione', *Quaderni del Dipartimento di filologia, linguistica, e tradizione classica* (Università degli studi di Torino) 9: 55–71.

Falkner, T. M. (1993), 'Making a Spectacle of Oneself: The Metatheatrical Design of Sophocles' *Ajax*', *Text and Presentation* 14: 35–40.

Fanfani, G. (2017), 'Moduli di rappresentazione corale nelle *Troiane* di Euripide', in F. Citti, A. Iannucci, and A. Ziosi (eds.) 2017, 31–47.

Fanfani, G. (2018), 'What Melos for Troy? Blending of Lyric Genres in the First *Stasimon* of Euripides' *Trojan Women*', in R. Andújar, T. Coward and Th. Hadjimichael (eds.) 2018, 239–63.

Faraone, C. A. (1994), 'Deianira's Mistake and the Demise of Heracles: Erotic Magic in Sophocles' *Trachiniae*', *Helios* 21.2: 115–35.

Farmer, M. C. (2017), *Tragedy on the Comic Stage* (New York: Oxford University Press).

Favi, F. (2019), 'The Title(s) of Menander's *Sikyonioi*', *Mnemosyne* 72, 335–9.

Ferrari, G. (2000), 'The Ilioupersis in Athens', *HSCPh* 100: 119–50.

Finglass. P. J. (2011), *Sophocles: Ajax* (Cambridge: Cambridge University Press).

Finglass, P. J. (2013), 'How Stesichorus Began His Sack of Troy', *ZPE* 185: 1–17.

Finglass, P. J. (2017), 'Euripides' *Oedipus*: A Response to Liapis', *TAPA* 147.1: 1–26.

Finglass, P. J., ed. (2018a), *Sophocles: Oedipus the King* (Cambridge: Cambridge University Press).

Finglass, P. J. (2018b), 'Gazing at Helen with Stesichorus', in A. Kampakoglou and A. Novokhatko, eds. (2018), 140–59.

Finglass, P. J. and L. Coo, eds. (forthcoming) *Fragmented Women: The Female Characters of Fragmentary Greek Tragedy* (Cambridge: Cambridge University Press).

Finglass, P. J. and A. Kelly, eds. (2015), *Stesichorus in Context* (Cambridge: Cambridge University Press).

Finkelberg, M. (2006), 'The City Dionysia and the Social Space of Attic Tragedy', in J. Davidson, F. Muecke and P. Wilson (eds.) 2006, 17–26.

Fiorentini, L. (2017), *Strattide: Testimonianze e frammenti* (Bologna: Pàtron Editore).

Fischer-Lichte, E. (2005) 'Embodiment. From Page to Stage: The Dramatic Figure', in W. Nöth, ed., *Semiotic Bodies, Aesthetic Embodiments, and Cyberbodies* (Kassel: Kassel University Press), 101–16.

Fisher, N. (2013), 'Erotic Charis: What Sorts of Reciprocity?', in E. Sanders (ed.) 2013, 39–65.

Foerster, R. and E. Richtsteig (1929), *Choricii Gazaei Opera* (Leipzig: Teubner).

Foley, H. P. (1980), 'The Masque of Dionysus', *TAPhA* 110: 107–33.

Foley, H. P. (1982a), 'Marriage and Sacrifice in Euripides' *Iphigeneia in Aulis*', *Arethusa* 15.1: 159–80.

Foley, H. P. (1982b), 'The Female Intruder, Reconsidered: Women in Aristophanes' *Lysistrata* and *Ecclesiazusae*', *CPh* 77: 1–21.

Foley, H. P. (1985), *Ritual Irony: Poetry and Sacrifice in Euripides* (Ithaca NY: Cornell University Press).

Foley, H. P. (1993), 'The Politics of Tragic Lamentation', in A. H. Sommerstein, S. Halliwell, J. Henderson and Z. Bernhard (eds.) 1993, 101–43.

Foley, H. P. (2001), *Female Acts in Greek Tragedy* (Princeton: Princeton University Press).

Foley, H. P. (2008), 'Generic Boundaries in Late Fifth-Century Athens', in M. Revermann and P. Wilson (eds.) 2008, 15–36.

Foley, H. P. (forthcoming), 'Heterosexual Bonding in the Fragments of Euripides', in P. Finglass and L. Coo (forthcoming).

Fontaine, M. and A. Scafuro, eds. (2014), *The Oxford Handbook of Ancient Comedy* (Oxford: Oxford University Press).

Ford, A. L. (1981), *A Study of Early Greek Terms for Poetry: Aoidē, Epos and Poiēsis* (PhD Diss.: Yale University).

Foucault, M. (1982), 'The Subject and Power', *Critical Inquiry* 8: 777–95.

Fowler, R. L. (1987), *The Nature of Early Greek Lyric: Three Preliminary Studies* (Toronto: University of Toronto Press).

Fox, R. L. (2004), *The Long March: Xenophon and the Ten Thousand* (New Haven: Yale).

Fraenkel, E. (1950), *Aeschylus: Agamemnon*. 3 vols. (Oxford: Oxford University Press).

Franco, C. (2014), *Shameless: The Canine and the Feminine in Ancient Greece*. Matthew Fox (tr.) (Oakland: University of California Press).

Frederiksen, R. (2002), 'The Greek Theatre. A Typical Building in the Urban Centre of the Polis?', in T. H. Nielsen (ed.) 2002, 65–124.

Frontisi-Ducroux, F. (1996), 'Eros, Desire, and the Gaze', in N. Kampen (ed.) 1996, 81–100.

Frontisi-Ducroux, F. (1997), 'Actéon, Ses Chiens, et Leur Maître', in B. Cassin and J.-L. Labarrière (eds.) 1997, 435–54.

Frontisi-Ducroux, F. (2007), 'The Invention of the Erinyes', in C. Kraus, S. Goldhill, H. P. Foley and J. Elsner (eds.) 2007, 165–76.

Funke, M. K. A. (2013), *Euripides and Gender: The Difference the Fragments Make* (PhD Diss.: University of Washington).

Furley, W. D. (2009), *Menander: Epitrepontes. BICS* Supp. 106 (London: Institute of Classical Studies, School of Advanced Study, University of London).

Furley, W. D. (2014), 'Aspects of Recognition in *Perikeiromene* and Other Plays', in A. H. Sommerstein (ed.) 2014, 106–15.

Furtwängler, A. (1884), 'Gorgones Und Gorgo', in W. H. Roscher (ed.) 1884, 1695–727.

Gagarin, M. (1976) *Aeschylean Drama* (Berkeley: University of California Press).

Bibliography

Gagné, R. and M. G. Hopman, eds. (2013), *Choral Mediations in Greek Tragedy* (Cambridge: Cambridge University Press).

Gallagher, R. L. (2003), 'Making the Stronger Argument the Weaker: Euripides, *Electra* 518–44', *CQ* 53: 401–15.

Gallagher, S., ed. (2011), *The Oxford Handbook of the Self* (Oxford: Oxford University Press).

Galli, M. (2010), 'Le immagini di Antigone: per un'archeologia delle emozioni', in A. M. Belardinelli and G. Greco (eds.) 2010, 59–70.

Gámez, L. R., ed. (1999), *Tragedy's Insights: Identity, Polity, Theodicy* (West Cornwall CT: Locust Hill Press) [=*Comparative Drama* 33.1].

Gantz, T. (1993), *Early Greek Myth: A Guide to Literary and Artistic Sources* (Baltimore: Johns Hopkins University Press).

Gardner, J. F. (1989), 'Aristophanes and Male Anxiety: The Defence of the Oikos', *G&R* 36: 51–62.

Garner, R. (1990), *From Homer to Tragedy: The Art of Allusion in Greek Poetry* (London: Routledge).

Garvie, A. F. (1969), *Aeschylus' Supplices: Play and Trilogy* (Cambridge: Cambridge University Press).

Garvie, A. F. (1986), *Aeschylus: Choephori* (Oxford: Oxford University Press).

Gennep, A. Van. (2004 [1906]), *The Rites of Passage*, trans. M. Vizedom and G. Caffee (London: Routledge).

Ghiron-Bistagne, P. (1976), *Recherches dur les acteurs dans la Grèce antique* (Paris: Les Belles Lettres).

Gianvittorio, L., ed. (2017), *Choreutika: Performing Dance in Archaic and Classical Greece* (Pisa and Rome: Biblioteca dei Quaderni Urbinati di Cultura Classica).

Gibert, J. (1995), *Change of Mind in Greek Tragedy* (Göttingen: Vandenhoeck & Ruprecht).

Gibert, J. (1997), 'Euripides *Heracles* 1351 and the Hero's Encounter with Death', *CPh* 92: 247–58.

Gibert, J. (1999/2000), 'Falling in Love with Euripides (*Andromeda*)', in M. J. Cropp, K. Lee and D. Sansone (eds.) 1999/2000, 75–91.

Gibert, J. (2003), 'Apollo's Sacrifice: the Limits of a Metaphor in Greek Tragedy', *HSCPh* 101: 159–206.

Gibert, J. (2011), 'Hellenicity in Later Euripidean Tragedy', in D. M. Carter (ed.) 2011, 383–401.

Gibert, J. (2017), 'Euripides and the Development of Greek Tragedy', in L. McClure (ed.) 2017, 42–58.

Gildenhard, I. and M. Revermann, eds. (2010), *Beyond the Fifth Century: Interactions with Greek Tragedy from the Fourth Century BCE to the Middle Ages* (Berlin and New York: de Gruyter).

Gill, C. (1996), *Personality in Greek Epic, Tragedy, and Philosophy: The Self in Dialogue* (Oxford: Clarendon Press).

Goette, H.. (1995), 'Griechischer Theaterbau der Klassik – Forschungsstand und Fragestellungen', in E. Pöhlmann (ed.) 1995, 9–48.

Goff, B. (2004), *Citizen Bacchae: Women's Ritual Practice in Ancient Greece* (Berkeley: University of California Press).

Goff, B. (2009), *Euripides: Trojan Women* (London: Duckworth).

Goffman, E. (1959), *Presentation of Self in Everyday Life* (Garden City NY: Doubleday).

Goldhill, S. (1986), *Reading Greek Tragedy* (Cambridge: Cambridge University Press).

Goldhill, S. (1987), 'The Great Dionysia and Civic Ideology', *JHS* 107: 58–76.

Goldhill, S. (1990), 'Character and Action, Representation and Reading. Greek Tragedy and Its Critics', in C. B. R. Pelling (ed.), *Characterization and Individuality in Greek Literature*, 100–27 (Oxford: Clarendon Press).

Goldhill, S. (2000), 'Civic Ideology and the Problem of Difference: The Politics of Aeschylean Tragedy, Once Again', *JHS* 120: 34–56.

Goldhill, S. and R. Osborne, eds. (1994), *Art and Text in Ancient Greek Culture* (Cambridge: Cambridge University Press).

Goldhill, S. and R. Osborne, eds. (1999), *Performance Culture and Athenian Democracy* (Cambridge: Cambridge University Press).

Goldman, H. (1910), 'The *Oresteia* of Aeschylus as Illustrated by Greek Vase-Painting', *HSCPh* 21: 111–59.

Gomme, A. W. and F.H. Sandbach (1973), *Menander: A Commentary* (London: Oxford University Press).

Goodwin, W. W. (1977), *A Greek Grammar*, 2nd ed. reprint (London: Macmillan).

Gould, J. (1978), 'Dramatic Character and "Human Intelligibility" in Greek Tragedy', *PCPS* 204 (24): 43–67.

Gould, J. (1980), 'Law, Custom, Myth: Aspects of the Social Position of Women in Classical Athens', *JHS* 100: 38–59.

Goward, B. (1999), *Telling Tragedy: Narrative Technique in Aeschylus, Sophocles and Euripides* (London: Duckworth).

Graf, F. (1985), *Nordionische Kulte: Religionsgeschichtliche und epigraphische Untersuchungen zu den Kulten von Chios, Erythrai, Klazomenai und Phokaia* (Rome: Schweizerisches Institut in Rom).

Graf, F., ed. (1998), *Ansichten griechischer Rituale. Geburtstag Symposium für Walter Burkert* (Stuttgart and Leipzig: Teubner).

Granata, F., L. Godart, G. Voza, G. Di Rauso and M. Centanni, eds. (2014), *Siracusa: Capitale del teatro* (Pachino: Erre).

Greco, E. (2011), 'Alla ricerca dell'Agora di Sparta', *ASAtene* 89: 53–77.

Greco, E. and O. Voza (2016), 'For a Reconstruction of the "Round Building" at Sparta as the Skias', in K. Zambas, V. Lambrinoudakis, E. Simandoni-Bournia and A. Ohnesorg (eds) (2016) Αρχιτέκων΅ τιμητικόσ τόμος για τον Καθηγητή Μανόλη Κορρέ (Athens: Melissa) 343–50.

Green, J. R. (1985), 'A Representation of the *Birds* of Aristophanes', *Greek Vases in the J. Paul Getty Museum*, Vol. 2 (Malibu CA: The J. Paul Getty Museum) 95–118.

Green, J. R. (2014), 'Regional Theatre in the Fourth Century', in E. Csapo, H. R. Goette, J. R. Green and P. Wilson (eds.) 2014, 333–69.

Gregory, J. (1999), *Euripides: Hecuba* (Atlanta: Scholars Press).

Grene, D. and R. Lattimore, eds. (1957). *Sophocles II: Ajax, The Women of Trachis, Electra and Philoctetes* (Chicago: Chicago University Press).

Griffin, J. (1998), 'The Social Function of Attic Tragedy', *CQ* 48: 39–61.

Griffith, G. T. (1935), *The Mercenaries of the Hellenistic World* (Chicago: University of Chicago Press).

Griffith, M. W. (2001), 'Antigone and Her Sister(s): Embodying Women in Greek Tragedy', in A. Lardinois and L. McClure (eds.) 2001, 117–36.

Griffith, M. W. (2013), *Aristophanes' Frogs* (Oxford: Oxford University Press).

Griffiths, A., ed. (1995), *Stage Directions: Essays in Ancient Drama in Honour of E. W. Handley* (London: Institute of Classical Studies).

Gruber, M. A. (2009), *Der Chor in den Tragödien des Aischylos: Affekt und Reaktion* (Tübingen: Gunter Narr).

Gutzwiller, K. (2000), 'The Tragic Mask of Comedy: Metatheatricality in Menander', *ClAnt* 19: 102–37.

Hackworth, R. (1938), 'Aristophanes, *Clouds* 534–6', *Classical Review* 52: 5–7.

Hall, E. (1989), *Inventing the Barbarian: Greek Self-Definition through Tragedy* (Oxford: Clarendon Press).

Hall, E. (1996), 'Is there a *Polis* in Aristotle's *Poetics*?', in M. Silk (ed.) 1996, 295–309.

Hall, E. (2000), 'Female Figures and Metapoetry in Old Comedy', in D. Harvey and J. Wilkins (eds.) 2000, 407–18.

Hall, E. (2006), *The Theatrical Cast of Athens: Interactions between Ancient Greek Drama and Society* (New York: Oxford University Press).

Hall, E. (2007), 'Tragedy Personified', in C. Kraus, S. Goldhill, H. P. Foley and J. Elsner (eds.) 2007, 221–56.

Bibliography

Hall, E. (2010), *Greek Tragedy: Suffering Under the Sun* (Oxford: Oxford University Press).

Halliwell, S. (1980), 'Aristophanes' Apprenticeship', *CQ* 30.1: 33–45.

Halporn, J. W. (1983), 'The Skeptical Electra', *HSCPh* 87: 101–18.

Hamilton, R. (1975), 'Neoptolemus' Story in the *Philoctetes*', *AJP* 96: 131–7.

Hamstead, S. (2012), 'On Blurring Boundaries in Sophokles' *Trachiniae*', in D. Rosenbloom and J. Davidson (eds.), *Greek Drama IV: Texts, Contexts, Performance*, 204–24 (Oxford: Aris & Phillips).

Handley, E. (1965), 'Notes on the *Sikyonios* of Menander', *BICS* 12: 38–62.

Hanink, J. (2014a), 'Crossing Genres: Comedy, Tragedy, and Satyr Play', in M. Fontaine and A. Scafuro (eds.) 2014, 258–77.

Hanink, J. (2014b), *Lycurgan Athens and the Making of Classical Tragedy* (Cambridge: Cambridge University Press).

Hansen, M. H. and T. H. Nielsen, eds. (2004), *An Inventory of Archaic and Classical Poleis* (Oxford: Oxford University Press).

Harris, E. M. (2014), '"Yes" and "No" in Women's Desire', in M. Masterson, N. S. Rabinowitz and J. Robson (eds.) 2014, 298–314.

Harrison, A. R. W. (1968), *The Law of Athens: The Family and Property* (Oxford: Clarendon Press).

Harrison, J. E. (³1922 [1903]), *Prolegomena to the Study of Greek Religion* (Cambridge: Cambridge University Press).

Harvey, D. and J. Wilkins, eds. (2000), *The Rivals of Aristophanes: Studies in Athenian Old Comedy* (London: Duckworth and The Classical Press of Wales).

Headlam, W. (1901), 'Notes on Euripides, II', *CR* 15: 98–108.

Headlam, W. (1906), 'The Last Scene of the *Eumenides*', *JHS* 26: 268–77.

Heath, M. (2009), 'Should There Have Been a *Polis* in Aristotle's *Poetics*?', *CQ* 59: 468–85.

Hedreen, G. (2016), *The Image of the Artist in Archaic and Classical Greece: Art, Poetry, and Subjectivity* (New York: Cambridge University Press).

Heiden, B. (1989), *Tragic Rhetoric: An Interpretation of Sophocles' Trachiniae* (New York: P. Lang).

Henderson, J. (1987), *Aristophanes: Lysistrata* (Oxford: Oxford University Press).

Henderson, J. (1991), *The Maculate Muse: Obscene Language in Attic Comedy* (Oxford: Oxford University Press).

Henderson, J., ed. and trans. (1998), *Aristophanes*. Vol. II (Cambridge, MA: Harvard University Press).

Henderson, J., ed. and trans. (2007), *Aristophanes*. Vol. V. (Cambridge, MA: Harvard University Press).

Henrichs, A. (1993), 'The Tomb of Aias and the Prospect of Hero Cult in Sophokles', *CA* 12: 165–80.

Henrichs, A. (1996), 'Dancing in Athens, Dancing on Delos: Some Patterns of Choral Projection in Euripides', *Philologus* 140: 48–62.

Henrichs, A. (2004), '"Let the Good Prevail": Perversions of the Ritual Process in Greek Tragedy', in P. Roilos and D. Yatromanolakis (eds.), *Greek Ritual Poetics*, 189–98 (Washington DC and Athens: Centre for Hellenic Studies, Trustees for Harvard University, Washington DC and Foundation of the Hellenic World, Athens, Greece).

Herington, J. (1985), *Poetry into Drama. Early Tragedy and the Greek Poetic Tradition* (Berkeley: University of California Press).

Hesk, J. (2003), *Sophocles: Ajax* (London: Bloomsbury).

Heubeck, A., S. West, and J. B. Hainsworth (1988), *A Commentary on Homer's Odyssey. Vol. I* (Oxford: Clarendon Press). Italian ed., 1981–2.

Higbie, C. (1997), 'The Bones of a Hero, the Ashes of a Politician: Athens, Salamis, and the Usable Past', *CA* 16: 278–307.

Hinds, S. (1998), *Allusion and Intertext: Dynamics of Appropriation in Roman Poetry* (Cambridge: Cambridge University Press).

Holst-Warhaft, G. (1992), *Dangerous Voices: Women's Laments and Greek Literature* (London: Routledge).

Holt, P. (1992), 'Ajax' Burial in Early Greek Epic', *AJP* 113: 319–31.

Hopman, M. G. (2012), *Scylla: Myth, Metaphor, Paradox* (Cambridge: Cambridge University Press).

Hordern, J. H. (2004), *Sophron's Mimes: Text, Translation, and Commentary* (New York: Oxford University Press).

Hornblower, S. (2013), *Herodotus, Histories Book 5* (Cambridge: Cambridge University Press).

Hornblower, S. and C. Pelling (2017), *Herodotus, Histories Book 6* (Cambridge: Cambridge University Press).

Horsfall, N. (2008), *Virgil, Aeneid 2* (Leiden: Brill).

Hose, M. (1990/91) *Studien zum Chor bei Euripides.* 2 vols. Beiträge zur Altertumsjunde, Bd. 10, Bd. 20 (Stuttgart: Teubner).

Hourmouziades, N. (1965), *Production and Imagination in Euripides: Form and Function of the Scenic Space* (Athens: Greek Society for Humanistic Studies).

Hubbard, T. K. (1991), *The Mask of Comedy: Aristophanes and the Intertextual Parabasis* (Ithaca, NY: Cornell University Press).

Huddilston, J. H. (1899), 'An Archaeological Study of the *Antigone* of Euripides', *AJA* 3: 183–201.

Hugoniot, C., F. Hurlet, and S. Milanezi, eds. (2004), *Le statut de l'acteur dans l'Antiquité grecque et romaine* (Tours: Presses Universitaires François–Rabelais).

Humphreys, S. (1993), *The Family, Women and Death: Comparative Studies*, 2nd edn. (Ann Arbor: University of Michigan Press).

Hunter, R. (2009), *Critical Moments in Classical Literature: Studies in the Ancient View of Literature and Its Uses* (Cambridge: Cambridge University Press).

Huys, M. (1997), 'Euripides and "The Tales of Euripides": Sources of the *Fabulae* of Ps.-Hyginus?', *APF* 43.1: 11–30.

Immerwahr, H. R. (2008), 'Aspects of Literacy in the Athenian Ceramicus', *Kadmos* 46.1/2: 153–98.

Inglese, L. (1992), '*Antigone* di Euripide: La trama e l'occasione', *RCCM* 34.2: 175–90.

Inglese, L. (1998), 'Euripide, Fragment 159 N²', *RCCM* 40.1–2: 133–6.

Irwin, E. (2005), *Solon and Early Greek Poetry: The Politics of Exhortation* (Cambridge: Cambridge University Press).

Jacoby, F. (1950), *Die Fragmente Der griechischen Historiker* (Leiden: Brill).

Jauss, H. R. (1982) *Towards an Aesthetic of Reception.* T. Bahti (tr.) (Minneapolis: University of Minnesota Press).

Jebb, R. C. (1892), *Sophocles: The Plays and Fragments*, Part I: *The Oedipus Tyrannus* (Cambridge: Cambridge University Press).

Jenkins, I. (1983), 'Is There Life After Marriage? A Study of the Abduction Motif in Vase-Paintings of the Athenian Wedding Ceremony', *BICS* 30: 137–45.

Jennings, V. and A. Katsaros (2007a), 'Introduction', in V. Jennings and A. Katsaros (eds.) 2007, 1–14.

Jennings, V. and A. Katsaros, eds. (2007b), *The World of Ion of Chios. Mnemosyne* Supp. 288 (Leiden: Brill).

Jones, J. (1980), *On Aristotle and Greek Tragedy* (Stanford: Stanford University Press).

Jones, W. H. S. (1959), *Pausanias: Description of Greece* (Cambridge MA: Harvard University Press).

Jouan, F. (1970), 'Le *Prométhée* d'Eschyle et l'*Héraclès* d'Euripide', *REA* 72: 317–31.

Jouan, F. (1992), 'Dionysos chez Eschyle', *Kernos* 5: 71–86.

Jouan, F. and H. Van Looy, eds. (1998–2003), *Euripide: Tragédies VIII: Fragments.* 4 vols. (Paris: Les Belles Lettres).

Just, R. (1989), *Women in Athenian Life and Law* (London: Routledge).

K.-A. = Kassel, R. and C. Austin 1983 (*Poetae Comici Graeci.* 8 vols.).

Bibliography

Kaibel, G. (1888), 'Scenische Aufführungen in Rhodos', *Hermes* 23: 268–78.

Kaimio, M. (2002), 'Erotic Experience in the Conjugal Bed: Good Wives in Greek Tragedy', in M. Nussbaum and J. Sihvola (eds.) 2002, 95–119.

Kambitsis, J. (1972), *L'Antiope d'Euripide* (Athens: Éditions Élie Hourzamanis).

Kamerbeek, J. (1959), *The Plays of Sophocles II:* Trachiniae (Leiden: Brill).

Kampakoglou, A. and A. Novokhatko, eds. (2018), *Gaze, Vision, and Visuality in Ancient Greek Literature* (Berlin/Boston: de Gruyter).

Kampen, N., ed. (1996), *Sexuality in Ancient Art: Near East, Egypt, Greece, and Italy* (Cambridge: Cambridge University Press).

Kannicht, R. (1972), 'Euripides' *Phaethon*', ed. J. Diggle, *Gnomon* 44: 1–12.

Kannicht, R. (2004), *Tragicorum Graecorum Fragmenta. Vol. V.1–2: Euripides* (Göttingen: Vandenhoeck & Ruprecht).

Kannicht, R. and B. Snell (1981), *Tragicorum Graecorum Fragmenta. Vol. II: Fragmenta Adespota* (Göttingen: Vandenhoeck & Ruprecht).

Karamanou, I. (2017a), *Euripides' Alexandros: Introduction, Text and Commentary.* Texte und Kommentare 57 (Berlin: de Gruyter).

Karamanou, I. (2017b), 'Euripides' Reception of Sophocles' *Antigone*', in D. Stuttard (ed.) 2017, 133–43.

Karanika, A. (2001), 'Memories of Poetic Discourse in Athena's Cult Practice', in S. Deacy and A. Villing (eds.) 2001, 277–91.

Kassel, R. and C. Austin (1983), *Poetae Comici Graeci.* 8 vols. (Berlin and New York: de Gruyter) [=K.-A.].

Katz, M. A. (1992), 'Ideology and "The Status of Women"', *History and Theory* 31: 70–97.

Kearns, E. (1989), *The Heroes of Attica. BICS* Supplement 57 (London: Institute of Classical Studies).

Kells, J. H. (1973), *Sophocles: Electra* (Cambridge: Cambridge University Press).

Kennedy, R. F., ed. (2017), *Brill's Companion to the Reception of Aeschylus.* (Leiden: Brill).

Kirk, G. S. (1990), *The Iliad: A Commentary. Vol. II* (Cambridge: Cambridge University Press).

Kitto, H. D. F. (1956), *Form and Meaning in Drama: A Study of Six Greek Plays and of Hamlet* (London: Methuen).

Kitto, H. D. F. (1961), *Greek Tragedy* (London: Methuen).

Klimek-Winter, R. (1993), *Andromedatragödien: Sophokles – Euripides – Livius – Andronikus Ennius – Accius. Text, Einleitung und Kommentar* (Stuttgart: Teubner).

Knox, B. (1979), *Word and Action. Essays on the Ancient Theater* (Baltimore: Johns Hopkins University Press).

Knox B. (1983), 'Sophocles and the *Polis*', in J. de Romilly (ed.), *Sophocle, Entretiens sur l'Antiquité Classique,* 29, 1–27 (Vandoeuvres-Genève: Fondation Hardt).

Konstan, D. (1999), 'The Tragic Emotions', in L. R. Gámez (ed.) 1999, 1–21.

Konstan, D. (2001), *Pity Transformed* (London: Duckworth).

Konstan, D. (2006), *The Emotions of the Ancient Greeks: Studies in Aristotle and Classical Literature* (Toronto: University of Toronto Press).

Konstantakos, I. M. (2011), 'Ephippos' *Geryones*: A Comedy between Myth and Folktale', *Acta Antiqua Academiae Scientarum Hungaricae* 51: 223–46.

Kopff, E. C. (1990), 'The Date of Aristophanes, *Nubes* II', *AJP* 111: 318–29.

Kourinou, E. (2000), *Σπάρτη. Συμβολή στὴν μνημειακὴ τοπογραφίας της* (Athens: Μεγάλη Βιβλιοθήκη).

Kourinou-Pikoula, E. (1992–8), 'Μνᾶμα γεροντείας', *Horos* 10–12: 259–76.

Kovacs, D. (1987), *The Heroic Muse: Studies in the Hippolytus and Hecuba of Euripides* (Baltimore: Johns Hopkins University Press).

Kovacs, D. (1989), 'Euripides, *Electra* 518–44: Further Doubts about Genuineness', *BICS* 36: 67–78.

Kovacs, D. (1994), *Euripides: Cyclops, Alcestis, Medea* (Cambridge, MA: Harvard University Press).

Kovacs, D. (1995), *Euripides: Children of Heracles, Hippolytus, Andromache, Hecuba* (Cambridge, MA: Harvard University Press).

Kovacs, D. (1997), 'Gods and Men in Euripides' Trojan Trilogy', *Colby Quarterly* 33: 162–76.

Kovacs, D. (2018), *Euripides: Troades* (Oxford: Oxford University Press).

Kowalzig, B. (2006), 'The Aetiology of Empire? Hero-Cult and Athenian Tragedy', in Davidson et al. (eds.) (2006), 79–98.

Kozak, L. and J. Rich, eds. (2006), *Playing Around Aristophanes* (Oxford: Aris & Phillips).

Kraus, C., S. Goldhill, H. P. Foley and J. Elsner, eds. (2007), *Visualizing the Tragic: Drama, Myth, and Ritual in Greek Art and Literature* (Oxford: Oxford University Press).

Kron, U., (1976), *Die Zehn Attischen Phylenheroen: Geschichte, Mythos, Kult und Darstellungen* (Berlin: Gebr Mann).

Krummen, E. (1998), 'Ritual und Katastophe: Rituelle Handlung und Bildersprache bei Sophokles und Euripides', in Graf (ed.) 1998, 296–325.

Labiano Illundain, J.M. (2004), 'Breves notas sobre el sufijo –ikós en la comedia aristofánica', in A. López Eire and A. Ramos Guerreira (eds.) 2004, 87–101.

Lacey, W. K. (1968), *The Family in Classical Greece* (London: Thames and Hudson).

LaCourse Munteanu, D. (2011), *Tragic Pathos: Pity and Fear in Greek Philosophy and Tragedy* (Cambridge: Cambridge University Press).

Laird, A., ed. (2006), *Ancient Literary Criticism* (Oxford: Oxford University Press).

Lamari, A. A. (2010), *Narrative, Intertext, and Space in Euripides'* Phoenissae (Berlin and Boston: de Gruyter).

Lamari, A. A., ed. (2015), *Reperformances of Drama in the Fifth and Fourth Centuries BC: Authors and Contexts* (Berlin and Boston: de Gruyter).

Lamari, A. A. (2017), *Reperforming Greek Tragedy: Theater, Politics, and Cultural Mobility in the Fifth and Fourth Centuries BC. Trends in Classics, Supplementary Vol. LII* (Berlin and Boston: de Gruyter).

Lambert, S. (2012), *Inscribed Athenian Laws and Decrees 352/1–322/1 BC: Epigraphical Essays* (Leiden: Brill).

Lammers, J. (1931), *Die Doppel- und Halbchore in der antiken Tragoödie* (Paderborn: Schöningh).

Lanza, D. (1963), 'L'*Alessandro* e il valore del doppio coro Euripideo', *SIFC* 34: 230–45.

Lape, S. (2004), *Reproducing Athens* (Princeton: Princeton University Press).

Lape, S. (2010), 'Gender in Menander's Comedies', in A. K. Petrides and S. Papaioannou (eds.) 2010, 51–78.

Lardinois, A. (1992), 'Greek Myths for Athenian Rituals: Religion and Politics in Aeschylus' *Eumenides* and Sophocles' *Oedipus Coloneus*', *GRBS* 33.4: 313–27.

Lardinois, A. and L. McClure, eds. (2001), *Making Silence Speak: Women's Voices in Greek Literature and Society* (Princeton: Princeton University Press).

Lauriola, R. (2009), 'The Greeks and the Utopia: An Overview through Ancient Greek Literature', *Revista Espaço Acadêmico* 97: 109–24.

Le Guen, B. (2014), 'Theatre, Religion, and Politics at Alexander's Travelling Royal Court', in E. Csapo, H. R. Goette, J. R. Green and P. Wilson (eds.) 2014, 249–74.

Lebeck, A. (1971), *The Oresteia. A Study in Language and Structure* (Cambridge MA: Harvard University Press).

Lee, K. H. (1976), *Euripides: Troades* (Basingstoke: MacMillan). Reprinted, 1997.

Leitao, D. (2012), *The Pregnant Male as Myth and Metaphor in Classical Greek Literature* (Cambridge: Cambridge University Press).

LeVen, P. A. (2014), *The Many-Headed Muse: Tradition and Innovation in Late Classical Greek Lyric Poetry* (Cambridge: Cambridge University Press).

Lévêque, P. (1955), *Agathon* (Paris: Les Belles Lettres).

Lewis, J. (2006), *Solon the Thinker: Political Thought in Archaic Athens* (London: Duckworth).

Bibliography

Liapis, V. (2014), 'The Fragments of Euripides' *Oedipus*: A Reconsideration', *TAPA* 144: 307–70.

LIMC = (1981), *Lexicon Iconographicum Mythologiae Classicae* (Zurich: Artemis).

Lloyd, M. (1986), 'Realism and Character in Euripides' *Electra*', *Phoenix* 40: 1–19.

Lloyd-Jones, H. (1961), 'Some Alleged Interpolations in Aeschylus' *Choephori* and Euripides' *Electra*', *CQ* 11: 171–84.

Lloyd-Jones, H. (1966), 'Menander's *Sikyonios*', *GRBS* 7: 131–57.

Long, A. A. (1968), *Language and Thought in Sophocles: A Study of Abstract Nouns and Poetic Technique* (London: Athlone Press).

López Eire, A. and A. Ramos Guerreira, eds. (2004), *Registros lingüísticos en la lenguas clásicas* (Salamanca: Classica Salmanticensia III. Ediciones Universidad de Salamanca).

Loraux, N. (1986), *The Invention of Athens*, tr. A. Sheridan (Cambridge, MA: Harvard University Press).

Loraux, N. (1991), *Tragic Ways of Killing a Woman*, tr. A. Forster (Cambridge, MA: Harvard University Press).

LSJ = Liddell, H. G., R. Scott, H. S. Jones and R. McKenzie (1996), *A Greek–English Lexicon*, 9th ed. (Oxford: Oxford University Press).

Lucas, H. (1937), 'Der Prolog der *Antigone* des Euripides', *Hermes* 72: 239–40.

Lulli, L. (2016), 'Elegy and Epic: A Complex Relationship', in L. Swift and C. Carey (eds.) 2016, 193–209.

Ma, J. (2004), 'You Can't Go Home Again: Displacement and Identity in Xenophon's *Anabasis*', in R. L. Fox (ed.) 2004, 30–45.

Maas, P. (1920), 'Wer singt bei Euripides *Hippol.* 58ff., 1102ff.?', *Sokrates* 8: 305.

MacCary, W. T. (1970), 'Menander's Characters: Their Names, Roles, Masks', *TAPA* 101: 277–90.

MacCary, W. T. (1972), 'Menander's Soldiers: Their Names, Roles, and Masks', *AJP* 93: 279–98.

MacDowell, D. M. (1990), 'The Meaning of ἀλαζών', in E. Craik (ed.) 1990, 287–92.

Macintosh, F., P. Michelakis, E. Hall and O. Taplin, eds. (2005), *Agamemnon in Performance 458 BC to AD 2004* (Oxford: Oxford University Press).

MacLachlan, B. (1993), *The Age of Grace: Charis in Early Greek Poetry* (Princeton: Princeton University Press).

Macleod, L. (2006), 'Marauding Maenads: The First Messenger Speech in the *Bacchae*', *Mnemosyne* 59: 578–84.

Major, W. E. (1997), 'Menander in a Macedonian World', *GRBS* 38: 41–74.

Major, W. E. (2006), 'Aristophanes and *Alazoneia*: Laughing at the Parabasis of the *Clouds*', *CW* 99: 131–44.

Major, W. E. (2013), 'Staging *Andromeda* in Aristophanes and Euripides', *CJ* 108.4: 385–403.

Mannack, T. (2001), *The Late Mannerists in Athenian Vase-Painting* (Oxford: Oxford University Press).

Mansfield, J. M. (1985), *The Robe of Athena and the Panathenaic Peplos* (PhD Diss.: University of California, Berkeley).

Mansfield N. (2000), *Subjectivity: Theories of the Self from Freud to Haraway* (New York: New York University Press).

Manuwald, G. (2004), 'Die ungleichen Schwestern in Plautus' *Poenulus*', in T. Bair (ed.) 2004, 215–33.

March, J. (1989), 'Euripides' *Bacchai*: A Reconsideration in the Light of the Vase Paintings', *BICS* 36: 33–65.

Marshall, C. W. (1996) 'Literary Awareness in Euripides and His Audience', in I. Worthington (ed.) 1996, 81–98.

Marshall, C. W. (1999/2000), 'Theatrical Reference in Euripides' *Electra*', *ICS* 24/25: 325–41.

Marshall, C. W. (2001), 'The Next Time Agamemnon Died', *CW* 95: 59–63.

Marshall, C. W. (2014), *The Structure and Performance of Euripides*' Helen (Cambridge: Cambridge University Press).

Marshall, C. W. (2015), 'Death and the Maiden: Human Sacrifice in Euripides' *Andromeda*', in V. D. Arbel, P. C. Burns, J. R. C. Cousland, R. Menkis and D. Neufeld (eds.) 2015, 131–7.

Marshall, C. W. and G. Kovacs, eds. (2012), *No Laughing Matter: Studies in Athenian Comedy* (London: Bristol Classical Press).

Marshall, H. R. (2012), '*Clouds*, Eupolis and Reperformance', in C. W. Marshall and G. Kovacs (eds.) 2012, 55–68.

Marshall, P. K. (1993), *Hyginus Fabulae* (Stuttgart: Teubner).

Martin, R. (1951), *Recherches sur l'agora grecque* (Paris: de Boccard).

Martina, A. (2016a), *Menandrea: Elementi e struttura della commedia di Menandro. Vol. II* (Pisa: Fabrizio Serra Editore).

Martina, A. (2016b), *Menandrea: Elementi e struttura della commedia di Menandro. Vol. III* (Pisa: Fabrizio Serra Editore).

Martindale, C. (1993), *Redeeming the Text: Latin Poetry and the Hermeneutics of Reception* (Cambridge: Cambridge University Press).

Masterson, M., N. S. Rabinowitz and J. Robson, eds. (2014), *Sex in Antiquity: Exploring Gender and Sexuality in the Ancient World* (London: Routledge).

Mastromarco, G. (2008), 'La parodia dell'*Andromeda* euripidea nelle *Tesmoforiazuse* di Aristofane', *CFC* 18: 177–88.

Mastronarde, D. J. (1994), *Euripides: Phoenissae* (Cambridge: Cambridge University Press).

Mastronarde, D. J. (1999–2000), 'Euripidean Tragedy and Genre: the Terminology and its Problems', in M. Cropp, K. Lee and D. Sansone (eds.) 1999–2000, 23–39.

Mastronarde, D. J. (2002), *Euripides: Medea* (Cambridge: Cambridge University Press).

Mastronarde, D. J. (2010), *The Art of Euripides: Dramatic Technique and Social Context* (Cambridge: Cambridge University Press).

Matheson, S. B. (1997), 'Hounded by Furies', *Yale University Art Gallery Bulletin*, 18–29.

Matthen, M. (2015), *The Oxford Handbook of the Philosophy of Perception* (Oxford: Oxford University Press).

Matthiessen, K. (2010), *Euripides, 'Hekabe'* (Berlin and New York: de Gruyter).

Maxwell-Stuart, P. G. (1973), 'The Appearance of Aeschylus' Erinyes', *G&R* 20.1: 81–4.

McCall, M. (1976), 'The Secondary Choruses in Aeschylus' *Supplices*', *CSCA* 9: 117–31.

McClure, L. (1999), *Spoken Like a Woman: Speech and Gender in Athenian Drama* (Princeton: Princeton University Press).

McClure, L., ed. (2017), *A Companion to Euripides* (Malden, MA: Wiley-Blackwell).

McHardy, F., J. Robson and D. Harvey, eds. (2005), *Lost Dramas of Classical Athens* (Exeter: University of Exeter Press).

Meier, C. (1988), *The Political Art of Greek Tragedy* (Baltimore: Johns Hopkins University Press).

Meineck, P., tr. (2000), *Aristophanes: Clouds* (Indianapolis and Cambridge, MA: Hackett).

Meineck, P. (2012), 'Combat Trauma and the Tragic Stage: 'Restoration' by Cultural Catharsis', *Intertexts* 16: 7–24.

Meineck, P., tr. (2014), *Sophocles. Philoctetes* (Indianapolis and Cambridge, MA: Hackett).

Meineck, P. (2016), 'Combat Trauma and the Tragic Stage: Ancient Culture and Modern Catharsis?' in V. Caston, S.-M. Weineck (eds.) 2016, 184–208.

Meineck, P. and D. Konstan, eds. (2014), *Combat Trauma and the Ancient Greeks* (New York: Macmillan).

Meineke, A. (1856), *Ioannis Stobaei Florilegium* (Leipzig: Teubner).

Meli, G., ed. (2007), *Teatri antichi nell'area del Mediterraneo: Atti del II convegno internazionale di studi la materia e i segni della storia Siracusa 13–17 ottobre 2004* (Palermo: Regione Siciliana, Assessorato dei beni culturali, ambientali e della pubblica istruzione, Dipartimento beni culturali ed ambientali ed educazione permanente).

Mesk, J. (1931), 'Die *Antigone* des Euripides', *WS* 49: 1–12.

Bibliography

Michelini, A. N. (1987), *Euripides and the Tragic Tradition* (Madison, WI: University of Wisconsin Press).

Moloney, E. (2014), '*Philippus in acie tutior quam in theatro fuit* . . . (Curtius 9.6.24): The Macedonian Kings and Greek Theatre', in E. Csapo, H. R. Goette, J. R. Green and P. Wilson (eds.) 2014, 231–48.

Moreau, A. (1994/5), 'Les Danaïdes de Mélanippidès: La Femme Virile', *CGITA* 8: 119–51.

Moretti, J.-C. (2014), 'The Evolution of Theatre Architecture Outside Athens in the Fourth Century', in E. Csapo, H. R. Goette, J. R. Green and P. Wilson (eds.) 2014, 107–37.

Moretti, L. (1960), 'Sulle didascalie del teatro attico rinvenute a Roma', *Athenaeum* 38: 263–82.

Morwood, J. (2001), *Oxford Grammar of Classical Greek* (Oxford: Oxford University Press).

Mossman, J. (1995), *Wild Justice: A Study of Euripides'* Hecuba (Oxford: Oxford University Press).

Mossman, J. (2001), 'Women's Speech in Greek Tragedy: The Case of Electra and Clytemnestra in Euripides' *Electra*', *CQ* 51: 374–84.

Most, G. W. (2006), *Hesiod: Theogony, Works and Days, Testimonia* (Cambridge, MA: Harvard University Press).

Mueller, M. (2016), *Objects as Actors: Props and the Poetics of Performance in Greek Tragedy* (Chicago: University of Chicago Press).

Müller, E. (1907), 'Die *Andromeda* des Euripides', *Philologus* 66: 48–66.

Murnaghan, S. (2017), 'The Euripidean Chorus', in L. McClure (ed.) 2017, 412–27.

Murray, A. T. (1999), *Homer: Iliad* (Cambridge MA: Harvard University Press).

Murray, O., ed. (1990), *Sympotica. A Symposium on the Symposion* (Oxford: Clarendon Press).

Muth, R., ed. (1962), *Serta Philologica Aenipontana* (Innsbruck: Institut fuir vergleichende Sprachwissenschaft).

Mylonas, G. E., ed. (1987), *ΦΙΛΙΑ ΕΠΗ ΕΙΣ ΓΕΩΡΓΙΟΝ Ε. ΜΥΛΩΝΑΝ. Vol. II* (Athens: Athenais Arhaiologike Hetaireia).

Nagy, G. (2013), 'The Delian Maidens and their Relevance to Choral Mimesis in Classical Drama', in R. Gagné and M. G. Hopman (eds.) 2013, 227–56.

Nauck, A. (1889), *Tragicorum Graecorum Fragmenta*, 2nd ed. (Leipzig: Teubner).

Neils, J. (1996a), 'Pride, Pomp, and Circumstance: The Iconography of Procession', in J. Neils (ed.) 1996, 177–97.

Neils, J., ed. (1996b), *Worshipping Athena: Panathenaia and Parthenon* (Madison WI: University of Wisconsin Press).

Neitzel, H. (1967), *Die dramatische Funktion der Chorlieder in den Tragödien des Euripides* (PhD Diss.: University of Hamburg).

Nelson, S. (2016), *Aristophanes and his Tragic Muse: Comedy, Tragedy and The Polis in 5th Century Athens* (Leiden: Brill).

Nervegna, S. (2013), *Menander in Antiquity: The Contexts of Reception* (Cambridge: Cambridge University Press).

Neumann, E. (1954), *The Origins and History of Consciousness* (New York: Bollingen Foundation, Inc.).

Newiger, H.-J. (1961), 'Elektra in Aristophanes' *Wolken*', *Hermes* 89: 422–30.

Nielsen, T. H., ed. (2002), *Even More Studies in the Ancient Greek Polis. Papers from the Copenhagen Polis Centre 6* (Stuttgart: Franz Steiner).

Nisetich, F. J. (1989), *Pindar and Homer* (Baltimore: Johns Hopkins University Press).

Nobili, C. (2016), 'Choral Elegy: The Tyranny of the Handbook', in L. Swift and C. Carey (eds.) 2016, 33–55.

Nocita, M. (2013), 'Qualche nota epigrafica su Roma: didascalie sceniche del Campo Marzio', *Mediterraneo Antico* 16: 597–608.

Nünlist, R. (1998), *Poetologische Bildersprache in der frühgriechischen Dichtung* (Stuttgart and Leipzig: Teubner).

Nünlist, R. (2004), 'Menander', in R. Nünlist, A. M. Bowie and I. De Jong (eds.) 2004, 297–305.

Nünlist, R., A. M. Bowie and I. De Jong, eds. (2004), *Narrators, Narratees, and Narratives in Ancient Greek Literature: Studies in Ancient Greek Narrative. Mnemosyne* Supp. 257 (Leiden: Brill).

Nussbaum, M. C. (2001), *The Fragility of Goodness: Luck and Ethics in Greek Tragedy and Philosophy*, rev. ed. (Cambridge: Cambridge University Press).

Nussbaum, M. and J. Sihvola, eds. (2002), *The Sleep of Reason: Erotic Experience and Sexual Ethics in Ancient Greece and Rome* (Chicago: The University of Chicago Press).

Oakley, J. and R. Sinos (2002), *The Wedding in Ancient Athens* (Madison, WI: University of Wisconsin Press).

Obbink, D. (2006), 'A New Archilochus Poem,' *ZPE* 156: 1–9.

Ogden, D. (2008), *Perseus* (London and New York: Routledge).

Olson, S. D. (1998), *Aristophanes: Peace* (Oxford: Oxford University Press).

Olson, S. D. (2002), *Aristophanes: Acharnians* (Oxford: Oxford University Press).

Olson, S. D. (2007), *Broken Laughter: Select Fragments of Greek Comedy* (Oxford: Oxford University Press).

Olson, S. D. (2015), 'On the Fragments of Eupolis' *Taxiarchoi*', in M. Taufer (ed.) 2015, 201–14.

Olson, S. D. (2016), *Eupolis. Heilotes – Chrysoun genos (frr. 147–325)* (Heidelberg: Verlag Antike).

Olson, S. D. (2017), *Eupolis, Testimonia and Auges – Demoi (frr. 1–146)* (Heidelberg: Verlag Antike).

Ormand, K. (1999), *Exchange and the Maiden: Marriage in Sophoclean Tragedy* (Austin: University of Texas Press).

Ormand, K., ed. (2012), *A Companion to Sophocles* (Malden, MA: Wiley-Blackwell).

Orth, C. (2009), *Strattis. Die Fragmente* (Berlin: Verlag Antike).

Orth, C. (2013), *Alkaios – Apollophanes. Einleitung, Übersetzung, Kommentar* (Heidelberg: Verlag Antike).

Orth, C. (2017), *Aristophanes. Aiolosikon – Babylonioi (fr. 1–100). Übersetzung und Kommentar* (Heidelberg: Verlag Antike).

Osborne, R. (1996), 'Desiring Women on Athenian Pottery', in N. Kampen (ed.) 1996, 65–80.

Osborne, R. and S. Hornblower, eds. (1994), *Ritual, Finance, Politics: Athenian Democratic Accounts Presented to David Lewis* (Oxford: Oxford University Press).

Owens, W. M. (2011), 'The Political Topicality of Menander's *Dyskolos*', *AJP* 132: 349–78.

Padel, R. (1990), 'Making Space Speak', in J. J. Winkler and F. I. Zeitlin (eds.) 1990, 336–65.

Pagano, V. (2010), *L'Andromeda di Euripide: edizione e commento dei frammenti* (Alessandria: Edizioni dell'Orso).

Page, D. (1972), *Aeschylus. Septem quae supersunt tragoediae* (Oxford: Clarendon Press).

Pagliaro, A. (1963), 'Il proemio dell'Iliade', in *Nuovi saggi di critica semantica* (Messina-Florence: G. d'Anna), 3–46.

Panagl, O. (1972), 'Zur Funktion der direkten Reden in den "dithyrambischen Stasima" des Euripides', *WS* 6: 5–18.

Papadimitropoulos, L. (2008), 'Causality and Innovation in Euripides' *Electra*', *RhM* 151: 113–26.

Papadopoulou, T. (2001), 'Representations of Athena in Greek Tragedy', in S. Deacy and A. Villing (eds.) 2001, 293–310.

Papastamati, S. (2017), 'The Poetics of *Kalos Thanatos* in Euripides' *Hecuba*: Masculine and Feminine Motifs in Polyxena's Death', *Mnemosyne* 70: 361–85.

Papazoglou, E. (2014), *Το πρόσωπο του πένθους: Η Ηλέκτρα του Σοφοκλή ανάμεσα στο κείμενο και την παράσταση* (Athens: Polis).

Papazoglou, E. (2019), 'Mechanisms of Female Exclusion: Women Between Ritual and Emotion' in T. Tsakiropoulou-Summers and K. Kitsi (eds.), *Women and the Ideology of Political Exclusion: From Classical Antiquity to the Modern Era*, 13245 (London: Routledge).

Park, A. (2017) 'Reality, Allusion, or Both? Cloud-women in Stesichorus and Pindar', in Arum Park (ed.), *Resemblance and Reality in Greek Thought: Essays in Honor of Peter M. Smith* (London: Routledge) 65–79.

Bibliography

Parke, H. W. (1977), *Festivals of the Athenians* (London: Thames & Hudson).

Parker, R. (1994), 'Athenian Religion Abroad', in R. Osborne and S. Hornblower (eds.) 1994, 339–46.

Parker, R. (1996), *Athenian Religion: A History* (Oxford: Oxford University Press).

Parker, R. (2007), *Polytheism and Society at Athens* (Oxford: Oxford University Press).

Paton, J. M. (1901), 'The *Antigone* of Euripides', *HSCPh* 12: 267–76.

Paton, W. R. (2010), *Polybius The Histories I Books 1–2*, rev. F. W. Walbank and C. Habicht (Cambridge MA: Harvard University Press).

Pedrick, V. and S. M. Oberhelman, eds. (2005), *The Soul of Tragedy: Essays on Athenian Drama* (Chicago: University of Chicago Press).

Pelling, C. B. R., ed. (1990), *Characterization and Individuality in Greek Literature* (Oxford: Oxford University Press).

Pelling, C. B. R. (1997a), 'Conclusion: Tragedy as Evidence, Tragedy and Ideology', in C. Pelling (ed.) 1997b, 213–35.

Pelling, C. B. R., ed. (1997b), *Greek Tragedy and the Historian* (Oxford: Oxford University Press).

Pepe, C. and G. Moretti, eds. (2015), *Le Parole dopo la Morte: Forme e funzioni della retorica funeraria nella tradizione greca e romana* (Trento: Università degli Studi di Trento).

Perris, S. (2011), 'Perspectives on Violence in Euripides' *Bacchae*', *Mnemosyne* 64: 37–57.

Perrone, S. (2019), *Cratete. Introduzione, traduzione e comment* (Göttingen: Vandenhoeck & Ruprecht).

Perusino, F. and M. Colantonio, eds. (2007), *Dalla lirica corale alla poesia drammatica: forme e funzioni del canto corale nella tragedia e nella commedia greca* (Pisa: Edizioni ETS).

Petersen, E. (1904), 'Andromeda', *JHS* 24: 99–112.

Petersmann, H. (1978), 'Mythos und Gestaltung in Sophokles' *Antigone*', *WS* 12: 67–96.

Petrides, A. K. (2014), *Menander, New Comedy and the Visual* (Cambridge: Cambridge University Press).

Petrides, A. K. and S. Papaioannou, eds. (2010), *New Perspectives on Postclassical Comedy. Pierides 2* (Newcastle upon Tyne: Cambridge Scholars Publishing).

Petrovic, A. (2013), 'An Epigram and a Treasury: On Sim. FGE Xxxiiib', *CQ* 63.2: 885–8.

Philippart, H. (1930), 'Iconographie des "Bacchantes" d'Euripide', *RBPh* 9: 5–72.

Phillips, K. M. (1968), 'Perseus and Andromeda', *AJA* 72: 1–23.

Phillips, T. (2015), 'Echo in Euripides' *Andromeda*', *Greek and Roman Musical Studies* 3: 53–66.

Pickard-Cambridge, A. W. (1988), *The Dramatic Festivals of Athens*, 2nd ed., rev. with a new supplement by J. Gould and D. M. Lewis (Oxford: Clarendon Press).

Platter, C. (2007), *Aristophanes and the Carnival of Genres* (Baltimore: Johns Hopkins University Press).

Podlecki, A. J. (1989), *Aeschylus: Eumenides* (Warminster: Aris & Phillips).

Podlecki, A. J. (2009), 'Echoes of the *Prometheia* in Euripides' *Andromeda*?', in J. R. C. Cousland and J. R. Hume (eds.) 2009, 77–91.

Pöhlmann, E., ed. (1995), *Studien zur Bühnendichtung und zum Theaterbau der Antike* (Frankfurt: Peter Lang).

Poilloux, J., N. M. Kontoleon, A. Scherer, D. Page, K. J. Dover, W. Bühler, E. K. H. Wistrand, B. Snell, O. Reverdin and M. Treu, (eds.) 1964, *Archiloque: sept exposés et discussions* (Geneva: Fondation Hardt).

Poli Palladini, L. (2013), *Aeschylus at Gela: An Integrated Approach* (Alessandria: Edizioni dell'Orso).

Porter, J. R. (1990), 'Tiptoeing through the Corpses: Euripides' *Electra*, Apollonius, and the *Bouphonia*', *GRBS* 31: 255–80.

Powell, A., ed. (1990), *Euripides, Women and Sexuality* (London: Routledge).

Prag, A. J. N. W. (1985), *The Oresteia: Iconographic and Narrative Tradition* (Chicago: Bolchazy-Carducci).

Prauscello, L. (2006), *Singing Alexandria: Music between Practice and Textual Transmission* (Leiden: Brill).

Preston, S. D. and de Waal, F. B. M. (2002), 'Empathy: Its Ultimate and Proximate Bases', *Behavioral and Brain Sciences* 25.1: 1–72.

Pritchett, W. K. (1987), 'The ΠΑΝΝΥΧΙΣ of the Panathenaia', in G. E. Mylonas (ed.) 1987, 179–88.

Raaflaub, K. (2014), 'War and the City: The Brutality of War and Its Impact on the Community', in P. Meineck and D. Konstan (eds.) 2014, 15–46.

Rabinowitz, N. S. (1993), *Anxiety Veiled: Euripides and the Traffic in Women* (Ithaca NY: Cornell University Press).

Rabinowitz, N. S. (2013), 'Woman as the Subject and Object of the Gaze in Tragedy', *Helios* 40.1–2: 195–221.

Rabinowitz, N. S. (2017), 'Trojan Women', in L. McClure (ed.) 2017, 199–213.

Race, W. H. (1997), *Pindar: Nemean Odes, Isthmian Odes, Fragments* (Cambridge, MA: Harvard University Press).

Race, W. (2014), 'Phaeacian Therapy in Homer's *Odyssey*', in P. Meineck and D. Konstan (eds.) 2014, 47–66.

Radding, J. (2015), 'Clytemnestra at Aulis: Euripides and the Reconsideration of Tradition', *GRBS* 55.4: 832–62.

Radt, S. (1977), *Tragicorum Graecorum Fragmenta. Vol. IV: Sophocles* (Göttingen: Vandenhoeck & Ruprecht).

Radt, S. (1985), *Tragicorum Graecorum Fragmenta. Vol. III: Aeschylus* (Göttingen: Vandenhoeck & Ruprecht).

Rau, P. (1967), *Paratragodia: Untersuchung einer komischen Form des Aristophanes* (Munich: Beck).

Reckford, K. J. (1985), 'Concepts of Demoralization in the *Hecuba*', in P. Burian (ed.) 1985, 112–28.

Redfield, J. M. (1979), 'The Proem of the *Iliad*: Homer's Art', *CP* 74: 95–110.

Rehm, R. (1994), *Marriage to Death: The Conflation of Wedding and Funeral Rituals in Greek Tragedy* (Princeton: Princeton University Press).

Rehm, R. (2002), *The Play of Space: Spatial Transformation in in Athenian Tragedy* (Princeton: Princeton University Press).

Reid, H., D. Tanasi and S. Kimbell, eds. (2017), *Politics and Performance in Western Greece: Proceedings of the Second Interdisciplinary Symposium on the Heritage of Western Greece* (Sioux City: Parnassos Press).

Revermann, M. (2006), *Comic Business: Theatricality, Dramatic Technique, and Performance Contexts of Aristophanic Comedy* (Oxford: Oxford University Press).

Revermann, M., ed. (2014), *The Cambridge Companion to Greek Comedy* (Cambridge: Cambridge University Press).

Revermann, M. and P. Wilson, eds. (2008), *Performance, Iconography, Reception: Studies in Honour of Oliver Taplin* (Oxford: Oxford University Press).

Rhodes, P. J. (2003), 'Nothing to Do with Democracy: Athenian Drama and the *Polis*', *JHS* 123: 104–19.

Rhodes, P. J. (2010), *A History of the Classical Greek World 478–323 BC*, 2nd edn. (Chichester: Wiley-Blackwell).

Rhodes, P. J. and R. Osborne (2003), *Greek Historical Inscriptions: 404–323 BC* (Oxford: Oxford University Press).

Richter, G. M. A. (1946), *Attic Red-Figured Vases: A Survey* (New Haven: Yale University Press).

Ringer, M. (1998), *Electra and the Empty Urn: Metatheater and Role Playing in Sophocles* (Chapel Hill: The University of North Carolina Press).

Ritchie, W. (1964), *The Authenticity of the Rhesus of Euripides* (Cambridge: Cambridge University Press).

Bibliography

Robert, C. (1878), 'Maskengruppen. Wandgemälde in Pompeji', *Archäologische Zeitung* 36: 13–24.

Robert, C. (1915), *Oidipus. Geschichte eines Poetischen Stoffs im griechischen Altertum* (Berlin: Weidmann).

Roberts, D. (1993), 'The Frustrated Mourner: Strategies of Closure in Greek Tragedy', in R. M. Rosen and J. Farrell (eds.) 1993, 573–89.

Robinson, E. W. (2011), *Democracy Beyond Athens* (Cambridge: Cambridge University Press).

Rogers, B. M. (2005), *Before Paideia: Representations of Education in Aeschylean Tragedy* (PhD diss.: Stanford University).

Rogers, B. M. (2013), 'Why *Didaskalia*?: The Language of Production in (and its Many Meanings for) Greek Drama', *Didaskalia* 10.62–9. http://didaskalia.net/issues/10/12/ (accessed 19 September 2019)

Roisman, H. M. (1997), 'The Appropriation of a Son: Sophocles' *Philoctetes*', *GRBS* 38: 127–71.

Roisman, H. M., ed. (2013), *The Encyclopedia of Greek Tragedy. Vol. III* (Malden MA: Wiley-Blackwell).

Roisman, J. (1997), 'Contemporary Allusions in Euripides' *Trojan Women*', *SIFC* 15: 38–46.

Roscher, W. H., ed. (1884), *Ausführliches Lexikon Der Griechischen Und Römischen Mythologie* (Leipzig: Teubner).

Rose, H. J. (1925), 'The Bride of Hades', *Classical Philology* 20.3: 238–42.

Rose, H. J. (1958), *A Commentary on the Surviving Plays of Aeschylus*. 2 vols. (Amsterdam: Noord-Hollandsche Uitgivers Maatschappij).

Rosen, R. M. (2000), 'Cratinus' *Pytine* and the Construction of the Comic Self', in D. Harvey and J. Wilkins (eds.) 2000, 23–39.

Rosen, R. M. (2006), 'Aristophanes, Fandom and the Classicizing of Greek Tragedy', in L. Kozak and J. Rich (eds.), 2006, 27–47.

Rosen, R. M. and J. Farrell, eds. (1993), *Nomodeiktes: Greek Studies in Honor of Martin Ostwald* (Ann Arbor: University of Michigan Press).

Rosenbloom, D. (2006), 'Empire and its Discontents: *Trojan Women, Birds*, and The Symbolic Economy of Athenian Imperialism', in J. Davidson, F. Muecke and P. Wilson (eds.) 2006, 245–71.

Rosenbloom, D. (2011), 'The Panhellenism of Athenian Tragedy', in D. M. Carter (ed.) 2011, 353–81.

Rosenbloom, D. (2012), 'Athenian Drama and Democratic Political Culture', in D. Rosenbloom and J. Davidson (eds.) 2012, 270–99.

Rosenbloom, D. (2014), 'The Politics of Comic Athens', in M. Fontaine and A. Scafuro (eds.) 2014, 297–319.

Rosenbloom, D. (2017), 'The Comedians' Aeschylus', in R. F. Kennedy (ed.) 2017, 4–87.

Rosenbloom, D. and J. Davidson, eds. (2012), *Greek Drama IV: Texts, Contexts, Performance* (Oxford: Aris & Philips).

Rosenmeyer, T. G. (2006), 'Ancient Literary Genres: a Mirage?', in A. Laird (ed.) 2006, 421–39.

Roux, J. (1973), *Euripide: Les Bacchantes*. 2 vols. (Paris: Les Belles Lettres).

Roy, J. (2004), 'The Ambitions of a Mercenary', in R. L. Fox (ed.) 2004, 264–88.

Ruffell, I. (2014), 'Character Types', in M. Revermann (ed.) 2014, 147–67.

Rusten, J. S., ed. (2011), *The Birth of Comedy: Texts, Documents, and Art from Athenian Comic Competitions, 486-280* (Baltimore: Johns Hopkins University Press).

Sanders, E., ed. (2013), *Erōs and the Polis: Love in Context. BICS* Supp.119 (London: Institute of Classical Studies).

Sanders, E., C. Thumiger, C. Carey and N. Lowe, eds. (2013), *Erōs in Ancient Greece* (Oxford: Oxford University Press).

Sanders, L. (1991), 'Dionysius I of Syracuse and the Origins of the Ruler Cult in the Greek World' *Historia* 40: 275–87.

Sansone, D. (2009), 'Euripides' New Song: The First Stasimon of Trojan Women', in J. R. C. Cousland and J. R. Hume (eds.) 2009, 193–203.

Sarian, H. (1986), 'Réflections Sur l'iconographie Des Érinyes Dans Le Milieu Grec, Italiote, et Étrusque', *Iconographie Classique et Identités Régionales, Bulletin de Correspondance Hellénique* 14, 25–35.

Schachter, A. (1994), *Cults of Boiotia 3. Potnia to Zeus, Cults of Deities Unspecified by Name. BICS* Supp. 38.3 (London: Institute of Classical Studies).

Scharffenberger, E. W. (1995), 'A Tragic Lysistrata?: Jocasta in the "Reconciliation Scene" of the *Phoenician Women', RhM* 138: 312–36.

Scharffenberger, E. W. (1996), 'Euripidean "Paracomedy": A Reconsideration of the *Antiope', Text and Presentation* 17: 65–72.

Scheid, J. and J. Svenbro (1996), *The Craft of Zeus: Myths of Weaving and Fabric* (Cambridge MA: Harvard University Press).

Schein, S.L. (2006), 'The *Iliad* and *Odyssey* in Sophocles' *Philoctetes*: Generic Complexity and Ethical Ambiguity', in J. Davidson, F. Muecke and P. Wilson (eds.) 2006, 129–40.

Schein, S. L. (2013), *Sophocles. Philoctetes* (Cambridge: Cambridge University Press).

Scodel, R. (2006), 'Aetiology, Autochthony, and Athenian Identity in *Ajax* and *Oedipus Coloneus*', in J. Davidson, F. Muecke and P. Wilson (eds.) 2006, 65–78.

Scodel, R. (2007), 'Lycurgus and the State Text of Tragedy', in C. R. Cooper (ed.) 2007, 129–54.

Scott, W. C. (1975), 'Two Suns Over Thebes: Imagery and Stage Effects in the *Bacchae', TAPhA* 105: 333–46.

Scott, M. (1995), 'The Character of Deianeira in Sophocles' *Trachiniae* 1', *AClass* 38: 17–27.

Scott, M. (1997), 'The Character of Deianeira in Sophocles' *Trachiniae* 2', *AClass* 40: 33–48.

Seaford, R. (1986), 'Wedding Ritual and Textual Criticism in Sophocles' *Women of Trachis', Hermes* 114 (1): 50–9.

Seaford, R. (1987), 'The Tragic Wedding', *JHS* 107: 106–30.

Seaford, R. (1988), 'The Eleventh Ode of Bacchylides: Hera, Artemis, and the Absence of Dionysos', *JHS* 108: 118–36.

Seaford, R. (1990a), 'The Structural Problems of Marriage in Euripides', in A. Powell (ed.) 1990, 151–76.

Seaford, R. (1990b), 'The Imprisonment of Women in Greek Tragedy', *JHS* 110: 76–90.

Seaford, R. (1993), 'Dionysus as Destroyer of the Household: Homer, Tragedy, and the Polis', in T. A. Carpenter and C. A. Faraone (eds.) 1993, 115–46.

Seaford, R. (1994), *Reciprocity and Ritual. Homer and Tragedy in the Developing City-State* (Oxford: Clarendon Press).

Seaford, R. (1996), *Euripides: Bacchae* (Warminster: Aris & Phillips).

Seaford, R. (2000), 'The Social Function of Attic Tragedy: A Response to Jasper Griffin', *CQ* 50: 104–19.

Seaford, R., J. Wilkins and M. Wright, eds. (2017), *Selfhood and the Soul: Essays on Ancient Thought and Literature in Honour of Christopher Gill* (Oxford: Oxford University Press).

Segal, C. P. (1969), 'Aristophanes' Cloud-Chorus', *Arethusa* 2: 143–61.

Segal, C. P. (1970), 'Protagoras' Orthoepeia in Aristophanes' "Battle of the Prologues" (*Frogs* 1119–97)', *RhM* 113.2/3: 158–62.

Segal, C. P. (1978), 'Pentheus and Hippolytus on the Couch and on the Grid: Psychoanalytic and Structuralist Readings of Greek Tragedy', *CW* 72 (3): 129–48.

Segal, C. P. (1984), 'Greek Tragedy, Writing, Truth and the Representation of the Self', in H. D. Evjen, ed., Mnēmai: *Classical Studies in Memory of Karl Hulley* (Chico, CA: Scholars Press), 41–67 [= (1986), *Interpreting Greek Tragedy: Myth, Poetry, Text* (Ithaca, NY: Cornell University Press), 75–109].

Segal, C. P. (1982), *Dionysian Poetics and Euripides'* Bacchae (Cambridge: Cambridge University Press).

Segal, C. P. (1990), 'Violence and the Other: Greek, Female, and Barbarian in Euripides' *Hecuba', TAPA* 120: 109–31. Reprinted in E. Segal 1993, 157–69.

Bibliography

Segal, C. P. (1993), *Euripides and the Poetics of Sorrow: Art, Gender, and Commemoration in Alcestis, Hippolytus, and Hecuba* (Durham, NC: Duke University Press).

Segal, C. P. (1998), *Sophocles' Tragic World: Divinity, Nature, Society* (Cambridge, MA: Harvard University Press).

Segal, C. P. (1999), *Tragedy and Civilization: An Interpretation of Sophocles* (Norman, OK: University of Oklahoma Press).

Segal, E., ed. (1983), *Oxford readings in Greek Tragedy* (Oxford: Oxford University Press).

Seidensticker, B. (2008), 'Character and Characterization in Greek Tragedy', in M. Revermann and P. Wilson (eds.), 2008, 333–48.

Seigel, J. (2005), *The Idea of the Self: Thought and Experience in Western Europe Since the Seventeenth Century* (Cambridge: Cambridge University Press).

Sfyroeras, P. (2008), 'πόθος Εὐριπίδου: Reading *Andromeda* in Aristophanes' *Frogs*', *AJP* 129: 299–317.

Shapiro, H. A. (1989), *Art and Cult Under the Tyrants in Athens* (Mainz am Rhein: von Zabern).

Shaw, M. (1975), 'The Female Intruder', *CP* 70: 255–66.

Shay, J. (1994), *Achilles in Vietnam: Combat Trauma and the Undoing of Character* (New York: Scribner).

Shay, J. (2002), *Odysseus in America: Combat Trauma and the Trials of Homecoming* (New York: Scribner).

Shear, J. L. (2001), *Polis and Panathenaia: The History and Development of Athena's Festival* (PhD Diss.: University of Pennsylvania).

Sherman, N. (2014), '"He Gave Me His Hand but Took My Bow": Trust and Trustworthiness in the *Philoctetes* and Our Wars', in P. Meineck and D. Konstan (eds.) 2014, 207–24.

Sidwell, K. (2009), *Aristophanes the Democrat* (Cambridge: Cambridge University Press).

Sienkewicz, T. J. (1978), 'Euripides' *Trojan Women*: An Interpretation', *Helios* 6: 81–95.

Silk, M. S., ed. (1996), *Tragedy and the Tragic: Greek Theatre and Beyond* (Oxford: Oxford University Press).

Silk, M. S. (2000), *Aristophanes and the Definition of Comedy* (Oxford: Oxford University Press).

Silk, M. S. (2013), 'The Greek Dramatic Genres: Theoretical Perspectives', in E. Bakola, L. Prauscello and M. Telò (eds.) 2013, 15–39.

Simas, A. (2016), 'Blood upon [Her] Eyes': Clytemnestra, the Erinyes, and the Gorgon in Aeschylus' *Oresteia*', Feminism and Classics VII: Visions. Seattle WA, May 19, 2016.

Slater, P. E. (2014), *The Glory of Hera* (Princeton: Princeton University Press).

Smith, J. A. (2003), 'Clearing up Some Confusion in Callias' *Alphabet Tragedy*: How to Read Sophocles' *Oedipus Tyrannus* 332–333 *et al*', *CPh* 98: 313–29.

Smith, O. L. (1976), *Scholia Graeca in Aeschylum quae exstant omnia pars I* (Leipzig: Teubner).

Smith, P. M. (1980), *On the Hymn to Zeus in Aeschylus'* Agamemnon (Chico, CA: Scholars Press).

Smith, R. S. and S. M. Trzaskoma (2007), *Apollodorus' Library and Hyginus' Fabulae: Two Handbooks of Greek Mythology* (Indianapolis: Hackett).

Smuts, A. (2008), 'The Desire–Frustration Theory of Suspense', *The Journal of Aesthetics and Art Criticism* 66: 281–90.

Snell, B. (1966), *Zu den Urkunden dramatischer Aufführungen* (Göttingen: Nachrichten der Akademie der Wissenschaften in Göttingen, Phil.-Hist. Klasse).

Snell, B. (1971), *Tragicorum Graecorum Fragmenta. Vol. I: Didascaliae Tragicae, Catalogi Tragicorum et Tragoediarum, Testimonia et Fragmenta Tragicorum Minorum* (Göttingen: Vandenhoeck & Ruprecht). 2nd ed., 1986.

Solmsen, F. (1967), 'Electra and Orestes: Three recognitions in Greek tragedy', *Medelingen der koninklijke Nederlandse Akad. van Wetenschappen* 30: 31–62.

Sommerstein, A. H. (1980), *Aristophanes: Acharnians* (Warminster: Aris & Phillips).

Sommerstein, A. H. (1982), *Aristophanes: Clouds* (Warminster: Aris & Phillips).

Sommerstein, A. H. (1985), *Aristophanes: Peace* (Warminster: Aris & Phillips).

Sommerstein, A. H. (1987), *Aristophanes: Birds* (Warminster: Aris & Phillips).

Sommerstein, A. H. (1989), *Aeschylus: Eumenides* (Cambridge: Cambridge University Press).

Sommerstein, A. H. (1994), *Aristophanes: Thesmophoriazusae* (Warminster: Aris & Phillips).

Sommerstein, A. H. (1996), *Aristophanes: Frogs* (Warminster: Aris & Phillips).

Sommerstein, A. H. (2002), 'The titles of Greek dramas', *SemRom* 5:1–16.

Sommerstein, A. H. (2008a), *Aeschylus: Fragments* (Cambridge, MA: Harvard University Press).

Sommerstein, A. H. (2008b), *Aeschylus: Oresteia* (Cambridge, MA: Harvard University Press).

Sommerstein, A. H. (2010a), *Aeschylean Tragedy*, 2nd ed. (London: Duckworth).

Sommerstein, A. H. (2010b), 'The History of the Text of Aristophanes', in Dobrov (ed.), 2010, 399–422.

Sommerstein, A. H., ed. (2014), *Menander in Contexts* (London: Routledge).

Sommerstein, A. H., S. Halliwell, J. Henderson and B. Zimmermann, eds. (1993), *Tragedy, Comedy and the Polis* (Bari: Levante Editori).

Sourvinou-Inwood, C. (1973), 'The Young Abductor of the Locrian Pinakes', *BICS* 20: 12–21.

Sourvinou-Inwood, C. (2004), 'Gendering the Athenian funeral: ritual reality and tragic manipulations', in D. Yatromanolakis and P. Roilos (eds.) 2004, 161–88.

Sourvinou-Inwood, C. (2011), *Athenian Myths and Festivals: Aglauros, Erechtheus, Plynteria, Panathenaia, Dionysia*, ed. R. Parker (Oxford: Oxford University Press).

Sparkes, B. A. (1991), *Greek Pottery: An Introduction* (Manchester: Manchester University Press).

Stama, F. (2014), *Frinico. Introduzione, Traduzione e Commento* (Heidelberg: Verlag Antike).

Stephanopoulos, T. K. (2012), 'Euripides oder Pseudo–Euripides?', *Logeion* 2: 100–20.

Stewart, E. (2017), *Greek Tragedy on the Move: The Birth of a Panhellenic Art Form c. 500–300 BC* (Oxford: Oxford University Press).

Stieber, M. C. (1994), 'Aeschylus' *Theoroi* and Realism in Greek Art', *TAPA* 124: 85–93.

Stieber, M. C. (2011), *Euripides and the Language of Craft* (Leiden: Brill).

Storey, I. C. (1993) 'The Date of Aristophanes' *Clouds II* and Eupolis' *Baptai*: A Reply to E. C. Kopff', *American Journal of Philology* 114: 71–84.

Storey, I. C. (2000), 'Appendix: The First Version of Clouds', in Meineck 2000, 115–19.

Storey, I. C. (2003), *Eupolis: Poet of Old Comedy* (Oxford: Oxford University Press).

Storey, I. C. (2010), 'Origins and Fifth-Century Comedy', in G. W. Dobrov (ed.) 2010, 179–225.

Storey, I. C. (2011), *Fragments of Old Comedy*. 3 vols. (Cambridge, MA: Harvard University Press).

Storey, I. C. and A. Allan (2005), *A Guide to Ancient Greek Drama* (Malden, MA: Blackwell).

Stuttard, D., ed. (2017), *Looking at Antigone* (London: Bloomsbury).

Suter, A. (2003), 'Lament in Euripides' *Trojan Women*', *Mnemosyne* 56: 1–28.

Sutton, R. F. (1981), 'Weddings on Attic Red-Figure Pottery', *AJA* 85: 220–1.

Sutton, R. F. (1997/98), 'Nuptial *Eros*: The Visual Discourse of Marriage in Classical Athens', *Journal of the Walters Art Gallery* 55–6: 27–48.

Swift, L. A. (2010), *The Hidden Chorus: Echoes of Genre in Tragic Lyric* (Oxford: Oxford University Press).

Swift, L. A. (2012), 'Archilochus the 'Anti–Hero'? Heroism, Flight and Values in Homer and the New Archilochus Fragment (P.OXY LXIX 4708)', *JHS* 123: 139–55.

Swift, L. A. (2014), 'Telephus on Paros: Genealogy and Myth in the "New Archilochus" Poem (P.Oxy 4708)', *CQ* 64: 433–47.

Swift, L. A. (2015), 'Stesichorus on Stage', in P. J. Finglass and A. Kelly (eds.) 2015, 125–44.

Swift, L. A. (2018), 'Competing Generic Narratives in Tragic Lyric', in R. Andújar, T. Coward and Th. Hadjimichael (eds.) 2018, 119–36.

Swift, L. A. and C. Carey, eds. (2016), *Iambus and Elegy. New Approaches* (Oxford: Oxford University Press).

Synodinou, K. (2005), *Εὐριπίδου Ἑκάβη*. 2 vols. (Athens: Daidalos-Zacharopoulos).

Taddei, A. (2014), 'Le Panatenee nel terzo stasimo degli *Eraclidi* (Eur. *Heracl.* 748–83). Rammemorazione rituale e identità corale', *Lexis* 32: 213–28.

Bibliography

Taplin, O. (1977), *The Stagecraft of Aeschylus* (Oxford: Clarendon Press).

Taplin, O. (1978), *Greek Tragedy in Action* (Berkeley: University of California Press).

Taplin, O. (1983), 'Tragedy and Trugedy', *CQ* 33: 331–3.

Taplin, O. (1986), 'Fifth-century Tragedy and Comedy: A Synkrisis', *JHS* 106: 163–74.

Taplin, O. (1987) 'Phallology, *Phylakes*, Iconography and Aristophanes', *Proceedings of the Cambridge Philological Society* 213: 92–104.

Taplin, O. (1993), *Comic Angels: And Other Approaches to Greek Drama Through Vase-painting* (Oxford: Oxford University Press).

Taplin, O. (1999), 'Spreading the Word through Performance', in S. Goldhill and R. Osborne (eds.) 1999, 33–57.

Taplin, O. (2007), *Pots & Plays: Interactions Between Tragedy and Greek Vase-painting of the Fourth Century B.C.* (Los Angeles: J. P. Getty Museum).

Taplin, I. (2017), 'The Syracusa Tragedy-Vase: Oedipus and his Daughters?', *engramma* 150, http://www.engramma.it/eOS/index.php?id_articolo=3303 (accessed 19 September 2019).

Taufer, M., ed. (2015), *Studi sulla commedia attica*. Paradeigmata 31 (Freiburg: Rombach).

Telò, M. (2007), *Eupolidis Demi* (Florence: Felice Le Monnier).

Telò, M. (2016), *Aristophanes and the Cloak of Comedy: Affect, Aesthetics, and the Canon* (Chicago: University of Chicago Press).

Thalmann, W. G. (2004), '"The Most Divinely Approved and Political Discord": Thinking about Conflict in the Developing Polis', *CA* 23: 359–99.

Thomson, G. (1966), *The Oresteia of Aeschylus* (Amsterdam: A. M. Hakkert).

Thumiger, Ch. (2006), 'Animal World, Animal Representation, and the "Hunting-Model": Between Literal and Figurative in Euripides' *Bacchae*', *Phoenix* 60: 191–210.

Thumiger, Ch. (2007), *Hidden Paths: Self and Characterization in Greek Tragedy: Euripides' Bacchae* (London: Institute of Classical Studies, School of Advanced Study, University of London).

Thumiger, Ch. (2013), 'Mad *Erōs* and Eroticized Madness in Tragedy', in E. Sanders, C. Thumiger, C. Carey and N. Lowe (eds.) 2013, 27–40.

Thury, E. M. (1985), 'Euripides' *Electra*: An Analysis Through Character Development', *RhM* 128: 5–22.

Tomaselli, S. and R. Porter, eds. (1986), *Rape* (Oxford: Blackwell).

Toohey, P. (1988), 'Archilochus' General (fr. 114W): Where Did He Come From?', *Eranos* 86: 1–14.

Toohey, P. and J. McClure (2013), 'Sexuality in Greek Tragedy', in H. M. Roisman (ed.) 2013, 1241–4.

Topper, K. (2007), 'Perseus, the Maiden Medusa, and the Imagery of Abduction', *Hesperia* 76.1: 73–105.

Torrance, I. (2011), 'In the Footprints of Aeschylus: Recognition, Allusion, and Metapoetics in Euripides', *AJP* 132: 177–204.

Torrance, I. (2013), *Metapoetry in Euripides* (Oxford: Oxford University Press).

Toutain, J. (1940), 'Le rite nuptial de l'*anakalypterion*', *REA* 42: 345–53.

Tracy, S. V. (1991), 'The Panathenaic Festival and Games: An Epigraphic Enquiry', *Nikephoros* 4: 133–53.

Traill, A. (2008), *Women and the Comic Plot in Menander* (Cambridge: Cambridge University Press).

Trendall, A. D. and T. B. L. Webster (1971), *Illustrations of Greek Drama* (London: Phaidon).

TrGF = (1974–2004), *Tragicorum Graecorum Fragmenta*. 5 vols. (Göttingen: Vandenhoeck & Ruprecht); *Vol. I* = B. Snell (1971, 1986), *Vol. II* = R. Kannicht and B. Snell (1981), *Vol. III* = S. Radt (1985), *Vol. IV* = S. Radt (1977, 1999), *Vol. V* = R. Kannicht (2004).

Trundle, M. (2013), 'The Business of War: Mercenaries', in B. Campbell and A. Tritle (eds.) 2013, 330–50.

Tyrrell, W. B. and L. J. Bennett (1998), *Recapturing Sophocles' Antigone* (Lanham, MD: Rowman & Littlefield).

Uidhir, C. M. (2011), 'An Eliminativist Theory of Suspense', *Philosophy and Literature* 35: 121–33.

Vahtikari, V. (2014), *Tragedy Performances Outside Athens in the Late Fifth and the Fourth Centuries BC* (Helsinki: Finnish Institute of Athens).

Vaio, J. (1964), 'The New Fragments of Euripides' *Oedipus*', *GRBS* 5: 43–55.

Verdenius, W. J. (1997), *Commentaries on Pindar. Vol. I* (Leiden: Brill).

Vermeule, E. (1966), 'The Boston Oresteia Krater', *AJA* 70.1: 1–22.

Vernant, J.-P. (1972), 'Ambiguïté et renversement; Sur la structure énigmatique d'Oedipe Roi', translated by J. Lloyd as 'Ambiguity and Reversal: On the Enigmatic Structure of *Oedipus Rex*' in J.-P. Vernant and P. Vidal-Naquet, 1988, 113–40.

Vernant, J.-P. (1991), 'The Individual Within the City-State', in F. I. Zeitlin, ed., *Mortals and Immortals. Collected Essays* (Princeton: Princeton University Press), 318–33.

Vernant, J.-P. and P. Vidal-Naquet (1972), *Mythe et tragédie en Grèce ancienne* (Paris: F. Maspero).

Vernant, J.-P. and P. Vidal-Naquet (1988), *Myth and Tragedy in Ancient Greece* (New York: Zone Books).

Vikatou, O., R. Frederiksen and S. Handberg (1914), 'The Danish–Greek Excavations at Kalydon, Aitolia: The Theatre. Preliminary Report from the 2011 and 2012 Campaigns', *Proceedings of the Danish Institute at Athens* 7: 221–34.

Visvardi, E. (2011), 'Pity and Panhellenic Politics: Choral Emotion in Euripides' *Hecuba* and *Trojan Women*', in D. M. Carter (ed.) 2011, 269–91.

Voza, G. (2001), 'Nuove ricerche sul teatro greco di Siracusa', in C. Basile and A. Di Natale (eds.) 2001, 207–10.

Voza, G. (2007), 'Teatro greco di Siracusa: stato delle conoscenze', in G. Meli (ed.) 2007, 72–80.

Voza, G. (2008), 'Siracusa – Teatro Greco: l'eccezionalità', *Numero Unico XLIV Ciclo Spettacoli Classici* (Syracuse: Fondazione INDA).

Voza, G. (2014), 'Teatro Greco a Siracusa, la solitudine dei numeri primi', in F. Granata, L. Godart, G. Voza, G. Di Rauso and M. Centanni (eds.) 2014, 18–49.

Wachsmann, S. (2012), 'Panathenaic Ships: The Iconographic Evidence', *Hesperia* 81: 237–66.

Wachsmuth, C. and O. Hense (1958), *Joannis Stobaei Anthologivm* (Berlin: Weidmann).

Walcot, P. (1984), 'Greek Attitudes toward Women: The Mythological Evidence', *G&R* 31: 37–47.

Walton, J. M. (2009), *Euripides: Our Contemporary* (Berkeley: University of California Press).

Webster, T. B. L. (1965), 'The *Andromeda* of Euripides', *BICS* 12: 29–33.

Webster, T. B. L. (1967a), *Monuments Illustrating Tragedy and Satyr Play. BICS* Supp. (London: Institute of Classical Studies).

Webster, T. B. L. (1967b), *The Tragedies of Euripides* (London: Methuen).

Weiss, N. A. (2018), *The Music of Tragedy: Performance and Imagination in Euripidean Theater* (Oakland CA: University of California Press).

Wender, D. (1974), 'The Will of the Beast: Sexual Imagery in the *Trachiniae*', *Ramus* 3: 1–17.

West, M. L. (1974), *Studies in Greek elegy and iambus* (Berlin: de Gruyter).

West, M. L. (1980), 'Tragica IV', *BICS* 27: 9–22.

West, M. L. (1990a), *Aeschyli Tragoediae cum incerti poetae Prometheo* (Stuttgart: Teubner).

West, M. L. (1990b), *Studies in Aeschylus* (Stuttgart: Teubner).

West, M. L. (2006), 'Archilochus and Telephus', *ZPE* 156: 11–17.

West, M. L. (2013), *The Epic Cycle: A Commentary on the Lost Troy Epics* (Oxford: Oxford University Press).

Westlake, H. D. (1953), 'Euripides' *Troades*: 205–229', *Mnemosyne* 6: 181–91.

White, J. W. (1909), 'The Iambic Trimeter in Menander', *CPh* 4: 139–61.

Whitehorne, J. E. G. (1978), 'The Ending of Euripides' *Electra*', *RBP* 56: 5–14.

Wilamowitz-Moellendorf, U. (1914), *Aeschyli Tragoediae* (Berlin: Weidmann).

Wiles D. (2000), *Greek Theatre Performance. An Introduction* (Cambridge: Cambridge University Press).

Wilfred, E. (2013), 'Staging *Andromeda* in Aristophanes and Euripides', *CJ* 108: 385–403.

Bibliography

Wilhelm, A. (1906), *Urkunden dramatischer Aufführungen in Athen* (Vienna: A. Hölder).

Wilk, S. R. (2000), *Medusa* (Oxford: Oxford University Press).

Wilkins, J. (1993), *Euripides: Heraclidae* (Oxford: Clarendon Press).

Willi, A. (2003), *The Languages of Aristophanes: Aspects of Linguistic Variation in Classical Attic Greek* (Oxford: Oxford University Press).

Wilson, E. R. (2004), *Mocked with Death: Tragic Overliving from Sophocles to Milton* (Baltimore: Johns Hopkins University Press).

Wilson, P. (2000), *The Athenian Institution of the Khoregia: The Chorus, the City and the Stage* (Cambridge: Cambridge University Press).

Wilson, P. (2009), 'Tragic Honours and Democracy: Neglected Evidence for the Politics of the Athenian Dionysia', *CQ* 59: 8–29.

Wilson, P. (2011), 'The Glue of Democracy? Tragedy, Structure, and Finance', in D. M. Carter (ed.) 2011, 19–43.

Wilson, P. (2015), 'The Festival of Dionysos in Ikarion: A New Study of *IG* I³ 254', *Hesperia* 84/1: 97–147.

Wilson, P. (2017), 'A Potted Political History of the Sicilian Theater (to ca. 300)', in H. Reid, D. Tanasi and S. Kimbell (eds.) 2017, 1–32.

Wilson, P. and O. Taplin (1993) 'The "Aetiology" of Tragedy in the *Oresteia*', *Proceedings of the Cambridge Philological Society* 39: 169–80.

Winkler, J. J. (1991), 'The Constraints of *Eros*', in C. A. Faraone and D. Obbink (eds.), Magika Hiera: *Ancient Greek Magic and Religion*, 214–43 (New York: Oxford University Press).

Winkler, J. J., and F. I. Zeitlin, eds. (1990), *Nothing to Do with Dionysus? Athenian Drama in its Social Context* (Princeton: Princeton University Press).

Winnington-Ingram, R. P. (1948), *Euripides and Dionysus: An Interpretation of the Bacchae* (Cambridge: Cambridge University Press).

Winnington-Ingram, R. P. (1969), 'Euripides: *Poiētēs Sophos*', *Arethusa* 2: 127–42.

Winnington-Ingram, R. P. (1980), *Sophocles: An Interpretation* (Cambridge: Cambridge University Press).

Witzke, S. (2016), 'Gendered Differences in the Recognition Plot: Menander's *Sikyonioi*', *EuGeStA* 6: 41–65.

Wohl V. (1998), *Intimate Commerce: Exchange, Gender, and Subjectivity in Greek Tragedy* (Austin: University of Texas Press).

Wohl, V. (2015), *Euripides and the Politics of Form* (Princeton: Princeton University Press).

Woodward, J. M. (1937), *Perseus: A Study in Greek Art and Legend* (Cambridge: Cambridge University Press).

Worthington, I., ed. (1996), *Voice into Text: Orality and Literacy in Ancient Greece* (Leiden: Brill).

Wright, E. (1986), *The Form of Laments in Greek Tragedy* (PhD Diss.: University of Pennsylvania).

Wright, M. (2005), *Euripides' Escape Tragedies: A Study of Helen, Andromeda, and Iphigenia among the Taurians* (Oxford: Oxford University Press).

Wright, M. (2010), 'The Tragedian as Critic: Euripides and Early Greek Poetics', *JHS* 130: 165–84.

Wright, M. (2012), *The Comedian as Critic: Greek Old Comedy and Poetics* (London: Bristol).

Wright, M. (2017), 'A Lover's Discourse: *Erōs* in Greek Tragedy', in R. Seaford, J. Wilkins and M. Wright (eds.) 2017, 219–42.

Xanthakis-Karamanos, G. (1980), *Studies in Fourth-Century Tragedy* (Athens: Academy of Athens).

Yatromanolakis, D. and P. Roilos, eds. (2004), *Greek Ritual Poetics* (Cambridge, MA: Harvard University Press).

Yossi, M. (1996), *Μύθος και λόγος στον Σοφοκλή* (Athens: Kardamitsa).

Zeitlin, F. I. (1986), 'Configurations of Rape in Greek Myth', in S. Tomaselli and R. Porter (eds.) 1986, 122–51.

Zeitlin, F. I. (1991), 'Euripides' *Hekabe* and the somatics of Dionysiac drama', *Ramus* 20: 53–94. Reprinted in Zeitlin 1996, 172–216.

Zeitlin, F. I. (1994), 'The Artful Eye: Vision, Ecphrasis, and Spectacle in Euripidean Theatre', in
    S. Goldhill and R. Osborne (eds.) 1994, 138–96, 295–304.
Zeitlin, F. I. (1996), *Playing the Other: Gender and Society in Classical Greek Literature* (Chicago:
    University of Chicago Press).
Zeitlin, F. I. (2005), 'Redeeming Matricide? Euripides Rereads the *Oresteia*', in V. Pedrick and
    S. M. Oberhelman (eds.) 2005, 199–225.
Ziegler, K. and W. Sontheimer (1967), *Der Kleine Pauly: Lexikon der Antike. Vol. II* (Stuttgart:
    A. Druckenmüller).
Zielinski, T. 1925. *Tragodoumenon Libri Tres* (Kraków).
Zimmermann, B., ed. (2001), *Rezeption des antiken Dramas auf der Bühne und in der Literatur*
    (Stuttgart: J. B. Metzler).
Zimmermann, C. (1993), *Der Antigone–Mythos in der antiken Literatur und Kunst* (Tübingen:
    Gunter Narr).

INDEX

Index

Index

www.ingramcontent.com/pod-product-compliance
Lightning Source LLC
Chambersburg PA
CBHW071501110726
47908CB00003B/688